Learning Relationships in the Classroom

Child Development in Families, Schools and Society 2

The companion volumes in this series are:

Cultural Worlds of Early Childhood
Edited by Martin Woodhead, Dorothy Faulkner and Karen Littleton

Making Sense of Social Development
Edited by Martin Woodhead, Dorothy Faulkner and Karen Littleton

These three readers are the core study material for students taking the course ED840 Child Development in Families, Schools and Society. This course may be taken as part of the Open University MA in Education programme. The course may also be taken as part of the Open University MSc in Psychology.

The Open University MA in Education

The Open University MA in Education is now firmly established as the most popular postgraduate degree for education professionals in Europe, with over 3500 students registering each year. The MA in Education is designed particularly for those with experience of teaching, the advisory service, educational administration or allied fields.

Structure of the MA

The MA is a modular degree and students are therefore free to select from a range of options the programme that best fits in with their interests and professional goals. Study in the Open University's Advanced Diploma and Certificate in Continuing Professional Development programmes can also be counted towards the MA. Successful completion of the MA in Education entitles students to apply for entry into the Open University Doctorate in Education (EdD) programme.

OU supported open learning

The MA in Education programme provides great flexibility. Students study at their own pace, in their own time, anywhere in the European Union. They receive specially prepared study materials, are supported by tutorials, and have opportunities to work with other students.

How to apply

The Professional Development in Education prospectus contains further information and application forms. To request your copy please write to the Course Reservations and Sales Centre, The Open University, PO Box 625, Walton Hall, Milton Keynes MK7 6AA, or telephone 01908 365302.

Learning Relationships in the Classroom

Edited by Dorothy Faulkner, Karen Littleton and Martin Woodhead

London and New York
in association with the
Open University

First published 1998
by Routledge
11 New Fetter Lane, London EC4P 4EE

Simultaneously published in the USA and Canada
by Routledge
29 West 35th Street, New York, NY 10001

Typeset in Garamond by RefineCatch Limited, Bungay, Suffolk
Printed and bound in Great Britain by
TJ International Ltd, Padstow, Cornwall

British Library Cataloguing in Publication Data
A catalogue record for this book is available from the British Library

Library of Congress Cataloguing in Publication Data
Learning relationships in the classroom / [edited by] Dorothy
    Faulkner, Karen Littleton, and Martin Woodhead.
        p.   cm.
    Includes bibliographical references and index.
    1. Teacher–student relationships.   2. Communication in education.
3. Group work in education.   I. Faulkner, Dorothy.   II. Littleton,
Karen.   III. Woodhead, Martin.
LB1033.L39   1999
371.102'3—dc21   98–13944
    T158260   CIP

ISBN 0-415-17373-6

Contents

Figures

Tables

Introduction

This collection contains studies on children's cognitive development from a socio-cultural perspective. A particular focus of this perspective has been to develop theoretical explanations of teaching and learning which take into account the many different social contexts in which children learn. The chapters in this book draw on a rich body of research on children and their teachers in different instructional contexts throughout the world and offer some fundamental insights into the nature of human cognition and its development. One of the most important of these insights has been the realisation that we need to develop a better understanding of the nature and functions of instructional discourse. Another has been that we need to pay attention to the nature of children's social relationships, and how interpersonal dynamics operate in teaching and learning exchanges.

The socio-cultural perspective contrasts with conventional, Piagetian and cognitive accounts of child development which were current in the 1960s and 1970s. These theoretical traditions describe cognitive development as a process of gradually emerging individual competencies. They also assume that intellectual development is stage-like and universal, and that it occurs in pretty much the same way in all children in all cultural settings. They fail to acknowledge, however, the respects in which children's knowledge, skills, beliefs and understandings are socially constructed through talk and language, and diverse processes of imitation, direct instruction, guided participation and collaborative construction.

Piaget's constructivist approach dominated the study of children's intellectual development in Europe and the United States throughout the 1960s and '70s. One of his key assumptions was that development takes place through the operations children carry out on their environment, (particularly the physical environment). His emphasis on the child's individual activity, combined with a maturationist approach, served to draw attention away from the significance of teaching and learning in development. His view was that teaching and instruction by adults (whether in informal settings such as the home, or formal settings such as the school) played at best a subordinate role; at worst, it was seen as interfering with processes of development.

Piaget's views on the developmental value of peer interactions between children, however, were more favourable. In his own work on moral development Piaget (1932) showed that peer interaction could lead to cognitive changes in children's understanding of morality and rules. More recently Piaget's colleagues have identified 'socio-cognitive conflict' as being important for cognitive growth. They are interested in the type of argument and discussion which takes place between children when they do not agree on how to explain some particular phenomenon, or when they challenge each other's perspectives and ideas, (e.g. Doise & Mugny, 1984). Despite the attention paid to social processes, these accounts remain fundamentally individualistic in their view of cognitive development.

The same is true of developmental psychologists working in the 1960s and '70s. These psychologists adopted a cognitivist (or information-processing) framework, and concentrated on observed changes in children's learning strategies, memory and knowledge organisation. They offered a decontextualised account of cognitive development based on administering specially designed tasks under laboratory-type conditions. Children were tested individually, and average performance measures for different age groups were taken to indicate developmental change. Children's learning in the everyday contexts of home and school was rarely studied, and the role of teaching and learning in development was seldom taken into account. Questions about whether children could learn from each other, or whether an older child could 'teach' a younger child, were simply not on the cognitivist agenda.

During the 1980s and '90s, however, the theories of the Russian psychologist Vygotsky (1962, 1978) came to exercise an increasingly important influence on contemporary developmental psychology. This influence has been twofold: first, through their exploration of Vygotsky's writings, child psychologists have begun to develop powerful and sophisticated theories and explanations of the role that teaching and instruction play in children's development. Unlike Piaget, Vygotsky placed great emphasis on both spoken and written language as the medium of instruction, of knowledge generation, and of cognitive change. Much contemporary research into classroom learning, therefore, has concerned itself with detailed analyses of the talk and discourse which takes place in formal and informal learning contexts. Second, it is now recognised that the study of children's development must take into account the social, cultural and historical contexts in which development is situated.

The readings in this collection have been selected as a representative sample of the large and growing body of research on teaching and learning carried out within what has come to be known as the 'Socio-cultural School' or, more simply, cultural psychology. The introductory chapters in Part I provide a theoretical overview of Vygotskian theory, and locate it in its socio-historical and socio-cultural framework. Chapters in Part II examine research which has drawn on this framework to analyse the teaching and learning interactions which take place between adults and children in the context of school class-rooms. Part III contains chapters describing experimental studies of peer interaction and collaborative learning. These chapters also compare Piagetian and Vygotskian accounts of the effects of peer interaction on cognitive development. Part IV examines the usefulness of these two approaches for understanding how children and their teachers construct knowledge through talk and language in different academic contexts.

In the opening chapter of Part I, Wertsch and Tulviste review aspects of Vygotsky's theory that have particular relevance for child psychologists today. They outline Vygotsky's views regarding the social origins and social nature of 'higher mental functions', and his claim that cognitive development has its origins in social interactions which in turn are shaped by particular cultural contexts and traditions. They contrast this view with 'traditional', Western psychological theories which have adopted the position (by implica-tion the Piagetian position) that mental processes and consciousness have their origin within the individual. Wertsch and Tulviste then go on to describe key Vygotskian concepts such as the *general genetic law of cultural development*; *intermental* and *intramental* processes; *internalisation*; and the *zone of proximal development* (ZPD). They discuss Vygotsky's analysis of the various functions of language, his 'developmental method', and his writings and research on culture and cognition. The final section of this chapter evaluates the relevance of Vygotsky's theory for contemporary developmental psycho-logists, and sets the scene for the following three chapters by Cole, Säljö and Gauvain

In Chapter 2 Cole's central question is, 'Does schooling or other forms of formal educational experience have particular cognitive consequences for the developing child?' In other words, is the cognitive development of children who live in cultures which operate formal, Western-type school systems qualitatively different from that of children belonging to other cultures? Drawing on the basic postulates of the socio-historical/cultural school, Cole develops the thesis that 'Culture is the unique medium of human existence'. Using the concepts of 'cultural mediation' and 'cultural artifacts' he gives a historical account of the development of writing systems and shows how formal systems of instruction and the development of literacy were a necessary consequence of this development. He reviews cross-cultural research compar-ing literate and non-literate societies and concludes that schooling and formal education do have particular consequences for the ways in which children think about the world. Cole goes on to identify features of schooling such as the use of written symbol systems and the unique nature of 'instructional' discourse, which are responsible for these consequences.

These themes are explored further in Chapter 3. Säljö develops the idea that human cognitive socialisation, or learning, requires children to 'appropri-ate' concepts which originate in the communicative practices of particular cultures. According to Säljö, 'human cognitive socialisation' is not a one-sided affair involving knowledge transmission from an expert (teacher) to a passive novice (learner). Following a socio-cultural perspective, he argues that learning and the development of cognition is best described as situated action mediated by the appropriation and mastery of communicative (e.g. spoken language) and technical tools or 'artifacts' (e.g. writing tools, measuring instruments, computers). His central questions are: 'How does technology reorganise interactions between pupils and teachers?' and 'Can technology create new educational environments?'. Whereas in the preceding chapter Cole illustrates these questions through the historical example of the development of writing systems, Säljö's emphasis is on the present and future potential of the computer and information technology to transform teaching and learning environments.

In the next chapter, Gauvain adopts Super and Harkness's (1986) concept of 'developmental niche' as a framework for organising cognitive developmental research in relation to culture. According to this framework each child's development is embedded within a particular cultural system. Cultural goals and values will guide and shape that child's cognitive activity in diverse ways in different socio-cultural contexts. For example, folk theories and beliefs about children's development influence the ways in which parents interpret and respond to children's behaviours. These beliefs determine the range and nature of the experiences made available to children and influence what are regarded as appropriate developmental goals. In societies which provide Western-style educational niches for their children, the ability to engage in decontextualised thinking, use particular educated discourses, and master the use of cultural artifacts are key developmental goals. Gauvain also argues that problem-solving practices are deeply influenced by cultural values. Using research on the development of mathematical knowledge as her example, she puts forward the now familiar thesis that material and symbolic tools act as 'cultural amplifiers' which can enhance human thinking and shape cognitive development.

The chapters in Part II illustrate how psychologists have applied Vygotskian theory to understanding teaching processes. Chapter 5 is taken from Tharp and Gallimore's (1988) book, *Rousing minds to life: teaching, learning and schooling in social context*. In this chapter they take the key Vygotskian concept of the 'zone of proximal development' and elaborate it into a theory of 'teaching as assisted performance'. They discuss how psychologists' detailed and systematic observation of dyadic interactions between parents and children has informed our understanding of the role of processes such as 'scaffolding' in informal teaching and learning contexts. A crucial question, however, is whether the theory has any real applications for classroom teaching, where sustained dyadic interchanges between teachers and learners are rare. The next two chapters address this question.

In Chapter 6, Mercer and Fisher describe the Spoken Language and New Technology (SLANT) project. The SLANT project investigated ways in which computer-based classroom activities could provide contexts for learning in British primary schools. It also evaluated how teachers manage pupil talk and discussion to mediate and support these learning activities. Mercer and Fisher argue that, although the neo-Vygotskian framework has generated powerful theories of teaching and learning, key concepts and principles such as scaffolding and the zone of proximal development have not been sufficiently well specified in practice. In this chapter they provide an operational definition of scaffolding and use it to analyse samples of classroom dialogue between teachers and pupils. They conclude that scaffolding is a useful concept for thinking about how teachers actively organise and support children's computer-based learning activities. The authors also discuss the role of the computer and computer-based instruction in the classroom. The findings of the SLANT project 'show that in practice the procedures and outcomes of any computer-based activity will emerge through the talk and joint activity of teacher and pupils. That is, the same software used by different combinations of teachers and pupils on different occasions will generate distinctive activities' (p. 128)

In the next chapter, Moll and Whitmore present a two-year case study of the development of language and literacy skills in a class of third grade (8–9-year-old) bilingual Mexican children. Using examples of the children's written work, they describe how the class teacher creates authentic social contexts which allow the children to explore the diverse purposes and uses of the oral and written conventions of the languages of their two cultures. The chapter describes practices which, according to Moll and Whitmore, capture some of the key elements of Vygotsky's theory. Although the concept of the zone of proximal development has usually been used in the context of dyadic teaching and learning exchanges, Moll and Whitmore propose that classrooms can give rise to 'collective' zones of proximal development and that it is incorrect to think of the ZPD as solely a characteristic of individual children. In classroom contexts the ZPD should be conceptualised as the zone where children engage in collaborative activity within specific social (discourse) environments. Moll and Whitmore argue that classrooms should be seen as socio-cultural systems which are actively created by teachers and students over time as they develop a history of shared understandings and engage in processes of knowledge creation.

In the final chapter of this section, Stone discusses the limitations of the scaffolding metaphor. 'Scaffolding' has been used as a portmanteau metaphor to describe what happens when an adult assists a child to carry out a task which he or she is not capable of accomplishing independently. Learning is said to have taken place when the child has mastered the various components of the task and can perform it independently. Like Mercer and Fisher, he criticises cultural psychologists for failing to pay attention to the specific mechanisms involved in this process. Stone argues that the success or otherwise of any teaching and learning exchange is crucially determined by the quality of the interpersonal relationship which exists between teacher and learner. Exchanges where partners in a dialogue are able to establish 'intersubjectivity', or shared meaning, and a common frame of reference are likely to be more successful than those where people are at cross-purposes. Establishing intersubjectivity, however, means that adults need to be sensitive to the fact that children, especially young children, may not have acquired an understanding of the sophisticated pragmatic conventions (e.g. 'prolepsis') which promote effective communication and dialogue. Stone also points out that shared understandings and common frames of reference are built up over a period of time as teachers and learners develop a working relationship. Research methodology and models of teaching and learning based on 'snapshot' studies of isolated teaching and learning exchanges have not been able to take these factors into account. The longitudinal research studies described by Mercer and Fisher and by Moll and Whitmore indicate how this can be achieved.

The chapters in Part III of the reader discuss the role of peer interaction in cognitive development. Unlike the two classroom observation studies presented in Chapters 6 and 7, the research reported in Part III is predominantly experimental. Nevertheless, the authors' aims have been to develop theories which can be tested in real-life educational settings. The chapter by Light and Littleton provides a state-of-the-art review of research on peer collaboration. They compare neo-Piagetian and neo-Vygotskian accounts of the influence of social context on the development of children's reasoning and problem-solving. According to both accounts, peer interaction has the potential to promote individual cognitive development. Light and Littleton point out, however, that joint problem-solving does not necessarily lead to cognitive gain. Not all children work well together, and not all tasks lend themselves to joint problem-solving. Factors such as individual and age-related differences in children's social and communicative skills have to be taken into account by teachers and researchers wishing to design supportive, collaborative learning environments.

A question of particular concern to both psychologists and educators is whether there is any benefit to children from working collaboratively with a peer over and above what can be achieved by working alone. In Chapter 10, Forman and Cazden describe a number of research studies which have investigated this particular question and present a detailed analysis of the working relationships which developed over a period of weeks between three pairs of 9-year-old children. Taking a Piagetian framework as their starting point, they compared the performance of these children on a series of scientific reasoning problems with that of children working alone on identical problems. They found that while all children solved the easier problems, only the children working in pairs were able to solve the more difficult ones. In the short term, subsequent individual tests showed that children who had worked in pairs fared no better than those who had worked alone. The study showed, however, that there was considerable variation in the quality of the working relationships which developed between the pairs of children. This may go some way towards explaining the finding that four months after the main study ended, both partners of the most successful pair had made equivalent cognitive gains. Forman and Cazden argue that from a neo-Piagetian perspective, this study does not provide much support for the hypothesis that peer interaction leads to cognitive gain. If a Vygotskian perspective is adopted, however, it becomes apparent that collaborative tasks provide children with valuable social and linguistic experiences which are not available to children working alone.

The research carried out by Forman and Cazden raises a number of important methodological and theoretical issues which have yet to be resolved. Many of these issues are discussed by Azmitia in Chapter 11. She starts by providing a summary of contemporary research on peer interaction, paying special attention to describing how negotiation processes, task difficulty, and the nature of the relationship between collaborators influence the processes and outcomes of 'peer-interactive minds'. Using evidence from studies such as those of Christine Howe and her research group, and also from her own studies of the influence of friendship on collaborative learning, Azmitia describes how children negotiate their roles and goals in relation to the tasks they have been set. She claims that children's ability to operate on each other's reasoning undergoes a major developmental shift between middle and late childhood. Over this time period children develop the ability to engage in particular forms of transactive dialogues which allow them to evaluate the merits of each other's reasoning, and identify inadequacies and contradictions between their own and their partners' thinking. Cognitive growth takes place when children attempt to resolve these contradictions and revise their own knowledge. Like Forman and Cazden, Azmitia draws on both Piagetian and Vygotskian theory to develop these arguments.

In later sections of her chapter Azmitia links the research on collaborative learning in childhood and adolescence with research which has focused on cognitive change in adulthood and old age. In addressing the theoretical and methodological issues that currently confront both fields she arrives at the interesting conclusion that '. . . our fascination with peer interacting minds may have led us to underestimate the contribution of solitary work and reflection to cognitive development, or at least to fail to recognize that cognitive development requires both social interaction and solitary reflection' (p. 227).

The various chapters in the final part of this reader return to a consideration of the ways in which teachers can guide the construction of knowledge through promoting effective group work in the classroom. As will have become apparent from the research on peer collaboration presented in the immediately preceding chapters, it is not sufficient to set groups of children to work on joint tasks in the hope that they will create for themselves conditions that lead to advances in their thinking and understanding. In Chapter 12, Baker-Sennett, Matusov and Rogoff explore the nature of children's creativity and group collaborative processes from a socio-cultural perspective. They observed groups of 7–9-year-old children developing a play based on a traditional fairy tale. Baker-Sennet *et al.* present a fascinating analysis of how one particular group of six girls' planning, organisation and ideas changed over one month. They also discuss the class teacher's role in structuring the task for her pupils. This teacher saw the task of creating a play as fulfilling two sets of aims: developing the children's literacy skills, and facilitating the development of the interpersonal problem-solving skills needed to cope with the social challenges of working as a group. Both of these aims were made explicit to the children, and throughout the chapter there are examples of how this particular teacher encourages her pupils to reflect on the interpersonal challenges which they encounter. This chapter provides an excellent example of what Tharp and Gallimore (Chapter 5) mean by teaching as assisted performance through the zone of proximal development. In this particular case, the girls are moving simultaneously through parallel social or interpersonal zones as well as creative, literary zones.

The next two chapters, by Driver *et al.* (Chapter 13), and Hatano and Inagaki (Chapter 14), examine the processes involved in children's construction of scientific knowledge. For Driver *et al.*, learning science means more than simply acquiring new scientific facts and understanding scientific theories. They view learning science as a socialisation process which enables children to participate in a particular cultural community, the knowledge community of scientists. A major part of this socialisation process involves assisting children's acquisition of the 'distinct discursive practices' (or ways of talking, thinking, reasoning and arguing) characteristic of scientific communities. Driver *et al.* argue that science classrooms should be seen as communities of enquiry which provide children with a cultural apprenticeship into the ways and means by which mature scientists construct their own disciplines. Again they highlight the crucial role of the teacher in structuring this socialisation process, and the chapter provides several examples of how teachers use talk and discussion to scaffold pupils' understanding of scientific concepts.

In Chapter 14, Hatano and Inagaki address two main questions: how a collective attempt to acquire knowledge takes place, and how much knowledge comes to be shared (acquired in common) through such attempts. In order to examine these questions they draw on observations of various classes of Japanese children finding out about scientific concepts such as buoyancy, the conservation of weight and animal habitats, through a method of science instruction called Hypothesis–Experiment–Instruction. This method is designed to encourage whole-class discussion and experimentation. The teacher's role is to act as a neutral chairperson during the students' discussion. A key feature of this method is that subgroups of children within the class (each holding different initial hypotheses about the topic under investigation) are encouraged to debate their case with other groups who hold a different position. This has the effect of children becoming quite partisan in defence of their own group's position, and Hatano and Inagaki present an analysis of how this influences children's comprehension and knowledge acquisition.

They claim that knowledge construction and collective comprehension activities are most likely to be successful when cognitive motivation and social (partisan) motivation operate in concert. They present experimental evidence on the extent to which individual students elaborate and revise their own ideas following collective comprehension activities. They conclude that two processes are involved here. First, during interaction students often collectively produce knowledge that they would not have been able to generate for themselves. This is assimilated into, or used to revise, their own knowledge base. Second, children are motivated to seek out and invent new knowledge for themselves as they reflect on inadequacies in their own comprehension highlighted through collective group discussion. Hatano and Inagaki's analysis is similar to Azmitia's (Chapter 11) argument that cognitive development requires solitary reflection as well as the social construction of knowledge through collective activity.

Crawford adopts a cultural psychological framework in Chapter 15 to examine how new forms of human activity (computer use) and technological tools (computers and information technology) present challenges to our understanding of how mathematical knowledge is constructed and how mathematics is taught in schools and universities. Traditionally, children have been required to learn mathematics 'in a form that is decontextualised from the human activities that engendered it'. Crawford suggests that in the 'information era' we should view mathematics education 'as a life long experience inextricably connected to other forms of cultural activity'. To illustrate this Crawford discusses an innovative twelve-week study of how computers, and the programming language LOGO, provided a new (social) context for children's mathematical activity in a class of 4–5-year-olds in an Australian pre-school. She also describes how the mathematical knowledge and understanding of a group of 12-year-old girls was radically transformed through their participation in an after-school computer club. In both contexts she provides examples of children constructing new mathematical insights through peer collaboration and collective activity. Using these and other examples (including that of a teacher training programme for mathematics teachers), Crawford develops a radical critique of traditional forms of mathematics education (as practised in some Australian schools) which orient students towards imitation, memorisation, and rote forms of problem solving. She claims that these approaches are outmoded, that they ignore the socio-cultural contexts in which practical mathematical activities take place, and that they neglect the personal needs and goals of children and the adults who teach them. Just as, historically, the development of symbolic notational systems and writing and calculating tools gave rise to educational systems which revolutionised human cognition (Cole, Ch. 2; Gauvain, Ch. 4), the new cultural tools of the information era offer the potential to change the ways in which teachers and learners think about and understand mathematical concepts.

References

Doise, W. & Mugny, G. (1984) *The social development of the intellect*, Oxford, Pergamon Press.

Piaget, J. (1932) *The moral judgement of the child*, London, Routledge & Kegan Paul.

Super, C.M. & Harkness, S. (1986) 'The developmental niche: conceptualisation at the interface of child and culture', *International Journal of Behavioural Development*, 9, 545–569.

Vygotsky, L.S. (1962) *Thought and language*, Cambridge, Mass., MIT Press.

Vygotsky, L.S. (1978) *Mind in society: the development of higher psychological processes*, Cambridge, Mass., Harvard University Press.

Part I

Cultural psychology
A framework for understanding teaching and learning

Chapter 1

L.S. Vygotsky and contemporary developmental psychology*

James V. Wertsch and Peeter Tulviste

Over the past decade there has been a major upsurge of interest in the ideas of Lev Semenovich Vygotsky (1896–1934). . . .

Our goal in this chapter is to review a few of Vygotsky's ideas that have particular relevance for contemporary developmental psychology and to see how these ideas can be extended in light of recent theoretical advances in the social sciences and humanities. Our discussion focuses primarily on two points in Vygotsky's theoretical approach: his claim about the social origins and social nature of higher (i.e., uniquely human) mental functioning and his uses of culture. In examining these points we also touch on his use of a developmental method and on his distinction between elementary and higher mental functioning.

Social origins of individual mental functioning

Perhaps the major reason for Vygotsky's current appeal in the West is his analysis of the social origins of mental processes. This is a theme that has reemerged with considerable force in Western developmental psychology over the past twenty years or so, and Vygotsky's ideas have come to play an important role in this movement.

In Vygotsky's view, mental functioning in the individual can be understood only by examining the social and cultural processes from which it derives. This involves an analytical strategy that may appear to some to be paradoxical at first glance. Namely, it calls on the investigator to begin the analysis of mental functioning in the individual by going outside the individual. As one of Vygotsky's students and colleagues, A.R. Luria, put it:

> In order to explain the highly complex forms of human consciousness one must go beyond the human organism. One must seek the origins of

* This is an edited version of a chapter that appeared in *An introduction to psychology*. London: Routledge, 1996.

conscious activity . . . in the external processes of social life, in the social and historical forms of human existence.

(1981, p. 25)

This view stands in marked contrast to the strong individualistic assumptions that underlie the bulk of contemporary Western research in psychology (see Sarason, 1981, for a critique of these assumptions).

Vygotsky's claims about the analytic priority to be given to social processes were in evidence throughout his career as a psychologist (basically the decade before his death from tuberculosis in 1934). For example, in one of his first articles from this period he asserted that "the social dimension of consciousness is primary in time and in fact. The individual dimension of consciousness is derivative and secondary" (Vygotsky, 1979, p. 30). . . .

Perhaps the most useful general formulation of Vygotsky's claims about the social origins of individual mental functioning can be found in his "general genetic law of cultural development."

Any function in the child's cultural development appears twice, or on two planes. First it appears on the social plane, and then on the psychological plane. First it appears between people as an interpsychological category, and then within the child as an intrapsychological category. This is equally true with regard to voluntary attention, logical memory, the formation of concepts, and the development of volition. . . . [I]t goes without saying that internalization transforms the process itself and changes its structure and functions. Social relations or relations among people genetically underlie all higher functions and their relationships.

(Vygotsky, 1981a, p. 163)

There are several aspects of this statement worth noting. The first is that the notion of mental functioning it presupposes differs from that which is typically assumed in contemporary Western psychology. Instead of beginning with the assumption that mental functioning occurs first and foremost, if not only, within the individual, it assumes that one can speak equally appropriately of mental processes as occurring *between* people on the intermental plane.[1] Indeed, it gives analytic priority to such intermental functioning in that intramental functioning is viewed as being derivative, as emerging through the mastery and internalization of social processes.

This fundamental difference in orientation is clearly manifested in how terms are used. In contemporary usage terms such as *cognition, memory*, and *attention* are automatically assumed to apply exclusively to the individual. In order to use these terms when speaking of processes carried out on the social plane, we must attach some modifier. This is the source of recent terms such as *socially shared cognition* (Resnick, Levine, and Behrend, 1991), *socially distributed cognition* (Hutchins, 1991), and *collective memory* (Middleton, 1987).

The need to use modifiers such as "socially shared" reflects the derivative, or nonbasic, status that mental functioning carried out on the social plane is assumed to have in contemporary paradigms.

In contrast to traditions in which individualistic assumptions are built into the very terms used to discuss psychological phenomena, Vygotsky's view was based in his claims about the social origins and "quasi-social nature" (Vygotsky, 1981a, p. 164) of intramental functioning. This orientation reflects an implicit rejection of the primacy given by individual functioning and the seemingly neat distinction between social and individual processes that characterize many contemporary approaches in psychology. In contrast to such approaches, Vygotsky viewed mental functioning as a kind of action (Wertsch, 1991) that may be carried out by individuals or by dyads and larger groups. Much like that of authors such as Bateson (1972) and Geertz (1973), therefore, this view is one in which mind is understood as "extending beyond skin." Mind, cognition, memory, and so forth are understood not as attributes or properties of the individual, but as functions that may be carried out intermentally or intramentally

Vygotsky's claims about the social origins of individual mental functioning surface in many ways throughout his writings. Two issues that have taken on particular importance in contemporary developmental psychology in the West are the "zone of proximal development" (Vygotsky, 1978, 1987) and "egocentric" and "inner speech" (Vygotsky, 1978, 1987). Each of these phenomena has taken on a sort of life of its own in the contemporary developmental literature, but from a Vygotskian perspective it is essential to remember how they are situated in an overall theoretical framework. In particular, it is important to remember that they are specific instances of more general claims about the social origins of individual mental functioning.

The zone of proximal development has recently received a great deal of attention in the West (e.g., Brown and Ferrara, 1985; Brown and French, 1979; Cole 1985; Rogoff, 1990; Rogoff and Wertsch, 1984; Tharp and Gallimore, 1988). This zone is defined as the distance between a child's "actual developmental level as determined by independent problem solving" and the higher level of "potential development as determined through problem solving under adult guidance or in collaboration with more capable peers" (Vygotsky, 1978, p. 86).

Vygotsky examined the implications of the zone of proximal development for the organization of instruction and for the assessment of intelligence. With regard to the former he argued that instruction should be tied more closely to the level of potential development than to the level of actual development: with regard to the latter he argued that measuring the level of potential development is just as important as the actual developmental level. He used the following example to illustrate his ideas about assessment:

Imagine that we have examined two children and have determined that the mental age of both is seven years. This means that both children solve tasks accessible to seven-year-olds. However, when we attempt to push these children further in carrying out the tests, there turns out to be an essential difference between them. With the help of leading questions, examples, and demonstrations, one of them easily solves test items taken from two years above the child's level of [actual] development. The other solves test items that are only a half-year above his or her level of [actual] development.

(Vygotsky, 1956, pp. 446–447)

Given this set of circumstances, Vygotsky (1956, p. 447) went on to pose the question, "Is the mental development of these two children the same?" In his view it was not:

From the point of view of their independent activity they are equivalent, but from the point of view of their immediate potential development they are sharply different. That which the child turns out to be able to do with the help of an adult points us towards the zone of the child's proximal development. This means that, with the help of this method, we can take stock not only of today's completed process of development, not only the cycles that are already concluded and done, not only the processes of maturation that are completed; we can also take stock of processes that are now in the state of coming into being, that are only ripening, or only developing.

(Vygotsky, 1956, pp. 447–448)

In such analyses, it is essential to keep in mind that the actual and potential levels of development correspond with intramental and intermental functioning, respectively. By doing so one can avoid the temptation to view the zone of proximal development simply as formulation for improving the assessment of individual mental functioning. Instead, it can be seen as having powerful implications for how one can *change* intermental, and hence intramental, functioning. This has been the key to intervention programs such as the "reciprocal teaching" outlined by Palincsar and Brown (1984, 1988).

As in the case of the zone of proximal development, Vygotsky's account of egocentric and inner speech reflects his more general concern with the sociocultural origins of individual mental functioning and has given rise to a spate of recent research (e.g., Berk, 1986; Berk and Garvin, 1984; Bivens and Berk, 1990; Bivens and Hagstrom, 1992; Diaz and Berk, 1992; Emerson, 1983; Kohlberg, Yaeger, and Hjertholm, 1968; Wertsch, 1979a, 1979b, 1985. Vygotsky claimed that inner speech enables humans to plan and regulate their action and derives from previous participation in verbal social interaction. Egocentric speech is "a [speech] form found in the transition from external to inner speech" (Vygotsky, 1934, p. 46). The appearance of ego-centric speech, roughly at the age of 3, reflects the emergence of a new self-regulative function similar to that of inner speech. Its external form reflects the fact that the child has not fully differentiated this new speech function from the function of social contact and social interaction.

As was the case in his account of the zone of proximal development Vygotsky's treatment of egocentric and inner speech is grounded in the assumptions spelled out in his general genetic law of cultural development. This is reflected at several points in his treatment. For example, let us turn once again to the terminology involved. Why did Vygotsky formulate his claims in terms of inner *speech* rather than in terms of *thinking, mental processes*, or some other commonly used label? The answer to this question lies in the assumptions about the social origins and quasi-social nature of intramental functioning. As was the case for other theorists in his milieu (e.g., Potebnya, 1922), Vygotsky's use of the term *speech* here reflects the fact that he viewed individual mental functioning as deriving essentially from the mastery and internalization of social processes.

Vygotsky's emphasis on the social origins of individual mental processes in this case emerges quite clearly in his analysis of the functions of language. He argued that "a sign is always originally a means used for social purposes, a means of influencing others, and only later becomes a means of influencing oneself" (Vygotsky, 1981a, p. 157). And focusing more specifically on the sign system of language, he argued that "the primary function of speech, both for the adult and for the child, is the function of communication, social contact, influencing surrounding individuals" (Vygotsky, 1934, p. 45). With regard to egocentric and inner speech Vygotsky argued that because these forms derive from "communication, social contact, influencing surrounding individuals," it follows that they should reflect certain properties of their intermental precursors, properties such as a dialogic structure. This is pre-cisely what he seems to have had in mind when he asserted that "egocentric speech . . . grows out of its social foundations by means of transferring social, collaborative forms of behavior to the sphere of the individual's psychological functioning" (Vygotsky, 1934, p. 45). Explications and extensions of this basic argument of how social, dialogic properties of speech characterize inner speech have been made by scholars such as Bibler (1975, 1981), Emerson (1983), and Wertsch (1980, 1985, 1991).

The role of a developmental method

A second theme in Vygotsky's work that has made it attractive to contempor-ary Western psychology is his use of a developmental, or genetic, method. His reliance on this method is reflected in the very title of his "general genetic law of cultural development." The fact that the law is formulated in terms of developmental transitions reflects his assumption that the most adequate way to understand human mental functioning is to trace it back through the developmental changes it has undergone. In his view,

> We need to concentrate not on the *product* of development but on the very *process* by which higher forms are established. . . . To encompass in research the process of a given thing's development in all its phases and changes – from birth to death – fundamentally means to discover its nature, its essence, for "it is only in movement that a body shows what it is." Thus, the historical [that is, in the broadest sense of "history"] study of behavior is not an auxiliary aspect of theoretical study, but rather forms its very base.
>
> (Vygotsky, 1978, pp. 64–65)

Vygotsky's account of a genetic method derived from several theoretical sources. For example, his debt to his contemporaries in psychology is reflected in the distinction he drew between description and explanation in psychology.

> Following Lewin, we can apply [the] distinction between the phenotypic (descriptive) and genotypic (explanatory) viewpoints to psychology. By a developmental study of a problem, I mean the disclosure of its genesis, its causal dynamic basis. By phenotypic I mean the analysis that begins directly with an object's current features and manifestations. It is possible to furnish many examples from psychology where serious errors have been committed because these viewpoints have been confused.
>
> (Vygotsky, 1978, p. 62)

Unlike many contemporary developmental psychologists, Vygotsky did not limit the application of his genetic analysis to ontogenesis. Instead, he viewed ontogenesis as one of several "genetic domains" (Wertsch, 1985) that must eventually be taken into consideration in order to provide an adequate account of human mental processes. In addition, he was concerned with phylogenesis, sociocultural history, and microgenesis (Wertsch, 1985). In his view, an adequate account of human mental functioning could be derived only through understanding how these various genetic domains operate within an integrated system. Vygotsky posited that change in each genetic domain is associated with a distinct set of explanatory principles.

> The use and "invention" of tools in humanlike apes crowns the organic development of behavior in evolution and paves the way for the transition of all development to take place along new paths. It creates *the basic psychological prerequisites for the historical development of behavior*. Labor and the associated development of human speech and other psychological signs with which primitives attempt to master their behavior signify the beginning of the genuine cultural or historical development of behavior.

Finally, in child development, along with processes of organic growth and maturation, a second line of development is clearly distinguished – the cultural growth of behavior. It is based on the mastery of devices and means of cultural behavior and thinking.

(Vygotsky and Luria, 1930, pp. 3–4)

In this view it is misguided to reduce the account of change in one genetic domain to the principles invoked in connection with another, a point associated with Vygotsky's basic antirecapitulationist orientation (Wertsch, 1991).

Vygotsky was particularly interested in "revolutionary," as opposed to evolutionary, shifts in development. For example, in outlining his account of the form of genetic transition involved in phylogenesis, sociocultural history, and ontogenesis, he argued:

> All three of these moments are symptoms of new epochs in the evolution of behavior and indications of a *change in the type of development itself.* In all three instances we have thereby selected turning points or critical steps in the development of behavior. We think that the turning point or critical moment in the behavior of apes is the use of tools; in the behavior of primitives it is labor and the use of psychological signs; in the behavior of the child it is the bifurcation of lines of development into natural-psychological and cultural-psychological development.

(Vygotsky and Luria, 1930, p. 4)

The tenets of Vygotsky's developmental approach provided the basic methodological framework within which all other aspects of his analyses were formulated.

Vygotsky's uses of culture

Up to this point our comments on the social origins and social nature of individual mental functioning have focused on a particular kind of social process. Specifically, we have concentrated on intermental functioning in the form of dyadic or small group processes and how it fits into Vygotsky's genetic analysis. This was a major focus of Vygotsky's thinking and certainly constitutes one of the ways in which mind may be said to extend beyond the skin in his approach. It has also been the concern of a great deal of Vygotsky-inspired research in contemporary Western psychology (e.g., Rogoff, 1990; Rogoff and Wertsch, 1984; Wertsch, 1979a).

There is a second, equally important sense, however, in which mental functioning may be said to extend beyond the skin in Vygotsky's writings, a sense that draws on his notion of culture. Mind extends beyond the skin in this second sense because human mental functioning, on the intramental as well as intermental plane, involves cultural tools, or mediational means. In contrast to the "unencumbering image of the self" that is presupposed by so much of contemporary psychology (Taylor, 1985; Wertsch, 1991), Vygotsky's account of culture suggests that humans are never as autonomous and as free of outside interference as it might at first appear. Instead, human mental functioning, even when carried out by an individual acting in isolation, is inherently social, or sociocultural, in that it incorporates socially evolved and socially organized cultural tools.

The two senses in which mental functioning may be said to extend beyond the skin are analytically distinct and hence require the use of different theoretical and methodological categories. However, in concrete human action they are inextricably linked, a point that surfaces in many forms throughout Vygotsky's writings. For example, the relationship between intermental functioning and culture is outlined in his statement that

> the word "social" when applied to our subject has great significance. Above all, in the widest sense of the word, it means that everything that is cultural is social. Culture is the product of social life and human social activity. That is why just by raising the question of the cultural development of behavior we are directly introducing the social plane of development.
>
> (Vygotsky, 1981a, p. 164)

From this statement one can see that Vygotsky understood culture as something that comes into concrete existence in social processes, and he viewed these social processes as providing the foundation for the emergence of individual mental processes. However, he did not assume that it is possible to reduce an account of culture to a set of principles that apply to intermental processes.

Despite the clear role that cultural tools played in Vygotsky's approach, his account of the more general category of culture is by no means well developed. Furthermore, the difficulties that arise in understanding his notion of culture are not primarily difficulties that can be resolved by correcting translations or by making more texts available. The fact is that, even though the school of psychology he founded came to be called the cultural-historical school in the Soviet Union in the 1930s, neither Vygotsky nor his followers provided extensive accounts of the notion of culture.[2]

An explication of Vygotsky's notion of culture must be based on an analysis of the role that culture played in his overall theoretical system. In this system Vygotsky gave the idea of mediation analytic priority over the notion of culture (as well as other themes; see Wertsch, 1985). Indeed, his analysis of culture is part of his attempt to elaborate the notion of mediation. In his view, a criterial feature of human action is that it is mediated by tools ("cultural tools") and signs ("psychological tools"). His primary concern was with the latter (what we are here calling "cultural tools"), and for that reason we shall focus primarily on "semantic mediation."

Basic to this perspective is Vygotsky's insight that the inclusion of psychological, or cultural, tools into human functioning fundamentally transforms this functioning. The incorporation of mediational means does not simply facilitate processes that would otherwise have occurred. Instead,

> by being included in the process of behavior, the psychological tool alters the entire flow and structure of mental functions. It does this by determining the structure of a new instrumental act, just as a technical tool alters the process of a natural adaptation by determining the form of labor operations.
>
> (Vygotsky, 1981b, p. 137)

According to Vygotsky (1981b):

> The following can serve as examples of psychological tools and their complex systems: language; various systems for counting; mnemonic techniques; algebraic symbol systems; works of art; writing; schemes, diagrams, maps, and mechanical drawings; all sorts of conventional signs; and so on.
>
> (p. 137)

In all cases, these are mediational means that are the products of sociocultural evolution and are appropriated by groups or individuals as they carry out mental functioning.

Vygotsky's tendency to approach the notion of culture via his account of mediation reflects the fact that he understood culture in terms of sign systems. He was primarily interested in one sign system, language. In his studies he focused on psychological processes that make use of natural language and on systems built on natural language – above all, prose and poetry (e.g., Vygotsky, 1971). At the same time, he showed a continuing interest in the use of non-verbal signs. For example, he often drew on examples having to do with the use of sign systems from traditional societies, such as tying knots to organize memory, and he was involved in A.N. Leont'ev's (1931) early research on children's and adults' use of pictures to assist performance in memory tasks (see Vygotsky, 1978).

Vygotsky was quite familiar with the general theories of culture that were being developed in his time by scholars in sociology, anthropology, and other disciplines. However, he chose not to incorporate them into his writings in any major way. Indeed, he firmly rejected the basic assumptions of the British evolutionary anthropologist that laws of individual mental functioning (i.e., laws of association) were adequate for explaining the historical development of culture, human behavior, and human thinking: Instead of assuming that human mental functioning remains basically the same across historical epochs, he argues that culture creates special forms of behavior, changes the functioning of mind, constructs new stories in the developing system of human behavior. . . . In the course of historical development, social humans change the ways and means of their behavior, transform their natural premises and functions, elaborate and create new, specifically cultural forms of behavior.

(Vygotsky, 1983, pp. 29–30)

. . . A first major fact about Vygotsky's notion of culture, then, is that it was motivated primarily by a concern with sign systems and their role in human mental functioning A second fact is that he held strongly to a evolutionist account of culture. In line with his mediation-based approach to culture, this fact was manifested in his comments on mediational means. These means were viewed as being capable of supporting more "rudimentary" and advanced levels of intermental and intramental functioning. A correlate of this was Vygotsky's concern with more and less developed cultures, primitive and modern cultures, people, minds, and so forth.

This evolutionist approach to culture reflects a kind of ethnocentric perspective, namely Eurocentrism, that makes it difficult to interpret some of the most interesting findings generated by cross-cultural studies. Vygotsky clearly regarded some cultures as inferior to others. It must be recognized, however, that he believed people in all cultures to be capable of, and indeed in need of, developing. For instance, he argued that education in Soviet Russia should aim at turning all children into "supermen" or "new [Soviet] men." The notion of a superman was of course borrowed from Nietzsche, but in Vygotsky's view, cultural, rather than biological, factors were capable of creating this new kind of human (Vygotsky, 1930).

In addition to their role in the ideological framework within which Vygotsky was operating, his evolutionist ideas were manifested in concrete ways in his empirical research. This is most apparent in his account of conceptual development. While arguing that all humans share a capacity to use language in a variety of ways, Vygotsky's assumption was that only more advanced groups had taken the evolutionary step necessary to use words in abstract, decontextualized ways. This assumption underlay several studies conducted by Luria (1976) in the 1930s in Soviet Central Asia that compared the performance of various cultural groups.

Vygotsky and Luria tended to interpret the results of these studies in terms of whether subjects were from primitive or advanced societies. They proceeded on the assumption that it is possible to characterize individuals and groups generally in terms of whether they use "scientific" versus "everyday" concepts (Vygotsky; 1987), rely on "abstract" versus "situational" thinking (Luria, 1976), and so forth. This is entirely consistent with Vygotsky's evolutionist approach to culture, according to which it is possible to rank cultures on some kind of scale from lower to higher.

In reanalyzing and extending the studies by Luria, authors such as Scribner and Cole (1981) and Tulviste (1986, 1991) argued that it is more accurate to interpret subjects' performance in these studies in terms of the demands of particular task settings than in terms of the general level of subjects' mental functioning or of a culture. Specifically, they demonstrated that the kinds of differences documented in subjects' performances are primarily attributable to differences in experience with the activity of a particular institutional setting, formal schooling. This is the crux of Scribner and Cole's (1981) "practice account of literacy" (p. 235). According to this account, subjects' exposure to the patterns of speaking and reasoning in formal instructional settings gives rise to a particular set of discourse and cognitive skills. Instead of assuming that these skills represent a general measure by which one can classify individuals and groups, Scribner and Cole emphasized that they are a particular form of literacy practice. The form of activity here contrasts, for example, with literacy practices, such as memorizing religious texts, that were found to be associated with other cognitive skills. . . .

The roots of this explication and extension of Vygotsky's ideas are to be found in the writing of Vygotsky himself. His claims about the situational specificity of mental functioning began to emerge only in the last years of his career, but they are clearly manifested in the differences between Chapters 5 and 6 of *Thinking and speech* (Vygotsky, 1987). Both chapters deal with the ontogenetic transition from "complexities" to "genuine," or "scientific," concepts. They differ, however, in what Vygotsky sees as relevant developmental forces. In Chapter 5 (based on research with Shif (1935) and written in the early 1930s, concept development is treated primarily in terms of intramental processes, that is, children's conceptual development as they move from "unorganized heaps" to "complexes" to "concepts."

In Chapter 6 (written in 1934) there is an essential shift in the way Vygotsky approached these issues. He clearly continued to be interested in intramental functioning, but he shifted to approaching concept development from the perspective of how it emerges in particular spheres of socioculturally situated activity. Specifically, he was concerned with how the forms of teacher–student intermental functioning encountered in the institutional setting of formal schooling provide a framework for the development of conceptual thinking.

This shift in Vygotsky's focus is an essential shift for two reasons. First, it was a move towards analyzing conceptual thinking in terms of its intermental precursors. This of course is in line with the argument he had used all along in connection with issues such as inner speech, and it follows naturally from his general genetic law of cultural development. Second, and more important for our purposes, it was a move toward recognizing that an account of the social origins of intramental functioning cannot stop with the intermental plane. Instead, the point is that the forms of mediated intermental functioning involved must themselves be recognized as being socioculturally situated with respect to activity settings and associated mediational means.

This transition in Vygotsky's thinking is important because it indicates a direction he was beginning to consider which, among other things, suggests a way out of the quandary of Eurocentrism. It suggests that instead of viewing particular forms of mental functioning as characterizing individuals or groups in a general way, these forms can be viewed as being characteristic of specific settings. As Tulviste (1991) noted, then, it follows that because individuals and groups are exposed to varieties of activity settings, we can expect them to master a heterogeneous set of mediational means and hence a heterogeneous set of mental processes.

Problems and prospects

There is little doubt that the renewed interest in Vygotsky's writings has had a powerful and positive influence on contemporary studies in developmental psychology. However, this by no means should be taken to indicate that there are no weaknesses in his approach or that revision and extension are not in order. In this final section, we touch on a few of these weaknesses and outline some ways in which they can be addressed.

The first of these concerns Vygotsky's Eurocentrism. In our opinion, Vygotsky made some major contributions to the discussion of historical differences in mental functioning, an issue that has seldom been addressed satisfactorily in psychology since his time. However, we believe that he tended to use the notion of a developmental hierarchy too broadly when trying to interpret differences in mental functioning. The result was a view in which modern European cultural tools and forms of mental functioning were assumed to be generally superior to the tools and functioning of their peoples. In many instances we believe it is more appropriate to view differences in terms of coexisting but qualitatively distinct ways of approaching a problem rather than as more or less advanced general levels of mental functioning.

As we noted in the preceding section, there are indications that Vygotsky was moving away from a view in which forms of mental functioning are viewed as properties that characterize the general level of individuals' and groups' functioning. In its place he seems to have been suggesting that particular forms of mental functioning are associated with particular institutionally situated activities. An implication of this is that it is more appropriate to characterize the mental functioning of individuals in terms of heterogeneity (Tulviste, 1986, 1991) or a "cultural tool kit" (Wertsch, 1991) of mental processes rather than in terms of a single, general level.

Reformulating mental functioning in terms of heterogeneity and cultural tool kits helps avoid the often ungrounded assumption that various individuals or groups can generally be ranked as inferior or superior to others. However, it still leaves unresolved the issue of what role developmental progression plays in mental processes. There is little doubt in most people's minds that there has been historical progress in at least certain forms of activities and the mental processes (e.g., reasoning) associated with them. For example, if one considers scientific knowledge about electricity, there is little doubt that the past two centuries have witnessed significant progress. It follows that *within specific domains of knowledge* certain activities, cultural tools, and forms of reasoning may be more advanced than others. One of the major challenges of a Vygotskian approach, then, is how to capture such facts about developmental progression without falling prey to ungrounded assumptions about the general superiority or inferiority of individuals or groups.

A second major issue in Vygotsky's approach that will require further attention emerges in his account of the ontogenetic domain. In formulating his notion of this domain, he argued that two lines of development – the cultural line and the natural line – come into contact and transform one another.

> The growth of the normal child into civilization usually involves a fusion with the processes of organic maturation. Both planes of development – the natural and the cultural – coincide and mingle with one another. The two lines interpenetrate one another and essentially form a single line of sociobiological formation of the child's personality.
>
> (Vygotsky, 1960, p. 47)

Although this general formulation continues to make a great deal of sense, the fact is that Vygotsky said very little and was quite unclear about the natural line of development. At some points he spoke of "organic growth and maturation" (Vygotsky and Luria, 1930, p. 4) when dealing with his line of development. This could refer to everything from the emergence of sensory abilities to motor skills to neurological development, but he did not specify which. In other places he seems to have been concerned with developmental changes that are not attributable directly to organic maturation on the one hand but are not cultural by his definition on the other. For example, he sometimes referred to changes in young children's abilities to use primitive tools, such as those outlined by Piaget (1952) in his account of the sensorimotor development having to do with new means to old ends.

Furthermore, Vygotsky said almost nothing about how the "elementary mental functioning" that grows out of the natural line of development might influence the "higher mental functioning" that derives from the mastery of cultural tools. Instead, he focused almost exclusively on ways in which cultural forces transform the natural line of development. In accordance with such a view, the natural line provides a kind of raw material whose fate is to be transformed by cultural forces.

A further problem with Vygotsky's account of the natural and cultural line in ontogenesis is that he viewed these lines as operating quite independently of one another during early phases of life. Since the time he made these claims, investigators such as Piaget (1952), Bower (1974), and Bruner (1976) have made major research advances that bring this assumption into question, and some of Vygotsky's own followers have taken a critical stance toward it. In reviewing Vygotsky's theoretical approach, A.N. Leont'ev and Luria noted that "after all, even in children at the very earliest ages mental processes are being formed under the influence of verbal social interaction with adults who surround them" (1956, p. 7).

Vygotsky's relatively unsophisticated view of the natural line of development can be traced largely to the dearth of theoretical and empirical research on infants available in the early decades of the twentieth century. However, it also reflects another problematic assumption that underlay his work. This is the assumption that the primary force of development comes from outside the individual. Whereas one of the reasons for Vygotsky's renewed influence in contemporary psychology is that his ideas provide a corrective to the tendency to isolate individuals from their sociocultural milieu, passages such as the following might seem to suggest that ontogenesis is solely a function of environment and leaves little room to consider the role of the active individual.

> The environment appears in child development, namely in the development of personality and specific human qualities, in the role of the source of development. Hence the environment here plays the role not of the situation of development, but of its source.
>
> (Vygotsky, 1934, p. 113)

Such passages in Vygotsky's writing seem to suggest that social and cultural processes almost mechanistically determine individual processes. This view minimizes the contributions made by the active individual. Among other things, it raises the question of how individuals are capable of introducing innovation and creativity into the system.

It is clear that Vygotsky has often been read in ways that make this a major problem. However, we believe that several points in his theoretical approach contradict such a reading. For the most part, these points do not emerge in the form of explicit counterstatements; instead, they surface in the assumptions about human action that underlie the entire framework of Vygotsky's approach. As we have stressed throughout this chapter, the notion of mediation by cultural tools plays a central role in his approach. This applies nowhere more forcefully than in his account of action. The basic form of action that Vygotsky envisioned was *mediated action* (Wertsch, 1991; Zinchenko, 1985). Such action inherently involves cultural tools, and these tools fundamentally shape it. However, this does not mean that such action can be reduced to or mechanistically determined by these tools and hence by the more general sociocultural setting. Instead, such action always involves an inherent tension between the mediational means and the individual or individuals using them in unique, concrete instances. . . .

The presentation and critique of Vygotsky we have outlined in this chapter should by no means be assumed to be exhaustive. Much more in the way of background and interpretation can be obtained by consulting the publications we listed in the first section. Furthermore, one should not assume that our interpretation and critique of Vygotsky's ideas are uncontested. Although there is widespread agreement that Vygotsky's ideas are extremely rich and have major implications for contemporary research in developmental psychology, there are also major differences among authors over how these ideas should be understood and applied. Perhaps the one thing that is clear to all, however, is that Vygotsky's writings are of more than historical concern. They are capable of providing the basis for major reformulations in developmental psychology today and hence are again proving their merit as classic texts.

Notes

1 In this article we use the terms *intermental* and *intramental* rather than *interpsychological* and *intrapsychological*, respectively. This follows the translation practices established in Vygotsky (1987) and contrasts with those found in earlier translated texts (Vygotsky, 1978, 1981a). *Intermental* and *intramental* are translations of the Russian terms *interpsikhicheskii* and *intrapsikhicheskii*, respectively.

2 The second part of the term *cultural-historical* has had better luck, notably in Scribner's (1985) analysis of "Vygotsky's uses of history," from which we borrowed to formulate the title of the present section.

References

Bateson, G. (1972). *Steps to an ecology of mind: A revolutionary approach to man's understanding of himself*. New York: Ballantine.

Berk, L.E. (1986). Relationship of elementary school children's private speech in behavioral accompaniment to task, attention, and task performance. *Developmental Psychology, 22*, 671–680.

Berk, L.E. and Garvin, R. (1984). Development of private speech among low-income Appalachian children; *Developmental Psychology, 20*, 271–286.

Bibler, V.S. (1975). *Myshlenie kak tvorchestvo* [Thinking as creation]. Moscow: Izdatel-'stvo Politicheskoi Literatury.

Bibler, V.S. (1981). Vnutrennyaya rech' v ponimanii L. S. Vygotsogo (Eshshe raz o predmete psikhologii) [Inner speech in L.S. Vygotsky's conceptualization (once again on the object of psychology)]. In *Nauchnoe tvorchestvo L.S. Vygotskogo i sovremennaya psikhologiva. Tezisy dokladov vsesoyuznoi konferentsii, Moskva, 23–25 iyunya 1981* [The scientific work of L.S. Vygotsky and contemporary psychology. Thesis of the presentations of an all-union conference, Moscow, June 23–25, 1981]. Moscow: Akademiya Pedagogicheskikh Nauk SSSR.

Bivens, J.A. and Berk, L.E. (1990). A longitudinal study of the development of elementary school children's private speech. *Merrill-Palmer Quarterly, 36*, 443–463.

Bivens, J.A. and Hagstrom, F. (1992). The representation of private speech in children's literature. In R.M. Diaz and L.E. Berk (eds), *Private speech: From social interaction to self-regulation* (pp. 159–177). Hillsdale, NJ: Erlbaum.

Bower, T.G.R. (1974). *Development in infancy*. San Francisco: Freeman.

Brown, A.L. and Ferrara, R. (1985). Diagnosing zones of proximal development. In J.V. Wertsch (ed.), *Culture, communication, and cognition: Vygotskian perspectives* (pp. 273–305). New York: Cambridge University Press.

Brown, A.L. and French, L.A. (1979). The zone of potential development: Implications for intelligence testing in the year 2000. *Intelligence, 3*, 255–277.

Bruner, J.S. (1976). Early social interaction and language acquisition. In H.R. Schaffer (ed.), *Studies in mother–infant interaction* (pp. 56–78). San Diego, CA: Academic Press.

Cole, M. (1985). The zone of proximal development: Where culture and cognition create each other. In J.V. Wertsch (ed.), *Culture, communication, and cognition: Vygotskian perspectives* (pp. 146–161). New York: Cambridge University Press.

Cole, M. and Scribner, S. (1974). *Culture and thought: A psychological introduction*. New York: Wiley.

Diaz, R.M. and Berk, L.E. (eds) (1992). *Private speech: From social interaction to self-regulation*. Hillsdale, NJ: Erlbaum.

Emerson, C. (1983). The outer word and inner speech: Bakhtin, Vygotsky, and the internalization of language. *Critical Inquiry, 10*, 245–264.

Geertz, C. (1973). *The interpretation of cultures*. New York: Basic Books.

Goudena, P. (1987). The social nature of private speech of preschoolers during problem solving. *International Journal of Behavioral Development, 10*, 187–206. .

Hutchins, E. (1991). The social organization of distributed cognition. In L.B. Resnick, J.M. Levine, and S.D. Teasley (eds), *Perspectives on socially shared cognition* (pp. 283–307). Washington, DC: American Psychological Association.

Kohlberg, L., Yaeger, J. and Hjertholm, E. (1968). Private speech: Four studies and a review of theories, *Child Development, 39*, 691–736.

Leont'ev, A.N. (1931). *Razvitie pamyati: Eksperimental'noe issledovanie vysshikh psikhologicheskikh funktsii* [The development of memory: Experimental research on higher psychological functions]. Moscow–Leningrad: Uchpedgiz.

Leont'ev, A.N. (1959). *Problemy razvitiya psikhiki* [Problems in the development of mind]. Moscow: Izdatel'stvo Moskovskogo Universiteta.

Leont'ev, A.N. (1981). The problem of activity in psychology. In J.V. Wertsch (ed.), *The concept of activity in Soviet psychology* (pp. 37–71). Armonk, NY: Sharpe.

Leont'ev, A.N. and Luria, A.R. (1956). Mirovozrenie psikhologii L.S. Vygotskogo [L.S. Vygotsky's outlook on psychology]. In L.S. Vygotsky, *Izbrannye psikhologicheskie issledovaniya* [Selected psychological investigations] (pp. 3–22). Moscow: Izdatel'stvo Akademic Pedagogicheskikh Nauk.

Luria, A.R. (1976). *Cognitive development: Its cultural and social foundation*. Cambridge, MA: Harvard University Press.

Luria, A.R. (1981). *Language and cognition* (J.V. Wertsch, ed.). New York: Wiley Intersciences.

Middleton, D. (1987). Collective memory and remembering: Some issues and approaches. *Quarterly Newsletter of the Laboratory of Comparative Human Cognition, 9*, 2–5.

Palincsar, A.S. and Brown, A.L. (1984). Reciprocal teaching of comprehension-fostering and comprehension-monitoring activities. *Cognition and Instruction, 1*, 117–175.

Palincsar, A.S. and Brown, A.L. (1988). Teaching and practicing thinking skills to promote comprehension in the context of group problem solving. *RASE, 9*, 53–59.

Piaget, J. (1952). *The origins of intelligence in children*. New York: International Universities Press.

Potebnya, A.A. (1922). *Mysl' i yazyk* [Thought and language]. Odessa, Ukraine: Gosudarstvennoe Izdatel'stvo Ukrainy.

Resnick, L.B., Levine, R., and Behrend, A. (1991). *Perspectives on socially shared cognition*. Washington, DC: American Psychological Association.

Rogoff, B. (1990). *Apprenticeship in thinking: Cognitive development in social context*. New York: Oxford University Press.

Rogoff, B. and Wertsch, J.V. (eds). (1984). Children's learning in the "zone of proximal development" In New directions for child development (no. 23). San Francisco: Jossey-Bass.

Sarason, S.B. (1981). An asocial psychology and a misdirected clinical psychology. *American Psychologist, 36*, 827–836.

Scribner, S. (1985). Vygotsky's uses of history. In J.V. Wertsch (ed.), *Culture, communication, and cognition: Vygotskian perspectives* (pp. 119–145). New York: Cambridge University Press.

Scribner, S. and Cole, M. (1981). *The psychological consequences of literacy*. Cambridge, MA: Harvard University Press.

Shif, Zh.I. (1935). *Razvitie nauchnykh ponyatii u shkol'nika: Issledovanie k voprosu umstvennogo razvitiya shkol'nika pri obuchenii obshchestvovedeniyu* [The development of scientific concepts in the school child: The investigation of intellectual development of the school child in social science instruction]. Moscow–Leningrad Gosudarstvennoe Uchebno-Pedagogicheskoe Izdatel'stvo.

Taylor, C. (1985). *Human agency and language. (Philosophical papers 1*. Cambridge: England, Cambridge University Press.

Tharp, R.G. and Gallimore, R. (1988). *Rousing minds to life*. New York: Cambridge University Press.

Tulviste, P. (1986). Ob istoricheskoi geterogennosti verbal'nogo myshleniya [The historical heterogeneity of verbal thinking]. In Ya. A. Ponomarev (ed.), *Myshlenie, obshchenie, praktika: sbornik nauchnykh trudov* [Thinking, society, practice: A collection of scientific works] (pp. 19–29). Yaroslavl, USSR: Yaroslavskii Gosudarstvennyi Pedagogicheskii Institut im. K.D. Ushinskogo.

Tulviste, P. (1991). *Cultural-historical development of verbal thinking: A psychological study*. Commack, NY: Nova Science Publishers.

Vygotsky L.S. (1930). Sotsialisticheskaya peredelka cheloveka [The socialist transformation of man]. *VARNITSO, 9–10*, 36–44.

Vygotsky, L.S. (1934). *Myshlenie i rech': Psikhologicheskie issledovaniya* [Thinking and speech: Psychological investigations]. Moscow and Leningrad: Gosudarstvennoe Sotsial'no-Ekonomicheskoe Izdatel'stvo.

Vygotsky, L.S. (1956). *Izbrannye psikhologicheskie issledovaniya* [Selected psychological investigations]. Moscow: Izdatel'stvo Akademii Pedagogicheskikh Nauk.

Vygotsky, L.S. (1960). *Razvitie vysshykh psikhicheskikh funktsii* [The development of higher mental functions]. Moscow: Izdatel'stvo Akademii Pedagogicheskikh Nauk.

Vygotsky, L.S. (1971). *The psychology of art*. Cambridge, MA: MIT Press.

Vygotsky, L.S. (1978). *Mind in society: The development of higher psychological processes* (M. Cole, V. John-Steiner, S. Scribner and E. Souberman, eds). Cambridge, MA: Harvard University Press.

Vygotsky, L.S. (1979). Consciousness as a problem in the psychology of behavior. *Soviet Psychology, 17*, 3–35.

Vygotsky, L.S. (1981a). The genesis of higher mental functions. In J.V. Wertsch (ed.), *The concept of activity in Soviet psychology* (pp. 144–188). Armonk, NY: Sharpe.

Vygotsky, L.S. (1981b). The instrumental method in psychology. In J.V. Wertsch (ed.), *The concept of activity in Soviet psychology* (pp. 133–143). Armonk, NY: Sharpe.

Vygotsky, L.S. (1983). *Sobranie sochinenii, Tom tretii. Problemy razvitiya psikhiki* [Collected works, Vol. 3: Problems in the development of mind]. Moscow: Izdatel'stvo Pedagogika.

Vygotsky, L.S. (1987). *Thinking and speech* (N. Minick, ed. and trans.). New York: Plenum (translation of Vygotsky, 1982b).

Vygotsky, L.S. and Luria, A.R. (1930). *Etyudy po istorii povedeniya: Obez'yana, primitiv, rebenok* [Essays on the history of behavior: Ape, primitive, child]. Moscow and Leningrad: Gosudarstvennoe Izdatel'stvo.

Wertsch, J.V. (1979a). From social interaction to higher psychological processes: A clarification and application of Vygotsky's theory. *Human Development, 22*, 1–22.

Wertsch, J.V. (1979b). The regulation of human action and the given-new organization of private speech. In G. Zivin (ed.), *The development of self-regulation through private speech* (pp. 79–98). New York: Wiley.

Wertsch, J.V. (1980). The significance of dialogue in Vygotsky's account of social, egocentric, and inner speech. *Contemporary Educational Psychology, 5*, 150–162.

Wertsch, J.V. (1985). *Vygotsky and the social formation of mind*. Cambridge, MA: Harvard University Press.

Wertsch, J.V. (1991). *Voices of the mind: A sociocultural approach to mediated action*. Cambridge, MA: Harvard University Press.

Zinchenko, V.P. (1985). Vygotsky's ideas about units of analysis of mind. In J.V. Wertsch (ed.), *Culture, communication, and cognition: Vygotskian perspectives* (pp. 94–118). New York: Cambridge University Press.

Chapter 2

Cognitive development and formal schooling

The evidence from cross-cultural research*

Michael Cole

> It is the dilemma of psychology to deal as a natural science with an object
> that creates history.
>
> (Ernst Boesch)

My goal in this chapter is to summarize the implications for understanding
cognitive development of the past three decades of intensive cross-cultural
research on the cognitive consequences of formal educational experience during middle childhood. . . .

Cross-cultural psychologists have (correctly, in my opinion) insisted that
evidence of cultural variation is of cardinal importance to the development of
a coherent psychological approach to human nature. However, the barriers to
including the category of culture in a unified science of psychology are
exceedingly difficult to overcome. In my opinion, eventual solution of this
problem requires that one formulate an approach to human nature that provides a clear conception of the role played by culture in general as a
theoretical/methodological foundation for the assessment of cultural variations. To my knowledge, the only existing school of psychology that has
developed such a formulation is that of the sociohistorical school. Hence, it is
to this set of ideas that I turn in order to provide the foundation for assessing
the topic of this chapter: How does formal schooling impact the process of
cognitive development?

Basic postulates of the sociohistorical school

The central role of culture in the sociohistorical school's approach to mind
and the special role that cross-cultural data played in the development of its
theories were clear in the earliest English publications of its ideas in the late

* This is an edited version of a chapter that appeared in *Vygotsky and education: Instructional
  implications and applications of sociohistorical psychology*. Cambridge: Cambridge University
  Press, 1990.

1920s and early 1930s (Leontiev, 1930; Luria, 1928, 1932; Vygotsky, 1929). Briefly (for a more extended discussion, see Cole, 1988), the fundamental postulate of their approach is that human psychological functions differ from the psychological processes of other animals because they are *culturally mediated, historically developing*, and arise from *practical activity*. Each term in this formulation is linked to the others. Taken as a whole, they provide a starting point for considering the special features of formal schooling as an activity context within which some human beings, in some cultural circumstances and some historical eras, develop.

1   Cultural mediation: The basic idea here, which can be traced back into antiquity and which forms the basis for a good deal of anthropological theorizing, is the notion that human beings live in an environment transformed by the artifacts of prior generations, extending back to the beginning of the species. The basic function of these artifacts is to coordinate human beings with the physical world and each other. As a consequence, human beings live in a "double world," simultaneously "natural" and "artificial." Culture, in this sense, must be considered the unique *medium* of human existence.

   Cultural artifacts are simultaneously ideal (conceptual) and material. They are ideal in that they contain in coded form the interactions of which they were previously a part. They exist only as they are embodied in material. This applies to language/speech as well as the more usually noted forms of artifact.

   In that they mediate interaction with the world, cultural artifacts can also be considered tools. As Luria (1928) put the matter early on, "Man differs from animals in that he can make and use tools. [These tools] not only radically change his conditions of existence, they even react on him in that they effect a change in him and his psychic condition" (pp. 493, 495).

2   The fact of cultural mediation fundamentally changes the structure of human psychological functions *vis-à-vis* animals. "Instead of applying directly its natural function to the solution of a particular task, the child puts between that function and the task a certain auxiliary means . . . by the medium of which the child manages to perform the task" (Luria, 1928, p. 495).

3   Cultural and therefore human psychological functions are historical phenomena.

   The history of one man's mastery over the regulation of the behavior of another repeats in many points his mastery over tools. It presupposes a change in the structure of behavior, which turns behavior directed to an end into behavior directed circuitously.

   (Leontiev, 1930, p. 59)

4   The basic unit for the study of psychological processes is practical activity. This idea is basic to what Vygotsky called the "cultural method" of thinking:

> human psychology is concerned with the activity of concrete individuals, which takes place either in a collective or in a situation in which the subject deals directly with the surrounding world of objects – i.e., at the potter's wheel or the writer's desk . . . if we removed human activity from the system of social relationships, it would not exist . . . the human individual's activity is a system in the system of social relations. It does not exist without these relations.
>
> (Leontiev, 1981, pp. 46–47)

5   Cultural mediation and grounding of thought in activity imply the context specificity of mental processes. As Vygotsky (1978) put it, "the mind is not a complex network of [general] capabilities, but a set of specific capabilities. . . . Learning . . . is the acquisition of many specialized abilities for thinking" (p. 83).

Four streams of history, four levels of development

In the early statements of their ideas, and in later applications, the founders of the sociohistorical school emphasized that a full theory of human development must take account of changes occurring simultaneously on four historical levels: the development of the species (*phylogeny*), the *history* of human beings since their emergence as a distinct species, *ontogeny* (the history of individual children), and *microgenesis*, the development of particular psychological processes in the course of experimental interactions in a single experimental session (e.g., the "psychological task").

Applied to the problem of cognitive development and formal schooling, this approach provides a rather well-specified framework of inquiry. First, one must inquire, at the phylogenetic level, what is the special general characteristic of *Homo sapiens* that underpins the specific form of activity called formal education. Second, at the historical level one must answer such questions as: Under what historical conditions did formal education arise? What are the social tasks that it evolved to fulfill, and what special means does it employ? Third, at the ontogenetic level one asks: What is the impact of involvement in formal school activity on individual development? Fifth, at the microgenetic level (which is the focus of the vast majority of research in educational psychology), how does the actual process of change in individual behavior occur within specific formal educational activity settings? Put differently, how is one to understand the moment-by-moment process of teaching/learning?

The phylogenetic level

For current purposes, this level is probably well enough specified in my brief summary of the basic postulates of the sociohistorical school. The special phylogenetic capacity of *Homo sapiens* is cultural mediation, the ability to act indirectly on the world via material/ideal artifacts and to communicate adaptively advantageous modifications to subsequent generations. The high-level pervasiveness of the capacity to create and use artifacts is a phylogenetic universal that attests to the "psychic unity" of our species.

The historical level

Though it must be argued that cultural mediation is a universal fact of our species, the development of specific forms of mediation (particular forms of activity employing particular mediational means) clearly is not. All cultures known to man have elaborated the basic potential of language and tool use, but not all cultures have developed the forms of activity that we refer to as formal schooling or the forms of mediation that we call literacy and numeracy.

Literacy and numeracy are direct extensions of the basic mediating capacity of language; sounds disappear as soon as they are spoken, and even the loudest speakers can project their voices over only a short distance. Language can be elaborated in myth and ritual to preserve information and make it available to later generations. In some systems (e.g., the tradition for teaching the large collection of hymns and rituals known as the Indian Vedas (Street, 1984), great accuracy can be achieved by oral recitation techniques, but at a tremendous cost in time and effort.

The essential advantage shared by all written notation systems is that they extend the power of language in time and space (Goody, 1977). Words that are written down can be carried great distances with no change in their physical characteristics. In like manner, writing systems freeze words in time: once written down, ideas and events can be returned to and contemplated time and again in their original form. In this respect, written notations are a form of memory. However, as both common sense and the evidence from research show, the actual way in which the potential of writing is realized depends crucially on the way in which it represents language and the way in which it enters into the mediation of activity.

A new mode of representation

When we look into the archaeological record, we can discern two distinct purposes of reading and writing: to regulate people's interactions with the physical world, and to regulate people's interactions with each other. The first of these purposes is illustrated by the bits of bone discovered in the vicinity of

Lascaux, in southern France, which was inhabited approximately 40,000 years ago. In the 1960s Alexander Marshak (1972) began to take an intense interest in these artifacts because of their patterned inscriptions. Previous scholars had assumed that they were used as decorations or perhaps represented no more than a form of doodling by people inhabiting the caves. By sitting at the mouth of the cave evening after evening and observing the rising moon, Marshak discovered that the cave dwellers were not doodling; they were making calendars.

A calendar is an excellent example of the way that written symbol systems can be used to regulate people's interactions with the physical environment. The key purpose of a calendar is prediction: How many days until winter? How many days until salmon return from the sea? Prediction is essential to control. Knowing when the salmon will arrive allows one to build fish traps and to set them in time to catch the fish; knowing when winter will arrive provides time to lay in provisions that enable one to survive the winter. Marshaks discovery is not an isolated one. Throughout the world archaeologists have discovered a variety of sophisticated calendrical devices – for example, Stonehenge – that were important for organizing people's activities.

A more immediate precursor of modern literacy is to be found in that part of the world now called the Middle East, where farming and the domestication of animals began some 10,000 years ago (Pfeiffer, 1972: Schmandt-Besserat, 1978). Once people discovered that they could collect and raise the seeds of food-bearing plants and that they could raise animals in captivity, they began to make permanent settlements. Permanent settlements permitted people to accumulate surplus goods to use in trade for things they could not grow or make themselves. It was in such early agricultural villages that archaeologists discovered a variety of small clay objects, such as the tokens found in the ancient Near East (Schmandt-Besserat, 1978). These tokens illustrate both of the fundamental features of writing systems in their most primitive aspect. First. because they "stood for" the actual objects – a circular token with lines on it might represent wool, for example, and a cone-shaped token might represent bread – they enabled people to keep track of their goods over time without having to count them over and over again. Second, because they were small and sturdy, they could be carried from one place to another as a kind of promissory note for purposes of trade. In either case, they were artificial signs that represented natural objects, allowing people more effectively to regulate their economic and social activities.

What makes these tokens of central importance to understanding the role of literacy and numeracy in human development is evidence that they are the direct antecedents of our system of writing. Moreover, the conditions under which this crude system of marked tokens became a full-blown writing system are the same ones that eventually gave rise to schools.

The origins of "Western" formal schooling

The system of tokens remained unchanged for several thousand years, during which time people continued to live in small villages or as nomads. Then, around 4000 BC, people discovered a means of smelting bronze that revolutionized their economic activities and social lives. Plows could be used to till the earth more deeply: extensive canals could be built to irrigate fields, and armies could be equipped with more effective weapons. For the first time, people could regularly grow substantially more food than they needed for their own use and could compel large numbers of other people to work for them. City-states arose where large numbers of people lived in close proximity to each other and separate from their sources of food.

The new form of life that arose with cities required a substantial division of labor. This made it impossible for everyone to interact on a face-to-face basis as they had when they lived in small, self-sufficient villages, and greatly increased the importance of their primitive systems of record keeping.

Side by side with the development of these early cities, token-based record-keeping systems rapidly evolved, allowing kings to monitor the wealth of their lands, the size of their armies, and the tax payments of their subjects. Under these new conditions, the early token system expanded to keep pace with the increased variety of things to be counted. This increase in the number of tokens made the entire system cumbersome. As a solution to this problem, people began to make pictures of the tokens on clay tablets instead of using the tokens themselves. This practice gave rise to cuneiform (*cuneiform* means, literally, to etch in clay).

This transformation in the medium of recording enabled a crucial change in how people began to relate inscribed symbols to objects. In the case of tokens, the tokens literally "stood for" objects. But when complicated transactions began to occur in the newly complex political and economic conditions of cities, the need arose to represent relationships among objects (such as *owe* or *paid*) as well as objects themselves. In these conditions, a revolutionary discovery was made. It is possible to represent the sounds of language using marks in clay just as it is possible to represent objects. (See Goody, 1987; Harris, 1986; Larsen, 1986, for more extended discussions of early writing systems, cuneiform in particular.)

The system of cuneiform writing that resulted from this discovery could not be mastered in a day. It required long and systematic study. Nevertheless, so important was the power associated with this new system of written communication that societies began to support young men who otherwise might be engaged directly in a trade or farming with the explicit purpose of making them "scribes," people who could write. The places where young men were brought together for this purpose were the earliest schools.

Fragmentary records of the activities in these early schools show that although they were very restricted and specialized in some ways they appear startlingly modern in others. As in modern schools, students were asked to copy out lists containing the names of various objects deemed important by their teachers and to spend a great deal of time memorizing the facts contained on such lists (see Table 2.1). In addition to learning the rudiments of writing and reading, these early students were learning something about the basic contents of the records that they were asked to keep so that they could act as civil servants once they graduated. Besides the financial benefits that derive from schooling, the ancients also believed that there was power to be had from the knowledge it produced. The basis of this knowledge is the ability to read, write, and solve problems in the economic and social spheres of life.

Modern children in elementary school in the 1980s still make lists, although they are more likely to be lists of the presidents of the United States or the spelling of words in which *e* comes before *i*. But the purposes to which this practice is to be put and the presumed advantages to be gained from study, no matter how boring, remain very much the same. As one father admonished his son, several thousand years ago,

> I have seen how the belaboured man is belaboured – thou shouldst set thy heart in pursuit of writing . . . behold, there is nothing which surpasses writing. . . .
> I have seen the metalworker at his work at the mouth of his furnace. His fingers were somewhat like crocodiles; he stank more than fish-roe. . . .
> The small building contractor carries mud. . . . He is dirtier than vines

Table 2.1 Examples from lists memorized in ancient and modern schools

Ancient		Modern	
Subject	Number	Subject	Number
Trees	84	Presidents of the US	40
Stones	12	States of the Union	50
Gods	9	Capitals of the states	50
Officials	8	Elements in the periodic table	105
Cattle	8	Planets in the solar system	9
Reeds	8		
Personal names	6		
Animals	5		
Leather objects	4		
Fields	3		
Garments	3		
Words compounded with *gar*	3		
Chairs	3		

Source: Adapted from Goody, 1977, p. 95.

or pigs from treading under his mud. His clothes are stiff with clay. . . .

Behold, there is no profession free of a boss – except for the scribe: he is the boss. . . .

Behold, there is no scribe who lacks food from property of the House of the King – life, prosperity, health!

(Quoted in Donaldson, 1978. pp. 84–85)

I have sketched only one line in the history of formal schooling, and it is certainly true that a great deal can be learned from comparison with systems that arose in different parts of the world using different means of representing language and privileging different social functions. However, the system in question represents a tradition of special relevance for the developing countries of Africa and South America with which I am familiar because its practices can be traced down to the present day via the later civilizations of Greece and Rome.

If I restrict myself to the case at hand, several points concerning the special organization of behavior peculiar to formal schooling stand out:

1   There is an intimate link between the development of schooling and the development of large urban centers engaged in trade and technologically sophisticated means of production.
2   There is a special mediational means, writing, that is essential to the activity of schooling. Writing is used to represent both language and physical systems (e.g., mathematics).
3   The activity settings where schooling occurs are distinctive in that they are removed from contexts of practical activity, and the requisite skills that will become the means of later activity are the goal.
4   There is a peculiar social structure to formal schooling in which a single adult interacts with many (often as many as 40 or 50, sometimes as many as 400) students at a time. Unlike most other settings for socialization, this adult is unlikely to have any familial ties to the learner, rendering the social relations relatively impersonal.
5   There is a peculiar value system associated with schooling that sets the educated person above his or her peers and which, in secular versions of formal education of the type I am focusing on, values change and discontinuity over tradition and community.

This characterization of the distinctive nature of the activity settings associated with formal schooling does not do justice to the full range of contexts that distinguish formal schooling from other contexts of socialization that might be considered educational in the broad sense (for more extended discussions, see Greenfield & Lave, 1982; Scribner & Cole, 1973). However, it is sufficient to permit us to pose more clearly the question before us: How does schooling influence cognitive development?

That issue can now be rephrased as follows. What are the consequences for later cognitive development of participation in contexts that have the characteristics of formal schooling in a society where formal schooling is an integral part of the political economy and a major institution for the socialization of children? Assuming that identifiable influences on cognitive development can be demonstrated, a series of subsequent questions can be addressed: Are the cognitive consequences of involvement in formal schooling general or specific? What aspects of schooling are responsible for such effects? Since it has already been shown that schooling arose historically as part and parcel of wider sociocultural changes, an inquiry into the cognitive impact of schooling naturally leads us to attempt to "unpackage" features of the experience of schooling such as its socioeconomic context, mediational means, etc., all of which might be expected to influence cognitive development.

The ontogenetic level

Barbara Rogoff's (1981) review of the literature on schooling and cognitive development provides a handy framework for discussion of the cognitive consequences of schooling as it has been studied in standard cross-cultural research.

> Schooled individuals have gained skills in the use of graphic conventions to represent depth in two-dimensional stimuli and in the fine-grained analysis of two-dimensional patterns. They have increased facility in deliberately remembering disconnected bits of information, and spontaneously engage in strategies that provide greater organization for the unrelated items. Schooled people are more likely to organize objects on a taxonomic basis, putting categorically similar objects together, whereas nonschooled people often use functional arrangements of objects that are used together. Schooled groups show greater facility shifting to alternative dimensions of classification and in explaining the basis of their organization. Schooling appears to have no effect on rule learning nor on logical thought as long as the subject has understood the problem in the way the experimenter intended. Nonschooled subjects seem to prefer, however, to come to conclusions on the basis of experience rather than relying on the information in the problem alone.

I will attempt to unpack this summary, beginning with the cases where schooling was said to have no impact, because these are the cases where the common phylogenetic heritage of the species results in forms of interaction with the world during ontogeny that are universal. The major body of research referred to here focuses on the development of operational thought in the Piagetian tradition.

Schooling and the development of logical operations

I believe that Rogoff is correct in her conclusion about the development of logical operations, but, as she is at some pains to point out, the matter has to be considered controversial. For purposes of discussion, I will assume that the logical operations in question are those that form the basis for Piagetian theory (Rogoff herself concentrated on cultural variations in response to logical syllogisms and concept learning based on logical relations). According to Inhelder and Piaget (1958):

> Although concrete operations consist of organized systems (classifica-tions, serial ordering, correspondences, etc.) [children at this age] proceed from one partial link to the next in a step-by-step fashion, without relating each partial link to all the others. Formal operations differ in that all of the possible combinations are considered in each case. Con-sequently, each partial link is grouped in relation to the whole; in other words, reasoning moves continually as a function of a "structured whole."
>
> (p. 16)

If we address first the question of concrete operations as embodied in the conservation tasks, it appears to be the case that schooling has no consistent influence on performance although in a few well-publicized cases (e.g., Greenfield & Bruner, 1966) the steady development of conservation among schooled children and its absence, among noneducated adults led to specula-tion that schooling might do more than accelerate rates of development (as Piaget (1970) speculated, it might actually be necessary for the development of concrete operations). This kind of result was picked up by Hallpike (1979), who claimed that adults in nonliterate societies, as a rule, fail to develop beyond pre-operational thought (a conclusion hotly denied by, among others, Jahoda, 1980).

The crucial phrase in Rogoff's review pertaining to performance on con-crete operations tasks is "as long as the subject has understood the problem in the way the experimenter intended." A number of years ago Dasen (1977) suggested that performance factors might interfere with the expression of concrete operational competence. In many, but not all, cases, modest amounts of conservation training were sufficient to improve performance markedly; it remained an open question if different kinds of training, or more training, would reveal the hypothesized competence (Dasen, Ngini, & Reschitzki, 1979). Greenfield's own research also points to situational factors that inter-fere with conservation judgments; when Wolof children poured water them-selves, conservation performance improved markedly.

Most notably, when university-trained African psychologists have con-ducted studies with Piagetian conservation tasks, they have found rates of development to be similar for schooled and nonschooled populations (Kamara

& Easley, 1977; Nyiti, 1976). Nyiti (1982) found a similar result when he contrasted the performance of Micmac (Canadian) children tested in English and Micmac.

Although there is room for disagreement, I believe that it is sensible to conclude that concrete operational thinking is not influenced by schooling; what is influenced is subjects' ability to understand the language of testing and the presuppositions of the testing situation itself.

At the level of formal operations, it is far more often concluded that schooling is a necessary, but not sufficient, condition for development. However, there is ample reason to question this conclusion as well. First, formal operations are rarely manifested by nonschooled subjects, and even highly schooled subjects are none too proficient (Neimark, 1975). Second, as Jahoda (1980) points out, when one moves outside of the narrow realm of the procedures used by Inhelder and Piaget (1958) in their monograph on formal operations, there is anecdotal, but persuasive, evidence that subjects can use formal operations.

My own belief appears to be close to that of Piaget (1972) (and, I believe, Jahoda, 1980). Formal operations are a universal achievement accompanying the change in social status from child to adult, but they will be manifest in specific domains of dense practice. As Jahoda notes, such practice is likely to be most dense in the domain of social relations. Consequently, it should come as no surprise that when Eric Erikson defines the process of identity formation, which is a hypothesized universal feature of the transition to adulthood, he seems to capture rather precisely the conception of a "structured whole" underpinning formal operations:

> In psychological terms, identity formation employs a process of simultaneous reflection and observations, a process taking place on all levels of mental functioning, by which the individual judges himself in the light of what he perceives to be the way others judge him in comparison to themselves and to a typology significant to them; while he perceives himself in comparison to them and to types that have become relevant to him.
>
> (1968, pp. 22–23)

Outside of contexts where individuals are actively thinking about their identities, in the absence of recording devices, full-blown formal operational thinking is probably a rarity in any culture. It will be associated with schooling as a normative part of scientific activities, but it almost certainly does not describe the actual thinking of trained scientists except under special circumstances where they need to check on their results or are working with auxiliary tools that help them to record and keep straight information (Latour, 1986). In the special sense that schooling expands the contexts of its use, then, formal operational thinking can be said to be influenced by schooling.

An interesting line of evidence in favor of this context-specific interpretation of formal logical skills comes from reasoning about logical syllogisms. In an early study, Luria (1934, 1976) demonstrated what appeared to be a strong relationship between formal schooling and syllogistic reasoning. Nonschooled Central Asian peasants responded to the syllogisms he posed in terms of their everyday knowledge, not the logical terms of the problem (the phenomenon referred to by Rogoff at the end of her summary). To take a famous example, when presented with a syllogism of the form, "In Siberia all the bears are white; my friend Ivan was in Siberia and saw a bear; what color was it?" nonschooled subjects answered to the effect, "I have never been to Siberia, so I cannot say what color the bear was; Ivan is your friend, ask him." This kind of response has now been recorded in many cultures among nonschooled peoples and has been shown to diminish quickly with a few years of schooling in favor of a response based on the logical requirements of the task (Cole, Gay, Glick, & Sharp, 1971; Scribner, 1975; Tulviste, 1979). To judge from such evidence, it appears that formal schooling promotes a distinctive kind of theoretical thinking, in line with expectations of the sociohistorical school as developed in the USSR.

Unhappily for the view that "empirical" thinking is replaced by "theoretical" thinking as a consequence of schooling, a substantial literature collected among college students in Great Britain and the United States shows that for slightly more complicated syllogisms responses are highly content-dependent. For example, Wason (1960) found that college students could solve a particular syllogism when it was embodied in a realistic question about postage stamps and envelopes but not when it was embodied in a hypothetical question about quality control at work. This same problem did not work for students in the United States, where one based on rules about the age of drinking worked quite well (D'Andrade, 1982).

Following D'Andrade, it seems best to conclude that cultural variations in the outcome of logical thinking are primarily the result of differences in the supply of well-formed content-based schemata that are brought to the task, for example, differences in cognitive content, not the presence of generalized thinking skills in one group that are absent in the other.

Information-processing skills

Within this category I include those tasks that Rogoff refers to as "fine-grained analysis of two-dimensional patterns," memory for disconnected bits of information, and classification. In each of these areas there is substantial evidence that exposure to schooling brings about changes in cognitive performance which are taken to be indicative of cognitive development when they are observed among children raised in industrially advanced countries where schooling and psychological testing are ubiquitous.

Analysis of two-dimensional patterns

Early research on perception of depth (summarized in Jahoda & McGurk, 1982) seemed to show that, whether they attended school or not, people from a wide variety of African cultures had difficulty perceiving two-dimensional representations of three-dimensional space. However, using more carefully constructed materials, Jahoda and McGurk found little difference across cultures, with even very small children displaying sensitivity to depth cues. In some cases (e.g., Dawson, 1967), there is evidence of improved performance for schooled populations, but performance was generally poor, and I am uncertain if schooling can be said to be a major factor in the development of the associated perceptual skills.

Other lines of evidence provide more support for Rogoff's generalization that formal schooling promotes skills in fine-grained analysis of two-dimensional figures. One source of support comes from research on the Ponzo illusion (two converging straight lines that are seen as parallel if interpreted three-dimensionally, as in the representation of railroad track). Wagner (1982) found that susceptibility to illusions increases as a consequence of schooling. Research on the embedded-figures test and other perceptual tasks using two-dimensional drawings also indicates a significant impact of schooling (Berry, 1976; Serpell, 1976).

Memory

A variety of evidence supports Rogoff's generalization that schooling promotes memory for unrelated materials (Cole & Scribner, 1977; Stevenson, 1982; Wagner, 1982). For example:

1   In repeated trials of free recall of common items that fall into culturally recognized categories, children with six or more years of schooling (Cole *et al.*, 1971) and adults with varying years of schooling (Scribner & Cole, 1981) remember more and cluster items in recall more than nonschooled comparison groups.
2   Short-term recall of item location increases as a function of schooling but not of age (Wagner, 1982).
3   Paired-associate learning of randomly paired items increases with schooling.

(Sharp, Cole, & Lave, 1979)

In addition, Stevenson (1982) reports a small positive effect of very small amounts of schooling on a battery of tasks that included various kinds of memory problems as well as visual analysis.

By contrast, schooling effects are generally absent in cases of recall of well-structured stories (Mandler, Scribner, Cole, & De Forest, 1980). They are also absent when the items to be paired in a paired-associate task are strongly associated with each other (Sharp *et al.*, 1979). Very short-term memory also seems unaffected by schooling; in Wagner's studies, most recently probed locations show no education effects (Wagner, 1974, 1978).

Classification and concept formation

A wide variety of studies have shown that schooled subjects are more likely to classify objects and pictures according to form (when such attributes as form, color, and function are used as possible bases for classification) and more likely to create categories that map onto taxonomic rather than functional attributes when these dimensions are put in competition with each other (Bruner, Olver, & Greenfield, 1966; Childs & Greenfield, 1982; Cole & Ciborowski, 1971; Serpell, 1976; Sharp *et al.*, 1979).

Interpretation: Are the effects specific or general?

The central question about such results is whether they signal something general about the cognitive capacities of educated children or relatively restricted outcomes of practice in specific cognitive skills explicitly trained in schools.

During the 1940s and 1950s, it was assumed that formal schooling promoted quite general forms of cognitive development. This assumption was widely shared by the founders of the United Nations (UNESCO, 1970) and underpinned the policies of developmental economics for several decades (Lerner, 1957; Inkeles & Smith, 1974).

Among academic researches, the "general change" position is represented by Greenfield and Bruner's (1966) early speculation (subsequently abandoned; see Greenfield, 1976) that schooling is a major institution by means of which some cultures "push cognitive development faster and further than others," but especially relevant to the present discussion is A. R. Luria's interpretation of his cross-cultural research, which is squarely in the "general cognitive change" camp. Luria (1976) characterized the goal of the research as an attempt to demonstrate that "many mental processes are social and historical in origin [and] that important manifestations of human consciousness have been directly shaped by the basic practices of human activity and the actual forms of culture" (p. 3).

Luria presents many interesting results in support of this thesis; in the areas of classification (colored threads, geometric figures, and various objects), logical deduction, and self-evaluation (roughly equivalent to what is now referred to as metacognition), traditional people responded to his tasks in ways systematically different from their neighbors who had been involved in collective agriculture and schooling.

Greatly simplified, the following conclusions are almost central: In the change from traditional agricultural life to collectivized labor in literate/ industrialized circumstances:

1 "Direct graphical-functional thinking" is replaced by at least the rudiments of "theoretical thinking."
2 The basic forms of cognitive activity go beyond fixation and reproduction of individual practical activity and cease to be purely concrete and situational, becoming a part of more general, abstractly coded, systems of knowledge.
3 These changes give rise not only to new forms of reasoning, restricted to logical premises free of immediate experience, but new forms of self-analysis and imagination as well.

Without dwelling on the complexities involved, I can point to two features of Luria's cross-cultural research that fail to fulfill the methodological requirements of the sociohistorical school. First, as we have commented elsewhere (Cole & Griffin, 1980), Luria neither studied nor modeled in his experiments the practical activity systems of the Uzbeki and Kazaki people and the psychological processes associated with them; hence, his interpretations were not grounded in an analysis of culturally organized activities. Instead, for purposes of psychological diagnosis he introduced distinctly Western European activity systems, in the form of psychological tests and interviews, which did not model local reality but served instead as measurements of generalized psychological tendencies for which there was a developmental interpretation in Western European societies.

Using this approach, Luria found that contact with European culture through either schooling or participation in Soviet-run collective enterprises increased the likelihood that traditional peasants would respond appropriately to his intellectual puzzles in Russian terms, but these results are basically silent with respect to possible analogues in indigenous practices. Such analogues might or might not exist, but the research Luria engaged in would, in principle, not be able to tell us which case fits reality.

The second, closely related problem, which becomes the focus when the sociocultural tradition is taken up in cross-cultural research by American investigators, is Luria's failure to restrict his conclusions to particular domains, instead appearing to claim that in general there is a change in the complexity of mediational mechanisms of cognition in the socioeconomic change from agricultural to industrial modes of production. Too often he seems to be concluding that the results he reports are independent of problem content and activity context, for example generalized cognitive changes. This kind of conclusion simultaneously undermines the well-established principles of the dependence of psychological process on living activity systems and renders adults who display such behaviors childlike in (inappropriate) terms.

As we have argued elsewhere, my colleagues and I believe that the data on the cognitive consequences of schooling at the level of individual behavior are best interpreted in context-specific terms (Cole *et al.*, 1971; Laboratory of Comparative Human Cognition, 1983). I will not repeat this argument in detail here. Suffice it to say that, insofar as the task environments used by psychologists to assess consequences of schooling for cognitive development take their structure and content from school-like tasks, it can hardly be surprising that people with extensive experience in school outperform those who have had no pertinent practice.

As discussed elsewhere (Jahoda, 1980; Laboratory of Comparative Human Cognition, 1983), a major shortcoming of the context-specific approach is that it fails to account for the apparent generality of cognitive change associated with context-specific experience. I will return to this important issue presently, but first we must address the final level of developmental change needed for a full account of schooling and cognitive development, the *microgenetic developments* that occur within formal educational activity settings.

The microgenetic level

Analyses of teaching/learning interactions in classrooms throughout the world yield a picture of very broad similarities, modified to some extent in some places by local practices (see, e.g., Spindler, 1980).

Four distinctive features of educational activity, already present in the schools of ancient Sumeria briefly described earlier, capture a good deal of the contemporary ethnographic picture.

First, formal schooling uses a distinctive mediational means, written symbol systems. In many discussions of the consequences of formal schooling in the past, literacy acquisition itself has been credited with causing advances in cognitive development, but in all such discussions literacy and schooling have been totally confounded. The conclusion we have reached on the basis of our analysis of literacy acquired in nonschools, Quranic schools, and English-style schools is that writing is a necessary, but not sufficient, explanation of schooling effects, be they context-specific or general.

This conclusion is based on the work of Scribner and Cole (1981) among the Vai people of northwestern Liberia. Many Vai (primarily men) are literate in an indigenous syllabic script, which they use mainly to write letters and to keep records either for personal use or for the affairs of small communities. Others are literate in the Quran, at least to the extent of being able to copy and recite verses, if not to use Arabic productively for non-religious purposes. Still others have attended school where they acquired literacy in English.

Though indigenous Vai literacy is clearly useful, and has a notable impact on Vai life, it is not used to master large bodies of knowledge that would otherwise be inaccessible to the individual, and the tested cognitive consequences of Vai literacy are correspondingly modest; the only item from Rogoff's summary that shows an impact of Vai literacy is the way that geometric figures are categorized – Vai literates sort such figures according to form and number more often than nonliterates.

The consequences of schooling summarized by Rogoff seem to depend on repeated practice in learning new material and mastering new information-processing procedures ("cognitive strategies"). The sheer mass of this knowledge requires that students learn how to commit large amounts of information to memory, to be used later to gain still more information, with no clear connection to everyday activities outside of school. Moreover, this information is structured according to category systems that are a part of the tradition that created modern science and bureaucratic institutions.

This aspect of the contexts of schooling appears, in my opinion, to be sufficient to explain most of the tested results comparing schooled and non-schooled children on memory and classification tasks.

The second conspicuous fact about schooling is the participant structure and the form of discourse that goes on there. Overwhelmingly, not just in the Arab world (Wagner & Lofti, 1980) but in American classrooms as well, a single teacher organizes recitations for large numbers of students. The material to be learned is broken down into units with a particular sequence, and the students must master lower-level steps to achieve higher-order ones. The larger purposes of this activity are observed; learning is for short-term information mastery goals.

Detailed studies of the way that language is used in schools reveal a distinctive pattern called instructional discourse. Instructional discourse differs from other ways in which adults and children speak in both its structure and its content. The central goals of instructional discourse are to give children information about the content of the curriculum and feedback about their efforts while providing teachers with information about their students' progress (Mehan, 1979).

One of the distinctive indicators of instructional discourse is the presence of the initiation–reply–evaluation sequence. This pattern starts when the teacher initiates an exchange, usually by asking a question; a student replies, and then the teacher provides an evaluation. An important feature of the initiate–reply–evaluate sequence is a form of questioning that is very rarely encountered outside of school, the "known-answer question" (Searle, 1969). When a teacher asks, "What does this say?" she is seeking information about what the child has learned, not about the state of the content in question. Children can ask questions just as they would at home, but very often when the teacher asks a question it is really a covert way to evaluate the student's progress. Learning to respond easily to known-answer questions, in addition to learning about the academic content of the curriculum, is an important early lesson of schooling (Mehan, 1979).

The special nature of language in school-based learning is also manifested in the emphasis that teachers place on linguistic form. Sometimes this emphasis on form may even occur at the expense of accuracy about content, making the entire exercise appear rather strange.

This set of practices, I believe (along with Rogoff, 1981, and Scribner, 1977), helps to account for the fact that only a very few years of schooling are sufficient to bring about a marked change in response to verbal logical problems. Such verbal logical problems map neatly onto the discourse of school with its motivated exclusion of everyday experience and its formal mode. Subjects who have attended school recognize the form and reply appropriately in its terms so long as the form of the syllogistic problem is simple enough. However, when the question becomes difficult, even educated adults, as D'Andrade (1982) clearly shows, fall back on everyday knowledge and modes of interpretation.

Sources of general cognitive effects

So far, the distinctive features of the microenvironment of schooling I have discussed motivate a context-specific interpretation of schooling's impact on cognitive development. It is important to ask if there is anything in the microenvironment that might reasonably be expected to have context-independent consequences. However, this discussion cannot get very far unless we complete the circle and inquire into the larger historical/cultural context within which schooling activity is embedded. General effects, according to the view our group has adopted, will depend crucially upon the extent to which forms of cognition mastered in one context are relevant in other contexts; put differently, "transfer" of school-based knowledge should be sought in the environment as well as in the transformed capacities within children's heads.

Three factors of educational activity have prima facie generality in the sense that they are relevant to behavior in a wide range of contexts (at least within industrially advanced countries). First, the medium of instruction, writing, is the medium of public life, aiding performance in a great many settings. Second, insofar as the content of the curriculum allows them more broadly to understand their particular historical circumstances, it will lead students to be more effective problem solvers when they are not in school. Third, the lexicon of every language carries within it the culture's theory about the nature of the world. Insofar as children's linguistic resources are expanded by exposure to words in many contexts, they gain access to the meaning systems of which those words are a part, meaning systems that have applicability beyond the school walls.

This is a very content-oriented view. The only quasi-cognitive process involved is the mastery of the written medium. Relatively speaking, I am unimpressed by the possibility that the specific cognitive strategies necessary for mastery of the curriculum have wide applicability across contexts, or that children master metacognitive abilities in school that transfer broadly. I am quite impressed, on the other hand, with evidence of greatly restricted transfer of problem-solving strategies and of the dependence of the quality of problem solving and other kinds of cognitive activity on content-based knowledge (for a more detailed justification of both these views, see Laboratory of Comparative Human Cognition, 1983).

General implications

If my view of the cognitive consequences of formal schooling is approximately correct, it cautions against the position, still easy to encounter in international development circles, that education will develop the minds of the world's nonliterate populations, thereby serving as the engine of economic and political development. Education provides new "tools of the intellect," to be sure. But without contexts of use, these tools appear to "rust" and fall into disuse.

It is my reading of the earliest origins of schooling in Sumeria that formal education could not be conceived of as a cause of the momentous sociopolitical-economic changes that took place there. Nor was it a simple effect; rather, it was an enabling condition along with many others. Schools evolved over many centuries, perhaps a thousand years, along with the social forms that they served and mediational means that made them possible. In short, formal schooling was an integral part of the social process.

That history is incredibly different from the situation of less-developed countries today, where schooling is an alien form, inserted into the social process by powerful outsiders within the past several decades, or at most 100 years. Less-developed countries have had no choice but to adopt formal schooling; it seemed to represent both a passkey to the modern world and the only hope of regaining national independence. But I think there is little doubt that widespread adoption of formal schooling has also been a source of social disruption and human misery.

Surveying the world today, we witness a number of attempts by less-developed countries to modify their educational systems, free of both the value systems and political control of outsiders. The ideology of development that underpinned development efforts in the 1950s and 1960s, including educational development, has been forcefully rejected by Muslim fundamentalism in the Near East. In a different form, that ideology is being rejected in West Africa in favor of a strategy of development consistent with the countries' own resources and national heritages. Perhaps the first shock wave of widespread formal schooling is passing. If this is so, perhaps a reevaluation of the relation between cognitive development and education along the lines suggested here will also provide useful ideas for policy makers who must be able not only to criticize the shortcomings of the past but to find a usable route to the future.

References

Berry, J. M. (1976). *Human ecology and cultural style*. New York: Sage-Halstead.

Bruner, J. S., Olver, R., & Greenfield, P. M. (1966). *Studies in cognitive growth*. New York: Wiley.

Childs, C. P., & Greenfield, P. M. (1982). Informal modes of learning and teaching: The case of Zinacanteco weaving. In N. Warren (Ed.), *Studies in cross-cultural psychology* (Vol. 2). New York: Academic Press.

Cole, M. (1988). Cross-cultural research in the socio-historical tradition. *Human Development, 31*, 137–157.

Cole, M., & Ciborowski, T. (1971). Cultural differences in learning conceptual rules. *International Journal of Psychology, 6*, 25–37.

Cole, M., Gay, J., Glick, J. A., & Sharp, D. (1971). *The cultural context of learning and thinking*. New York: Basic Books.

Cole, M., & Griffin, P. (1980). Cultural amplifiers reconsidered. In D. Olson (Ed.), *Social foundations of language and thought*. New York: Norton.

Cole, M., & Scribner, S. (1977). Developmental theories applied to cross-cultural cognitive research. *Annals of the New York Academy of Sciences, 285*, 366–373.

D'Andrade, R. (1982). Reason vs. logic. Paper presented at the Symposium on the Ecology of Cognition, Greensboro, NC.

Dasen, P. R. (Ed.) (1977). *Piagetian psychology: Cross-cultural contributions*. New York: Gardner.

Dasen, P. R., Ngini, L., & Reschitzki, L. (1979). Cross-cultural studies of concrete operations. In L. H. Eckensberger, W. J. Lonner, & Y. H. Poortinga (Eds.), *Cross-cultural contributions to psychology*. Amsterdam: Swetz & Zeitlinger.

Dawson, J. L. M. (1967). Cultural and physiological influences upon spatial-perceptual processes in West Africa (Pt. 1). *International Journal of Psychology, 2*, 115–128.

Donaldson, M. (1978). *Children's minds*. New York: Norton.

Erikson, E. H. (1968). *Identity: Youth and crisis*. New York: Norton.

Goody, J. (1977). *Domestication of the savage mind*. Cambridge: Cambridge University Press.

Goody, J. (1987). *The interface between the written and the oral*. Cambridge: Cambridge University Press.

Greenfield, P. M. (1976). Cross-cultural research and Piagetian theory: Paradox and progress. In K. F. Riegel and J. A. Meacham (Eds.), *The developing individual in a changing world: Historical and cultural issues* (Vol. 1). Chicago: Aldine.

Greenfield, P. M., & Bruner, J. S. (1966). Culture and cognitive growth. *International Journal of Psychology, 1*, 89–107.

Greenfield, P. M., & Lave, J. (1982). Cognitive aspects of informal education. In D. A. Wagner & H. Stevenson (Eds.), *Cultural perspectives on child development*. San Francisco: Freeman.

Hallpike, C. R. (1979). *The foundations of primitive thought*. New York: Oxford University Press.

Harris, R. (1986). *The origin of writing*. London: Duckworth.

Inhelder, B., & Piaget, P. (1958). *The growth of logical thinking from childhood to adolescence*. New York: Basic Books.

Inkeles, A., & Smith, D. H. (1974). *Becoming modern*. Cambridge, MA: Harvard University Press.

Jahoda, G. (1980). Theoretical and systematic approaches in cross-cultural psychology. In H. C. Triandis & W. W. Lambert (Eds.), *Handbook of cross-cultural psychology: Vol. 1. Perspectives*. Boston: Allyn & Bacon.

Jahoda, G., & McGurk, H. (1982). The development of picture perception in children from different cultures. In D. A. Wagner and H. W. Stevenson (Eds.), *Cultural perspectives on child development*. San Francisco: Freeman.

Kamara, A. I., & Easley, J. A., Jr. (1977). Is the rate of cognitive development uniform across cultures? A methodological critique with new evidence from Themne children. In P. R. Dasen (Ed.), *Piagetian psychology: Cross-cultural contributions*. New York: Gardner.

Laboratory of Comparative Human Cognition (1983). Culture and cognitive development. In P. H. Mussen (Ed.), *Carmichael's handbook of child development* (Vol. 1). New York: Wiley.

Laboratory of Comparative Human Cognition (1986). The contribution of cross-cultural research to educational practice. *American Psychologist, 41*, 1049–1058.

Larsen, M. (1986). Writing on clay: From pictograph to alphabet. *Quarterly Newsletter of the Laboratory of Comparative Human Cognition, 8*(1), 3–10.

Latour, B. (1986). *Laboratory life: The construction of scientific facts*. Princeton, NJ: Princeton University Press.

Leontiev, A. N. (1930). Studies of the cultural development of the child: 3. The development of voluntary attention in the child. *Journal of Genetic Psychology, 37*, 52–81.

Leontiev, A. N. (1981). *Problems in the development of mind*. Moscow: Progress.

Lerner, D. (1957). *The passing of traditional society*, New York: Free Press.

Luria, A. R. (1928). The problem of the cultural development of the child. *Journal of Genetic Psychology, 35*, 493–506.

Luria, A. R. (1932). *The nature of human conflicts*. London: Liveright.

Luria, A. R. (1934). The second psychological expedition to Central Asia. *Journal of Genetic Psychology, 41*, 255–259.

Luria, A. R. (1976). *Cognitive development*. Cambridge. MA: Harvard University Press.

Mandler, J. M., Scribner, S., Cole, M., & De Forest, M. (1980). Cross-cultural invariance in story recall. *Child Development, 51*, 19–26.

Marshak, A. (1972). *The roots of civilization: The cognitive beginnings of man's first art, symbol, and notation*. New York: McGraw-Hill.

Mehan, H. (1979). *Learning lessons*. Cambridge, MA: Harvard University Press.

Neimark, E. D. (1975). Intellectual development during adolescence. In F. D. Horowitz (Ed.), *Review of child development research* (Vol. 4). Chicago: University of Chicago Press.

Nyiti, R. M. (1976). The development of conservation in the Meru children of Tanzania. *Child Development 47*, 1122–1129.

Nyiti. R. (1982). The validity of "cultural differences explanations" for cross-cultural variation in the note of Piagetian cognitive development. In D. A. Wagner & H. W. Stevenson (Eds.), *Cultural perspectives on child development*. San Francisco: Freeman.

Pfeiffer, J. (1972). *The emergence of man*. New York: Harper & Row.

Piaget, J. (1970). Piaget's theory. In P. H. Mussen (Ed.), *Carmichael's handbook of child psychology* (3rd ed.). New York: Wiley.

Piaget, J. (1972). Intellectual evolution from adolescence to adulthood. *Human Development, 15*, 1–12.

Rogoff, B. (1981). Schooling and the development of cognitive skills. In H. C. Triandis & A. Heron (Eds.), *Handbook of cross-cultural psychology* (Vol. 4). Boston: Allyn & Bacon.

Schmandt-Besserat, D. (1978). The earliest precursor of writing. *Scientific American, 238*, 50–59.

Scribner, S. (1975). Recall of classical syllogisms: A cross-cultural investigation of errors on logical problems. In R. Falmagne (Ed.), *Reasoning: Representation and process*, Hillsdale, NJ: Erlbaum.

Scribner, S. (1977). Modes of thinking and ways of speaking: Culture and logic reconsidered. In P. N. Johnson-Laird & P. C. Wason (Eds.), *Thinking: Readings in cognitive science*. Cambridge: Cambridge University Press.

Scribner, S., & Cole, M. (1973). Cognitive consequences of formal and informal education. *Science, 182*, 553–559.

Scribner, S., & Cole, M. (1981). *The psychology of literacy*. Cambridge, MA: Harvard University Press.

Searle, J. (1969). *Speech acts*. Cambridge: Cambridge University Press.

Serpell, R. (1976). *Culture's influence on behavior*. London: Methuen.

Sharp, D. W., Cole, M., & Lave, C. (1979). Education and cognitive development: Evidence from experimental research. *Monographs of the Society for Research in Child Development, 44* (Serial No. 178).

Spindler, G. D. (1980). *Doing the ethnography of schooling*. New York: Holt, Rinehart & Winston.

Stevenson, H. W. (1982). Influences of schooling on cognitive development. In D. A. Wagner and H. W. Stevenson (Eds.), *Cultural perspectives on child development*. San Francisco: Freeman.

Street, B. V. (1984). *Literacy in theory and practice*. Cambridge: Cambridge University Press.

Tulviste, P. (1979). On the origins of theoretic syllogistic reasoning in culture and the child. *Quarterly Newsletter of the Laboratory of Comparative Human Cognition, 1*(4), 73–80.

UNESCO. (1970). *Literacy 1967–9: Progress throughout the world.*

Vygotsky, L. S. (1929). The problem of the cultural development of the child (pt. 2). *Journal of Genetic Psychology, 36*, 414–434.

Vygotsky, L. S. (1978). *Mind in society*. Cambridge, MA: Harvard University Press.

Wagner, D. A. (1974). The development of short-term and incidental memory: A cross-cultural study. *Child Development, 45*, 389–396.

Wagner, D. A. (1978). The effects of formal schooling on cognitive style. *Journal of Social Psychology, 106*, 145–151.

Wagner, D. A. (1982). Ontogeny in the study of culture and cognition. In D. A. Wagner and H. W. Stevenson (Eds.), *Cultural perspectives on child development*. San Francisco: Freeman.

Wagner, D. A., & Lofti, A. (1980). Learning to read by "rote" in the Quranic schools of Yemen and Senegal. Paper presented at the meeting of the American Anthropological Society, Washington, DC.

Wason, P. C. (1960). Regression in reasoning. *British Journal of Psychology, 4*, 471–480.

Wertsch, J. V. (Ed.) (1985). *Culture, communication, and cognition.* Cambridge: Cambridge University Press.

Whiting, B. (1976). The problem of the packaged variable. In K. F. Riegel & J. A. Meacham (Eds.), *The developing individual in a changing world: Historical and cultural issues* (Vol. 1), The Hague: Mouton.

Chapter 3

Thinking with and through artifacts

The role of psychological tools and physical artifacts in human learning and cognition*

Roger Säljö

Cognition and human practices: a sociocultural approach

For most researchers in the areas of cognition and learning, thinking was, until recently, construed as "an individual act bounded by the physical facts of brain and body" (Resnick, 1991, p. 1). . . . In a cognitivist perspective, cognition is decontextualized from physical (and communicative) action and treated as a mental entity that causes action but is somehow not part of it. Culture, context, and social life in general have been conceived as entities that "influence" cognition, but they have not been seen as constitutive elements of human thinking. The social situatedness and sensitivity of human sense-making and action that have been brought into focus in so much research in various fields during the past years, remain inexplicable, and context is still widely considered "a nuisance variable" rather than "an integral aspect of cognitive events" (Rogoff, 1984, p. 3, cf., e.g., Chaiklin & Lave, 1993; Nunes, Schliemann, & Carraher, 1993). At a general level the present situation in cognitive research implies that the relationship between the social and collective levels of human activity on the one hand, and individual action on the other, is difficult to address.

There are many ways to formulate the differences between a sociocultural approach to human cognition and communicative action on the one hand, and those assumptions that dominate mainstream cognitivist approaches on the other. . . . Vygotsky (1986) attempted to create the foundations for an understanding of thinking that is not premised on the assumption that cognition is exclusively a private and internal mental process disconnected from action in social life. Instead thinking relies on the use of modes of understanding the world – intellectual tools and signs – that are collective in nature, and it is in itself a social practice in which these tools are put to use for specific purposes. Thinking is thus not something that lies "behind" or "under" individual action; it is an integral part of human practices.

* This is an edited version of a chapter that appeared in *Learning in humans and machines: towards an interdisciplinary learning science*, Oxford: Pergamon/Elsevier Science, 1996.

Thinking and the use of tools

One of the significant features of a sociocultural perspective on human think-ing and learning that makes it stand out as an alternative to dualist positions within cognitivism is the assumption of the centrality of *mediation* and the role of *tools* – psychological as well as technical – in human practices. The concept of mediation refers to the fact that our relationship with the outside world is always mediated by signs and artifacts. We do not encounter the world as it exists in any neutral and objective sense outside the realm of human experience. We learn to interact with it by means of the signs and tools provided by our culture and in terms of which phenomena make sense. In this sense, human cognitive socialization – learning and development – is a process of appropriating concepts that originate in communicative practices in our culture. In other words, the world is pre-interpreted for us by previous generations, and we draw on the experiences that others have made before us.

Tools serve as mediational means, i.e., they – metaphorically speaking – stand between the individual and the world. The most important psycho-logical tool is language, which is the prime device for rendering the world intelligible and for communicating our intentions to others. Language here does not refer to a formal system but should be conceived as a semiotic resource providing signs that can be flexibly and creatively used in social practices.

> In contrast to many contemporary analyses of language, which focus on the structure of sign systems independent of any mediating role they might play, a sociocultural interpretation presupposes that one conceives of language and other sign systems in terms of how they are a part of and *mediate* human action.
>
> (Wertsch, 1991, p. 29; italics in original)

An important corollary of this position is that language is first and fore-most a system that serves purposes of coordinating human activities; it is a means of action and a practical resource rather than a device for contemplat-ing the world *in vacuo* (Marková, 1982; Silverman & Torode, 1980). Concepts and words do not mean anything in and by themselves, language use and the construction of meaning are always social processes dependent on people who interact, and meaning is always relative to options and constraints that are present in social situations. "A word is a bridge thrown between myself and another," as Voloshinov (1973, p. 86) puts it. And consequently, if "one end of the bridge depends on me, then the other depends on my addressee. A word is a territory shared by both addresser and addressee, by the speaker and his interlocutor" (ibid.). Communication is thus always a two-sided affair in which speakers (or writers) and listeners (or readers) actively contribute to create what can be "conceived of as an *inter-subjectively established social reality*"

(Rommetveit, 1973, p. 25; italics in original). Communication in this perspective is never an issue of simply reproducing meaning but rather is an active and in some sense creative process in which past experiences are brought to bear on whatever is talked about.

The concept of mediation and the role of language in this context have obvious links to current discussions within various constructivist positions on the nature of human concept formation as well as to concepts such as representation and processing used in cognitivist traditions. In cognitivist approaches, representation is held to be an inner image or a mental model (Johnson-Laird, 1983) that the mind creates when confronted with an object or an event and that matches this object. An additional tenet is that "cognitive representations are perceptually based, and that perception is basically realistic" (Edwards & Potter, 1992, p. 19), which implies that representations are often conceived as copies of whatever is out there. In contrast to this, a sociocultural approach would emphasize how discourse enters into our perceptions and thinking, and how conceptualizations of phenomena reflect distinctions that are discursive in origin rather than present in objects as such (Bergqvist & Säljö, 1994; Säljö & Bergqvist, 1997). The somewhat archaic expression "verbal thinking" that Vygotsky uses points to the continuity between communication and thinking that reflects this position. As the individual is socialized into a particular culture, there is a "close correspondence between thought and speech" (1986, p. 80). Thinking implies operating with psychological tools that originate in language and that allow for adequate and sensitive evaluations of what are situationally appropriate modes of describing or understanding an object or a phenomenon. There is no assumption of decontextualized and unverifiable correspondences between mental images and an outside reality.

An obvious implication of the perspective outlined above is thus that thinking to a large extent is achieved through talk. Thus, not only can we assume that there is a continuity between what goes on inside and outside the heads of individuals in terms of the semiotic resources used for thinking, it is also obvious that talk is a mode of thinking that is vital in almost every setting. As Hutchins & Palen (1997) put it, "natural language as a medium for creating representations is a language of thought" (p. 2). The obviousness of the fact that thinking goes on between individuals and by means of discourse often escapes researchers as a result of the sharp line of division maintained within a dualist position where thinking is construed as pursued in brain structures rather than by means of linguistic resources. Consider as an example the following two excerpts taken from a classroom in which students in secondary school are working on the problem of producing a statute-book in which the *"laws that were considered to be of primary importance for living safely in our society"* (Bergqvist, 1990, p. 94, italics in original) were to be listed and discussed. In the first excerpt (see Table 3.1) we find the students cooperating on this task by enumerating different kinds of offenses that the statute book should specify.

Table 3.1 Excerpt of dialogue about statutes

2	Hanna 1:	Burglary, should I write that down? Should I write burglary?
3	Nina 1:	Yes! (impatiently) Wait! Assault, murder, theft, robbery. That's only this kind of thing . . . Is there no other . . . eh (laughs) eh . . . embarrassing, no bu
4	Hanna 2:	Eh . . . eh . . . well, hit and run. Hit and run, we talked about that earlier on.
5	Nina 2:	Well traffic and such.
6	Hanna 3:	Drunken driving.
7	Nina 3:	Let's just write down lots . . . dru . . . drunkenness (giggling)
8	Hanna 4:	Dangerous . . . drunken . . .
9	Nina 4:	Shoplifting, yes.
10	Hanna 5:	Dangerous driving, or whatever it's called

Source: Bergqvist, 1990, p. 98.

The two girls Nina and Hanna here operate in a manner which could equally well be conceived as an internal dialogue within one individual. They coordinate their thinking within the context of a shared institutional activity, and they negotiate what is considered as significant contributions and valid representations of a criminal act. Their talking can be conceived as thinking, and their thinking is very clearly carried out by means of sociocultural resources which are linguistic in nature. When Nina in her first statement in this excerpt establishes with some embarrassment that they have been limiting themselves to violent activities and wants to change their line of thinking, her interlocutor responds by suggesting "hit and run" as another example of a candidate crime. This particular example, which is an adequate contribution, however, can also be conceived as representing an act of physical violence. Nina therefore continues by taking "hit and run" as an additional example, but also by exploiting it as a resource for moving the conversation into the area of traffic, where they should be able to find lots of other offenses that would fit into the task they have to do.

Thinking is thus socially distributed by means of language (and other tools; see below), and talk is a most productive and significant vehicle for cognitive activities. It should not be conceived merely as a medium in which whatever is "inside" the cognitive system of an individual is represented, as is so often done in research, for instance when data are being collected through interviews, "think-aloud" protocols, or when experiments being conducted (cf. Elbers, 1991: Elbers & Kelderman, 1994; Grossen, 1993). Another example from the same corpus of data that further illustrates how thinking is a discursive process and has to be understood as occurring between individuals is shown in Table 3.2. Here a group of four secondary school students working on the same issue as above are engaged in the activity of finding a technical term for a particular offense. In his first comment, Robert gives a description in everyday language of this offense – destruction – but at the same time he makes clear that there is a term which in technical, legal

Table 3.2 Excerpts from a dialogue on statute law

729	Robert 181:	What's destruction called? It's called something special.
730	Eva 218:	We already have destruction once.
731	Inga 163:	Offense.
732	Robert 182:	No-o.
733	Eva 219:	Well, it does have a special name.
734	Robert 183:	Ye-es.
735	Inga 164:	Damage.
736	Robert 184:	Yes!!
	Ralf 154:	
	Eva 220:	
737	Eva 221:	Good Inga!
738	Robert 185:	Damage!! Oh, that's good Inga!!

Source: Bergqvist, 1990, p. 101.

parlance is the expected one. What triggers this discussion is a cognitive – and communicative – situation.

Again, this interactive sequence can very well be understood as somehow representing what would go on within an individual in a similar problem-solving situation. When attempting to find the term that they are searching for, individuals oscillate between internal "verbal" thinking and externalizing their thoughts in explicit language to make what they think public. There is no sense in which our psychological understanding of interactions of this kind would be improved by positing internal thinking as somehow being pursued at a totally different level of description in terms of processes and mechanisms that would lie "under" or "behind" discursive action.

Psychological tools and learning

The role of psychological tools in human learning is thus fundamental. By acquiring concepts and discursive tools, we appropriate ways of understanding reality that have developed within particular discursive practices in different sectors in a complex society. When faced with identical problems or situations, people differing in expertise will construe the objects very differently depending on the conceptual frameworks they are familiar with and are able to draw upon. What is a chaotic and completely unintelligible picture to an outsider, as in the case of an X-ray, is highly meaningful and relevant for action for the expert nurse or physician. Even though individuals may be exposed to identical stimuli, these will mean very different things depending on experiential backgrounds and the conceptual resources we bring to the situation when deciphering the X-ray or any other cultural tool. . . .

This example illustrates that representation is not a passive process of creating a mental image in a picture-like fashion. Rather, conceptual resources constitute objects and events for us in accordance with criteria utilized in specific human practices. Furthermore, conceptual knowledge is action-oriented and developed to serve as functional devices in social practices: "applying a concept to something enables me to act in ways that I otherwise could not" (Harré & Gillett, 1994, p. 41). Since modern society is characterized by a multitude of social and institutional practices in activity systems such as production, science, bureaucracies, schools, health care and many others, events and objects are construed in many different ways to serve different purposes. To learn is to appropriate psychological tools and conceptual resources that fit certain needs in ongoing activities rather than to internalize a "neutral" image of the world.

Artifacts and cognition[1]

Tools such as paper and pencil, newspapers and books and the wonders of modern information technology mediate reality for us in a wide range of activities; in an obvious sense our actions are performed by means of technical tools rather than by direct intervention in physical reality. Thus, we remember by writing things down in notebooks and calendars, and whenever we need to retrieve a telephone number, a code for the teller machine or whatever, we consult our notebook. When counting the money in our cheque account, there is nowhere we can go to count the money; rather we consult the record of the cheque account produced by the bank or we look in the cheque book that we keep ourselves. The use of a computer and software in a problem-solving situation may alter the nature of cooperation between learners in joint problem-solving and facilitate "co-construction of knowledge" (cf. Barbieri & Light, 1992; Light, Littleton, Messer & Joiner, 1994) by offering representations that provide concrete backgrounds for verbal interaction on how to plan, negotiate, and so on.

The potential of the computer to transform both the nature and organization of the classroom is discussed by Cole and Griffin (1987), who contrast two metaphors for computer–student interaction. The first metaphor they discuss assumes that the computer is an agent, operating as a "partner in dialogue." This view implies that the student–computer system can be viewed as an analogue to the student–teacher system, with the computer replacing the teacher. Within the framework provided by this perspective it is important to look at the computer's potential for providing structured hints, well-timed feedback, and a wealth of factual knowledge. It is this metaphor, they suggest, that underlies the bulk of research on computers and education at the present time. The second metaphor they discuss is of the computer as a "medium," not replacing people, but "reorganizing interactions among people," creating new environments in which children can be educated and grow by discovering and gaining access to the world around them. This metaphor emphasizes the potential of computers for reorganizing instruction within the classroom and for making possible the extension of education beyond the classroom (Cole & Griffin, 1987, pp. 45–46).

It is this second metaphor, that of computer as "medium," which is of interest from the point of view of a sociocultural approach to psychology. Clearly, cultural psychology is not interested in computer technology simply as a new vehicle for transmitting knowledge or as a new way of providing exploratory environments. Rather, it is concerned with how computers uniquely transform the way in which human cognitive activity is organized. To date there has been very little research on this; thus there is a pressing need to consider the special relevance of computers for reordering the contexts of education by reorganizing interactions among people. For example, we need to understand how the use of educational software serves to reorganize the social processes of children's joint problem solving (Crook, 1992). Keogh and Barnes (1994) have started to investigate this issue by comparing the nature of the talk and joint activity observed in same- or mixed-gender pairs of children engaged in an identical language problem-solving task (involving the assembly of a poem from a jumbled collection of phrases) presented either on or off the computer. Their findings highlight the impact that the presence of the computer has on the activity of the mixed-gender pairs: boys dominate the task when it is presented on the machine, whereas the activity is distributed more equally between the pair members when the task is off-computer.

We also need to know how such technology reorganizes the interactions among pupils and teachers. As Mercer notes:

> the quality of understanding that learners acquire through the use of information technology in the classroom is not, and never will be, determined by the quality of the "interface" between the learner and the technology. Quality of understanding, the nature of educational knowledge, is determined by a much more complex contextual system which is inseparable from how education is defined in our culture . . . this culturally-based contextual system is continually created and re-created in the classroom through interactions between teachers and learners.
>
> (Mercer, 1993, p. 37)

When it comes to computer use, however, many children know more than their teacher. One investigation of "expert" children and "novice" teachers (Shrock & Stepp, 1991) took the form of a naturalistic study of the social interaction surrounding a microcomputer in an American elementary school classroom. The teacher was relatively inexperienced in computer use and so designated a child "expert" as the resource person for students learning to use the computer. The observed negative effects on the role definition of "teacher" and the frequency of interactions not conducive to learning led the researchers to warn of the potential danger of child experts becoming "gate-keepers" of knowledge and competing authority figures in the classroom. Clearly, then, the use of technology in the classroom may facilitate a different kind of social dynamic between pupil and teacher, and future research will need to pay particular attention to the teacher/pupil discourse in classroom settings where new technology is taken as a focal point (Crook, 1992, p. 225).

As well as reorganizing interactions between people, computer technology has the potential to create new educational environments. Consider, for example, the opportunities offered by computer-mediated communication. Here computer technology can support joint activities which may need to be separated in time and space. In this situation the network provides a common storage area which can be referred to by collaborating pupils in different groups or from different classrooms. It may allow different generations of pupils to "leave tracks" that become a resource for new cohorts.

In an interesting sense this configuration furnishes new media for the organization of common knowledge within the community of learners. Pupils are thereby given new opportunities to participate within that community – this might apply to networking infrastructures related at the level of primary school or at the level of undergraduate departments. Such technology also opens up the possibility for the extension of education beyond the classroom. As Crook (1992, p. 221) puts it, this "form of communication opens up exchanges between children who are growing up and learning in, perhaps, very different cultural contexts," and "it can also create real audiences for their work and a real possibility of intellectual co-ordination with peers in pursuit of joint projects."

But although computers have the potential to reorganize learning inter-actions in a variety of significant ways, everyday experience suggests that social institutions have a remarkable capacity for "neutralizing" the effects of new developments, technological or otherwise. Classrooms may prove to be too well "buffered" to be much affected by computers and indeed may assimi-late computers entirely into their existing ways of doing things. Only time will tell whether computer technology will radically alter the ways in which children's thinking is developed and extended (cf. Cole, 1991).

In a very fundamental sense, we think with and through artifacts. In human practices there is an intricate interplay between tools and physical activities. The experienced carpenter attempting to establish how much wood will be needed when repairing the wall of a wooden house will make a drawing of the building and make his calculations by means of this paper-and-pencil version of the house. There will be no need to measure the wall more than once, since the drawing – if done with adequate precision – mediates the wall in a functional manner. Most further reasoning can be done without measuring the real object.

Technical tools thus extend, or rather transform, the capacities for physical and intellectual action that were bestowed upon human beings by nature, as it were. With tools such as paper and pencil, calculators, binoculars, computers, and telephones, tasks that would be burdensome, maybe even impossible, to perform become manageable. In the creation of human culture, toolmaking can be seen as one of the most powerful achievements. The difference between digging with one's hands and with a shovel of some kind or between hunting by throwing stones and using a bow and an arrow are profound also from a psychological point of view. Changing tools alters the structure of work activity (Scribner & Cole, 1981, p. 8) and, thus, the cognitive and communicative requirements of our actions. Through the use of tools, the human environment is fundamentally transformed and new modes of organizing habitats and social life become possible. We no longer have to follow the rhythms and demands of nature; rather, we can actively transform and control the physical environment to the needs we perceive. . . .

Situating thinking in human practices

It follows from what has been said above that learning in a sociocultural perspective can be described as the appropriation and mastery of communicative (including conceptual) and technical tools that serve as mediational means in social practices. These tools are the products of culture and they thus represent the experiences of previous generations. At the same time, however, even physical artifacts contain knowledge that is of a conceptual and thus discursive origin. Tools such as a compass or a watch contain symbolic resources that represent the world in categories that are clearly human in origin; the compass gives directions in degrees and the watch in units such as seconds, minutes and hours. Even technical devices can thus to a large extent be seen as extensions of what were originally human conceptual tools, although these resources have now been built into physical equipment.

In recent research by scholars such as Suchman (1987; Suchman & Trigg, 1993). Hutchins (1994), Goodwin (1997), and many others, this perspective of studying cognition as situated action and as tool-mediated has been taken further in interesting ways. In a series of studies, Hutchins (Hutchins & Palen, 1997) has explored the interdependence between human action and technological tools in environments such as cockpits and the pilot house on board modern naval ships. In the latter context, Hutchins points out how the long history of navigation implies a continuity in the psychological and even some technological tools that are used. The task of navigating a modern ship is socially distributed and divided between individuals performing actions that imply reading instruments, coordinating information, and making decisions on a continuous basis whenever the ship is at sea. Instruments such as nautical charts, an alidade, telephones and other communication devices, watches, echo-sounding equipment, and several others are necessary for this complex activity, which involves up to six people working together intensely when navigating in narrow waters. The cognitive part of this work is very clearly achieved by thinking, by communicating, and by consulting instruments that account for the world in a manner that is productive for this

particular activity. Thus, the task of navigating and "its computational properties are determined in large part by the structure of the tools with which the
navigators work" (p. 43), and the cognitive dimension is precisely what
unites people and instruments in a socially organized practice. Thought is
shaped by and implemented in a collective activity in a particular setting, and
we will learn little about cognition in real world events if we assumed that
"cognitive activity has to be crammed into the individual mind" (p. 62) and
described in a language that refers to hypothetical entities and processes that
in mysterious ways differ from what can be observed in interaction. As
Hutchins argues, "the properties of groups of minds in interaction with each
other, or the properties of the interaction between individual minds and
artifacts in the world, are frequently at the heart of intelligent human performance" (ibid.), and there is nothing more fundamental to cognition than
that. . . .

Conclusions

Throughout this chapter, I have been arguing for understanding human
learning and cognition by means of a unit that is identical to what Goodwin
(1997), following Goffman, refers to as a "situated activity system" (p. 6). In
such systems, cognition and learning have to be accounted for by analyzing a
socially purposeful and situated activity which is maintained through
practices that integrate physical tools and instruments, communicative
(including cognitive) activities, rules, and traditions of participant roles and
contributions, and criteria of success and failure. Thinking will be understood
as pursued in conjunction with artifacts, and the exact modes in which cognition and practical action are shared between actors and mediational means
become objects of analysis rather than something that can be taken for
granted by means of a priori restricting cognition to what takes place inside
the heads of individuals.

By analyzing learning in terms of the roles and responsibilities given to
people within situated activity systems, it becomes possible to understand
how individuals expand their intellectual repertoires and practical skills
through participation in collective activities rather than through absorbing
information *in vacuo*. Expertise will be seen as something that is publicly
displayed and shaped within the context of socially meaningful activities,
rather than as something that is of a strictly internal and mental nature.

. . . The assumption that individuals carry knowledge, procedures, and
skills from one context to another to apply them to new problems represents
an unreasonable position. As has been argued above, thinking is part of a
situated activity system, and as the situation changes so will the mediational
means and the modes in which problems are structured and perceived. In
situated activity systems, the constitution of a problem is a creative and most
significant activity, and the determination of what is problematic about an

instance is not necessarily visible from an analysis of the problem as such. Encountering a task inside or outside the workplace or the school may dramatically transform our perceptions of it and the range of solutions that appear reasonable. In fact, whether we encounter a problem in the context of a mathematics lesson or a social science lesson may alter our assumptions of what are appropriate modes of dealing with it (Säljö & Wyndhamn, 1993).

. . . The task for a systematic research approach to the issue of learning in complex settings becomes precisely one of studying how a problem is understood and constituted, and what kinds of structuring resources individuals rely on when dealing with it (cf. Newman, Griffin, & Cole, 1984). We shall learn little by continuing to assume that learning can be understood as a simple process in which decontextualized pieces of information and conceptual knowledge are taken from one context to the next in a mechanical fashion. Modern situated activity systems are far too dynamic and complex to allow for such simple assumptions to serve as productive and inspiring theoretical guidelines.

Notes

1 I am grateful to Paul Light, Department of Psychology, University of Southampton and Karen Littleton, Department of Psychology, Open University for substantial contributions to this section.

References

Barbieri, M.S., & Light. P. (1992). Interaction, gender and performance on a computer-based problem-solving task. *Learning and Instruction, 2(3)*, 199–214.

Bergqvist, K. (1990). Doing schoolwork. Task premises and joint activity in the comprehensive classroom. *Linköping Studies in Arts and Science, 55*. Linköping: University of Linköping.

Bergqvist, K., & Säljö, R. (1994). Conceptually blindfolded in the optics lab. Dilemmas of inductive learning. *European Journal of Psychology of Education, 9(2)*, 149–158.

Chaiklin, S., & Lave, J. (1993). *Understanding practice. Perspectives on activity and context*. New York: Cambridge University Press.

Cole, M. (1991). A cultural theory of development: What does it imply about the application of scientific research? *Learning and Instruction, 1(3)*, 187–200.

Cole, M., & Griffin, P. (1987). *Contextual factors in education: Improving science and mathematics education for minorities and women*. Madison: Wisconsin Center for Education Research.

Crook, C. (1992). Cultural artefacts in social development: The case of computers. In H. McGurk (Ed.), *Childhood social development: Contemporary perspectives*. Hove: Lawrence Erlbaum.

Edwards, D., & Potter, J. (1992). *Discursive psychology*. London: Sage.

Elbers, E. (1991). The development of competence and its social context. *Educational Psychology Review, 3*, 73–99.

Elbers, E., & Kelderman, A. (1994). Ground rules for testing: Expectations and misunderstandings in test situations. *European Journal of Psychology of Education, 9 (2)*, 111–120.

Goodwin, C. (1997). The blackness of black: Color categories as situated practice. In C. Pontecorvo, L. Resnick, & R. Säljö (Eds.), *Discourse, tools, and reasoning: Situated cognition and technologically supported environments* (preliminary title). New York: Springer.

Grossen, M. (1993). Negotiating the meaning of questions in didactic and experimental contracts. *European Journal of Psychology of Education, 8(4)*. 451–471.

Harré, R., & Gillett, G. (1994). *The discursive mind*. London: Sage.

Hutchins, E. (1994). *Cognition in the wild*. Cambridge, MA: MIT Press.

Hutchins, E., & Palen, V. (1997). Constructing meaning from space, gesture, and talk. In C. Pontecorvo, L. B. Resnick, & R. Säljö (Eds.), *Discourse, tools, and reasoning: Situated cognition and technologically supported environments*. New York: Springer.

Johnson-Laird, P. (1983). *Mental models*. Cambridge, MA: Harvard University Press.

Keogh, T., & Barnes, P. (1994, September). Computers versus paper: girls versus boys. Paper presented at the International Conference of Group and Interactive Learning, University of Strathclyde.

Light, P., Littleton, K., Messer, D., & Joiner, R. (1994). Social and communicative processes in computer-based problem solving. *European Journal of Psychology of Education, 9(2)*, 93–110.

Marková, I. (1982). *Paradigms, thought, and language*. Chichester: Wiley.

Mercer, N. (1993). Computer-based activities in classroom contexts. In P. Scrimshaw (Ed.), *Language, classrooms and computers*. London: Routledge.

Newman, D., Griffin, P., & Cole, M. (1984). Social constraints in laboratory and classroom tasks. In B. Rogoff & J. Lave (Eds.), *Everyday cognition: Its development in social context*. Cambridge, MA: Harvard University Press.

Nunes, T., Schliemann, A., & Carraher, D.W. (1993). *Street mathematics and school mathematics*. Cambridge: Cambridge University Press.

Resnick, L.B. (1991). Shared cognition: Thinking as social practice. In L. Resnick, J.M. Levine, & S. Teasley (Eds.), *Perspectives on socially shared cognition*. Washington, DC: American Psychological Association.

Rogoff, B. (1984). Introduction: Thinking and learning in social context. In B. Rogoff & J. Lave (Eds.), *Everyday cognition: Its development in social context*. Cambridge, MA: Harvard University Press.

Rommetveit, R. (1973). *On message structure*. London: Wiley.

Rommetveit, R. (1992). Outlines of a dialogically based social-cognitive approach to human cognition and communication. In A. Heen-Wold (Ed.), *The dialogical alternative: Towards a theory of language and mind*. Oslo: Scandinavian University Press.

Säljö, R., & Bergqvist, K. (1997). Seeing the light: Discourse and practice in the optics lab. In C. Pontecorvo, L. B. Resnick & R. Säljö (Eds.), *Discourse, tools, and reasoning: Situated cognition and technologically supported environments*. New York: Springer.

Säljö, R., & Wyndhamn, J. (1993). Solving everyday problems in the formal setting: An empirical study of the school as a context for thought; In S. Chaiklin & J. Lave (Eds.), *Understanding practice. Perspectives on activity and context*. Cambridge, MA: Harvard University Press.

Scribner, S., & Cole, M. (1981). *The psychology of literacy*. Cambridge, MA: Harvard University Press.

Shrock, S., & Stepp, S. (1991). The role of child micro-computer experts in an elementary classroom: A theme emerging from a naturalistic study. *Journal of Research on Computing in Education, 23*, 545–559.

Silverman, D., & Torode, B. (1980). *The material word*. London: Routledge & Kegan Paul.

Suchman, L. (1987). *Plans and situated actions. The problem of human machine communication*. Cambridge: Cambridge University Press.

Suchman, L., & Trigg, R. (1993). Artificial intelligence as craftwork. In S. Chaiklin & J. Lave (Eds.), *Understanding practice. Perspectives on activity and context*. Cambridge: Cambridge University Press.

Voloshinov, V.N. (1973). *Marxism and the philosophy of language*. [L. Matejka & I.R. Titutnik, Trans.]. New York: Seminar Press.

Vygotsky, L.S. (1986). *Thought and language*. [A. Kozulin, Trans.] Cambridge, MA: MIT Press.

Wertsch, J.V. (1991). *Voices of the mind*. Cambridge, MA: Harvard University Press.

Chapter 4

Thinking in niches

Sociocultural influences on cognitive development*

Mary Gauvain

In all societies throughout the world, most children grow up to be competent members of their community. This impressive phenomenon – and indeed it is impressive – is dependent on an inherent human ability to develop intellectual and social skills adapted to the circumstances in which the individual develops. In addition, it relies on cultural practices that support and maintain desired patterns of development. This chapter is concerned with two questions pertaining to this process: How do children develop the skills and knowledge to become competent members of their community? How are cultures uniquely suited to support and lead this development?

To explore these questions, I consider the role of culture in the development of thinking by focusing on culturally devised ways of supporting the development and maintenance of valued cognitive skills. The chapter takes as its primary inspiration the idea of the "developmental niche" introduced by Super and Harkness (1986). They use this concept to characterize the psychological structure of the human ecosystem that guides children's social development. A central purpose of the present chapter is to extend the notion of the developmental niche to the study of cognitive development and thereby to provide a framework for organizing cognitive developmental research from a sociocultural perspective. A second purpose is to illustrate these ideas by drawing on research extant in the developmental literature. An assumption underlying this analysis is that culture is a central component of all human functioning. Thus, a connection between culture and cognitive development should be evident in all research on cognitive development. . . . This is because despite theoretical and methodological challenges, consideration of culture is necessary whenever individuals are asked to perform in relation to some situation or apparatus or interaction that draws meaning from culture, as they are in most psychological research. Whether a developmental psychologist is exploring short-term microgenetic or long-term ontogenetic changes, prior experiences with a set of materials, a type of task, a pattern of

* This is an edited version of an article that appeared in *Human Development*, vol. 38, 1995.

interaction, or a group of participants are important in understanding the origins and development of the target behavior(s). Materials, tasks, interactions, and people represent and derive meaning from the culture from which they come. Thus, the child's experience reflects his or her history within a culture. The extent to which history, culture, and social experience should be considered depends on the topic and the questions asked. The main point is that the behaviors that are observed are not independent of the social history and cultural processes that guided the child in the development and organization of these behaviors. From this perspective, developmental researchers have much to gain from incorporating a cultural perspective in their work.

Cognitive development in sociocultural context

Two important questions can be asked about mental development. The first, the most familiar to researchers, is how the mind as an organized system both functions and grows. This question is not independent of another one, however: How does the individual mind connect with the minds of others? Human beings are social animals, and the connectedness between individual thinkers is a nontrivial aspect of mental life. This connection not only helps organize and sustain the human intellect: it also serves as a template for cognitive growth. To the benefit of the organism (but perhaps to the bane of researchers), this connection has evolved in such a way that individual mental life and its sociocultural context are virtually seamless.

A sociocultural or sociohistorical analysis brings this connection more clearly into view (Cole, 1990; Laboratory of Comparative Human Cognition, 1983; Rogoff 1990: Saxe, 1991). In such analyses, cognitive development is considered as a fundamentally social and cultural process that reflects the coordination of biological capabilities and constraints with cultural values and opportunities. These two contributions to development, the biological and the cultural, inform and refine each other over time. Human beings learn to think about and solve problems in their everyday lives through the appropriation, use, and adaptation of social practices, materials, and symbolic tools developed by their culture. Individuals play an active, directive role in this process as their developing capabilities set the stage and the boundaries for development within a cultural context (Rogoff, 1990; Whiting & Edwards, 1988). And whatever cultural arrangements exist at any given point in time contain to some degree the coordinations that preceded them (Cole, 1990; Geertz, 1973). In Faulkner's words, "The past is never past, it is always with us."

The inextricable connection between human biological processes, cultural systems of meaning and action, and their joint passage through time and historical circumstances constitutes the landscape of human development. The goal of a cultural developmental psychology is to search out universals of human development while at the same time remaining cognizant of the social and historical processes that give these universals form and meaning. In this way, a historically based, sociocultural view brings both differences and commonalities into relief. Although in the case of any specific accomplishment, one contributor – the biological, the social, or the historical – may be more evident or influential than another, these localized developments should not obscure the interdependent roles of all three. From the perspective of the developing individual, none of these contributors can function without the others.

The developmental niche

Super and Harkness (1986) have proposed the concept of "developmental niche" as a means of considering simultaneously the psychological and cultural contributions to human development. They place the child's development and cultural processes within a single framework, with human development embedded within a cultural system. As an organizing theme, Super and Harkness adapt a concept from biological ecology – the "ecological niche" – and use it to describe the relation between organisms and their environments. The developmental niche is similar to its counterpart in biology in that the physical and social environment is a defining feature of an organism and its development. For humans, this ecological setting is a social-psychological nexus that provides organisms with regulation and direction for development by means of the cultural system in which they live and grow.

It is not only the organism that provides structure and direction to development. Culture also possesses structure and direction, and it is through the conjoining of these two organized systems that human development unfolds. This conception of development directs attention away from the solitary organism or the environment as units of study and toward the continuing and changing fit between regularities in the cultural system and those in the organism over the course of growth. As in biology, growth or change is a function of both the structure of the organism and the environment, with the direction and pattern of change reflecting the coordination of these two forces.

Super and Harkness (1986) identify three subsystems of the developmental niche that connect human developmental processes directly to the culture – the physical and social settings of development, the customs of child care, and the psychology of caregivers. These subsystems simultaneously emphasize the psychological contributions of the participants and the context in which these develop. They provide a basis for categorization of empirical studies. For example, research on the influence of adult–child and peer interaction on development, as well as investigations of the role of the family, the neighborhood, and the classroom in organizing and channeling development, emphasize the physical and social setting of the niche. Child care customs are the focus of much current developmental research, as evidenced in studies of the developmental consequences of home-based versus out-of-home care for young children and the influence of maternal employment on child development. The psychology of the caregiver is receiving increased attention in research on parental belief systems, parenting styles, maternal guidance, and the role of parents as emotional regulators for children. The concept of developmental niche can serve as an organizing frame linking these and other contemporary areas of research to each other, in addition to providing a connection between these subsystems and the larger cultural system.

A major challenge in understanding the transaction between cognitive development and sociocultural processes lies in specifying the linkages between them more precisely. The role that parents and other social agents play in directing cognitive development is important and the type of research referred to earlier may further understanding of this process. However, the subsystems described by Super and Harkness (1986) are more suited to examining social than cognitive development. Although they argue that cultural regularities "provide material from which the child abstracts the social, affective, and cognitive rules of the culture" (p. 552), it is unclear what cognitive rules exist, how these rules are abstracted to guide cognitive performance, and, most important for the present discussion, how these rules are related to cognitive development. In the remainder of this chapter, we explore how the idea of the developmental niche may be extended to apply to cognitive development.

Cognitive subsystems of the developmental niche

In this section, three subsystems of the developmental niche are discussed. Each may serve as a sociocultural frame within which thinking develops. These subsystems describe ways in which culture penetrates cognitive activity and development across various levels of psychological functioning and experience. They also bring together several areas of developmental research that have touched either directly or indirectly on culture and cognitive development but have not been integrated within an overall framework. The three subsystems are: (a) activity goals and values of the culture and its members: (b) historical means provided by the culture, such as material and symbolic tools for satisfying these goals and values; and (c) higher-level structures, such as scripts, routines, and rituals, that instantiate cultural goals and values in socially organized ways and thereby connect individual members to each other and to cultural goals and values in the course of everyday practices. These subsystems provide both opportunities for and constraints on cognitive development. They thereby help support and extend human thinking in ways suited to the values and requirements of a culture. . . .

Activity goals and values of the culture

Central to a sociohistorical approach is the idea that human behavior and thinking occur within meaningful contexts, as people conduct purposeful goal-directed activities (Leont'ev, 1981; Rogoff, 1982; Vygotsky, 1978; Wertsch, 1985). Behavior does not occur in a vacuum but in a meaningful confluence of material, social, and individual resources organized to accomplish a goal. Research has shown that the purpose for conducting an activity may influence how the activity is organized, which in turn may influence learning (Frese & Sabini, 1985; Gauvain & Rogoff, 1986; Leont'ev, 1981; Zinchenko,1981).

Although the importance of considering activity structure, including the task goal and the means for reaching this goal, is well-established in psychological research, the connecion between activity structure, cultural practices, and cognitive development remains relatively unexplored. This oversight is serious, since culture provides both opportunities for and constraints on human action by defining activities and their structure. These activities are the workspaces of cognitive growth. In order to understand what a person is trying to do while solving a problem, it is important to examine the activity being performed both as a meaningful whole and in relation to the cultural and social practices in which this skill has been developed and is used.

Recent research on the connection between practical activites and cognitive functioning demonstrates how an individual's daily activities are goal-directed and reflect the culture within which that individual participates. In their work with Brazilian street children, Carraher *et al.* (1985) and Saxe (1991) have shown that mathematical activity is handled differently, and more successfully, when the goal of the calculation is meaningful. For instance, the candy sellers observed by Saxe (1991) displayed better arithmetic skills when their calculations were linked to their principal motive to make money. Scribner *et al.* (1984) demonstrated that workers in a milk-processing plant relied on their extensive spatial knowledge of the plant to shape their work assignment so that it was handled more efficiently, a common goal among workers and employers in Western communities. Finally, Rand (1968) found that taxi drivers and pilots drew different types of city maps reflecting the types of goal-directed actions in which each participated.

Cultural values and human activity

In addition to goal-directed action, some system of values guides members of a culture in selecting and shaping cognitive activity. Values related to cooperation and competition, individualism, sex roles, traditionalism, and other cultural concerns have been discussed extensively in the psychological and sociological literature. They clearly influence cognition and its development. . . . For example, theories or beliefs about children and how they develop influence the ways in which parents interpret and respond to their children's behaviors (Goodnow, 1985; Goodnow *et al.*, 1984), and these may be related to later developmental outcomes, such as academic performance when children enter school (Hess *et al.*, 1980).

Cultural values also contain tacit understandings about what is an appropriate goal or what a good performance should look like (Goodnow, 1990). Such assumptions are often unspoken, and may in many instances be unconscious (Bargh, 1990). But they nevertheless help guide human action along particular courses toward particular ends. Along these lines, Goodnow (1976) suggests that certain features of intellectual performance, such as generalization, completeness of problem solutions, and conventional interpretations of tasks and task solutions, reflect the goals and values of a culture. For instance, the propensity among thinkers in Western communities to generalize information may hinge upon cultural values that regard a search for universals or principles across events as important and worthy of pursuit (Cole, 1985). . . .

The cultural context also helps determine human action by prescribing socially appropriate ways of participating in and managing cognitive activity. For instance, whether a task is performed to satisfy a practical purpose or is primarily for evaluation is determined by cultural requirements, oftentimes presented through cultural institutions. Similarly, whether challenging tasks are typically performed alone or with the assistance of someone more experienced is culturally influenced. These practices are rooted in cultural values and beliefs about mental activity and its development. Such values and beliefs take form in specific activities, primarily through the goals that organize action and the means that are used to support action. It is in this way that problem-solving practices are deeply entwined with cultural values and the activities and goals that stem from these values. And within cultures, various contexts or institutions may distinguish themselves by the goals they set for human action. For instance, participation in Western-type schooling imposes particular patterns of goals on intellectual performance (Cole, 1985; Goodnow, 1976; Rogoff, 1981a).

Culture and goal-directed action

Cultural goals and beliefs are evident in the form or organization of knowledge that children develop. A cross-national team of researchers (Hatano *et al.*, 1993) studied the development of biological knowledge among children in three cultures (Japan, Israel, and the United States) and found similarities in biological knowledge across these groups. However, results also showed differences across the communities reflecting differing cultural beliefs regarding living and nonliving entities, linguistic encoding of this information, and children's exposure to scientific and nonscientific views of vitality.

Cultural goals with respect to social interaction, and the values underlying

them, can affect the nature and outcome of cognitive activity that is conducted socially (Ellis and Gauvain, 1992). Mackie (1980, 1983) compared the
effects of social interaction on performance on a Piagetian spatial reasoning
task among two groups of New Zealand children. Pakehas (of European
descent) and Polynesians (of Maori and Pacific Island descent). Traditional
Polynesian society promotes group goals and conformity in social interaction
over individual pursuits. Polynesian children learn to avoid interpersonal
conflict, value membership in a group, and obey older and more authoritative
children (Graves and Graves, 1979, cited in Mackie, 1983). Mackie predicted
that Polynesian children would benefit less from social interaction than
Pakehas children because they would be less likely to engage in the kind
of verbal discussion critical to sociocognitive conflict. Nonconserving
Polynesian children were more passive in their interactions, particularly when
paired with more advanced partners, and they showed less improvement than
their Pakehas counterparts. The goals of the interaction differed in the two
groups, reflecting differing cultural values regarding social discourse. These
differences affected children's opportunities for learning in a social context.

The implication of these examples is that activities and the goals and
values that guide them are expressions of culture. A sociocultural framework
focused on human activity as the level of analysis may further understanding
of how human intelligence is organized over the course of development to fit
with the requirements and opportunities of the culture in which development
occurs. However, a focus on activities and activity goals does not suggest that
goals are always completely formulated in advance or are unchangeable. Some
goals may purposely be left unspecified, enabling a person to take advantage
of opportunities that arise in the course of action to refine the goal. For
example, in planning everyday activities, skilled planners often begin with an
idea of how to work toward a goal and then refine the plan and the goal
opportunistically in accord with constraints and opportunities in the physical
and social environment (Rogoff *et al.*, 1987). Saxe's (1991) study of Brazilian
candy sellers illustrates this point:

> Sellers' mathematical goals are not consciously planned by the sellers nor
> are they determined by the conventions and artifacts of the practice.
> Rather the goals emerge in the practice, as sellers attempt to address their
> larger economic objective of making money.
>
> (p. 35)

The sellers' emergent activity goals may entail adjusting pricing to infla-
tion, immediate consumer demands, or other conditions of the marketplace.
As goals are formulated and refined in the course of action, they rely on
information and support provided by the culture to help steer the action in
ways suited to the community in which the action occurs. Thus, whether

goals are set in advance or completed during action, culture helps define, modify, and evaluate them.

As a final point, the study of psychological activities and activity goals in relation to culture and development may also facilitate examination of an issue that has vexed cognitive developmentalists for decades – the issue of transfer. Examination of connections across activities, such as how an activity changes over time and how traces of the means or goals of prior activities are inserted in current or planned activities, may help illuminate continuity in human intellectual growth (Rogoff, 1992). In fact, one of the consolidating links connecting intellectual functioning across activities is the cultural system of meaning within which human activity resides. It is this system of meaning and intention that connects human actions over time and place.

Historical means for satisfying cultural goals and values

Material and symbolic tools and resources are developed and used by cultures to support mental activity. As such, they play a central role in the development and organization of cognitive skill. Through the use of culturally developed tools for thinking, a person's mental functioning acquires an organized link to sociohistorically formulated means and operations. This transmission occurs through cultural tools and involvement with more experienced cultural members who use and convey the use of these tools to new members. Cole and Griffin (1980) refer to such tools as cultural amplifiers, that is, techniques or technological features provided by a culture that alter the approaches individual members of the culture use in solving problems posed by their environments. Thus, not only do material tools such as computers, symbolic systems such as language, or notational systems such as number enhance human thinking. More important, they may transform thinking. In so doing, they shape cognitive development in unique ways.

Maps and mathematical tools

Developing competence at using material and symbolic tools that support cognitive activity is an important developmental achievement with critical consequences for the development of thinking. For example, if a person knows how to use a map or navigational tool of some sort, extensive travel will not only be more successful; it also becomes more likely. . . .

Developmental researchers have examined the influence of a variety of tools, both material and symbolic, on cognitive development. Research on the development of map-reading skills demonstrates that even preschoolers can acquire some integrated knowledge about the relative positions of locations from a map and this knowledge can aid subsequent navigation (Uttal and Wellman, 1989). In this case, an external, symbolic representation – a map – mediates and enhances cognitive activity. School-age children are clearly not expert map users; full competence in map reading may not be acquired until adolescence (Presson, 1987), depending on the type of map and cultural opportunities available for developing these skills (Gauvain, 1993). Nonetheless, the point is that children's success or failure on a mapping task is not only reflective of their spatial or representational skills. It also reflects skill and practice with a system of representation – a tool – available within a particular cultural context.

An area of cognitive development that incorporates extensive use of symbolic and material tools is mathematical skill. Material tools to support mathematical activity have existed throughout history (Ascher, 1991) and continue to be developed. Slide rules, calculators, computers, abacuses, and number tables are obvious examples. Adoption of innovative tools to support mathematical activity is not always without reservation, however. For example, the impact of calculators and computers on mathematical learning is a topic of current debate. Such concerns are not new. The chalkboard was greeted with skepticism by mathematics instructors at the turn of the century, who worried that its use in the classroom might lead to less reliance on mental calculation. These concerns reflect the strong connection between learning and the material tools that support it.

One of the best demonstrations of the connection between material tools and mental processes is provided by Stigler and colleagues, who examined the relation of skill at using the abacus and the process of mental calculation (Stigler, 1984; Stigler et al., 1986). By comparing abacus users' reports of their progress at intermediate steps of mental calculation and their progress when performing the same calculation using the abacus. Stigler (1984) discovered that intermediate and expert abacus users employed a "mental abacus" when they calculated solutions in their heads. Furthermore, his comparison of errors made by abacus users and errors made by American students unfamiliar with the abacus who relied on Arabic numerals showed patterns consistent with the characteristics of the operators in the respective systems. Further research by Stigler et al. (1986) demonstrated that abacus skill enhances both mental calculation skills and conceptual understanding of the number system. This research provides support for the contention that through the provision of material and symbolic tools, cultures provide ways of managing immediate problem-solving situations as well as ways of representing and thinking about the domain of knowledge that these tools support.

Historical tracks of a notational system

Beyond providing material support for mathematical thinking, symbolic tools also become integrated with the development and organization of thinking over time. Consider how a shift in the established notational systems for recording and calculating sums directed the development and organization of mathematical thinking during the early Renaissance. During the thirteenth and fourteenth centuries, Italian merchants were exposed to the Hindu-Arabic numeral system and its method of computation by a young scholar of the time, Leonardo of Pisa, also known as Fibonacci (Swetz, 1987). Leonardo wrote a book that detailed this notational system as well as its commercial applications. In particular, he recognized that this system was easily adapted to the complicated bookkeeping procedures that were increasingly vital to the rapidly developing commerce in the region. Soon after this book appeared, the merchant houses of Italy replaced the Roman numerals they were then using in their account books with Hindu-Arabic symbols and gradually eliminated the counting board (or computing table) and tally system that were used to support calculations with Roman numerals. This board was a form of abacus that had similar operational properties. It was complicated and cumbersome to use and was mastered and passed on by a relatively small number of teachers. In contrast, the algorithms associated with Hindu-Arabic numerals could be easily learned and performed without elaborate equipment. They relied on the use of pen and ink, which is readily transportable and had the additional benefit of making ciphering more public than it had been with the counting board system. Not surprisingly, because of the ease with which this system could be mastered and used, it posed a threat to the established computing means of the time. Yet, despite attempts to suppress and sanction their use. Hindu-Arabic numerals gradually supplanted the prior calculation system in Europe. And Italian merchants soon dominated Europe in both this new accounting form and in trade. Interestingly, some remnants of the earlier calculation system remain to this day. For example, the concept of "carrying" a number over to the next column has its origins in the abacus, where a physical transfer or "carrying" of counters to the next position is used to accommodate a larger number (Swetz, 1987).

The purpose in recounting this history is to place the findings of Stigler and colleagues in a broader historical framework. Recall that the American students, the non-abacus users in Stigler's (1984) study, were slower at mental calculation than the intermediate and expert abacus users. However, only the expert abacus users were more accurate over all the addend problems (2-, 3-, 4-, and 5-digit addends) than the non-abacus users. It seems that one cognitive consequence of the change in notational and ciphering systems introduced during the Renaissance may have been a reorganization of mental calculation. Swetz (1987) notes that as use of the Hindu-Arabic system spread, skill at calculating mentally became less important and skill at manipulating numerals on paper became more important. Thus, it appears that the differential skill of the abacus and non-abacus users in contemporary research may have origins in the notational shift introduced during the thirteenth and fourteenth centuries. Abacus use improves the mathematical skill of experts in ways consistent with the requirements of the apparatus and the practice that the abacus affords. The calculation skill of non-abacus users, in particular their reliance on pencil-and-paper calculations, is consistent with the notational system they use.

Although it apparently constrained the development of mental-calculation skills, the Hindu-Arabic notational system helped lay the foundations for other developments in mathematics. Because this system relies on writing mathematical operations out in a form that is commonly understood, it is possible to reexamine calculations later for mathematical patterns and structure. According to Swetz (1987), this notational system, in conjunction with printing, which enforced standardization of mathematical terms and symbols, paved the way for further computational and symbolic advances in mathematics.

Mathematical tools and the development of mathematical thinking

. . . An example of the relation between tools and mathematical thinking is drawn from developmental psychology and directly illustrates the link between symbolic tools and developmental competence. Miller and Stigler (1987) demonstrated that features of a numbering system influence the development of counting skills. They compared the acquisition of counting in American and Taiwanese preschool and early school-age children. They hypothesized that the counting tools in the English and Chinese languages were differently suited to the task of learning to count. In particular, they hypothesized that certain number names in the English language, such as specialized compound terms like the "teen" numbers and nonstandard terms like "eleven," may interfere with children's ability to generate consistent counting rules. Number terms in Chinese are more standardized than in English.

Results support this hypothesis. Chinese children made fewer counting errors than American children, and the errors the American children made were most often associated with counting junctures involving the less standard number names. Miller and Stigler concluded that the difficulty young American children have when learning to count may, in large part, reflect peculiarities of English more than an underlying cognitive confusion. However, they also pointed out that these patterns may not have resulted solely from linguistic differences. Chinese and American children are reared in communities that place different emphases on counting and mathematical skills more generally. Together, the symbolic, linguistic tools that cultures provide for developing counting skills and the cultures' promotion of these skills merge with the child's developing capabilities in ways that shape the development of these skills.

As this example shows the particular arrangements supporting the development of thinking, namely the material and the symbolic tools used, were only meaningful when located in the larger sphere of cultural practices and values. These tools are an inherent aspect of thinking that reflect the culture in which development occurs. In all of these cases, the tools, whether material or symbolic, and the thinking were merged. Attention to the historical processes by means of which cultural goals and values are satisfied in these activities is critical for understanding the patterns of cognitive development observed. Yet, in much psychological research one side of the problem-solving effort – in these cases the spatial or mathematical thinking – is regarded as inside the head and therefore the "stuff" of psychology, while the other side – the map or paper or notational system – is seen as outside the head and not critical to examine. This division obscures the fact that the thinking and the tools are part of the same problem-solving process. To examine thinking by considering one and not the other is to ignore part of the problem-solving process itself.

Higher-level structures that instantiate goals and values in everyday practice

Social processes affect the cognitive opportunities that arise over the course of development. The importance of social processes in cognitive development has not gone unnoticed by developmental researchers, and in recent years there has been an upsurge of research activity on this topic. Despite general acceptance of the idea that cognitive development is strongly influenced by social processes, the related link between social and cultural processes is less well established. This omission is problematic in that the form that social processes assume in order to transmit what can and should be learned in any particular community is largely determined by the cultural values and practices regarding social interaction and social institutions in that community. Culture provides the norms and institutions that organize the process and outcome of social transmissions.

Conventions for organizing and communicating knowledge

One critical historical means by which individual development is organized in ways to satisfy cultural goals and values is found in the conventions that are used within a community to organize and communicate knowledge. A central developmental task is the acquisition of skills for organizing knowledge and communicating it in understandable ways to others (Shatz, 1983). These skills not only help people organize their knowledge for effective use; they also allow people to share their knowledge with one another and thereby connect members of a community to each other. In fact, a prerequisite for participation in many of the sociocultural processes essential for intellectual growth may be the development of skill in the conventional forms of organizing and communicating knowledge.

Illustrations of the intricate connection between cultural patterns of organizing and communicating knowledge and cognitive development exist in the developmental literature, although they are not often couched in these terms. For example, research on the development and use of scripts (Nelson and Gruendel, 1981) treats the acquisition of culturally organized knowledge as a critical developmental achievement. The developmental study of pragmatics also supports the general claim that cultural practices of organizing and communicating knowledge form much of the substrate of development. Of course, the specific content of scripts or pragmatic conventions reflects a unique culture, but the point remains that the development of skill in conventional forms of communication is central to cognitive development. Descriptions of culturally defined conversational prescriptions, for example, appear throughout the developmental literature. Rogoff (1981b) provides a fascinating example in her descriptions of the ways in which Mayan children address peers versus elders. As another example, preschool children's relative inexperience with certain communicative conventions has been frequently cited as an explanation for their failure on Piagetian (Donaldson, 1978) and other cognitive tasks (Siegel, 1991).

Research on the development of spatial thinking well illustrates the role of cultural conventions in the development and organization of knowledge. Spencer and Darvizeh (1983) found route descriptions provided by British and Iranian preschoolers to differ. Descriptions provided by Iranian 3-year-olds living in Britain included more vivid and fuller accounts of the sites along a route but less directional information than those provided by British children. This difference suggests that as early as 3 years of age children are displaying some of the values of their cultural community with respect to presentation of spatial information to others.

Gauvain and Rogoff (1989) studied the development of children's use of one pragmatic convention for describing large-scale space, the "mental tour" (Linde and Labov, 1975), in relation to spatial memory. A mental tour is a system for organizing complex spatial information in a linear fashion, as if the space were being mentally traversed. It contains information about the temporal and spatial contiguity of areas in the space. In the Gauvain and Rogoff (1989) study, 6- and 9-year-old children explored a laboratory-constructed funhouse, guided by instructions either to study the overall arrangement of the funhouse (the layout) or the best way for getting through the funhouse (the route). They were later asked to describe the space. Few age differences appeared in memory of the funhouse. However, the descriptions provided by older children were mostly in the form of "mental tours," resembling those of adults (Linde and Labov, 1975), regardless of whether these children received instructions to study the layout or the route. Younger children provided mental-tour descriptions only when they were instructed to attend to the route. Otherwise, their descriptions were nonspatial in character, tending to contain a list of places without reference to spatial relations.

It appears that with development children become increasingly skilled at using pragmatic conventions for organizing and communicating spatial knowledge. Whether conventions such as mental tours are universal in appearance or form is an open question. Certainly the experiences this skill relies on are universal. Children throughout the world have increasing opportunity with development to navigate through and use large-scale space. Greater skill in using the mental-tour convention may reflect increasing practice with age in following spatial directions, in self-guided wayfinding, and in receiving feedback from others when providing spatial descriptions. Communicative conventions such as this may play an important role in conveying spatial information to listeners, and listeners may respond to their use in meaningful ways and even expect and rely on them when spatial information is provided. One of the interesting developmental aspects of this process is an age-increasing demand from others for presenting spatial information in certain conventional forms.

The evidence reviewed thus far indicates that ways of speaking are influenced by cultural conventions and that use of these conventions changes with development. The more intriguing question is whether these conventional forms influence the process of thinking and its development. This is a difficult question to answer, but some suggestive evidence, also in the area of spatial cognition, exists. Levinson (1992) studied spatial thinking among the Guugu Yimithirr, an Aboriginal community in Eastern Australia. In representing spatial information, the Guugu Yimithirr language does not rely on the use of relativistic terms. Rather, it encodes spatial information in absolute position in accordance with cardinal directions. An example is in order:

> In Guugu Yimithirr, in order to describe someone as standing in front of a tree, one says some thing equivalent to "George is just North of the tree" . . . or to ask someone to turn off the camping gas stove "turn the knob West" and so on.
>
> (Levinson, 1992, p. 3)

In a series of studies involving skill at dead-reckoning (pointing to out of-sight locations) in the desert and reproducing object arrangements on table tops in adjacent rooms, Levinson found that Guugu Yimithirr speakers identified and reconstructed spatial information according to the absolute rather than relative positioning of objects. Even when not speaking, they behaved in ways consistent with their communicative conventions for describing space. The rapidity and precision with which they provided absolute spatial information led Levinson to conclude that their spatial visual encoding must reflect absolute orientation consistent with the linguistic form. Although these data do not explain how development occurs, they suggest that it involves the coordination of visual and linguistic coding in ways suited to the cultural community and that such encoding may affect the thinking process. The fact that these observations were made among a people who have long been known to possess extraordinary spatial skill (Davidson, 1979; Kearins,

1976, 1981) is noteworthy. The existence of superior spatial skill and the need for such skill in the harsh environs inhabited by Aboriginal peoples of Australia for the last 40,000 years begs the question of how communicative systems and cognitive systems coordinate over time and place.

Coventions for organizing and conveying knowledge appear to be an inherent aspect of thinking and to reflect the culture in which development occurs. Although examination of cultural variation in the development and use of such conventions is of interest, our concern here is with how such processes reflect the juncture of developing capabilities, such as spatial knowledge, and culturally valued and practiced methods of organizing and communicating this knowledge. Understanding the role that higher-level structures, such as scripts and communicative conventions, play in organizing the child's mind and connecting it to the minds of others is an important task. The developmental consequences, both cognitive and social, of appropriating culturally prescribed ways of speaking is thus one goal of a sociocultural approach to cognitive development. Better understanding of the appropriation process will inform researchers as they try to interpret children's performance on any task that relies on culturally influenced ways of organizing or communicating knowledge – a characteristic of most tasks used in research settings.

Formal and informal social interaction practices

In addition to conventions for organizing and communicating knowledge, cultures also provide organized patterns of social interaction that influence the development of cogninve skill. These patterns have been the focus of much research in recent years, largely inspired by Vygotsky's sociohistorical perspective. For Vygotsky, higher mental functions have their origin in human social life as children interact with more experienced members of their culture. This process involves a child as an active participant working with a more competent partner to solve a problem. To facilitate children's participation and learning, more experienced partners target their assistance to a child's zone of proximal or potential development (Vygotsky, 1978), exposing children to increasingly more complex understanding and activity than they are capable of on their own. Thus, the more experienced partner encourages and supports a child in using his or her current capabilities to extend the child's skill to higher levels of competence.

Social opportunities are not resources for cognitive growth in the same way that the material world is, however. Unlike the material world, the social world provides the developing mind with a dynamic and mutually generated context that originates in and is maintained through the contributions and goals of the participants. Involvement with others, either at play or at work, creates opportunities for individuals to evaluate and refine their understanding as they are exposed to the thinking of others and as they participate in creating some form of shared understanding with others. And the form of learning that children are capable of in these social encounters depends on the perspective-taking skills of the child, which change over the course of development (Tomasello *et al.*, 1993).

Some research on the influence of adult–child and peer collaboration on cognitive development has concentrated specifically on the sociocultural nature of these interactions. For example, Ochs and Schiefflin (1984) have studied the various forms that language learning takes in different cultural communities. They argue that becoming a competent community member largely entails the acquisition of knowledge and social practices through language development and exchange and suggest that this is the primary way in which children acquire culture. Laosa (1978, 1980) has examined mother–child problem solving in Latino and Euro-American families, identifying relations among culture, maternal education, social class, and maternal teaching strategies. More recently, Gutierrez and Sameroff (1990) have studied the relation of acculturation and maternal beliefs among Latino and Euro-American mothers to the cognitive assistance mothers provide for their children. Finally, Serpell *et al.* (1993) have observed relations between child-rearing beliefs and mother–child interaction in two ethnically different communities in urban Baltimore.

Dyadic interaction and direct parental guidance during joint cognitive activity, common themes in contemporary developmental research, may reflect practices and values with unique ties to the contemporary culture of the USA and perhaps even to particular subgroups within this community (Rogoff, 1990). In all communities, the everyday lives of children require involvement with others. Some communities place great emphasis on dyadic involvement, whereas in others children are involved in larger social groups for many of their daily experiences. Where dyadic interaction is not the norm, the imposition of dyadic interaction for research purposes may yield data affected by the reactions of both child and adult to being isolated from the usual social group (Rogoff *et al.*, 1991; Sostek *et al.*, 1981) or to being asked to be conversational partners when this is not a customary practice (Bowerman, 1981; Heath, 1983). These concerns do not imply that adult–child dyadic interaction should be discarded as an area of study. However, they do suggest that dyadic interactional processes may be a particular cultural response to more general developmental needs.

The challenge in understanding the role of social interaction in human development is to identify and examine both levels of the process – one pertaining to unique cultural patterns of development and the other to universal requirements and processes of human growth. Despite variation across communities, the process of social interaction reflects two universal developmental themes – the prolonged dependence of immature human organisms on more mature members and the press within cultures to maintain valued knowledge and skills via new members. The exact forms these themes take vary, especially across communities having differing approaches to factors such as adult–child interaction, kinship organization, or formal schooling. The point is that without cultural analysis it is not clear whether a psychological process represents a unique cultural response to universal requirements of the species or whether it is a universal form.

Sociocultural influences beyond the dyad

The focus so far has been on the influence of direct dyadic interaction on the development of cognitive skill. Yet less direct social processes make up a substantial portion of the cognitive opportunities children encounter. In fact, the primary power that parents and other more experienced community members exert over cognitive development, especially in the years after infancy, may not be in direct dyadic exchanges with children. Rather, it may be through control over the network composition and boundaries of children's social and mental life (Parke and Bhavnagri, 1989; Whiting, 1980). Children's opportunity to observe the practices of more mature community members – what Lave and Wenger (1991) refer to as legitimate peripheral participation – is an important avenue of cognitive development. Variation exists in the ways in which children are involved in the mature practices of their communities (Morelli et al., 1993; Whiting & Edwards, 1988), with patterns reflecting both short- and long-term goals and values of the culture (LeVine, 1977). Cultural factors also influence how peers interact (Ellis and Gauvain, 1992), and efforts to incorporate cultural values into peer learning programs in the classroom have been successful (Tharp and Gallimore, 1988).

An illustration of how research beyond the dyad may be informative has to do with how the practical actions of children, as guided by their parents, contribute to the development of spatial skills. Munroe and Munroe (1971) found a relationship between the distance children played from their village in Kenya and their skill on spatial tasks. A longitudinal follow-up (Munroe et al., 1985) indicated that directed distance from home, (i.e., travel undertaken while engaging in an activity away from the home area such as herding, running errands to neighboring villages, or weeding crops in the field), and not free-time distance from home (i.e., playing in non-adult-defined or directed activities), was the important contributor to boys' skill on several spatial tests. For these children, adult-directed and child-conducted activity facilitated the development of spatial skill. This result suggests that the assistance provided by adults in framing the activity was important for skill development. This assistance pertained to the overall goal of the activity and did not supplant the children's active control of actions to attain the goal. The opportunity for children to move through and view space under their own control guided by a superordinate structuring from adults was associated with spatial skill. Perhaps adult assistance in developing this skill may be more beneficial when it provides a goal and leaves the means of exploration to the child. This activity requires mental involvement on the part of the child and may lead to different types of developmental opportunities, compared to unstructured play or activities structured entirely by adults.

Finally, other more structural systems of interaction, such as formal institutions of learning, also intersect with the development of cognitive skills. The complex relation between schooling and cognitive development has been the object of extensive study (Cole *et al.*, 1976; Greenfield & Lave, 1982; Nerlove & Snipper, 1981; Rogoff, 1981a; Saxe, 1991; Stevenson, 1982). Although it is well established that schooling and Western values associated with schooling may affect the development of cognitive skills in important ways, the historical connection across social institutions in which development occurs, and how institutions coordinate their "developmental responsibilities" over time, are an important component of sociocultural analysis. For instance, how can we understand the involvement or lack of involvement of American parents in their children's homework, relative to parents in Japan, without considering the historical roots wherein social responsibility for fostering intellectual growth was explicitly distributed across societal agencies in these two cultures? . . .

To advance understanding of cognitive development, social and historical influences on cognitive development must be considered in far broader terms than is currently the norm. Characterizing cultural opportunities of a social interactional and social institutional nature and identifying their specific connection to cognitive development is a primary task for the next decade of developmental research.

Conclusions

In this chapter, a set of cultural subsystems or niches have been proposed as a conceptual aid to researchers interested in sociocultural influences on cognitive development. In the course of everyday life, human beings engage in meaningful goal-directed activities that reflect the goals and values of their culture. These activities often involve historically devised means, such as material and symbolic tools; higher-level structures, such as scripts, rituals, and communicative conventions; and formal and informal social interaction practices, provided by the culture. Through these activities, cultural goals and values are transmitted across generations and help guide the direction and course of cognitive development. The approach advocated here highlights the connection between cognitive development and its sociocultural context by adopting a framework within which both aspects of the developmental process are considered simultaneously. It does not treat culture as either an independent or dependent variable, but rather as the overarching context of cognitive development.

A central purpose of this chapter has been to illustrate the utility of this approach and not merely to criticize traditional avenues of investigation. In fact, the approach intersects with and complements a range of developmental concerns. Although the extent to which cultural considerations can be incorporated into traditional views of development is unclear, it would be foolhardy to dismiss a long history of careful research rooted in such traditions simply because it did not take into account cultural influences on development. Thus, a difficult task for the future is the reconciliation of findings from nonculturally based research with culturally based investigations of the same and related phenomena. By drawing on developmental literature, much of which was not intended to focus directly on culture, this chapter illustrates how this may be accomplished. . . . By developing conceptual frameworks in which social and historical systems of interacting and supporting thinking are an inextricable part of cognitive development, developmental researchers may make this task an easier one.

References

Ascher, M. (1991). *Ethnomathematics: A multicultural view of mathematical ideas.* Pacific Grove, CA: Brooks Cole.

Bargh, J.A. (1990). Auto-motives: Preconscious determinants of social interaction. In E.T. Higgins & R.M. Sorrentino (Eds.), *Handbook of motivation and cognition.* New York: Guilford Press.

Bowerman, M. (1981). Language development. In H.C. Triandis & A. Heron (Eds). *Handbook of cross-cultural psychology* (Vol. 4). Boston: Allyn & Bacon.

Bruner, J.S. (1986). *Actual minds, possible worlds.* Cambridge, MA: Harvard University Press.

Carraher, T.N., Carraher, D.W. & Schliemann, A.D. (1985). Mathematics in the streets and in schools. *British Journal of Developmental Psychology*, *3*, 21–29.

Cole, M. (1985). Mind as a cultural achievement: Implications for IQ testing. In E. Eisner (Ed.), *Learning and teaching the ways of knowing: Eighty-fourth yearbook of the National Society for the Study of Education.* Chicago: National Society for the Study of Education.

Cole, M. (1990). Cultural psychology: A once and future discipline? In J. J. Berman (Ed.), *Nebraska Symposium on Motivation: Cross-cultural perspectives* (Vol. 37). Lincoln: University of Nebraska Press.

Cole, M., & Griffin, P. (1980). Cultural amplifiers reconsidered. In D.P. Olson (Ed.), *The social foundations of language and thought.* New York, Norton.

Cole, M., Sharp, D.W., & Lave, C. (1976). The cognitive consequences of education. *Urban Review, 9*, 218–233.

Davidson, G.R. (1979). An ethnographic psychology of aboriginal cognition. *Oceania, 49*, 270–294.

Donaldson, M. (1978). *Children's minds.* New York: Norton.

Ellis, S., & Gauvain, M. (1992). Social and cultural influences on children's collaborative interactions. In L.T. Winegar & J. Valsiner (Eds.), *Children's development within social context* (Vol. 2). Hillsdale, NJ: Erlbaum.

Frese, M., & Sabini, J. (1985). *Goal directed behavior: The concept of action in psychology.* Hillsdale, NJ: Erlbaum.

Gauvain, M. (1993). The development of spatial thinking in everyday activity. *Developmental Review, 13*, 92–121.

Gauvain, M., & Rogoff, B. (1986). Influence of the goal on children's exploration and memory of large-scale space. *Developmental Psychology, 22*, 72–77.

Gauvain, M., & Rogoff, B. (1989). Ways of speaking about space: The development of children's skill at communicating spatial knowledge. *Cognitive Development, 4,* 295–307.

Geertz, C. (1973). *The interpretation of culture.* New York: Basic Books.

Goodnow, J.J. (1976). The nature of intelligent behavior: Questions raised by cross-cultural studies. In L. B. Resnick (Ed.), *The nature of intelligence,* Hillsdale, NJ: Erlbaum.

Goodnow, J.J. (1985). Change and variation in parents' ideas about childhood and parenting. In I.E. Sigel (Ed.), *Parental belief systems: The psychological consequences for children.* Hillsdale, NJ: Erlbaum.

Goodnow, J.J. (1990). The socialization of cognition. In J.W. Stigler, R.A. Shweder, & G. Herdt (Eds.), *Cultural psychology.* New York: Cambridge University Press.

Goodnow, J.J., Cashmore, J., Cotton, S., & Knight, R. (1984). Mothers' developmental timetables in two cultural groups. *International Journal of Psychology, 19,* 193–205.

Greenfield, P., & Lave, J. (1982). Cognitive aspects of informal education. In D.A. Wagner & H.W. Stevenson (Eds.), *Cultural perspectives on child development.* San Francisco: Freeman.

Gutierrez, J., & Sameroff, A. (1990). Determinants of complexity in Mexican-American and Anglo-American mothers' conceptions of child development. *Child Development, 61,* 384–394.

Hatano, G., Siegler, R.S., Richards, D.D., Inagaki, K., Stavy, R., & Wax, N. (1993). The development of biological knowledge: A multi-national study. *Cognitive Development, 8,* 47–62.

Heath, S.B. (1983). *Ways with words.* New York: Cambridge University Press.

Hess, R.D., Kashiwagi, K., Azuma, H., Price, G.G., & Dickson, W.P. (1980). Maternal expectations for mastery of developmental tasks in Japan and the United States. *International Journal of Psychology, 15,* 259–271.

Inkeles, A., & Smith, D.H. (1974). *Becoming modern.* Cambridge, MA: Harvard University Press.

Kearins, J.M. (1976). Skills of desert children. In G.E. Kearney & D.W. McElwain (Eds.), *Aboriginal cognition: Retrospect and prospect.* Canberra: Australian Institute of Aboriginal Studies.

Kearins, J.M. (1981). Visual spatial memory in Australian aboriginal children of desert regions. *Cognitive Psychology, 13,* 434–460.

Laboratory of Comparative Human Cognition. (1983). Culture and cognitive development. In P. Mussen (Series ed.), W. Kessen (Vol. ed.), *Handbook of child psychology: Vol 1. History, theory, and methods* (4th ed.). New York: Wiley.

Laosa, L.M. (1978). Maternal teaching strategies in Chicano families of varied educational and socioeconomic levels. *Child Development, 49,* 1129–1135.

Laosa, L.M. (1980). Maternal teaching strategies in Chicano and Anglo-American families: The influence of culture and education on maternal behavior. *Child Development, 51,* 759–765.

Lave, J., & Wenger. E. (1991). *Situated learning: Legitimate peripheral participation.* New York: Cambridge University Press.

Leont'ev, A.N. (1981). The problem of activity in psychology. In J.W. Wertsch (Ed.), *The concept of activity in Soviet psychology.* Armonk, NY: Sharpe.

LeVine, R.A. (1977). Child rearing as cultural adaptation. In P.H. Leiderman, S.R. Tulkin, & A. Rosenfeld (Eds.), *Culture and infancy.* New York: Academic Press.

Levinson, S.C. (1992). Language and cognition: The cognitive consequences of spatial description in Guugu Yimithirr. Unpublished manuscript. Max Planck Institute for Psycholinguistics, Nijmegen, The Netherlands.

Linde, C., & Labov, W. (1975). Spatial networks as a site for the study of language and thought. *Language, 51*, 924–939.

Mackie, D. (1980). A cross-cultural study of intra- and interindividual conflicts of centrations. *European Journal of Social Psychology, 10*, 313–318.

Mackie, D. (1983). The effect of social interaction on conservation of spatial relations. *Journal of Cross-Cultural Psychology, 14*, 131–151.

Miller, K.F., & Stigler, J.W. (1987). Counting in Chinese: Cultural variation in a basic cognitive skill. *Cognitive Development, 2*, 279–305.

Morelli, G.A., Rogoff, B., & Angelillo, C. (1993). Cultural variation in children's work and social activities. Paper presented at the biennial meeting of the Society for Research in Child Development, New Orleans.

Munroe, R.H., Munroe, R.L., & Brasher, A. (1985). Precursors of spatial ability: A longitudinal study among the Logoli of Kenya. *The Journal of Social Psychology, 125*, 23–33.

Munroe, R.L., & Munroe, R.H. (1971). Effect of environmental experience on spatial ability in an East African society. *The Journal of Social Psychology, 83*, 15–22.

Nelson, K., & Gruendel, J. (l981). Generalized event representations: Basic building blocks of cognitive development. In M.E. Lamb & A.L. Brown (Eds.), *Advances in developmental psychology* (Vol. 1). Hillsdale, NJ: Erlbaum.

Nerlove, S.B., & Snipper, A.S. (1981). Cognitive consequences of cultural opportunity. In R.H. Munroe, R.L. Munroe, & B.B. Whiting (Eds.), *Handbook of cross-cultural human development.* New York: Garland STPM Press,

Ochs, E., & Schiefflin, B. (1984). Language acquisition and socialization: Three developmental stories and their implications. In R. Shweder & R. LeVine (Eds.), *Culture and its acquisition.* Chicago: University of Chicago Press.

Parke, R.D., & Bhavnagri, N.P. (1989). Parents as managers of children's peer relationships. In D. Belle (Ed.), *Children's social networks and social supports.* New York: Wiley.

Presson, C.C. (1987). The development of spatial cognition: Secondary uses of spatial information. In N. Eisenberg (Ed.), *Contemporary topics in developmental psychology.* New York: Wiley.

Rand, G. (1968). Pre-Copernican views of the city. *Architectural Forum, 131*, 76–81.

Rogoff, B. (1981a). Schooling and the development of cognitive skills. In H.C. Triandis & A. Heron (Eds.), *Handbook of cross-cultural psychology* (Vol. 4). Rockleigh, NJ: Allyn & Bacon.

Rogoff, B. (1981b). Adults and peers as agents of socialization: A Highland Guatemalan profile. *Ethos, 9*, 18–36.

Rogoff, B. (1982). Integrating context and cognitive development. In M.E. Lamb & A.L. Brown (Eds.), *Advances in developmental psychology* (Vol. 2). Hillsdale, NJ: Erlbaum.

Rogoff, B. (1990). *Apprenticeship in thinking.* New York: Oxford University Press.

Rogoff, B. (1992). Three ways to relate person and culture: Thoughts sparked by Valsiner's review of *Apprenticeship in thinking*. *Human Development, 35*, 316–320.

Rogoff, B., Gauvain, M., & Gardner, W. (1987). The development of children's skill adjusting plans to circumstances. In S.L. Friedman, E.K. Scholnick, R.R. Cocking (Eds.), *Blueprints for thinking: The role of planning in cognitive development*. Cambridge: Cambridge University Press.

Rogoff, B., Mistry, J., Goncu, A., & Mosier, C. (1991). Cultural variation in the role relations of toddlers and their families. In M.H. Bornstein (Ed.), *Cultural approaches to parenting*. Hillsdale, NJ: Erlbaum.

Saxe, G. (1991). *Culture and cognitive development: Studies in mathematical understanding*. Hillsdale, NJ: Erlbaum.

Scarr, S. (1992). Cultural lenses on mothers and children. In L. Friedrich-Cofer (Ed.), *Human nature and public policy*. New York: Praeger.

Scribner, S., Gauvain, M., & Fahrmeier, E. (1984). Use of spatial knowledge in the organization of work. *The Quarterly Newsletter of the Laboratory of Comparative Human Cognition, 6*, 32–34.

Serpell, R., Baker, L., Sonnenschein, S., & Hill, S. (1993). Contexts for the early appropriation of literacy: Caregiver meanings of recurrent activities. Paper presented at the annual meeting of the American Psychological Society, Chicago.

Shatz, M. (1983). Communication. In P. Mussen (Series ed.), J.H. Flavell, & E.M. Markman (Vol. eds.), *Handbook of child psychology: Vol. 3. Cognitive development* (4th. ed.). New York: Wiley.

Siegel, M. (1991). *Knowing children: Experiments in conversation and cognition*. London: Erlbaum.

Sostek, A.M., Vietze, P., Zaslow, M., Kriess, L., van der Waals, F., & Rubinstein, D. (1981). Social context in caregiver–infant interaction: A film study of Fais and the United States. In T.M. Field, A.M. Sostek, P. Vietz, & P.H. Leiderman (Eds.), *Culture and early interactions*. Hillsdale, NJ: Erlbaum.

Spencer, C., & Darvizeh, Z. (1983). Young children's place-descriptions, maps and route-finding: A comparison of nursery school children in Iran and Britain. *International Journal of Early Childhood, 15*, 26–31.

Stevenson, H.W. (1982). Influences of schooling on cognitive development. In D.A. Wagner & H.W. Stevenson (Eds.), *Cultural perspectives on child development*. San Francisco: Freeman.

Stigler, J.W. (1984). Mental abacus: The effect of abacus training on Chinese children's mental calculations. *Cognitive Psychology, 16*, 145–176.

Stigler, J.W., Chalip, L., & Miller. K.F. (1986). Consequences of skill. The case of abacus training in Taiwan. *American Journal of Education, 94*, 447–479.

Super, C.M., & Harkness, S. (1986). The developmental niche: A conceptualization at the interface of child and culture. *International Journal of Behavioral Development, 9*, 545–569.

Swetz, F.J. (1987). *Capitalism and arithmetic*. La Salle, IL: Open Court.

Tharp, R.G., & Gallimore, R. (1988). *Rousing minds to life: Teaching, learning, and schooling in social context*. Cambridge: Cambridge University Press.

Tomasello, M., Kruger, A.C., & Ratner, H.H. (1993). Cultural learning. *Behavioral and Brain Sciences, 16*, 495–552.

Uttal, D.H., & Wellman, H.M. (1989). Young children's representation of spatial information acquired from maps. *Developmental Psychology, 25*, 128–138.

Vygotsky, L.S. (1978). *Mind in society.* Cambridge, MA: Harvard University Press.

Wertsch, J.V. (1981). *The concept of activity in Soviet psychology.* Armonk, NY: Sharpe.

Wertsch, J.V. (1985). *Culture, communication, and cognition: Vygotskian perspectives.* Cambridge: Cambridge University Press.

Whiting, B.B. (1980). Culture and social behavior: A model for the development of social behavior. *Ethos, 8,* 95–116.

Whiting, B.B., & Edwards, C.P. (1988). *Children of different worlds: The formation of social behavior.* Cambridge, MA: Harvard University Press.

Zinchenko, P.I. (1981). Involuntary memory and the goal-directed nature of activity in Soviet psychology. In J.V. Wertsch (Ed.), *The concept of activity in Soviet psychology.* Armonk, NY: Sharpe.

Part II

Teaching and learning

Scaffolding and the zone of proximal development

Chapter 5

A theory of teaching as assisted performance*

Roland Tharp and Ronald Gallimore

The development of cognition in society

Schools have much to learn by examining the informal pedagogy of everyday life. The *principles* of good teaching are no different for school than for home and community. When true teaching is found in schools, it observes the same principles that good teaching exhibits in informal settings.

Long before they enter school, children are learning higher-order cognitive and linguistic skills. Their teaching takes place in the everyday interactions of domestic life. Within these goal-directed activities, opportunities are available for more capable members of the household to assist and regulate child performances. Through these mundane interactions, children learn the accumulated wisdom and the cognitive and communicative tools of their culture. They begin to develop functional cognitive systems; they begin to generalize their new skills to new problems and to novel aspects of familiar situations; they learn how to communicate and think.

In this formal socialization, neither communication nor cognition is the subject of direct instruction. Children's participation is sustained by the adults assuming as many of the strategic functions as are necessary to carry on (Wertsch, 1979, 1985). Children often are unaware of the goal of the activity in which they are participating, but at the earliest levels this is not necessary to learning. The caretakers' guidance permits children to engage in levels of activity that could not be managed alone. The pleasures of the social interaction seem sufficient to lure a child into the language and cognition of the more competent caregiver (Bernstein, 1981).

The process begins early, much earlier than was once thought, and takes place mainly without the conscious awareness of the participants (Ochs, 1982). Without awareness, a caregiver may engage in a collaborative enterprise with the most profound implications for the development of a

---

* This is an edited version of a chapter that appeared in *Learning to Think*, London: Routledge, 1991.

participating child. Revealed in the interpersonal exchanges are the precursors of cognitive and communicative functions that will some day be self-regulated by the child and it is through such mundane interactions that children learn the cognitive and communicative tools and skills of their culture. This insight from Vygotsky has the most profound implications for how we think about development and teaching:

> From the very first days of the child's development his activities acquire a meaning of their own in a system of social behaviour and, being directed towards a definite purpose, are refracted through the prism of the child's environment. The path from object to child and from child to object passes through another person. This complex human structure is the product of a developmental process deeply rooted in the links between individual and social history.
>
> (Vygotsky, 1978; 30)

Thus, to explain the psychological, we must look not only at the individual but also at the external world in which that individual life has developed. We must examine human existence in its social and historical aspects, not only at its current surface. These social and historical aspects are represented to the child by people who assist and explain, those who participate with the child in shared functioning:

> Any function in the child's cultural development appears twice, or in two planes. First it appears on the social plane, and then on the psychological plane. First it appears between people as an interpsychological category, and then within the child as an intrapsychological category. This is equally true with regard to voluntary attention, logical memory, the formation of concepts, and the development of volition.
>
> (Vygotsky, 1978: 163)

The process by which the social becomes the psychological is called *internalization*: "The process of internalization is not the *transferral* of an external activity to a preexisting, internal plane of consciousness : It is the process in which this plane is *formed*" (Leont'ev, 1981: 57). The individual's "plane of consciousness" (i.e., higher cognitive processes) is formed in structures that are transmitted to the individual by others in speech, social interaction, and the processes of cooperative activity. Thus, individual consciousness arises from the actions and speech of others.

However, children reorganize and reconstruct these experiences. The mental plane is not isomorphic with the external plane of action and speech. As the external plane is internalized, transformations in structure and function occur. In this regard, Vygotsky's thought is closer to that of Piaget than to others. For example, Vygotsky expressly denies Watson's assumption that the internal speech of thinking is identical with external speech save for the vocalization. A child does learn to speak by hearing others speak – indeed, learns to think through hearing others speak – but as private speech sinks "underground" into thought, it is abbreviated and finally automatized into a form that bears little surface resemblance to speech itself. This transformation of form is a part of the developmental process.

The child is not merely a passive recipient of adult guidance and assistance (Baumrind, 1971; Bell, 1979; Bruner, 1973); in instructional programs, the active involvement of the child is crucial (Bruner, 1966). To acknowledge the inventive role of the child in transforming what is internalized, some developmentalists have begun to use the term *guided reinvention* – a term that connotes both social learning and cognitive reconstructivist arguments. Fischer and Bullock (1984) credit Vygotsky for having best anticipated the guided reinvention perspective, which expressly excludes the extreme positions found in some versions of modern social learning and cognitive-stage theories. Guided reinvention

> acknowledges the social learning theorists' insistence that social guidance is ubiquitous. It also acknowledges, however, the Piagetian insight that to understand is to reconstruct. Thus, guided reinvention elaborates the theme that normal cognitive development must be understood as a collaborative process involving the child and the environment.
>
> (Fischer and Bullock, 1984: 112–13)

In summary, the cognitive and social development of the child (to the extent that the biological substrate is present) proceeds as an unfolding of potential through the reciprocal influences of child and social environment. Through guided reinvention, higher mental functions that are part of the social and cultural heritage of the child will move from the social plane to the psychological plane, from the intermental to the intramental, from the socially regulated to the self-regulated. The child, through the regulating actions and speech of others, is brought to engage in independent action and speech. In the resulting interaction, the child performs, through assistance and cooperative activity, at developmental levels quite beyond the individual level of achievement. In the beginning of the transformation to the intramental plane, the child need not understand the activity as the adult understands it, need not be aware of its reasons or of its articulation with other activities. For skills and functions to develop into internalized, self-regulated capacity, all that is needed is performance, through assisting interaction. Through this process, the child acquires the "plane of consciousness" of the natal society and is socialized, acculturated, made human.

The zone of proximal development

Assisted performance defines what a child can do with help, with the support of the environment, of others, and of the self. For Vygotsky, the contrast between assisted performance and unassisted performance identified the fundamental nexus of development and learning that he called the zone of proximal development (ZPD).

It is conventional and correct to assess a child's developmental level by the child's ability to solve problems unassisted – this is the familiar protocol of standardized assessment, such as the Stanford-Binet. The child's *learning*, however, exceeds the reach of the developmental level and is to be found by assessing those additional problems that the child can solve with social assistance.

The distance between the child's individual capacity and the capacity to perform with assistance is the ZPD, which is

> *the distance between the actual developmental level as determined by individual problem solving and the level of potential development as determined through problem solving under adult guidance or in collaboration with more capable peers.* The zone of proximal development defines those functions that have not yet matured but are in the process of maturation, functions that will mature tomorrow but are currently in an embryonic state. These functions could be termed the "buds" or "flowers" of development rather than the "fruits" of development.
>
> (Vygotsky, 1978: 86; italics in original)

In contemporary neo-Vygotskian discussions, the concept of the ZPD has been extended to a more general statement, in which the "problem solving" of the preceding quotation is understood to mean performance in other domains of competence (Cazden, 1981; Rogoff and Wertsch, 1984). There is no single zone for each individual. For any domain of skill, a ZPD can be created. There are cultural zones as well as individual zones, because there are cultural variations in the competencies that a child must acquire through social interaction in a particular society (Rogoff, 1982). Boys in Micronesia, where sailing a canoe is a fundamental skill, will have a ZPD for the skills of navigation, created in interaction with the sailing masters. A girl in the Navajo weaving community will have experiences in a zone not quite like any ever encountered by the daughters of Philadelphia. Whatever the activity, in the ZPD we find that assistance is provided by the teacher, the adult, the expert, the more capable peer. Through this assistance,

> learning awakens a variety of internal developmental processes that are able to operate only when the child is interacting with people in his

environment and in cooperation with his peers. Once these processes are internalized, they become part of the child's independent developmental achievement.

(Vygotsky, 1978: 90)

Distinguishing the *proximal zone* from the *developmental level* by contrasting assisted versus unassisted performance has profound implications for educational practice. It is in the proximal zone that teaching may be defined in terms of child development. In Vygotskian terms, teaching is good only when it *"awakens and rouses to life those functions which are in a stage of maturing, which lie in the zone of proximal development"* (Vygotsky, 1956; 278; quoted in Wertsch and Stone, 1985; italics in original).

We can therefore derive this general definition of teaching: *Teaching consists in assisting performance through the ZPD. Teaching can be said to occur when assistance is offered at points in the ZPD at which performance requires assistance.*

By whom performance is assisted is less important than that performance is achieved, and thereby development and learning proceed. To the extent that peers can assist performance, learning will occur through that assistance. In terms of pedagogy, assistance should be offered in those interactional contexts most likely to generate joint performance.

Vygotsky's work principally discusses children, but identical processes can be seen operating in the learning adult. Recognition of this fact allows the creation of effective programs for teacher training and offers guidance for organizational management of systems of assistance. Developmental processes, arising from assisted performance in the ZPD, can be observed not only in the ontogenesis of the individual but also in the microgenesis of discrete skills as they develop throughout the life course. . . .

Paths through the zone

The transition from assisted performance to unassisted performance is not abrupt. We can again use the example of an interaction between a father and a daughter who cannot find her shoes; the father asks several questions ("Did you take them into the kitchen? Did you have them while playing in your room?"). The child has some of the information stored in memory ("not in the kitchen; I think in my room"); the father has an interrogation strategy for organizing retrieval of isolated bits of information in order to narrow the possibilities to a reasonable search strategy. The child does not know how to organize an effective recall strategy; the father knows the strategy, but he does not have the information needed to locate the shoes. Through collaboration, they produce a satisfactory solution. When the child is older, perhaps the father will have to say less ("Well, think of where you last saw the shoes"), leaving the more specific interrogation to the now self-assisting strategies of the child. This example of memory function provides an account of the origins of what are typically called metacognitive processes (Brown, 1978; Wertsch, 1978).

The developmental stages of higher cognitive, communicative, and social functioning always involve new systemic relationships among more basic functions. Vygotsky's discussions of higher-order mental processes all emphasize the shifting nature of such relationships during the course of development (Vygotsky, 1987). Attentional processes may be used as an example. In the first days of school, children can solve even simple problems only if attentional processes are brought into a new relationship with perception and memory. The attention capacity of the child entering kindergarten may be in the ZPD, so that a 5-year-old is capable of attending to teacher instruction and direction, but only if a rich diet of teacher praise is available. The teacher praise assists the child's attending by both cueing and reinforcing it. With time, the amount of praise required may be expected to decline (Tharp and Gallimore, 1976). As the capacity for attending advances through the ZPD, assistance often is provided by peers, who may remind a daydreamer that attention to the teacher is wise. For most pupils, after the third grade, assistance by either teachers or peers is rarely needed; attention processes can be invoked when the situation is judged appropriate; they have become self-regulated.

The development of any performance capacity in the individual also represents a changing relationship between self-regulation and social regulation. We present problems through the ZPD in a model of four stages. The model focuses particularly on the relationship between self-control and social control.

The four stages of the ZPD

Stage I: Where performance is assisted by more capable others

Before children can function as independent agents, they must rely on adults or more capable peers for outside regulation of task performance. The amount and kind of outside regulation a child requires depend on the child's age and the nature of the task: that is, the breadth and progression through the ZPD for the activity at hand.

Wertsch (1978, 1979, 1981, 1985) has pointed out that during the earliest periods in the ZPD, the child may have a very limited understanding of the situation, the task, or the goal to be achieved; at this level, the parent, teacher, or more capable peers offers directions or modeling, and the child's response is acquiescent or imitative. Only gradually does the child come to understand the way in which the parts of an activity relate to one another or to understand the meaning of the performance. Ordinarily, this understanding develops through conversation during the task performance. When some conception of the overall performance has been acquired through language or other semiotic processes, the child can be assisted by other means – questions, feedback, and further cognitive structuring. Consider a child perplexed by the myriad pieces of a puzzle. Thus, the adult might say, "Which part of the puzzle will you start to do?" The child may respond by putting in all the wheels, and thus see a truck take shape. Such assistance of performance has been described as *scaffolding*, a metaphor first used by Wood, Bruner, and Ross (1976) to describe the ideal role of the teacher. Greenfield (1984) noted that the characteristics of the carpenter's scaffold indeed provide an apt analogy for the teaching adult's selective assistance to a child. She added that scaffolding is similar to the concept of "behavior shaping," except in one important way. Shaping simplifies a task by breaking it down into a series of steps toward the goal. Scaffolding, however, does not involve simplifying the task; it holds the task difficulty constant, while simplifying the child's role by means of graduated assistance from the adult/expert (Greenfield, 1984).

Scaffolding is a concept that has been of unusual importance to the study of child development. However appealing this metaphor may be, the field has advanced to the point that a more differentiated concept can be developed. For example, scaffolding suggests that the principal variations in adult actions are matters of quantity – how high the scaffold stands, how many levels it supports, how long it is kept in place. But many of the acts of the adult in assisting the child are qualitatively different from one another. "Sometimes, the adult directs attention. At other times, the adult holds important information in memory. At still other times, the adult offers simple encouragement" (Griffin and Cole, 1984: 47).

The various means of assisting performance are indeed qualitatively different. By discussing these different means of assisting performance, we have the opportunity to connect neo-Vygotskian ideas with a broader literature of American and British psychology.

For the present, we can discuss the issue in terms of the various kinds of assistance that are regular features of Stage I. Rogoff (1986) discusses some of these issues in terms of *structuring situations*. Even before interacting with the child, a parent or teacher assists by an age grading of manipulanda: the choice of puzzles, the selection of kindergarten tasks, and the selection of appropriate tools and materials for an apprentice are all important features of assisting performance.

In addition to grading manipulanda, the assistor provides a "grading" of tasks, by structuring tasks into sub-goals and sub-sub-goals. The Saxe, Gearhart, and Guberman (1984) work on assisting children to learn to count is an example of structuring a teaching situation by careful task analysis and sub-goal selection, until the entire script is assembled back from its parts.

During Stage I, a child (or an adult learner) may not conceptualize the goal of the activity in the way that the adult assistor does (Figure 5.1). A child's initial goal might be to sustain a pleasant interaction or to have access to

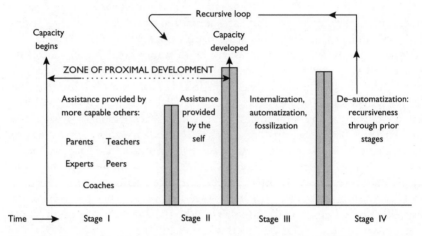

Figure 5.1 Genesis of performance capacity: progression through the ZPD and beyond

some attractive puzzle items, or there might be some other motive that adults cannot apprehend. As interaction proceeds, different goals and sub-goals emerge and change as the participants work together. The adult may shift to a subordinate or superordinate goal in response to ongoing assessment of the child's performance. The child's goals will also shift in response to adult help and their growing intersubjectivity. In a careful analysis of such interactions, Saxe and associates concluded that because the goal structure is located

> neither in the head of the mother nor in that of the child, this goal structure is negotiated in the interaction itself. Thus, the emergent goal structure simultaneously involves the child's understandings and the historical achievements of culture as communicated by the mother. . . . As children generate coherent means to achieve these socially negotiated goals, they create for themselves a system of representation that reflects achievements that have been generated in our culture's social history.
>
> (Saxe *et al.*, 1984: 29)

The shifting of goals by the adult to achieve intersubjectivity is the fundamental reason that a profound knowledge of subject matter is required of teachers who seek to assist performance. Without such knowledge, teachers cannot be ready promptly to assist performance, because they cannot quickly reformulate the goals of the interaction; they cannot map the child's conception of the task goal onto the superordinate knowledge structures of the academic discipline that is being transmitted. This fundamental aspect of interaction in the ZPD will emerge repeatedly in our analysis of teaching and the development of teaching.

During Stage I, we see a steadily declining plane of adult responsibility for task performance and a reciprocal increase in the learner's proportion of responsibility. This is Bruner's fundamental "handover principle" – the child who was a spectator is now a participant (Bruner, 1983: 60). The developmental task of Stage I is to transit from other-regulation to self-regulation. The transit begins while performance is still being carried out on the interpsychological plane of functioning, because the child can begin to use language exchanges with the adult to engender assistance. For example, in the analysis of joint puzzle-solving, the child can begin to ask the adult for strategic direction (e.g., "Which part do I do next?") (Wertsch, 1979: 19).

Indeed, by asking questions and adopting other sub-routines of the adult's assistance, children gradually take over the actual structuring of the task and thereby acquire not only the performance but also the process of transfer of the performance (Rogoff, 1986). The adult's task is accurately to tailor assistance to the child by being responsive to the child's current effort and understanding of the task goal. By asking "Which part do I do next?" the child begins to influence the level of help provided. *This assists the adult to assist.* Children, and other learners, are never passive recipients of adult or teacher input. As infants, they attracted adult attention through cries, smiles, and other responses. "Rocking and walking are not only effective ways of calming babies but also provide them with adult legs to move on and with access to new scenes of regard that yield information about the environment" (Rogoff, Malkin, and Gilbride, 1984: 32).

"Legs" of a different kind are needed to solve puzzles, learn to read, and acquire all the other skills that have their origins in social interaction. But at each stage, the developing child contributes to the success of an activity. Asking for strategic direction is, in this sense, no different than the infant's cry that makes locomotion possible. In both cases, the child's partial performance provides adult assistance, thus permitting an achievement not possible without the collaborating other.

The task of Stage I is accomplished when the responsibility for tailoring the assistance, tailoring the transfer, and performing the task itself has been effectively handed over to the learner.

Of course, this achievement is gradual, with progress occurring in fits and starts. The line between any two stages in the diagram of the ZPD is represented as a zone itself.

Stage II: Where performance is assisted by the self

If we look carefully at the child's statements during this transition, we see that the child

> has taken over the rules and responsibilities of both participants in the language-game. These responsibilities were formerly divided between the adult and child, but they have now been taken over completely by the

child. The definitions of situation and the patterns of activity which formerly allowed the child to participate in the problem-solving effort on the interpsychological plane now allow him/her to carry out the task on the intrapsychological plane.

(Wertsch, 1979: 18)

Thus, in Stage II, the child carries out a task without assistance from others. *However, this does not mean that the performance is fully developed or automatized.*

This point can be seen most clearly at the level of individual, ontogenetic development. In neo-Vygotskian theory, whether we consider the genesis of a particular performance capacity (microgenesis) or the development of an individual (ontogenesis), the same four stages describe the preponderance of self-control/social-control relationships. During Stage II, the relationships among language, thought, and action in general undergo profound rearrangements – ontogenetically, in the years from infancy through middle childhood. By the age of 2 years or so, child behavior can be inhibited by adult speech ("Don't kick!"). In the next stage of development, this same *self* instruction ("Don't kick!") also inhibits the kicking impulse. Control is passed from the adult to the child speaker, but the control function remains with the overt verbalization. The transfer from external to internal control is accomplished by transfer of the manipulation of the sign (e.g., language) from others to the self.

The phenomenon of self-directed speech reflects a development of the most profound significance. According to Vygotsky, and his follower Luria, once children begin to direct or guide behavior with their own speech, an important stage has been reached in the transition of a skill through the ZPD. It constitutes the next stage in the passing of control or assistance from the adult to the child, from the expert to the apprentice. What was guided by the other is now beginning to be guided and directed by the self.

There is now substantial experimental and observational evidence (Gallimore *et al.*, 1986; Tharp, Gallimore, and Calkins, 1984; Watson and Tharp, 1988) that a major function of self-directed speech is "self-guidance, that its developmental origins have to do with early social experiences, and that it increases under task circumstances involving obstacles and difficulties" (Berk and Garvin, 1984: 24; Berk, 1986). Developmental analysis places self-assistance as a stage in the ZPD.

Self-control may be seen as a recurrent and efficacious method that bridges between help by others and fully automated, fully developed capacities. Meichenbaum (1977) sought to teach self-instruction to children with deficient self-control. "Impulsive" children were taught to instruct themselves with cognitive strategies (e.g., "Go slow and be careful") before and during a variety of performance tasks; they demonstrated improved performance in such tasks as paper-and- pencil mazes. For children older than 6 years, semantic meaning efficiently mediates performance (Gal'perin, 1969).

Children also employ self-directed vocalization to assist performance under conditions of stress of task difficulty (Berk, 1986; Berk and Garvin, 1984; Kohlberg, Yaeger, and Hjertholm, 1968; Roberts, 1979; Roberts and Mullis, 1980; Roberts and Tharp, 1980).

Thus, for children, a major function of self-directed speech is self-guidance. This remains true throughout lifelong learning. At the microgenetic level, when we consider the acquisition of some particular performance capacity, adults during Stage II consistently talk to themselves, and indeed assist themselves in all ways possible. The self-conscious, systematic use of self-directed assistance strategies is one of the most vigorous movements in applied psychology (Watson and Tharp, 1988).

Self-speech is more than instrumental in skill acquisition; it is itself an aspect of cognitive development of the most profound sort (Diaz, 1986); it forms the basis for writing and thus is transformed into the highest forms of communication available to the literate life (Elsasser and John-Steiner, 1977).

Stage III: Where performance is developed, automatized, and "fossilized"

Once all evidence of self-regulation has vanished, the child has emerged from the ZPD into the *developmental stage* for that task. The task execution is smooth and integrated. It has been internalized and "automatized." Assistance, from the adult or the self, is no longer needed. Indeed, "assistance" would now be disruptive. It is in this condition that instructions from others are disruptive and irritating; it is at this stage that self-consciousness itself is detrimental to the smooth integration of all task components. This is a stage beyond self-control and beyond social control. Performance here is no longer developing; it is already developed. Vygotsky described it as the "fruits" of development, but he also described it as "fossilized," emphasizing its fixity and distance from the social and mental forces of change.

Stage IV: Where de-automatization of performance leads to recursion back through the ZPD

The lifelong learning by any individual is made up of these same regulated, ZPD sequences – from other-assistance to self-assistance – recurring over and over again for the development of new capacities. For every individual, at any point in time, there will be a mix of other-regulation, self-regulation, and automatized processes. The child who can now do many of the steps in finding a lost object might still be in the ZPD for the activities of reading, or any of the many skills and processes remaining to be developed in the immature organism.

Furthermore, once children master cognitive strategies, they are not obligated to rely only on internal mediation. They can also ask for help when stuck, for example, in the search for lost items of attire. During periods of difficulty, children may seek out controlling vocalizations by more competent others (Gal'perin, 1969). Again, we see the intimate and shifting relationship between control by self and control by others.

Even for adults, the effort to recall a forgotten bit of information can be aided by the helpful assistance of another, so that the total of self-regulated and other-regulated components of the performance once again resembles the mother-and-child example of shared functioning. Even the competent adult can profit from regulation for enhancement and maintenance of performance.

Indeed, enhancement, improvement, and maintenance of performance provide a recurrent cycle of self-assistance to other-assistance. A most important consideration is that *de-automatization and recursion* occur so regularly that they constitute a Stage IV of the normal developmental process. What one formerly could do, one can no longer do. This de-automatization may be due to slight environmental changes or individual stress, not to mention major upheavals or physical trauma. The analogy between microgenesis and ontogenesis is again clear; at the end of life, capacities fall into general decline. After de-automatization, for whatever reason, if capacity is to be restored, then the developmental process must become recursive.

The first line of retreat is to the immediately prior self-regulating phase. We have already discussed how children doing more difficult problems talk to themselves about it more, and quite competent adults can recall talking themselves through some knotty intellectual problem or through the traffic patterns of a strange city. Making self-speech external is a form of recursion often effective in restoring competence. A further retreat, to remembering the voice of a teacher, may be required. "Hearing the voice of the teacher" has been shown to be one of the middle stages in the development of complex skills (Gallimore *et al.*, 1986). Intentionally recurring to that point in the zone – consciously reconjuring the voice of a tutor – is an effective self-control technique.

But in some cases no form of self-regulation may be adequate to restore capacity, and a further recursion – the restitution of other-regulation – is often required. The readiness of a teacher to repeat some earlier lesson is one mark of excellent teaching. The profession of assisting adults (psychotherapy) is now a major Western institution. In all these instances, the goal is to reproceed through assisted performance to self-regulation and to exit the ZPD again into a new automatization.

Responsive assistance

In the transition from other-assistance to self-assistance (and automatization) there are variations in the means and patterns of adult assistance to the child. At the earlier phases, assistance may be frequent and elaborate. Later, it occurs less often and is truncated. Adult assistance is contingent on and responsive to the child's level of performance. In the earliest stages, when the child does not comprehend the purpose of an activity or see the connection between component steps, adult help tends to be relatively narrow in focus: "Pick up the blue one, and put it next to the yellow one."

As the child's comprehension and skill increase, adults begin to abbreviate their help (Rogoff and Gardner, 1984; Wertsch and Schneider, 1979). The adult may say something like "OK, what else could you try?". Such a truncated bit of help may prompt the child to take another look at the model of the puzzle, or scan the finished part, or poke through the pile of pieces for a different one. In narrative retelling, the adult may ask if the child remembers any more of the story, whereas earlier queries were about more specific details ("What did the other brother do?") (McNamee, 1979).

If the truncated guidance fails, the adult may add additional hints, testing to find that minimum level of help the child needs to proceed. This continual adjustment of the level and amount of help is *responsive to the child's level of performance and perceived need.* Assisting adults appear to keep in mind the overall goal of the activity, to stay related to what the child is trying to do. New information or suggestions are made relevant to furthering the child's current goal, and at the same time furthering the overall goal.

The tuning of adult assistance appears to begin quite early. For example, Cross (1977) studied 16 children ranging in age from 19 to 32 months. Although the average difference among their mean lengths of utterance (MLU) was only two words, correlations between mothers' speech adjustments and child speech levels ranged from 0.65 to 0.85. More significantly, the best predictor of mother adjustments to child utterances was the mean of the 50 longest utterances (out of 500), *not* the MLU for the entire 500. The mothers' MLUs were, on average, about three morphemes longer than their children's and less than half a morpheme longer than the children's longest utterances. The mothers probably were tracking their children's best performance, which probably was at or near the capacity level for the age of the children. This suggests that mothers' contingent speech adjustments are well "tuned" to the leading edge of child communicative competence – to the ZPD of social communication.

For older children, responsive adult assistance can become quite varied within a single episode of collaborative activity – and the reciprocity of adult–child interactions quite complex. Attempts by assisting adults to assess a child's readiness for greater responsibility often are subtle and embedded in the ongoing interaction, appearing as negotiations of the division of labor. For example, in Rogoff's study (1986), at the beginning of sessions, mothers often provided redundant information to ensure correct performance; this decreased over the session, as in the study of Wertsch and Schneider (1979). Mothers and children used hesitation, glances, and postural changes, as well as errors by the children, to adjust relative responsibilities for problem-solving. For example, one mother encouraged her child to determine where the next item went. When the child hesitated, the mother turned slightly toward the correct location. When the child still hesitated, the mother glanced at the correct location and moved the item slightly toward its intended location. Finally, she superficially rearranged other items in the correct group, and with this hint the child finally made the correct placement. Thus, the mother encouraged greater responsibility by the child and masked her assistance as random activity rather than correction of error, adjusting her support to the child's level of understanding.

However, patient, contingent, responsive, and accurately tuned adult assistance does not always occur. A major variable here is the nature of the task or performance. If efficient production is needed, the adult will likely be more directive and less tolerant of such costly child errors as failing to correctly care for animals on which the family's survival is partly dependent (Wertsch, Minick, and Arns, 1984). In joint productive activities of some importance, a child's participation may be relatively passive – observing the adult/expert carry out the task, and joining in to help at those points where the child's skill matches the task demands. This is the classic pattern of informal teaching that has been described in the anthropological literature for 50 years (Fortes, 1938).

But when the development of independent child skill is defined as a goal, the pattern of assistance provided by the adult is more responsive, contingent, and patient. The adult graduates the assistance, responsive to the child's performance level: the more the child can do, the less the adult does (Wertsch et al., 1984).

This illuminates an important pedagogical principle. "Assistance" offered at too high a level will disrupt child performance and is not effective teaching. Once independent skill has been achieved, "assistance" becomes "interference." For this reason, our definition of teaching emphasizes that *teaching can be said to occur when assistance is offered at points in the ZPD at which performance requires assistance.* Careful assessment of the child's abilities, relative to the ZPD and the developmental level, is a constant requirement for the teacher. This becomes imperative when we remember that the processes of development are recursive.

Assisted performance: child, parent, and teacher

As common as assisted performance is in the interactions of parents and children, it is uncommon in those of teachers and students. Study after study has documented the absence in classrooms of this fundamental tool for the teaching of children: assistance provided by more capable others that is responsive to goal-directed activities.

The absence of assisted performance in schools is all the more remarkable because most teachers are members of the literate middle class, where researchers have most often found such interactions. Why is it that this adult–child pattern – no doubt a product of historical, evolutionary processes – is so seldom observed in the very setting where it would seem most appropriate? Such interactions can be found in every society, in the introduction of children to any task. But this basic method of human socialization has not generally diffused into schools. Why?

There are two basic reasons. First, to provide assistance in the ZPD, the assistor must be in close touch with the learner's relationship to the task. Sensitive and accurate assistance that challenges but does not dismay the learner cannot be achieved in the absence of information. Opportunities for this knowledge, conditions in which the teacher can be sufficiently aware of the child's actual, inflight performing, simply are not available in classrooms organized, equipped, and staffed in the typical pattern. There are too many children for each teacher. And even if there is time to assess each child's ZPD for each task, more time is needed – time of interaction, for conversation, for joint activity between teachers and children. Occasionally, now and through history, these opportunities have existed: the classical Greek academies, Oxford and Cambridge, the individual tutorial, the private American school with classes of seven or less. But all involve a pupil–teacher ratio that exceeds the politicians' judgment of the taxpayers' purse. Public education is not likely to reorganize into classrooms of seven pupils each.

This does not make the case hopeless. Emerging instructional practices do offer some hope of increased opportunities for assisted performance: the increased use of small groups, maintenance of a positive classroom atmosphere that will increase independent task involvement of students, new materials and technology with which students can interact independent of the teacher.

There is a second reason that assisted performance has not diffused into the schools. Even when instructional practices allow for increased use of assisted performance, it will not necessarily appear as a regular feature of a teacher's activity. It may not be practiced even by those teachers who are from homes and communities where, outside of school, such interactions are commonplace. It will not necessarily be forthcoming from teachers who themselves provide assisted performance for their own children. Even with the benefits of modern instructional practice, there is still too large a gap between the conditions of home and school. Most parents do not need to be trained to assist performance; most teachers do.

References

Baumrind, D. (1971) "Current patterns of parental authority," *Developmental Psychology Monographs 4:* 99–103.

Bell, R. Q. (1979) "Parent, child, and reciprocal influences," *American Psychologist 34:* 821–6.

Berk, L. E. (1986) "Relationship of elementary school children's private speech to behavioral accompaniment to task, attention, and task performance," *Developmental Psychology* 22: 671–80.

Berk, L. E. and Garvin, R. (1984) "Development of private speech among low-income Appalachian children," *Developmental Psychology* 20: 271–86.

Bernstein, L. E. (1981) "Language as a product of dialogue," *Discourse Processes* 4: 117–47.

Brown, A. L. (1978) "Knowing when, where and how to remember: A problem of metacognition," in R. Glaser (ed.) *Advances in Instructional Psychology* 1, pp. 77–165, Hillsdale, NJ: Erlbaum.

Bruner, J. S. (1966) *Toward a Theory of Instruction*, Cambridge, MA: Harvard University Press.

Bruner, J. S. (1973) "Organization of early skilled action," *Child Development* 44: 1–11.

Bruner, J. S. (1983) *Child's Talk: Learning to Use Language*, New York: Norton.

Cazden, C. B. (1981) "Performance before competence: Assistance to child discourse in the zone of proximal development," *Quarterly Newsletter of the Laboratory of Comparative Human Cognition* 3(1): 5–8.

Cross, T. G. (1977) "Mothers' speech adjustments: The contribution of selected child listener variables," in C. E. Snow and C. A. Ferguson (eds) *Talking to Children: Language Input and Acquisition*, pp. 151–88, Cambridge: Cambridge University Press.

Diaz, R. M. (1986) "The union of thought and language in children's private speech," *Quarterly Newsletter of the Laboratory of Comparative Human Cognition* 8(3): 90–7.

Elsasser, N. and John-Steiner, V. P. (1977) "An interactionist approach to advancing literacy," *Harvard Educational Review* 47: 355–69.

Fischer, K. W. and Bullock, D. (1984) "Cognitive development in school-aged children: Conclusions and new directions," in W. C. Collins (ed.) *Development during Middle Childhood: The Years from Six to Twelve*, pp. 70–146, Washington, DC: National Academy Press.

Fortes, M. (1938) "Education in Taleland," *Africa 1*, 11(4): 14–74.

Gallimore, R., Dalton, S., and Tharp, R. G. (1986) "Self-regulation and interactive teaching: The impact of teaching conditions on teachers' cognitive activity," *Elementary School Journal* 86(5): 613–31.

Gal'perin, P. (1969) "Stages in the development of mental acts," in M. Cole and I. Malzman (eds), *A Handbook of Contemporary Soviet Psychology* pp. 249–73, New York: Basic Books.

Greenfield, P. M. (1984) "A theory of the teacher in the learning activities of everyday life," in B. Rogoff and J. Lave (eds), *Everyday Cognition: Its Development in Social Contexts*, pp. 117–38, Cambridge, MA: Harvard University Press.

Griffin, P. and Cole, M. (1984) "Current activity for the future: The Zo-ped," in B. Rogoff and J. V. Wertsch (eds), *Children's Learning in the "Zone of Proximal Development"* (New Directions for Child Development, no. 23, pp. 45–64), San Francisco: Jossey-Bass.

Kohlberg, L., Yaeger, J., and Hjertholm, E. (1968) "Private speech: Four studies and a review of theories," *Child Development* 39: 691–736.

Leont'ev, A. N. (1981) "The problem of activity in psychology," in J. V. Wertsch (ed.), *The Concept of Activity in Soviet Psychology*, pp. 37–71, Armonk, NY: M. E. Sharpe.

McNamee, G. D. (1979) "The social interaction origins of narrative skills," *Quarterly Newsletter of the Laboratory of Comparative Human Cognition* 1(4): 63–8.

Meichenbaum, D. (1977) *Cognitive Behavior Modification: An Integrative Approach*, New York: Plenum Press.

Ochs, E. (1982) "Talking to children in western Samoa," *Language in Society* 11: 77–104.

Roberts, R. N. (1979) "Private speech in academic problem-solving. A naturalistic perspective," in G. Zivin (ed.), *The Development of Self-regulation through Private Speech*, pp. 295–323, New York: Wiley.

Roberts, R. N. and Mullis, M. (1980) "A component analysis of self-instructional training," paper presented at the annual convention of the Western Psychological Association, Honolulu.

Roberts, R. N. and Tharp, R. G. (1980) "A naturalistic study of children's self-directed speech in academic problem-solving," *Cognitive Research and Therapy* 4: 341–53.

Rogoff, B. (1982) "Integrating context and cognitive development," in M. E. and A. L. Brown (eds), *Advances in Developmental Psychology*, vol. 2, pp. 125–70, Hillsdale, NJ: Lawrence Erlbaum Associates.

Rogoff, B. (1986) "Adult assistance of children's learning," in T. E. Raphael (ed.) *The Contexts of School-based Literacy,* pp. 27–40, New York: Random House.

Rogoff, B. and Gardner, W. (1984) "Adult guidance of cognitive development," in B. Rogoff and J. Lave (eds), *Everyday Cognition: Its Development in Social Contexts*, pp. 95–116, Cambridge, MA: Harvard University Press.

Rogoff, B., Malkin, C., and Gilbride, K. (1984) "Interaction with babies as guidance in development," in B. Rogoff and J. V. Wertsch (eds), *Children's Learning in the "Zone of Proximal Development"* (New Directions for Child Development, no. 23, pp. 30–44), San Francisco: Jossey-Bass.

Rogoff, B. and Wertsch, J. (eds) (1984) *Children's Learning in the "Zone of Proximal Development"*, (New Directions for Child Development, no. 23), San Francisco: Jossey-Bass.

Saxe, G. B., Gearhart, M., and Guberman, S. R. (1984) "The social organization of early number development," in B. Rogoff and J. V. Wertsch (eds) *Children's Learning in the "Zone of Proximal Development"* (New Directions for Child Development, no. 23, pp.19–30), San Francisco: Jossey-Bass.

Tharp, R. G. and Gallimore, R. (1976) "The uses and limits of social reinforcement and industriousness for learning to read" (technical report no. 60), Honolulu: Kamehameha Schools/Bishop Estate, Kamehameha Early Education Program.

Tharp, R. G., Gallimore, R., and Calkins, R. P. (1984) "On the relationships between self-control and control by others," *Advances en Psicologia Clinical Latinamericano* 3: 45–58.

Vygotsky, L. S. (1956) *Izbrannie psibhologicheskie issledovania* (Selected psychological research), Moscow: Izdatel'stvo Akadamii Pedagogicheskikh Nauk.

Vygotsky, L. S. (1978) *Mind in Society: The Development of Higher Psychological Processes*, in M. Cole, V. John-Steiner, S. Scribner, and E. Souberman (eds and trans.), Cambridge, MA: Harvard University Press.

Vygotsky, L. S. (1987) *Collected Works of L S. Vygotsky: vol. 1: Problems of General Psychology* (trans. N. Minick; series eds Robert W. Reiber and Aaron S. Carton), New York: Plenum Press. (Original work published in 1982 in Russian.)

Watson, D. R. and Tharp, R. G. (1988) *Self directed Behavior* (5th edn), Monterey, CA: Brooks/Cole.

Wertsch, J. V. (1978) "Adult–child interaction and the roots of metacognition," *Quarterly Newsletter of the Laboratory of Comparative Human Cognition* 2(1): 15–18.

Wertsch, J. V. (1979) "From social interaction to higher psychological process: A clarification and application of Vygotsky's theory," *Human Development* 22: 1–22.

Wertsch, J. V. (1981) *The Concept of Activity in Soviet Psychology*, Armonk, NY: M. E. Sharpe.

Wertsch, J. V. (ed.) (1985) *Vygotsky and the Social Formation of Mind*, Cambridge, MA: Harvard University Press.

Wertsch, J. V., Minick, N., and Arns, F. A. (1984) "The creation of context in joint problem-solving," in B. Rogoff and J. Lave (eds) *Everyday Cognition: Its Development in Social Contexts*, pp. 151–71, Cambridge, MA: Harvard University Press.

Wertsch, J. V. and Schneider, P. J. (1979) "Variations of adults' directives to children in a problem solving situation," unpublished manuscript, Evanston, IL: Northwestern University.

Wertsch, J. V. and Stone, C. A. (1985) "The concept of internalization in Vygotsky's account of the genesis of higher mental functions," in J. V. Wertsch (ed.) *Culture, Communication and Cognition: Vygotskian Perspectives*, pp.162–79, New York: Cambridge University Press.

Wood, D. J., Bruner, J. S., and Ross, G. (1976) "The role of tutoring in problem solving," *Journal of Child Psychology and Psychiatry* 17(2): 89–100.

Chapter 6

How do teachers help children to learn?

An analysis of teachers' interventions in computer-based activities*

Neil Mercer and Eunice Fisher

Introduction

The purpose of this chapter is to describe and explain the style and function of the interventions made by teachers when children are doing computer-based activities in their classrooms. We believe that achieving a better understanding of such aspects of teaching is necessary for the most effective use of the new technology in schools and could also contribute to the development of better "classroom-based" methods for the initial and in-service training of teachers. This chapter also reflects our concern with the adequacy of available theoretical models of learning and instruction, and specifically with the relationship between those theoretical accounts and the practice of teaching and learning as it is actually carried out in schools and elsewhere. We will argue that the "neo-Vygotskian" approach offers the best available basis for the development of a conceptual framework for understanding teaching and learning in classroom settings. We will then use that approach in an analysis of specific examples of teachers' interventions in children's computer-based activity using observational data from a current research project. By doing so we hope to shed light on the nature of the teaching and learning process and relate theoretical concepts to the realities of classroom education.

Some central features of the neo-Vygotskian perspective

We are using the term "neo-Vygotskian" to refer to a theoretical approach to the study of learning and cognitive development which draws heavily, though not exclusively or literally, on the work of Vygotsky (Mercer, 1991a, 1992). Others have called this approach "cultural psychology" (Crook, 1991), "socio-cognitive-developmental theory" (Smith, 1989) and "the socio-historical approach" (Newman, Griffin, & Cole, 1989). The essence of this approach is to treat learning and cognitive development as culturally based, not just culturally influenced, and as social rather than individualized

* This is an edited version of an article that appeared in *Learning and Instruction*, vol. 2, 1992.

processes. It highlights communicative aspects of learning, whereby knowledge is shared and understandings are constructed in culturally formed settings.

Compared with other theories of learning and cognition, the neo-Vygotskian approach has certain attractive features for researchers who are concerned with the use of computers for learning and instruction in schools, which can be summarized as follows.

First, most theories of learning and cognitive development have focused on the individual to the extent that cultural and interactional factors in learning and development are marginalized or even ignored. In recent years, critical attention has focused on the inherent "individualism" of Piagetian theory, and on the marginal role attributed to language, culture, and social interaction in the empirical research of Piaget and his followers (see e.g., Edwards & Mercer, 1987; Mercer, 1991a, 1992; Walkerdine, 1984). In research into computer-based learning, the influence of Piagetian ideas has been particularly strong. This is well exemplified by the work of Papert (1980), who promotes a radical "discovery-learning" approach to learning through LOGO, in which the child's relationship with a human teacher is supplanted by an individualized computer-based learning environment.

Other more recently developed approaches to cognitive development share the same individualistic emphasis. For example, much of the "cognitive science" which has been so influential in America (e.g., Resnick, 1987; Simon, 1980, 1981) is based on a narrow, individualistic definition of learning (see Newman et al., 1989, and Edwards, 1991, for a critical discussion). There is also little evidence of a culturally based approach to learning having influenced the design of educational software. In contrast, because neo-Vygotskian theory gives a central and prominent place to communicative and cultural factors, it seems better suited to the needs of researchers who wish to study learning and instruction in a social context, and also to those concerned with the implementation and design of software for classroom use. In particular, it offers interesting possibilities for theoretical development in the study of "situated learning" with computers, especially if such research focuses on children's problem-solving practice in schools (see Lave, 1992) and the process of learning through "cognitive apprenticeship" (Collins, Brown, & Newman, 1990).

Second, neo-Vygotskian theory offers both a theory of learning *and* a theory of instruction. In all societies, talk is the prime medium for sharing knowledge, and one through which adults influence the representations of reality which children eventually adopt. Neo-Vygotskian theory deals directly with this essential feature of learning and instruction in school. It encourages the view that to communicate with others through speech is to *engage in a social mode of thinking*.

We therefore believe that a neo-Vygotskian framework offers a suitable basis for an educationally relevant theory of learning and instruction. However, its principal concepts (the zone of proximal development and "scaffold-ing"; discussed below) have not yet been properly defined for classroom research. Although the concepts are now in common use in discussions of educational processes, they were developed in observational research on parent–child interactions (Bruner, 1978; Wertsch, 1985; Wood, Bruner, & Ross, 1976), and only subsequently applied to educational settings by draw-ing analogies between learners at home and in school and between the sup-portive activities of parents and teachers (e.g., Bruner, 1985, 1986). Some educational researchers have therefore suggested that the concepts themselves cannot map well on to the pedagogic realities of classroom education. David McNamara (personal communication) comments that "the theory implies that each child's 'scaffold' or ZPD is different and that the teacher must treat each child's learning individually . . . this is probably an unrealistic aspiration as far as most teachers and most classes are concerned." Smith (1989) points to the lack of relevant empirical exemplification of the theory's explanatory value. Whilst we accept the grounds for these criticisms, we see them as a stimulus for research rather than as a reason to forsake the neo-Vygotskian framework. For all its current weaknesses, it represents the only available theoretical perspective which is potentially capable of handling teaching and learning as culturally based, "situated" activity. Through the research pre-sented in this chapter we hope to advance further its empirical validity and educational relevance.

Two key concepts in the neo-Vygotskian framework

The essential psychological asymmetry of the teaching and learning relation-ship may be said to be represented in two neo-Vygotskian concepts: the *zone of proximal development* and *scaffolding*.

The zone of proximal development (ZPD)

The zone of proximal development (ZPD) is "the distance between the actual developmental level as determined by independent problem solving and the level of potential development as determined through problem solving under adult guidance or in collaboration with more able peers" (Vygotsky, 1978, p. 86). We believe that the concept represents two basic and essen-tial aspects of human development. One is that learning with assistance or instruction is a common and important feature of human mental develop-ment. The second is that the limits of a person's learning or problem-solving ability can be expanded by providing the right kind of assistance or instruction.

Within a neo-Vygotskian framework, learning and problem-solving are seen as context-bound processes, so that the level of understanding achieved by individuals in specific settings is recognized to be, in part at least, a function of those settings as dynamic contexts for cognitive activity (Crook, 1991). Thus what appear to be variations in the ability of a child to solve "the same" problem across different experimental settings (for example, as described by Donaldson, 1978) might best be explained in terms of variations between the implicit contextual frameworks surrounding those tasks. As Newman, Griffin, & Cole (1989) argue, a great deal of psychological research is flawed because researchers have naively accepted that experimental tasks can be defined independently of the intersubjective contexts in which they are performed.

References to the ZPD are increasingly common in developmental and educational research; but it seems to us that there is a danger that the term is used as little more than a fashionable alternative to Piagetian terminology or the concept of IQ for describing individual differences in attainment or potential. In our view, such usages miss the essence of the concept, and lose its radical implications for the study of learning. The limits of the ZPD for any particular child on any particular task will be established in the course of an activity, and one key factor in establishing those limits will be the quality of the supportive interventions of a teacher. That is, the ZPD is not an attribute of a child (in the sense that, say, IQ is considered to be) but rather an attribute of an event. It is the product of a particular, situated, pedagogical relationship. Through establishing a ZPD, a teacher or researcher may gain valuable insights into how a child may be encouraged to progress. But children do not carry their ZPDs with them when they leave a classroom, and a new task with a different teacher may generate quite different "zones" for the same group of children.

This brings us to the second concept, that of "*scaffolding*." In the context of parental tutoring, Bruner (1978) uses the term to refer to steps taken by an adult to *reduce the degrees of freedom* in carrying out some task so that a child can concentrate on the difficult skill he or she is in the process of acquiring. It represents the kind and quality of cognitive support which an adult can provide for a child's learning – a form of "vicarious consciousness" (as Bruner also put it) which anticipates the child's own developing understanding. As such, it clearly relates to the concept of the zone of proximal development. We and our associates, involved in both educational research and the in-service training of teachers, have found the concept of "scaffolding" a very useful tool in analytic discussions of teachers' pedagogic strategies (see e.g., Fisher, 1991; Maybin, Mercer, & Stierer, 1992; Mercer, 1991b). Teachers also seem to find the concept very appealing, perhaps because it resonates with their own intuitive conceptions of what it means to intervene successfully in children's learning. It has also begun to appear in studies of computer-based learning. However, it has been used without being operationally defined for the classroom, and so is used loosely and given a variety of covert interpretations. For example, Hoyles, Healy, & Sutherland (1991, p. 219), in their study of pupil discussion in computer-based learning say, "We refer to scaffolding as 'hooks' available in any setting which assist pupils in overcoming significant obstacles in the generalization process," while Emihovich and Miller (1988), in a study of young children being instructed in the use of LOGO, employ the term only to refer to teachers' express guidance, through talk, of the children. Bruner's own application of it to the relationship between teacher and pupil (Bruner, 1985) is achieved simply by drawing an analogy between the discourse of parental tutoring and that of classroom teaching. If we start from the position that the concept of "scaffolding" *is* potentially applicable to classroom education, the essential problem is to decide what counts as "scaffolding" and what is merely "help." Is "scaffolding" a description of a particular kind of teacher behavior (whatever its outcome for the pupil), or a label that can be applied to any kind of teacher intervention which is followed by learning success for a pupil? Maybin *et al.* (1992) offer the following hypothetical formulation:

> ["Scaffolding"] is not just any assistance which helps a learner accomplish a task. It is help which will *enable a learner to accomplish a task which they would not have been quite able to manage on their own*, and it is help which is *intended to bring the learner closer to a state of competence which will enable them eventually to complete such a task on their own* . . . To know whether or not some help counts as "scaffolding", we would need to have at the very least *some evidence of a teacher wishing to enable a child to develop a specific skill, grasp a particular concept or achieve a particular level of understanding.* A more stringent criterion would be to require *some evidence of a learner successfully accomplishing the task with the teacher's help.* An even more stringent interpretation would be to require *some evidence of a learner having achieved some greater level of independent competence as a result of the scaffolding experience* (that is, demonstrating their increased competence or improved level of understanding in dealing independently with some subsequent problem).

Method

Within our research into teaching and learning in classrooms, one area of special interest has been the study of how computer-based activities are incorporated into the social interactive life of school classrooms (Fisher, 1991; Mercer, 1991c). Most recently this interest has generated the SLANT (Spoken Language and New Technology) Project, which was set up in 1990 to investigate how primary school children talk when they are working together at the computer. The main aims of the project are:

- to identify ways in which computer-based classroom activities provide contexts for learning through talk and for developing children's use of talk for learning;
- to describe the range and quality of the talk observed;

- to relate our analysis of the talk to the design of computer-based learning tasks (including the nature of the software used);
- to provide information about the role of a teacher in mediating and supporting such activities;
- to assist teachers in developing and refining their practice.

   With the aim of obtaining data on a variety of ages of children, urban/rural locations, curriculum-related topics, and educational software packages, ten schools and fifteen teachers were chosen from those who had responded to initial enquiries from the project to schools in four eastern counties of England. The design of the project was based on a notion of close partnership between the researchers in the central team and the primary teachers in whose classrooms the research was to be carried out. All the teachers were experienced teachers, but most of them were not "computer experts." Only two had special responsibility for IT in their schools. At initial meetings, researchers explained to teachers that the project was primarily concerned with examining the potential of various computer activities for generating discussion between children (as described above). The teachers then developed activities (usually in discussion with a researcher) which would fit in with and, it was hoped, enhance their normal curriculum activities. After spending some time in more general observation in the classrooms, the researchers made video recordings of one or more groups of children doing the activities, usually over a series of lessons. In this way, 50 children aged between 5 and 12 were recorded working at the computer, on a range of activities based on software which included word-processing packages, adventure games, simulations, databases, and mathematics programs. Once the research was under way, regular meetings between teachers and researchers (which usually involved the viewing of recently recorded data) often led to new ideas for activities and to further recording. Researchers and teachers also talked about the activities with the children involved. The scope, aims, and rationale for SLANT are described in more detail in Mercer, Phillips, & Somekh (1991).

Teacher interventions

It has become increasingly apparent to SLANT researchers that, in order to identify the contextual factors which encourage different kinds of discourse, it is necessary to examine the total activity, including the way the teacher has set up the task and how she then supports its progress. This has led us to focus on the kinds of intervention that teachers make in pupils' activity in order to help them continue and complete the learning task in hand. In the current chapter we are concerned only with teachers' *interventions* in computer-based activities which are already under way, and not with the ways that teachers "set up" or initially "frame" activities before pupils start them (as discussed in Fisher, 1991; Mercer, 1991b, 1992).

Relevant here is the work of Emihovich and Miller (1988), who in a small-scale, "experimental teaching" investigation analyzed the discourse of teaching and learning when two pairs of 5-year-old children were instructed in the use of LOGO by a teacher (one of the researchers). One of their aims was to demonstrate an effective role for the teacher in LOGO learning, and the nature of the experimentation involved was to design a set of "cognitive teaching acts" which the teacher-researcher self-consciously employed in attempting to "scaffold" the children's learning. These acts were "acts" in the sense that the term has been employed by discourse analysts (Mehan, 1979; Sinclair & Coulthard, 1975); that is, single utterances which initiated verbal exchanges with the pupils. Thus, through the use of a "meta-elicit" act like "Remember what those were for?", the teacher elicits from the child information previously learned. Their main finding was that the children became increasingly able to take strategic responsibility for their LOGO activity, and that while the number of teacher-led exchanges remained high throughout, the children's learning was mirrored by an increase over time of verbal exchanges initiated and directed by the children themselves.

Certain distinctive features of computer-based activities in school are important for any analysis of teacher interventions. One is the physical separation of the work done at the computer from the "mainstream" activity of the class. Even when it is within the classroom (as seems generally to be the case in primary schools), the computer is likely to be at the side (near an electric socket and out of harm's way), with children often seated with their backs to the rest of the class. This makes it easier for an observer to see when the teacher makes contact with the group as well as requiring the teacher to make a definite move if she is to see what the children are doing. The opportunities for teachers to make useful interventions, and relative frequency of different kinds of interventions will certainly vary with the nature of the software and the activities in which it is embedded. For example, Emihovich and Miller (1988) suggest that when tasks and problems (and children's responses to them) are dynamically represented on the screen, as in LOGO problem-solving tasks, teachers may more easily be able to make an explicit connection between talk, thought, and action than in activities where the effect of children's decisions are not so graphically represented.

Another feature of computer work seems to be that children (and possibly adults also) are prepared to work for longer-than-usual periods of time, even when their work fails to be productive. Consequently the physical separation mentioned above, together with the fact that it is not always easy for a teacher to identify what has gone on already, make the timing and nature of intervention even more crucial than it would be with other types of classroom activity. Other researchers have reported on the nature and importance of intervention, and have emphasized the need for strategies which change over time and in relationship to the complexity of the task with which the pupils are involved. Hoyles and Sutherland (1989) found that, whereas pupil requests for teacher intervention decreased as pupils became more experienced in using LOGO, teachers chose to intervene more often as the tasks which they had set became more complex. Their interventions were sometimes aimed at directing pupils, but more often were attempts to encourage pupils to reflect on what they were doing. Similarly, Fraser, Burkhardt, Coupland, Phillips, Pimm, and Ridgeway (1990), also working in mathematics classes, found that teachers gradually relinquished the managing role and took on more of a *counselling*, *fellow pupil*, or *resource* role.

Teaching and learning in progress

In this section we will take three transcribed sequences of classroom discourse and, for each, attempt to do the following things:

1   Provide some background information about the educational settings from which it was taken, with special reference to the curriculum goals being pursued and the relationship of the work being done to prior activity and that planned for the immediate future (to the extent that these were made available to us through discussion with the teachers involved);
2   Use a conceptual framework based upon neo-Vygotskian theory (as expounded above) to analyze the sequence as a piece of teaching-and-learning.

The sequences have been expressly chosen from our data to illustrate the features of teaching and learning which we wish to discuss. They are taken from actual lessons and embody strategies used by the teachers of their own volition, though sometimes as the result of their reflections during the progress of the project. Our wider observations support the view that these sequences are not odd or atypical examples of teacher activity, but we do not wish to claim them as representative of the "teaching styles" of particular teachers.

Sequence 1 (below) was recorded in a class in which the children were using computers in pairs to pursue a specific task set by their teacher. In the preceding weeks, the class had spent some time learning different ways of representing the natural environment, including making three-dimensional models and drawing maps on the computer using the software package *Paintspa* (which enables free drawing on the screen through the use of the "mouse"). In fact, many of the children in the class found the computer-based part of the activity difficult, probably because it was their first experience of using *Paintspa* and of using a "mouse." It was the stated aim of the teacher that the children should be learning not only how to model and map the village, but should learn about the relationship between alternative modes of representation and how to transpose information from one mode to another.

In this sequence, two 8-year-old girls (Louise and Harriet) were trying to reproduce on the computer screen a map of a particular three-dimensional model village which the members of the class had constructed. By the beginning of this sequence, the girls had been working for about 20 minutes. It begins at a point where, having marked out the basic structure of the village, they were putting in some of the buildings. However, they were unsure how to mark each type of building so that it would be identifiable on the map. Although they had had some difficulties (several of which had been observed by the teacher from a distance), Sequence 1 contains the first intervention by the teacher since she gave the girls the initial explanation of what they had to do. (Note: In all the discourse sequences, the following transcription conventions apply: T = teacher. Simultaneous speech is marked by [. Additional information about observed activities is in parentheses and italics. The talk has been punctuated to make it more comprehensible to the reader.)

Sequence 1: Mapping a village

1	Louise:	Mrs O . . . (*Teacher comes over to the girls*) [Do you have to put
2		"H" now?
3	Harriet:	[Oh, it's undoing, its
4		undoing.
		(*referring to what's happening on screen*)
5	Louise:	Put "H" in the house
6	T:	Well, what other way can you do it?
7	Louise:	Well, you could, um
8	Harriet:	It wasn't "H" anyway, it was a school, weren't it?
9	T:	Right. What other way can you think? You need to [have a key.
10	Louise:	[You can, you
11		can colour it in, what, some colour can't you?
12	T:	Right. Well, we're going to be using the colour printer, right, so
13		you could do just that, then.
14	Louise:	Shall we?
15	Harriet:	One of the, some of the blocks are too small
16	T:	Yeah
17	Harriet:	And the gaps
18	T:	(*Watching as Harriet operates the mouse*) Yeah. That's right.
19		Good. OK. Make sure you don't do them grey otherwise they'll
20		look like roads. Yeah, that's fine.
21	Harriet:	And what you've got to think about is what colour this (*she*
22		points to an item on the screen) is going to be.
23	Harriet:	I'll do that one yellow.
24	T:	Some of it's garden and some of it's grass. (*T walks away*)

The talk in Sequence 1 has many features which are typical of teachers' interventions in children's activity at the computer. The aim of the teacher seems to be to encourage the children's own efforts at solving problems, rather than to offer ready solutions. For example, in line 1, the girls ask the teacher a direct question. Although the teacher has intervened at the request of the pupils, she responds with a question of her own (line 6) in which she asks *them* to suggest a possible strategy, and so elicits a minimal response from the girls (lines 7 and 8). In performing this elicitation, she does not comment directly on the girls' idea of putting "H" in the houses to mark them, but elaborates the requirements of the task in hand. She then repeats her question and goes on to suggest a strategy for dealing with their problem (line 9). She confirms Louise's interpretation of her suggestion (that such a key could be based on colours) and adds the additional relevant information that a colour printer is to be used (lines 12–13). So in the latter part of this sequence her talk consists of comments on the quality of pupils' activity and of reiterations and elaborations of the requirements of the task.

With a fairly open-ended task such as this one (in that a variety of mapping styles and formats would be acceptable), there are no single "right answers." The teacher's manner of intervention allows the children to explore the software and develop their own strategies for completing the task, but prevents them floundering or getting discouraged by difficulties which are beyond their technical or conceptual expertise. The concept of the ZPD would seem to be relevant to an analysis of this kind of teaching and learning event. The teacher had planned the task as one which would "stretch" the children but which they should be able to accomplish with some support. Once the activity was begun, she had to make judgments, presumably based on her assessment of Louise and Harriet's competence in general and on the evidence of their progress on this particular task, about how much additional support she needed to provide. Louise and Harriet did go on to produce a satisfactory map, with a colour key.

Having described the teacher's supportive activity, we might now ask: is it appropriate to call this kind of activity "scaffolding"? The effect of the teacher's interventions is certainly to "reduce the degrees of freedom" of the task. To go a little further, from what we know of this sequence, it would seem that we can satisfy some of the criteria of Maybin et al. (1992) for the use of that term (as set out previously). We can satisfy the requirement of knowing that Louise and Harriet "would not have been quite able to manage on their own" if we accept their own judgment on the matter (the sequence begins with their appeal to the teacher for help). It would seem indisputable that the teacher is offering "help which is intended to bring the learner(s) to a state of competence which will enable them to complete such a task on their own." We also have some evidence (in the form of the teacher's stated intention) of "a teacher wishing to enable a child to develop a particular skill . . . or achieve a particular level of understanding." Furthermore, we can satisfy the more stringent criterion requiring "some evidence of a learner successfully accomplishing the task with the teacher's help." What we cannot do is satisfy the most stringent criterion of subsequent "independent competence," because Louise and Harriet did not go onto do an unsupported version of the same kind of task during the period of our observations (the lack of such evidence is, of course, virtually a paradigmatic limitation of naturalistic/ observational research: see the experimental studies of Newman *et al.*, 1989). Our conclusion, therefore, is that – in the absence of any other apt terminology – "scaffolding" is indeed an appropriate term to use here.

With some computer-based activities, it might well be argued that the software itself provides an element of "scaffolding" for the pupils' learning. Certainly, some kinds of software, like adventure games and problem-solving programs, provide *structure* and *guidance* for activity, and such programs also often provide *feedback* to children on their actions (features that are all usually emphasized in the teachers' manuals which accompany most educational software). However, because any educational software that we have observed in use offers, at best, a very limited set of "feedback" responses to children's input, and since such responses are often a poor match for the problems actually encountered by children in the classroom, we do not feel that the use of the term "scaffolding" is appropriate. Moreover, we have observed that (a) pupils often get into difficulties in spite of information or guidance offered by a program, and (b) it is precisely at such times that a teacher's supportive intervention is sought and received. This is well illustrated in the next sequence (Sequence 2), which comes from the same class as Sequence 1. On this occasion, a group of three children (aged 8) were playing a game called *Nature Park Adventure*. This software is highly structured, in that children have to complete successfully a mathematical problem at the end of each stage of the adventure before they can proceed. Just before the start of Sequence 2, they reached a stage which required them to choose from a selection of coins (shown on the screen) so that they had the correct money to purchase two carrots at 12 pence each. They spent some time selecting a combination of coins, but as they erroneously concluded that they needed a total of 12 pence, not 24 pence, the computer informed them that they had the wrong answer. The children reached an impasse and were showing obvious signs of frustration, when the teacher (who has been observing them from a distance) came across and stood behind the group as they faced the computer screen.

Sequence 2: Buying carrots

1 *Harriet:* (*to teacher*) What shall we do? We can't (*inaudible remark*)
2 *Tom:*   It's only 12p
3 *Harriet:* Last time we pressed 10 and 2 and nothing happened, and then
4   we pressed 5p and 5p and]
5 *T:*   [Right. Read it out, Harriet.
6 *Harriet:* (*Reading from the screen*) If a carrot costs 12 pence which coins

7   would you use to pay for 2 ca- oh, for two carrots, ooh.
                     (*Teacher laughs and walks away*).

The children then proceeded to solve the problem with ease. Clearly it was not their arithmetical skills which were lacking but, as the teacher immediately realized, they had failed to read the question properly. She did not respond directly to Harriet's question (line 1), but instead she obtained a reiteration of the task by eliciting a response from the child (lines 5–7). In directing them to read the instructions, she made available to them support which was already there, but which in this case was useless to them without her guidance. From her tone of voice, it seemed that this was a type of mistake which she, and they, had encountered before. She responded by implicitly invoking a simple but golden rule of problem-solving in school: *read the question properly!*

The teacher's intervention in Sequence 2 meets several of the criteria of Maybin *et al*. (1992) for "scaffolding." She is helping the children accomplish a specific task at which they were not succeeding on their own, and they go on to complete it successfully. We do not have evidence that they go on to achieve greater independent capability at solving such problems, but it is clear that the teacher's help is of a kind intended to help them do so. That is, it is help which does not provide a direct solution to their problem but which instead focuses their attention on the detail of the problem and on an important aspect of dealing with all such problems. She wants them not only to correct their mistakes, but also to learn from them. This brings us, in an intriguing way, back to the concept of the ZPD. Within some paradigms of learning and some educational ideologies, a problem-solving task which can only be done with a teacher's help would be judged as poorly designed or ill-suited to the children's needs. However, from a neo-Vygotskian perspective the necessity of a teacher's support can be seen as a virtue, because it is only when "scaffolding" is required that we can infer that a child is working in a zone of proximal development. Put more simply, neo-Vygotskian theory suggests that any task which children are able to accomplish without any assistance at all is unlikely to be one which encourages them to work to the limits of their intellectual capabilities!

In both Sequence 1 and Sequence 2, we can see a teacher supporting children's learning by not merely helping them but by providing a structure which enables them to help themselves. In both sequences, the teacher's intervention is a response to a perceived problem on the part of the children: she helps them to "sort things out" and then leaves them to resume independent activity. In the next sequence (Sequence 3), the teacher's intervention is less reactive and more directive. The computer-based activity was part of a larger scheme of work on traditional fairy tales, within which the teacher wanted these 6/7-year-old children to develop an understanding of the structure of such stories and how characters in them are typically (and stereotypically) represented. She also wanted the children to develop their understanding of a real audience for such stories, as represented by the young children in the nursery class of the school. The computer-based task which she used to pursue these aims was for the children to design and use an "overlay" for the keyboard which would transform it into a "concept keyboard." The nursery children could use this concept keyboard to select a limited set of words to make sentences and so create their own fairy stories. From our discussions with the teacher, we know that she also intended this computer-based activity to fulfill the aim of developing the computing skills of her pupils, and so to enable them to fulfill National Curriculum targets in Design and Technology.

Eight pupils in the class were working on this task in pairs, and the teacher supported their activity by going round to each pair in turn. With each pair, she would observe the current state of their progress, draw attention to certain features and use them to raise issues related to the successful completion of the activity. With all four pairs, her interventions dealt with the following task-specific issues:

1   The relationship of the design of the overlay to the computer keys which it was intended to cover.
2   The need to design an overlay which would generate appropriate sequences of words (so that "beginning words" were in the left-hand column, with suitable following words in the next column, and so on).
3   The need to select words which were appropriate for the younger children in terms of difficulty and interest.

Sequence 3 is an example of one such of her interventions with two girls, Carol and Lesley, in which the teacher begins her intervention by asking for information about the task.

Sequence 3: Designing a concept keyboard

1	T:	(Standing behind the pair of pupils) So what are you going to put
2		in this one? (points to a blank square on their overlay)
3	Carol:	[(inaudible mutters)
4	Lesley:	[(inaudible mutters)
5	T:	Come on, think about it
6	Lesley:	A Dragon?
7	T:	A dragon, Right. Have you got some words to describe a dragon?
8	Carol:	[No
9	Lesley:	[No
	T:	(Reading from their overlay and pointing to the words as she does so)
10		"There is a little amazing dragon." They could say that, couldn't
11		they?

12 *Carol:*   [Yes
13 *Lesley:*   [Yes
(*Carol and Lesley continue working for a short while, with the teacher making occasional comments*)
14 *T:*   Now let's pretend it's working on the computer. You press a
15   sentence and read it out for me Lesley.
16 *Lesley:*   (*pointing to the overlay as she reads*) "Here . . . is . . . a . . .
17   wonderful . . ."
18 *T:*   Wait a minute
19 *Lesley:*   "Princess . . ."
20 *T:*   (*turning to Carol*) Right, now you do one. You read your
21   sentence.
22 *Carol:*   (*pointing to overlay*) "Here . . . is . . . a little . . . princess"
23 *T:*   Good. What do you need at the end of the sentence, so that the
24   children learn about [how
25 *Lesley:*   [Full stop
26 *T:*   Full stop. We really should have allowed some space for a full
27   stop. I wonder if we could arrange . . . When you actually draw
28   the finished one up we'll include a full stop. You couldn't
29   actually do it. We'll put it there. (*She writes in a full stop on the*
30   overlay) so that when you, can you remember to put one in? So
31   what are the children going to learn? That a sentence starts with a
                . . .?
33 *Lesley:*   Capital letter
34 *T:*   And finishes with?
35 *Lesley:*   A full stop.
36 *T:*   And it's showing them (*she moves her hand across the overlay*
37   *from left to right*) What else is it showing them about sentences?
38   That you start? On the?
39 *Lesley:*   On the left
40 *T:*   And go across the page (*She again passes her hand from left to right*
                across the page).

Sequence 3 includes many examples of the kinds of discourse identified by Edwards and Mercer (1987, 1988) as representative of the intellectual relationship between teachers and children. Selecting particular themes, the teacher elicits responses from the pupils which draw them along a particular line of reasoning on that theme (a line of reasoning consonant with her own goals for the activity: lines 1, 2, 5, 7, 10). Moreover, she *cues* some of those responses heavily through the form of her questions (e.g., "That a sentence starts with a . . . ?": lines 31–32) and by her gestures (passing her hand from left to right: lines 36–37). In pursuing this line of reasoning, she has to elaborate the requirements of the activity, and in fact goes on to redefine those requirements (in relation to the inclusion of a "full stop" on the overlay: lines

26–30). She also defines the learning experience as one which is shared by her and the children through her use of "we."

In Sequence 3, we can see how a teacher uses talk, gesture, and the shared experience of the piece of work in progress to draw the children's attention to salient points – the things she wishes them to do, and the things she wishes them to learn. The nature of her intervention is to remind pupils of some specific requirements of the task in hand, and so guide their activity along a path which is in accord with her predefined curriculum goals for this activity. It is worth noting that this kind of interaction is very different in style from much of her teaching (as observed elsewhere), when she encourages free-ranging discussion and in which she plays a much less dominant role. We know that she saw this activity as a demanding one for the children (they had spent only one session using a manufactured keyboard overlay before beginning to design their own), and she was anxious that they all did manage to produce workable models. Her teaching style in the interventions she made can be seen as clear attempts to reduce the "degrees of freedom" of the activity so as to ensure that its demands did not exceed the capabilities of the children and so that the possible directions and outcomes of their efforts were constrained to accord with the specific goals she had set. In fact, we know that Lesley and Carol did produce a satisfactory overlay, and went on to teach the nursery children how to use it.

The prime justification for employing the concept of "scaffolding" in an analysis of the process of teaching-and-learning must be that it helps distinguish some kinds of teaching-and-learning from others. Sequence 3 shows an adult effectively performing the role of teacher without employing a traditional, didactic "chalk and talk" pedagogy or using only the kind of nondirective learning support strategies associated with "discovery learning" and certain "progressive" approaches to primary education. What we see in that sequence is also clearly not apprenticeship learning of the "sitting with Nellie" kind, rarely encountered in school but common in craft training, where a novice is expected to acquire skills and understanding simply through observation and working in parallel with an expert. We could describe what we see as "scaffolded" learning if (following Maybin et al., 1992) we are satisfied that (a) Carol and Lesley could not have succeeded without the teacher's interventions; (b) the teacher is aiming for some new level of independent competence on the children's part; and (c) the teacher has the acquisition of some specific skill or concept in mind. We are satisfied that these conditions are met. Furthermore, we also have evidence of the children successfully completing the task in hand and even (though the evidence is not very "hard") of their success in going on to deal independently with a subsequent related problem (i.e., teaching the nursery children to use the keyboard).

Conclusions and discussion

On the relevance and applicability of neo-Vygotskian concepts

Early in this chapter we argued that one of the most attractive features of neo-Vygotskian theory is that it conceptualizes the process of cognitive change as one of "teaching-and-learning" (or "learning-and-instruction") rather than dealing with "learning" as an individualized activity. It is, moreover, a theory which accords significance to the communicative, cultural contexts in which learning takes place. As education is first and foremost a matter of cognitive socialization (rather than a process of individual discovery), this theory would appear to offer a more appropriate explanatory framework for research into learning in classrooms than other contemporary psychological theories. We accepted, however, that neo-Vygotskian concepts needed to be given more precise formulations if they were to be used to explain classroom events.

For the concept of "scaffolding" we took up a formulation offered by Maybin et al. (1992). Our view is that this definition is sufficiently elaborated to allow researchers to discuss and explain differences in the quality of intellectual support which teachers provide for pairs or groups of learners working at the computer, while sufficiently stringent to exclude some kinds of "help" provided by teachers. Through applying this formulation of the concept, we have been able to show how teachers use talk to influence children's activities so that the success or failure of those activities does not hinge entirely on the relationship between the children and the computer.

More generally, we have used the concept to describe how teachers attempt to support children's problem solving without taking over complete responsibility for it.

It is probably in making a direct conceptual link between two very different aspects of the teacher's involvement with pupils' learning that the concept of "scaffolding" offers most to educational research. These aspects are (i) the pursuit of curriculum-related goals for learning and (ii) the use of specific discourse strategies for intervening in children's learning. The concept focuses attention on how, and how well, a teacher can actively organize and support children's learning without relying on didactic instruction or mere "shaping" through feedback. An obvious extension of the research described here would be to relate the relative incidence of the kinds of interventions teachers make to the progress of children through specific tasks.

Our discussion of teachers' cognitive support in this chapter deals only with strategic response rather than the planning and design of activity. That is (with the exception of Sequence 3) we have not considered here how cognitive support for an activity may be set up in advance by a teacher in the way a task is defined in practical terms (e.g., choice of software), organized (e.g., which children should work together), related to other learning experiences (e.g., to other work on a particular topic, or to children's broader interests) and how the task is introduced and explained by the teacher to the children. Aspects of such planning should probably be considered as part of "scaffolding," as it may well be that some of the more profound aspects of pedagogical decision-making (e.g., what curriculum goals are actually to be pursued through a task, and how these goals may be adapted to the needs of particular children) are made at that stage.

The second concept, the zone of proximal development, also embodies a view of the developing child or learner as someone whose learning achievements are situationally determined. We have offered observational data which illustrate how teachers attempt to provide a supportive contextual framework, and to do so in ways which reflect their judgments about *how much help the children need to perform to the limits of their capabilities*. For the psychology of learning and cognitive development, this concept challenges views of problem-solving ability or "cognitive level" as something abstract and non-task-specific. It invites us to consider how learning tasks *as social events* constrain or extend the cognitive potential of learners. For educational psychologists, classroom researchers, and teachers, it also encourages an approach to the monitoring of individual children's capabilities which focuses on supported development rather than "decontextualized" individual performance. In practice, children's development might be gauged as they progress through a series of related activities, carried out in the continuity of shared classroom experience, in terms of the extent to which the children become increasingly able to function with diminishing amounts of teacher support. Where special diagnosis is required owing to a child's learning difficulties, an approach such as this could be very useful.

However, the ZPD seems to us to have limited applicability in research directly concerned with the quality of teaching and learning in classrooms. One obvious reason is that practical circumstances force most teachers to plan activities on the scale of classes or groups, not individuals. The notion of any group of learners having a common ZPD seems untenable! Perhaps classroom researchers and teachers need instead a conceptualization of the ways that the organizing actions and interventions of a teacher are related to the creation of a learning culture in the classroom, and hence to the cognitive advancement of the members of a group or class as a whole. If we shift focus from the strengths and weaknesses of individual learners and instead consider how well a class or group of pupils and their teacher function as a "community of enquiry" (Prentice, 1991) as they progress through a series of curriculum-based activities, we may be more able to identify in what directions members of that class or group could be collectively expected and encouraged to advance. We believe that the conceptualization of what might be called the *synergy* of a learning group should be an important theoretical goal for research into learning and instruction.

On the nature of computer-based activity in the classroom

A common view, held by teachers, software designers, and many education technology researchers, is that the nature of any computer-based learning activity is almost entirely defined by the software. Teachers typically attribute the failure or success of any activity to "good" or "poor" programs. Although software is of course a defining influence on activities (to greater or lesser extents for different kinds of programs: compare, say, some adventure games with word-processing packages), our observations show that in practice the procedures and outcomes of any computer-based activity will emerge through the talk and joint activity of teacher and pupils. That is, the same software used by different combinations of teachers and pupils on different occasions will generate distinctive activities. These distinctive activities will operate to different timescales, generate different problems for pupils and teachers, and will almost certainly have different learning outcomes. Apart from the software itself, the main defining influence on the structure and outcomes of a computer-based activity will be that of the teacher, through any initial "setting up" of the activity, through the nature of the interventions he or she makes during the activity, and through the ways (before and after the time spent at the screen) that pupils are enabled to relate the activity to other educational experience. As Crook (1991) suggests, there is a need for the computer to:

> become a topic of classroom discourse such that the experience can be interpreted and blended into the shared understanding of the participants. This is a more demanding and perhaps more intrusive role for the teacher than has otherwise been identified.
>
> (p. 87)

We should not decry or attempt to diminish the powerful influence of the teacher on computer-based learning activities, for the teacher's responsibility is to ensure that children's computer-based experience contributes to their education. That responsibility cannot be delegated to even the most sophisticated software, or to the children themselves. If we can describe and evaluate the ways that teachers attempt to "scaffold" children's learning with computers, we might then be able to help teachers to perform that role more effectively and also contribute to the design of more "classroom-friendly" software.

References

Bruner, J. (1978). The role of dialogue in language acquisition. In A. Sinclair, R. Jarvella, & W. J. M. Levelt (Eds.), *The child's conception of language* (pp. 241–256). New York: Springer.

Bruner, J. (1985). Vygotsky: A historical and conceptual perspective. In J. V. Wertsch (Ed.), *Culture, communication and cognition: Vygotskian perspectives* (pp. 21–34). Cambridge: Cambridge University Press.

Bruner, J. (1986). *Actual minds, possible worlds*. London: Harvard University Press.

Collins. A., Brown, J. S., & Newman, S. (1990). Cognitive apprenticeship: Teaching students the crafts of reading, writing and mathematics. In L. B. Resnick (Ed.), *Knowing, learning and instruction: Essays in honor of Robert Glaser* (pp. 121–136). Hillsdale, NJ: Erlbaum.

Crook, C. (1991). Computers in the zone of proximal development: Implications for evaluation. *Computers in Education*, 17, 81–91.

Donaldson, M. (1978). *Children's minds*. London: Fontana.

Edwards, D. (1991). Categories are for talking: On the cognitive and discursive bases of categorization. *Theory and Psychology*, 1, 515–542.

Edwards, D., & Mercer, N. (1987). *Common knowledge: The development of understanding in the classroom*. London: Methuen.

Edwards, D., & Mercer, N. (1988). Discourse, power and the creation of shared knowledge: How do pupils discover what they are meant to? In M. Hildebrand-Nilshon, & G. Ruckriem (Eds.), *Proceedings of the First International Congress on Activity Theory* (Vol.3, pp. 9–36). Berlin: CIP.

Emihovich, C., & Miller, G. (1988). Talking to the turtle: A discourse analysis of Logo instruction. *Discourse Processes*, 11, 182–201.

Fisher, E. (1991). The teacher's role in teaching with the computer. Unit 8 of *EH232 Computers and Learning*. Milton Keynes: Open University Press.

Fraser, R., Burkhardt, H., Coupland, J., Phillips, R., Pimm, D., & Ridgeway J. (1990). Learning activities and classroom roles with and without the micro-computer. In O. Boyd-Barrett & E. Scanlon (Eds.), *Computers and learning* (pp. 205–230). Milton Keynes: Open University Press.

Hoyles, C., & Sutherland, R. (1989). *Logo mathematics in the classroom*. London: Routledge.

Hoyles, C., Healy, L., & Sutherland, R. (1991). Patterns of discussion between pupil pairs in computer and non-computer environments. *Journal of Computer-Assisted Learning*, 7, 210–228.

Lave, J. (1992). Word problems: A microcosm of theories of learning. In P. Light & G. Butterworth (Eds.), *Context and cognition* (pp. 74–93). Hemel Hempstead: Harvester-Wheatsheaf.

Maybin, J., Mercer, N., & Stierer, B. (1992). "Scaffolding" learning in the classroom. In K. Norman (Ed.), *Thinking voices: The work of the National Oracy Project*. London: Hodder & Stoughton for the National Curriculum Council.

Mehan, H. (1979). *Learning lessons*. Cambridge, MA: Harvard University Press.

Mercer, N. (1991a). Accounting for what goes on in classrooms: What have neo-Vygotskians got to offer? *British Psychological Society Education Section Review*, 15, 61–67.

Mercer, N. (1991b). Learning through talk. In *Talk and learning 5–16: An inservice pack on oracy for teachers* (pp. A5–A10). Milton Keynes: Open University Press.

Mercer, N. (1991c). Computers and communication in the classroom. Unit 7 of *EH232 Computers and Learning*. Milton Keynes: Open University Press.

Mercer, N. (1992). Culture, context and the construction of classroom knowledge. In

P. Light & G. Butterworth (Eds.), *Context and cognition* (pp. 28–46). Hemel Hempstead: Harvester-Wheatsheaf.

Mercer, N., Phillips, T., & Somekh, B. (1991). Spoken language and the new technology: The SLANT project. *Journal of Computer-Assisted Learning* 7, 195–202.

Miller, G., & Emihovich. C. (1986). The effects of mediated programming on pre-school children's self-monitoring. *Journal of Educational Computing Research*, 2, 283–97.

Newman, D., Griffin, P., & Cole, M. (1989). *The construction zone*. Cambridge: Cambridge University Press.

Papert, S. (1980). *Mindstorms: Children, computers and powerful ideas*. New York: Basic Books.

Prentice, M. (1991). A community of enquiry. In *Talk and learning 5–16: An inservice pack on oracy for teachers* (pp. A28–A31). Milton Keynes: Open University Press.

Resnick, L. B. (1987). *Education and learning to think*. Washington, DC: National Academy Press.

Simon, H. A. (1980). Cognitive science. The newest science of the artificial. *Cognitive Science*, 4, 33–46

Simon, H. A. (1981). *The sciences of the artificial*. Cambridge, MA: MIT Press.

Sinclair, J., & Coulthard, R. (1975). *Towards an analysis of discourse: The English used by teachers and pupils*. London: Oxford University Press.

Smith, L. (1989). Changing perspectives in developmental psychology. In C. Desforges (Ed.), *Early childhood education* (BPS Monograph series No. 4). Edinburgh: Scottish Academic Press.

Vygotsky, L. S. (1978). *Mind in society*. Cambridge, MA: Harvard University Press.

Walkerdine, V. (1984). Developmental psychology and the child-centred pedagogy: The insertion of Piaget into early education. In J. Henriques, W. Hollway, C. Urwin, C. Venn, & V. Walkerdine, *Changing the subject* (pp. 153–201). London: Methuen.

Wertsch, J.V. (1985). *Culture, communication and cognition: Vygotskian perspectives*. Cambridge: Cambridge University Press.

Wood, D., Bruner, J., & Ross, G. (1976). The role of tutoring in problem-solving. *Journal of Child Psychology and Child Psychiatry*, 17, 89–100.

Chapter 7

Vygotsky in classroom practice

Moving from individual transmission to social transaction*

Luis C. Moll and Kathryn F. Whitmore

In this chapter we present a case study of a third-grade bilingual classroom.[1] The students in the class are primarily working-class Mexican children, and the school is located within their neighborhood in a southwestern city of the United States. We have selected this classroom for discussion because its activities do not fit well or easily into current discussions of "guided practice" or "assisted performance" derived from Vygotskian theory, especially from dyadic interpretations of his concept of the zone of proximal development. Hence this chapter demonstrates how practice can exceed, as well as inform and elaborate, our theoretical notions.

By presenting the classroom analysis we emphasize what we consider to be a more dynamic and encompassing notion of Vygotsky's zone of proximal development. We are, of course, not the first to suggest that current interpretations of this concept may be too narrow.[2] Griffin and Cole (1984), for example, have suggested that "English-speaking scholars interpret the concept more narrowly than Vygotsky intended, robbing it of some of its potential for enabling us to understand the social genesis of human cognitive processes and the process of teaching and learning in particular" (p. 45).

Valsiner (1988) has pointed out that Vygotsky's intent in his introductory explanation of the zone of proximal development was much broader, to "get across to his pedagogically-minded listeners (or readers) a more basic theoretical message: . . . the interdependence of the process of child development and the socially provided resources for that development" (p. 145). Vygotsky used this concept to emphasize the importance – in fact the inseparability – of sociocultural conditions for understanding thinking and its development (Minick, 1989; Moll, 1990b; Vygotsky, 1978, 1987; Wertsch, 1985). Hence he viewed thinking not as a characteristic of the child only, but of the child-in-social-activities with others (Minick, 1985). In terms of classroom learning, Vygotsky specifically emphasized the relation between thinking and

---

* This is an edited version of a chapter that appeared in *Contexts for learning: sociocultural dynamics in children's development*, Oxford: Oxford University Press, 1993.

what we would call the social organization of instruction (Moll, 1990b). He wrote about the "unique form of cooperation between the child and the adult that is the central element of the educational process" and how by this inter-actional process "knowledge is transferred to the child in a definite system" (Vygotsky, 1987, p. 169). It is these systemic properties of instruction that Vygotsky thought provided a special socialization of children's thinking.

In particular, Vygotsky concentrated on the manipulation of language as an important characteristic of formal schooling. He thought that formal instruction in writing and grammar, by refocusing attention from the content of communication to the means of communication, provided the foundations for the development of conscious awareness and voluntary control of impor-tant aspects of speech and language (Minick, 1987). He believed that schooled discourse represented a qualitatively different form of communica-tion from everyday discourse because words act not only as means of com-munication, as they would in everyday talk, but as the object of study. During classroom interactions the teacher directs the children's attention to word meanings and definitions and the systematic relation among them that constitutes an organized system of knowledge. Formal instruction, then, with its special organization and discourse, through its social and semiotic medi-ations, provides children with the resources to develop the capacity to con-sciously manipulate and voluntarily control crucial sociocultural symbolic systems.

The above theory suggests that it is incorrect to think of the zone as solely a characteristic of the child or of the teaching, but of the child engaged in collaborative activity within specific social (discourse) environments. From our perspective, the key is to understand the social transactions that make up classroom life. Within this analysis the focus of study is on the *sociocultural system* within which children learn, with the understanding that this system is mutually and actively created by teachers and students. What we propose is a "collective" zone of proximal development. As we illustrate with our case study, it is this interdependence of adults and children, and how they use social and cultural resources, that is central to a Vygotskian analysis of instruction.

Understanding classrooms as sociocultural systems

This case study presents data collected during weekly classroom observations over two academic school years in a bilingual third-grade classroom.[3] It is a special classroom that provides rich data for a Vygotskian interpretation. The teacher describes herself as a "whole-language" teacher. Central to this approach is a view of literacy as the understanding and communication of meaning (e.g., Goodman & Goodman, 1990). Both comprehension and expression are built and developed collaboratively by students and teachers through functional, relevant, meaningful language use. Therefore a major instructional goal of the teacher is to make the classroom a highly literate environment in which many language experiences can take place and different types of "literacies" can be used, understood, and learned by the students. This approach rejects the typical reduction of reading and writing into skill sequences transmitted in isolation or in a successive, stage-like manner (including such practices as having children sit quietly, follow mundane directions, only read assigned texts, fill out work sheets, and take tests). Rather, it emphasizes the creation of authentic social contexts in which children use, try out, and manipulate language as they make sense and create meaning. The role of the teacher is to mediate these social contexts, in a Vygotskian sense, so that through their own efforts children assume full control of diverse purposes and uses of oral and written language.

Such classrooms, then, allow insights into the social processes of literacy development that are unavailable in more typical settings. It is this process of social mediation that we want to highlight here: not the creation of individual zones of proximal development but of collective, interrelated zones of proximal development as part of a transactive teaching system. The knowledge about subject matter is learned through different types of social relationships facilitated by the teacher. This process is mediated in the sense that the teacher controls it strategically to engage students in different aspects of reading and writing. It is also mediated in the sense that the teacher creates future contexts in which children can consciously apply in new ways what they are learning.

Furthermore, this classroom is a bilingual one, using English and Spanish. The teacher's goal is to create conditions for learning the second language that are "additive," that is, perceived by all as a positive addition to a first language, with a strong emphasis on communication for academic purposes. In particular, there is an attempt to integrate written language in either the students' first or second language as part of every academic activity, where books are read in both languages and the students are free to write in their language of choice. For example, it is common for a student to read a book in English and write a summary in Spanish, or vice versa.

When presenting the case study we first describe a "typical day" to give the reader a good sense of the classroom's daily routine, the social system that is in place. Included is a description of a thematic unit centered on Native Americans that the teacher and students jointly develop. This unit illustrates well how the teacher creates diverse circumstances for the children to use and apply their considerable intellectual and linguistic resources. We see these theme units as dynamic contexts within which the children learn by manipulating knowledge and provide the teacher and themselves with many opportunities to evaluate how well they are using reading and writing as tools for analysis and for thinking. In our terms, these units are made up of connected zones of proximal development within which the children constantly redefine themselves as learners.

Typical day: creating a literate community

The classroom community includes 27 children (12 boys and 15 girls) who come from either the neighborhood or "barrio" surrounding the school (16 children) or who travel from other neighborhoods in the city (11 children) as part of a magnet desegregation program.[4] As is common in bilingual class-rooms, there is considerable diversity in the children's language and literacy abilities. Fifteen of the children are monolingual English speakers and readers. Of these children, two (Sarah and Brooke) are rapidly learning to speak, read, and write Spanish. Elizabeth is the only English-dominant bilingual speaker, and she reads in both languages. Nine children are bilingual. Of the nine, Veronica, Susana, and Lupita are reading and writing in both languages; Francisco, Raymundo, and Roberto read both but are clearly Spanish-dominant; and Rosario, David, and Ana are Spanish-only readers. Jaime is a Spanish-dominant speaker who came into the classroom in the fall speaking only Spanish and by the end of the year spoke and read some English as well. Acuzena is a monolingual Spanish speaker. She arrived in the United States from Mexico in the spring and reads only Spanish.

Each day for this classroom begins in the patio area of the school, where children, staff, and faculty meet to share announcements, sing, and recite the Pledge of Allegiance. After this morning ritual, the children enter the class-room, noisily put away their things, greet each other in English and Spanish, and move to the group meeting area in the center of the room. The teacher finds a chair, and the group quiets for announcements, calendar and weather information, and a discussion of the schedule for the day. She reads aloud to the children in either English or Spanish at least once each day.

After the opening story, the class moves into math centers. Little direction is necessary to get the children and adults moving around the classroom, gathering materials, and settling into four math groups located at various places in the classroom. This classroom is a functionally organized setting. There are several large tables in the room that, along with the ample amount of carpeted floor area, provide work space for the children and adults. Cubicles and cupboards are used by the children as storage space for their personal belongings, but the school supplies (pencils, paper, crayons, and the like) are shared by the classroom community. They are all within easy access of the children and are clearly labeled in both languages. A piano, loft, and the teacher's hidden desk allow children places to hide away to work, read, and visit.

Following math centers, the children usually go outside for recess, although some students request permission to stay inside to continue writing projects, illustrate books, catch up on assignments, and work on their second language. Roberto and Rafael ask to work on a collaborative book; Brooke asks to practice reading in Spanish; and Shelley finishes a filmstrip project. These children work independently, and the teacher uses this time to prepare for upcoming activities, plan with the student teacher, or interact with children inside or outside on the playground.

The children reconvene at the meeting area before they move into a language arts block that consists of a period of sustained silent reading (which the teacher calls DEAR: Drop Everything And Read), literature study groups, and writing workshop. The children are continuing studies of several authors. While the teacher and the student teacher meet with two of the literature groups, the other children either meet in their own author-centered literature groups independently or do DEAR.

DEAR in this classroom means an extended period of time (at least 15 to 30 minutes) spent reading any material of choice. The children and adults all read, and the reading materials are extensive and varied in type, topic, and language. The teacher frequently selects a piece of adolescent literature to read for her graduate children's literature courses. Newspapers are available and are usually the choice of the student teacher and the teacher assistant. They share articles with each other, chatting as they would over the breakfast table at home. Children read magazines, chapter books (books long enough to be segmented into chapters with few if any illustrations), books authored and published by students and the whole class, picture books, comic books, and nonfiction books. Children settle in comfortably with friends or alone during DEAR, finding niches under the loft or piano or lying on the floor. The DEAR period is not entirely silent, although it is subdued. Sometimes music plays in the background, and children enthusiastically share information and illustrations as they read.

The children and adults must use print to complete activities and "live" successfully in this highly literate classroom environment. The daily schedule is revised each morning and referred to by all participants throughout the day, for instance. Evidence of group learning, as recorded on charts and other public documents, includes the following: webs representing brainstorming sessions,[5] data collected during math and science experimentation, and ongoing records of thematically organized activities. They include lists of questions children generate at the outset of each new theme. Reading and writing are not only subjects in this classroom but essential aspects of the classroom's intellectual and functional daily life.

The teacher uses literature study groups to provide social reading experiences that complement the personal reading experience provided by DEAR. These study groups enable the children to share their reactions, analyses, and questions about children's trade books with their peers and teachers. The materials for literature study groups vary greatly and provide a wealth of opportunity for choice for the readers, as well as a wide assortment of literary examples. During an author's study group, the teacher supplied over 50 different books in text sets according to author, for example. The children read silently, individually, or with a friend, before their groups meet for discussion. In addition to reading a variety of literature during literature study groups, the children learn biographical information about authors and illustrators, compare pieces of writing, extend their reading into writing and illustrations through literature logs and other writing projects, analyze plots, characters, settings, and other literary elements, and create story maps, among other activities. Literature groups are organized according to the interests and choices of the children, in contrast to traditional "reading groups," which are organized homogeneously by reading "ability." The groups allow children opportunities to study and enjoy literature with readers of all abilities, as well as readers of two languages, and provide them with frequent opportunities to mediate each other's learning through shared literacy experiences.

The following examples, taken from the transcripts of literature groups about popular children's authors William Steig and Byrd Baylor, reveal the nature of interactions that characterize this component of the curriculum. The teacher (T) opens the first session of the Steig group by eliciting the children's reactions to one of his books:

T:	*Sylvester and the Magic Pebble.* What did you guys think about this story?
Rita:	I think they cared a lot for him.
T:	What do you mean? You mean his parents?
Rita:	Yes
T:	What made you think that when you read the story?
Rita:	Because they really worried about him.
T:	Who else wants to share something? I'd like to hear everybody's ideas. Then we can decide what we want to talk about. Sarah?
Sarah:	I think he got the idea of it when he was little, or maybe one of his friends got lost or something?
T:	What do you mean, he got the idea?
Sarah:	He got the idea for his parents to think that Sylvester got lost.
T:	You're talking about where William Steig might have gotten his ideas.
Sarah:	Yes.
T:	That maybe something like this happened to him or someone he knew. A lot of times authors get their ideas from real life things, don't they? Jon, what did you think about this story?
Jon:	It was like a moral story. It's like you can't wish for everything. But, in a sense, everything happened to him when he was panicking.
T:	When did you think he panicked?
Jon:	Well, when he saw the lion, he started to panic.
Richard:	And he turned himself into a rock.
Jon:	Yeah. He said, "I wish I were a rock."
T:	Right. And it happened, didn't it?

Richard:	It was stupid of him.
T:	So maybe he wasn't thinking far enough ahead? What would you have wished instead of a rock?
Richard:	A plane. A plane.
T:	An airplane? That would've been a good wish.
Sarah:	I would wish him to disappear.
T:	Wish the lion to disappear?
Jon:	I would wish the lion could turn into a tiny gnat and fly away.
Rita:	I wish he turned into a bird.

Note how the students contributed different levels of interpretation of the story in response to the teacher's open request. She summarizes the discussion thus far, saying, "Look at all the different kinds of things you had to say. Rita talked about the characters in the story and what they must have been feeling. Sarah took the author's point of view. And you saw it as a particular kind of story, Jon, as a moral story." The teacher asks the students to reflect on their reactions and justify them, and she is explicit about her goals. Note that she refers to the literature logs the students keep on the stories they have read.

T:	What did you say in your log about the story when you wrote in your log yesterday?
Richard:	That it was a good book.
T:	Why would you say this was a good story?
Richard:	I don't know.
T:	I guess what I want is for kids to know why they think something is a good story.

As the discussion progresses the children use each other, their experiences, the text, and other stories they have read to mediate their understanding of the story. Throughout, the teacher participates in the discussion, revealing her thinking, contributing her observations along with the students, and elaborating on the children's comments.

As the talk continues, Sarah initiates a discussion to clarify her understanding of the text, and the group recalls the details of the plot to seek an answer. In the following segment of the transcript it is particularly interesting that after Sarah initiates an in-depth discussion she listens quietly to the group interpretation of the text. The teacher takes a notably quiet place in the lively discussion as well; in fact, twice her attempts to participate are interrupted by children. Eventually, Sarah verbalizes a conclusion to her own question.

Sarah:	I was thinking, at the end, I always get mixed up, because when they have the rock on him, does Sylvester wish himself back, or do his parents?
Richard:	Sylvester does!

Rita:	No, they do!
Richard:	Sylvester does! Sylvester does!
T:	Can you find in the book where . . .
Richard:	It's right here, it's right here.
T:	Wait a second. And Richard if you will . . .
Richard:	It says, "'I wish I were myself again. I wish I were my real self again,' thought Sylvester."
Jon:	Yes.
Rita:	But his parents did that too.
Richard:	But he said . . .
Rita:	They found the pebble and they . . .
Richard:	Put it on him.
T:	Do you remember how the magic had to work?
Jon:	It would have to be on Sylvester.
T:	What was the only way the pebble worked?
Richard:	If it was on the person.
T:	If you had it in your hand, right?
Richard:	Or on you.
T:	So if he's a rock, he can't hold the pebble.
Jon:	But he could support it.
Sarah:	Yeah, he wished himself back.

As the discussion of the story continues, the children and the teacher explore several themes and interpretations that come about from a shared reading of the text. The discussion includes what the story might be like in another genre, such as a novel, how the action in the story alternates between panic and calm, and if the changing colors in the illustrations depict the changing seasons and why that would be important to the story. Near the end of the session, the teacher discusses with the students what they want to plan to do next. The teacher negotiates with the group, drawing on what has captivated them about the piece of literature. It is the teacher's way of facilitating the students' ownership of the discussion and purpose of the literature group.

Reading and writing merge during another author study about Byrd Baylor's work. After spending several days reading from a set of Baylor's books, Ilinca, Rita, and Mariah come together to discuss their impressions of the books, the commonalities across texts, and how they might share their reading with the rest of the class. Here again, the teacher mediates the children's understandings by using their ideas, questions, and interests to help them focus on meaningful discussions and presentations.

Ilinca:	All the books are deserty. They all have to do with the desert — mostly the plants and animals.
Mariah:	All the desert scenes look like they were painted with watercolors.

Rita: What I liked best was the lettering, the print. It was like in poetry. It doesn't have anything to do with poetry. Well, maybe a little. It sounded like poetry.

T: Poetry doesn't have to rhyme. It's more a way of expressing feelings and describing things. Do you think Byrd Baylor was expressing her feelings about the desert?

Rita: I can tell she's a gentle person. It sounds like she cares about the desert and doesn't want it destroyed.

Mariah: I read about Byrd Baylor in that newspaper article. She lives in the desert. Her house is kind of Indian style.

Ilinca: Maybe we could write about the desert, a plant, or animal and make it look like poetry like Byrd Baylor does. I like being in the desert. Could I write about being in the desert?

T: Yes, of course. That sounds like a wonderful way to share what you have learned with the rest of the class.

Mariah: And we could make pictures like the books too.

The group then spends time studying Peter Parnall's illustrations (in the Baylor books) more carefully, noticing how he uses simple lines and little color, and how only some parts of the plants and animals are detailed. They are not sure how to go about writing in a style similar to Byrd Baylor. The teacher suggests that first they simply write something about the desert that expresses their own feelings. She does the same, and then demonstrates breaking her prose into shortened segments to establish the rhythm that makes it more poetic. The children are pleased with the results. Here are some examples of the children's writing:

I love
to watch the hawk soar
through the sky
and the coyotes howl
at night.
The rabbits hop
from cactus to cactus.
                    by Sarah

The coyote
eats by day and
the coyote howls
by night.
The coyote
goes out in the
middle of the
night to find

his prey. At
the time of
dawn, he comes
home, with good
things to eat.
The mother
says (in coyote
words) I was
worried. – Don't
worry, be happy.
I thought
you got
caught. Who
me? Never.
                    by Jon

As a participant in such literature groups, rather than solely the leader, the teacher strives to respond as a reader, to move beyond traditional comprehension questions, and to expand on teachable moments. Most remarkable is the teacher's trust of the children's questions and ideas. She clearly does not have a predetermined agenda for discussions and resulting projects but assists the children as a more experienced participating reader in the group to summarize their ideas, merge their questions, and conceptualize ways to present their learning to themselves and others. This important role of the teacher demonstrates her trust of children's transactions with the text and with each other, and her continuous sharing of control with them in curriculum development.

DEAR and literature studies transform into a writing workshop (WW) with a quiet direction or by turning off and on the lights. Materials and work partners change, and quiet talking about reading becomes active discussion about writing projects, illustration, and publication.[6] At the piano bench, Racheal and Lupita finish a conference with the student teacher about spelling and return to the publication process. Their story represents an interesting collaboration. Racheal, a monolingual English speaker, approached Lupita and invited her to join her in a project so that they could produce a bilingual book, Lupita being bilingual and biliterate. Their joint story concerns a young English-speaking girl who encounters a monolingual Spanish-speaking girl and the problems they face as they develop a relationship. In the course of their dialogue, Racheal says, "Lupita, you know what we should do?" and suggests a minor revision. "No, that won't sound good," counters Lupita. "Okay, you're right," Racheal adds, "I'm not good at the Spanish, Lupita" "You're not? Then just do the letters," comforts Lupita.

Jaime and Roberto are nestled under the loft. They are busy writing letters during WW time. The letters, written in Spanish, are headed across the room to David and Raymundo, who are scrunched under the study carrels. Jaime and Roberto are writing to them "because they don't want to be our friends, and we want them to," confides Roberto.

Meanwhile, Susana and the teacher are at the computer, putting a story on the word processor for final publication. Across the room a group of girls sit at a table covered with final projects deeply involved in an author's circle, reading their writing to one another, asking each other questions, and making revisions in their texts. Ana and the teacher assistant confer elsewhere about punctuation and spelling for a final draft. The room is busy with papers, pencils, markers, and crayons as children work at real authoring and illustrating.

The descriptions above only briefly touch on the variety of literacy events taking place simultaneously in this classroom. Many students have more than one project going on at one time, and their writing (in English, Spanish, or both) includes a variety of genres and styles. The teacher believes children are readers and writers, and she strives to support and enhance their continued development and success. As she states, she and her colleagues are "working hard to give the kids the knowledge that they can be learners." The students are trusted to select appropriate materials, writing topics, and language(s) for literacy activities. The teacher helps the children take risks with difficult materials and new genres and formats for reading and writing, with the aim of expanding their developing abilities. She describes the process of attending to traditional skills within a classroom emphasizing writing as a process:

> I keep almost everything that the kids write, so that I'm real aware of what things they are trying out when they are writing. If I see a lot of children exploring something, then I will do a short class lesson [about a skill]. We did that with quotation marks. There were a lot of kids trying to put conversations into their stories, but they don't use punctuation and they don't use speech carriers and you couldn't tell who was talking. So we spent a couple of days doing written conversations. The kids did them with each other in class, and they were also asked to do it with their parents at home. And then in the classroom we talked about how you put [the punctuation] in so you can tell who is talking. Then the kids went back and did that with their written conversations. I have seen that in their writing since then some of the kids are really starting to use the ideas we practiced. The speech carriers appeared right away, they were less sure what to do with the little marks, but some of the kids are using them now. And if I see them I say, "Oh, I see you are using quotation marks in your story." So most of the teaching about writing takes place along that line.

She continues by explaining how they use the children's reading to develop their writing:

Also, we look as readers. We might look at how an author uses a particular stylistic kind of thing or how poets use things like alliteration and try out some more guided kinds of writing. We do some pattern kinds of writing sometimes when we're exploring things like that. And kids may or may not pick up things on their own when it comes to their writing, but I certainly see a lot of growth. And the spelling development is there, too, because I don't teach the spelling program either, and the kids are beginning to trust that they will learn to spell.

The children determine which language(s) they will use to read and write. The teacher ensures that the students develop strong literacy strategies in their first language, whether it be English or Spanish, as it serves as the basis for second language development. The children's desires to read and write in a second language are fostered, encouraged, and supported. Such efforts are facilitated by paired reading between students and between students and adults. Regardless of the language of choice, however, the emphasis on using literacy to make meaning remains the same.

A few minutes before noon, the children get ready for lunch. They put away writing materials and gather at the meeting area once again. The teacher takes a moment to comment on the morning's activities and set the stage for the afternoon. Frequently, the teacher's philosophy is shared during such moments, allowing the children open insight into her beliefs about learning. "Talking is probably the most important thing we do in here because you learn the most when you can talk while you work," the teacher tells the students.

Thematic unit: Native Americans

When the children return from their lunch period, they become involved in work organized around thematic content. The theme under way is Native Americans. The teacher explains how much control the children have over the topics that form part of these theme studies:

> The theme cycles are pretty much controlled, the topics anyway, by the kids. Right away at the beginning of the year we go through a group brainstorm process where the kids will put out anything they are interested in studying, and we group things together. We put sharks and whales in the list together with someone [who] said ocean, so that related topics are chunked together. And then the kids are asked to vote for their ten most favorite, and those are the ones that we do as group theme cycles for the year. I put my things on the list, too.

Other topics chosen for intensive study during the year have been fairy tales, astronomy, ancient Egypt, and the ocean. As the teacher explains it, the theme studies involve both individual and collaborative projects among the students:

> [It] usually starts with some kind of a web, sometimes the kids would share what they already know, I usually ask them to generate lists of questions of what they want to know about and that helps arrange centers or activities, knowing what they're interested in, what their areas are. With the Native American unit we are doing right now, the kids wanted to do some independent research projects, but they also wanted to do centers. The reports they'll produce will probably be a page or a couple of pages, and we talked about binding them into a book for the library, because we found very little information in our school library to help us.

Based on the type of planning just described, the teacher collects wide and varied literacy materials to fill the classroom with information in both Spanish and English. Approximately 100 trade books, pieces of art, posters, and artifacts about Native Americans find their way into the classroom from the teachers, support staff, parents, and the children themselves.

The teacher makes use of the children's interests and ideas as she plans the learning experiences that will form part of the theme units. The themes involve large groups, small groups, and individual activities, and they integrate all subject areas. The organizational web (Figure 7.1) illustrates the Native American theme as a whole.

Each theme culminates in some form of a product or demonstration of the group's learning. For example, the Native American theme produced a

Figure 7.1 Organizational web: Native American theme

published class book that included all of the children as coauthors and a detailed bibliography.

Four centers are included in the Native American theme study. At one side of the room, Angel, Roberto, Jaime, and Francisco are learning about corn. On their table is a basket containing blue and yellow corn chips to taste, a collection of trade books in English and Spanish about corn, a corn legend, and a colorful basket of squash and Indian corn. The teacher briefly joins the children to explain the procedure. When she leaves, the children taste the corn chips, read a book about corn, and write about each experience. The books are varied in style and language, and the children cheer when the teacher explains that she found a Spanish translation of one of the books for them (*Corn is Maize*, by Aliki).

Across the room, Rafael and Susana work with the teacher assistant on weaving. Each child has a forked branch that serves as the frame for the work. The teacher assistant helps the children select colors, measure the appropriate amount of yarn, and begin the weaving. Spanish dominates their casual and comfortable conversation as the children methodically weave colors of yarn around the natural looms. In the basket on their table are books about weaving and a diagram that labels the components of weaving in both languages, as well as the weaving materials.

In another center the children view a variety of film strips. The children are using this center as a resource for their ongoing research projects by viewing the films, including helpful information in their reports, and documenting them in their bibliographies.

The fourth center involves the children who are working on individual research projects. These children and the teacher are seated around two tables that are covered with bins of books categorized according to topic, 3×5 note cards, and children's work folders in manila envelopes.

Lupita, who is researching the Sioux, is reading a trade book in English called *Plains Indians*, concentrating on a section called "Games and Pastimes." As she reads, she records relevant information in Spanish on an index card. Her work provides a good example of the research process involved in this theme. The class as a large group began the theme by discussing and webbing the content they wanted to learn through their study. The result of their discussions is represented in Figure 7.2.

The students then create a web of information they want to know about their individual topics and write questions to guide their research. Examples of Lupita's questions are presented in Figure 7.3. The children may read and write in either language or a combination of the two, as Lupita's activities illustrate. As the children look for answers to their questions in resource materials, they record pertinent information on their cards, as shown in Figure 7.4.

Additionally, they record the books they use on a reference sheet that asks for information about the title, author, call number, and whether they will

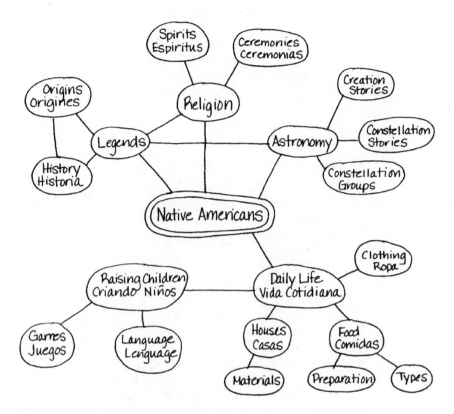

Figure 7.2 Class web: Native American theme

use the book for information or will not use the book. These sheets will become a bibliography when their upcoming reports are finished. Lupita's partial bibliography is depicted in Figure 7.5.

Upon completion of the research, the children create a second individual web summarizing the information they have obtained as a way to monitor their own learning and write their reports. This entire process is graded by the teacher according to the quality of the questions, the first web, the resource list, the note keeping, the final report, the final web, and a composite overall grade. The children's final reports are bound in a published book to donate to the school's library, where it will be catalogued and shelved for the rest of the school to utilize as a reference document. Lupita's report is shown in Figure 7.6.

Other children in the class follow a similar procedure. Consider Veronica, a Spanish-dominant bilingual child, who is studying the Yaqui Indians. The teacher is sitting with her, reading to her from an adult-level book written in English (*Southwestern Indian Tribes* by Tom Bahti). After she reads a passage,

Lupita

Me gustaria, saber sobre
el tribu Siux.

¿En que teritorio vivian?

~~¿Porque no quirian a
la gente blanca?~~

¿Porque se pintaban
las caras y sus
caballos?

¿Que se, significaban
las plumas en sus
cabeza?

¿Porque sus jefes
tenian nombres
de animal?

¿Tenian una manera
especial de aser la
ropa?

Lupita

I would like to know about the Sioux tribe.
In what territory did they live?
Why did they not like white people?
Why did they paint their faces and their horses?
What was the meaning of the feathers in their heads?
Why did their chiefs have animal names?
Did they have a special way of making clothes?

Figure 7.3 Lupita's questions about Native Americans [7]

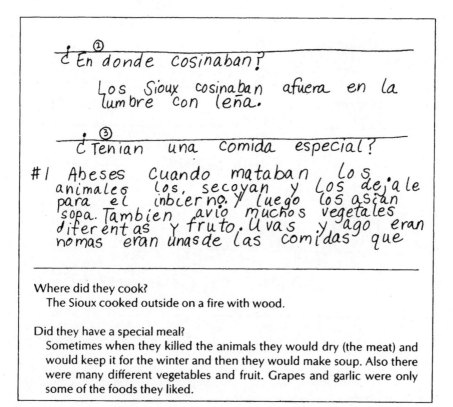

¿ En donde cosinaban?

Los Sioux cosinaban afuera en la lumbre con leña.

¿ Tenian una comida especial?

#1 Abeses Cuando mataban los animales los, secoyan y los deja le para el inbcerno. Y luego los asian sopa. Tambien avio muchos vegetales diferentas y fruto. Uvas y ago eran nomas eran unas de las comidas que

---

Where did they cook?
The Sioux cooked outside on a fire with wood.

Did they have a special meal?
Sometimes when they killed the animals they would dry (the meat) and would keep it for the winter and then they would make soup. Also there were many different vegetables and fruit. Grapes and garlic were only some of the foods they liked.

Figure 7.4 Lupita's research cards[7]

the teacher translates the ideas into Spanish and discusses them with Veronica in terms of her research questions. The teacher is absorbed in the process herself; she is a co-researcher with Veronica, eager to learn and discuss new knowledge with her student. Veronica incorporates a second source of information in her research project: She has interviewed a Yaqui teacher assistant in the school and kept a written record of her interview questions and the responses she elicited, which are incorporated into her final report; the interview is documented in her bibliography.

Richard and Evan are at the opposite end of the table studying the Anasazi. They are searching for information about weapons and how the Anasazi defended themselves. Richard finds a picture of an "atlatl," a missile launcher used for hunting, and they decide to use it for their answer. Each boy traces the illustration, cuts it out and tapes it to his index card. Evan finishes taping his and says, "This is cool," as he hurries over to Jason at another table to share what he has learned. Jason is discussing the Sioux and responds to Evan saying, "The Anasazi didn't trade with the white men. The Sioux just needed

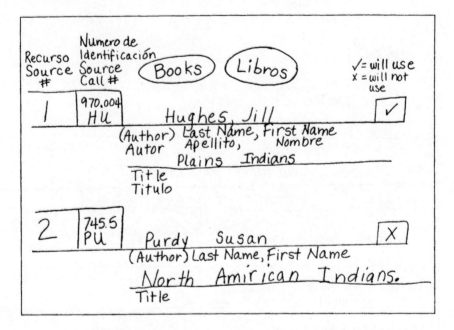

Figure 7.5 Lupita's bibliography

to buy iron for weapons, and they did the rest." Talk centered around the content of study is frequent and natural.

From the initial web, through the intermediate stages of planning, center activity, research work, and publication, the theme studies include authentic, captivating, integrated learning experiences, where the children use literacy to search for knowledge and to present their ideas to others in the classroom community and in the school.

Discussion

This classroom, organized into center activities, literacy events, and theme research projects, is structured so that children may work in various ways to accomplish their individual and group academic goals There is no limit to what the children may learn about Native Americans or themes centered around other concepts. There is no ceiling on the possible level of intellectual work or the learning potential of the children. The teacher allows and encourages children to stretch their abilities and to take risks with new experiences, materials, and challenges. Simultaneously, the design of the curriculum and the participation of the teacher support the children and ensure success, acting as a safety net for those children who take risks, especially in their second language. Throughout, the children are perceived not only as active

LOS INDIOS SIOUX

por María Guadalupe

Yo se llamo María Guadalupe y quise aprender del tribu Sioux porque casi no se mucho de ese tribu. Aprendí de los juegos que jugaban. También aprendí de los vegetales que comían y los nombres de los jefes.

Los Sioux vivían cerca del Trin River. Los Sioux no hacían muchas canastas.

A veces, cuando mataban los animales, los secaban y los dejeban para el invierno. Luego lo hacían sopa. También había muchos vegetales diferentes y frutz. Uvas y ajo eran unas de las cosidas que les gustaban. Los Sioux cocinaban afuera en la lumbre.

Estos son unos de los nombres de los jefes del tribu Sioux: Sitting Bull – jefe del tribu Sioux, Chief Ball – Hunkpapa Teton, Chief Red Horn Bull – Ogalala, and Rain-in-the-face.

También aprendí los juegos de los Sioux. Uno se llama "tiren lo del caballo" que jugaban antes de cazar o de peliar. Jugaban tirando a otros al suelo. También había otros juego que dos hombres tenían que poner un palo por un hoyo. El que ponía el palo por el hoyo primero ganaba.

THE SIOUX INDIANS

by Maria Guadalupe

My name is Maria Guadalupe and I wanted to learn about the Sioux Tribe because I hardly know anything about that tribe. I learned about the games they played. I also learned about the vegetables which they ate and the names of their chiefs.

The Sioux lived near the Trin river. The Sioux did not make many baskets.

Sometimes, when they killed animals, they dried them and left them for winter. Later they would make them into soup. Also there were many different vegetables and fruits. Grapes and garlic were some of the foods which they liked. The Sioux cooked outside on a fire.

These are some of the names of the chiefs of the Sioux tribe: Sitting Bull – chief of the Sioux tribe, Chief Ball – Hunkpapa Teton, Chief Red Horn Bull – Ogalala, and Rain-in-the-face.

I also learned the games of the Sioux. One was called "pull him off the horse" which they played before hunting or fighting. They played by throwing others to the floor. There was also another game in which two men had to place a stick in a hole. The one that put the stick in the hole first would win.

Figure 7.6 Lupita's final report

participants in their own learning but are encouraged to be responsible for their own academic development and behavior; and they are actively involved in diverse classroom activities. The classroom is socially and culturally organized to support and advance those goals.

The curriculum indicates a value placed on the children's learning *processes* as well as on completing products. With the Native American theme, the children not only learn information about their theme of study, but they learn the valid procedures of research. These third-grade children are responsible for conceiving their own questions, guiding their own learning with bi-literate materials and experiences, and following a sophisticated research sequence. They are expected to display skills at using reference materials and to articulate their awareness of the reasons for keeping records of reference materials. The research process culminates in a report, wherein children learn to produce a piece of writing in a specific genre at the same time that they are providing the school library with real, researched, referenced information. The research process will be repeatedly initiated by the children as they explore other subject areas in the future.

Bilingualism in this classroom is both a goal and a powerful resource for learning; it is an integral part of their classroom community and a means for children to expand their literate and social experiences. In the study centers and groups, Spanish is used interchangeably with English, so the children learning English can both understand the content in their dominant language and expand their vocabulary and comprehension in their second language. Whenever appropriate, information is recorded in either language, with decisions for language choice made by the children and the teacher. The teacher strives to provide the children with materials in English and Spanish because they expand the children's literate worlds and to use their bilingualism to create interesting, advanced conditions for literacy use and language learning. In general, however, the students' and teacher's bilingualism is used as a resource to expand opportunities to obtain, create, and communicate knowledge and to develop the social relationships so essential to this classroom's work.

The materials in the classroom form part of the collective zone, serving as cultural mediators, helping to extend the amount and type of learning possible for any child. Included in the materials for the Native American unit, for example, are a great number of books, such as information books, legends, cookbooks, music and art books, and many pieces of children's literature of various genres that deal with Native American topics. Many of the books are at an adult level. The children read these books selectively and glean information pertaining to their self-selected topics and specific questions. The books are sometimes difficult, but the teacher assumes that with her assistance the students can read and use them. This point is illustrated by the interaction between Veronica and the teacher, described above. The teacher helped Veronica, a dominant-Spanish speaker and reader, translate and discuss a difficult text from English into Spanish, rather than assuming that Veronica could not handle the information or that she needed an easier task.

Although adult-directed lessons are relatively rare in this classroom, there is definitely adult involvement in the children's work. The teacher's guidance is purposely mediated, almost hidden, embedded in the activities. It is clear that the teacher assumes a variety of roles during the course of a day and even during one theme. These roles can be succinctly described as follows:

1   As *guide and supporter*, the teacher is crucial for helping children take risks, focus their questions and ideas, and translate them into manageable activities, ensuring that each child finds academic success.
2   As *active participant in the learning*, the teacher can research theme topics along with the children, combining her own content questions with demonstrations of the research process.
3   As *evaluator* of the children's individual and collective development, the teacher uses anecdotal records, notations of children's individual interests, and reflections about transcripts from literature study groups, and demonstrates her knowledge about children and learning.
4   As *facilitator*, the teacher utilizes conscious planning of the environment, curriculum, and materials to provide functional and purposeful uses for language, literacy, and learning processes.

All of these teacher roles constitute mediation.

An essential factor contributing to the success of this classroom and its value for interpreting Vygotskian theory is the reality that children have considerable control over virtually all aspects of their own learning experience. They select groups, reading materials, writing topics, theme topics, and language to use for each. They generate their research questions and negotiate their learning tasks with their teacher. The teacher allows and promotes this sharing of power, based on her trust of them as learners. She explains it as follows:

> It's taken a lot of trust to give control to the children, but I think that I've really been rewarded in the long run. The day may not run smoothly, and it may not look organized to people who are not knowledgeable about what is going on in the classroom; but I think the learning that is going on on the children's behalf and on my own is much more genuine and meaningful when it is like that.

The teacher's trust in the children's abilities enables her to set high expectations for them; their trust in her allows them to take risks, experiment, and collaborate with her in learning. Learning in this classroom is not only an individual achievement but a joint accomplishment between adults and children.

Practice informing theory

We have depicted a classroom characterized by a complex but coordinated set of practices that form part of a third-grade curriculum. These practices capture some key elements of Vygotsky's concept of a zone of proximal development but, as we have tried to show, in a broader and much more socially distributed fashion. This classroom contains elements that may exceed Vygotsky's formulation or, at the very least, shed light on how narrowly we may have been interpreting and applying his ideas.

When we examine the practices that constitute our case study it becomes evident that the usual definition of the zone of proximal development is pretty barren; it cannot help interpret what goes on in this diverse, yet systematic, classroom. Limitations are largely overcome when the concept is understood as part of a broader theoretical framework that takes the development of mind in social practice as its central problematic (Minick, 1989). It then becomes clear that the zone is itself a mediating concept, a "connecting" concept, as Bruner (1987) suggested, that helps integrate Vygotsky's more encompassing theoretical view (for more detailed discussions see Minick, 1989; Moll, 1990a; Valsiner, 1988).

One aspect of this broader view is particularly relevant to our case study: the centrality of the concept of mediation to Vygotsky's formulations, including not only social interactions but semiotic mediations. This semiotic emphasis brings with it a focus on meaning as central to human activity (e.g., Bakhurst, 1986) that is often ignored during discussions of the zone. The emphasis is usually on the transmission of skills from adult to child, as is the case with typical classrooms. Yet our case study suggests that a different, more transactional view of the zone is possible, one that focuses on the co-construction of meaning as facilitated by the various activities that make up classroom life.

Central to this formulation is the emphasis on the active child developing the cultural means to assist his or her own development. In our case study the children select topics for study at the beginning of the year, choose books to read and issues to analyze, specify research questions to address, use literacy in various ways as part of classroom activities, create texts for authentic purposes, and publicly display their learning, including the development of novel products, based on their real questions about the world. The role of the adult is to provide mediated assistance, indirect help, that does not displace the direction and control children give to the tasks and activities. The goal of this mediated assistance is to make children consciously aware of how they are manipulating the literacy process, achieving new means, and applying their knowledge to expand their boundaries by creating or reorganizing future experiences or activities. Our case study suggests that an apt definition of the zone, at least as applied to classroom analysis, must include the active child appropriating and developing new mediational means for his or her own learning and development.

Finally, our case study highlights issues about social relationships and teaching that are not usually considered within Vygotskian formulations, especially as they relate to education. We have mentioned the importance of the sharing of control between teacher and students, the development of mutual trust, the importance of the authenticity of materials and tasks, the types of discourse that make up learning events, the use of bilingualism as a resource, and the teacher's and students' perception of their roles as learners. We consider these qualitative issues in educational practice. We studied them holistically, as separate issues and in relation to how they form the classroom's social and cultural system. Our methods included participant observations, interviews of teachers and students, collection of materials, and audiotape and videotape analyses. We find these methods indispensable if the units of study are active subjects within diverse and dynamic social environments. These methods are fully compatible with Vygotsky's developmental emphasis, his insistence on a historical method, and his focus on how humans use cultural resources as tools to transform the present into the future.

Notes

1 This case study formed part of a much broader study that included household observations and close collaboration with teachers for analyzing and developing classroom practices (e.g., Moll & Greenberg, 1990). Portions of this chapter were included in the project's reports to the funding agency, the Office of Bilingual Education and Minority Language Affairs, Department of Education. We appreciate their support.

2 For additional discussions of this key theoretical concept, see, e.g., del Río and Alvarez (1988); Minick (1985, 1987); Moll (1990a); Palacios (1987); Rivière (1984); Rogoff and Wertsch (1984); Tharp and Gallimore (1988); Valsiner (1988); Vygotsky (1978, 1987); Wertsch (1985).

3 Kathryn F. Whitmore conducted these observations. For purposes of this chapter we have collapsed several observations into a description of one representative day, concentrating primarily on language arts activities. We would like to thank the teacher for sharing with us her observations, transcripts of lessons, and the writing of the students. She actively collects data in her own classroom not only as part of her graduate studies but to understand better how she is teaching and how the children are learning. She has been our teacher as well.

4 Readers not familiar with the politics of race in the United States may not know this term. In brief, it is usually meant to depict a school located in a Black or Latino neighborhood that has been made attractive to Anglo-Saxon families because of a special characteristic, for example, an emphasis on teaching with computers. The hope is that these families will voluntarily send their children there to integrate what would otherwise be an ethnically or racially segregated school. Alternatively, desegregation schools may be located in predominantly Anglo neighborhoods, and minority children are bussed into the school. All

desegregation programs receive additional funding and programs, including such personnel as fine arts teachers, counselors, and librarians.

5 Many elementary classrooms use webs, which resemble spider webs in their final design, to record information and questions. Webbing is especially helpful as a visual tool for categorization and organization of ideas. An example of a content theme web is Figure 7.2.

6 Writing workshop is part of a process approach to writing that is becoming common in classrooms in the United States. It involves the following steps: topic selection, composition of a first (rough) draft, sharing the draft with friends and readers, revision of the draft, editing in a conference with the teacher or teacher assistant, illustration if appropriate, and final publication. Final products are usually shelved in the classroom library for open reading.

7 The translation of Lupita's writing is not a literal one. For example, it is difficult to capture invented spellings from one language to another. Consequently, the translation is void of miscues and invented spellings.

References

Bakhurst, D. J. (1986). Thought, speech and the genesis of meaning: on the 50th anniversary of Vygotsky's Myslenie i Rec' [Speech and Thinking]. *Studies in Soviet Thought, 31*, 102–29.

Bruner, J. (1987). Prologue to the English edition. In R. Rieber & A. Carton, (eds.) *L. S. Vygotsky. Collected works* (Vol. 1, pp. 1–16) (N. Minick, transl.). New York: Plenum.

del Río, P., & Alvarez, A. (1988). Aprendizaje y desarollo: la teoría de attividad y la zona de desarollo proximo [Learning and development: activity theory and the zone of proximal development]. In C. Coll (ed.). *Psicología de la educación* [Psychology of education] (pp. 1–34). Madrid: Alianza.

Goodman, Y., & Goodman, K. (1990). Vygotsky in a whole language perspective. In L. C. Moll (ed.). *Vygotsky and education* (pp. 223–50). Cambridge: Cambridge University Press.

Griffin, P., & Cole, M. (1984). Current activity for the future: the zo-ped. In B. Rogoff & J. Wertsch (eds.). *Children's learning in the "zone of proximal development"* (pp. 45–64). San Francisco: Jossey-Bass.

Minick, N. (1985). L. S. Vygotsky and Soviet activity theory: new perspectives on the relationship between mind and society. Unpublished doctoral dissertation, Northwestern University.

Minick, N. (1987). Implications of Vygotsky's theories for dynamic assessment. In C. S. Lidz (ed.). *Dynamic assessment* (pp. 116–40). New York: Guilford Press.

Minick, N. (1989). Mind and activity in Vygotsky's work: an expanded frame of reference. *Cultural Dynamics, 2,* 162–87.

Moll, L. C. (ed.). (1990a). *Vygotsky and education.* Cambridge: Cambridge University Press.

Moll, L. C. (1990b). Introduction. In L. C. Moll (ed.). *Vygotsky and education* (pp. 1–30). Cambridge: Cambridge University Press.

Moll, L. C., & Greenberg, J. (1990). Creating zones of possibilities: combining social contexts for instruction. In L. C. Moll (ed.). *Vygotsky and education* (pp. 319–48). Cambridge: Cambridge University Press.

Palacios, J. (1987). Reflexiones en torno a las implicaciones educativas de la obra de Vygotski [Reflections in terms of the educational implications of Vygotsky's work]. In M. Siguán (ed.). *Actualidad de Lev S. Vygotski* [Actuality of Lev S. Vygotsky] (pp. 176–88). Barcelona: Anthropos.

Rivière, A. (1984). La psicología de Vygotski [The psychology of Vygotsky.] *Infancia y Aprendizaje, 27–28*(3–4), 7–86.

Rogoff, B., & Wertsch, J. (eds.) (1984). *Children's learning in the "zone of proximal development"* (pp. 7–18). San Francisco: Jossey-Bass.

Tharp, R., & Gallimore, R. (1988). *Rousing minds to life: teaching, learning and schooling in social context.* Cambridge: Cambridge University Press.

Valsiner, J. (1988). *Developmental psychology in the Soviet Union.* Sussex, Brighton: Harvester Press.

Vygotsky, L. S. (1978). *Mind in society.* Cambridge, MA: Harvard University Press.

Vygotsky, L. S. (1987). Thinking and speech. In R. Rieber & A. Carton, (eds.), *L. S. Vygotsky. Collected Works* (Vol. 1, pp. 39–285) (N. Minick, transl.). New York: Plenum.

Wertsch, J. V. (1985). *Vygotsky and the social formation of mind.* Cambridge. MA: Harvard University Press.

Chapter 8

What is missing in the metaphor of scaffolding?*

C. Addison Stone

The scaffolding metaphor

In 1976, Wood, Bruner, and Ross (1976) introduced the term *scaffolding* in the context of an analysis of adult–child interaction. They used the term as a metaphor for the process by which an adult assists a child to carry out a task beyond the child's capability as an individual agent. They described scaffolding as consisting of the adult's "'controlling' those elements of the task that are initially beyond the learner's capacity, thus permitting him to concentrate upon and complete only those elements that are within his range of competence." They argued, furthermore, that "the process can potentially achieve much more for the learner than an assisted completion of the task," and that it could result in "development of task competence by the learner at a pace that would far outstrip his unassisted efforts." . . . The mechanism assumed to lead to this success was summarized in a companion paper by Wood and Middleton (1975, p. 190).

> The instruction serves to mark or highlight . . . task appropriate actions, providing [the child] with feedback which, though consistent with his actions, might not be inferred by him alone in the face of the many other competitors for relevance and attention which confront him. As he enacts and perfects such isolated task constituents, uncertainty about what to do and what to anticipate as a consequence of his actions diminishes, at least with regard to a subset of the task. This further frees the child to consider the wider or related task constraints and operations. At best, this process continues until he becomes acquainted with and skilled in all aspects of task activity to the point where he can initiate and control his own behaviour in the absence of an instructor.

In this early analysis of scaffolding, then, emphasis was placed on the

* This is an edited version of a chapter that appeared in *Contexts for learning: sociocultural dynamics in children's development*, Oxford: Oxford University Press, 1993.

adult's role as a support for the child for accomplishing the goal via task analysis and practice with subcomponents. The result was seen as independent functioning on the part of the child.

Limitations of the metaphor

The initial discussions of scaffolding were focused on identifying and describing instances of such interactions and on documenting their effectiveness in instilling new capabilities in the child. At the time, little attention was paid to the mechanism by which this transfer of responsibility from the adult to the child was accomplished.[1] In contrast, more recent discussions of the concept of scaffolding have included a greater emphasis on mechanisms of transfer (variously termed transfer of control, internalization, and appropriation).[2] Much of this work has been influenced directly by the work of Vygotsky.

Although Wood and his colleagues did not draw explicitly on Vygotsky's work when formulating their ideas concerning scaffolding, there are clear parallels to Vygotsky's concept of the "zone of proximal development" (ZPD) (Vygotsky, 1978, 1987). . . . Indeed for many the term scaffolding has come to be synonymous with the process of adult–child interaction within the ZPD.

A persisting limitation of the metaphor of scaffolding, however, relates to the specification of the communicative mechanisms involved in the adult–child interaction constituting the scaffolding process. These mechanisms are crucial to Vygotsky's theoretical framework. The purpose of the present chapter is to highlight some of the specific communicative mechanisms involved in the scaffolding process and, more generally, to explore certain implications of extending a Vygotskian-inspired analysis of scaffolding. These implications include the argument that the effectiveness of interactions (and therefore the potential for new learning) within the ZPD varies as a function of the interpersonal relationship between the participants.

Scaffolding as semiotic interaction

When analyzing the learning that takes place in the ZPD, Vygotsky (1987) argued generally that the mechanism involves the transfer of task responsibility from the social (intermental) level to the individual (intramental) level. In essence, the child's task approach comes to be mediated by the verbal and nonverbal directives provided by the adult during the interaction. This process is not, however, a simple matter of the child's literally "internalizing" the interchange between himself and the adult, as has been implied by some authors. Indeed, it is not even clear what such a process of literal internalization would look like. Instead, Vygotsky appeared to have in mind a much more subtle semiotic process, one that might be called "appropriation of meaning," or "semiotic uptake" (Wertsch & Stone, 1985).

To appreciate the spirit and implications of Vygotsky's analysis of internalization, it is useful to build on concepts from the field of linguistics. . . . One such concept that seems to have some promise as a means of making sense of certain communicative dynamics within the ZPD is that of "prolepsis" (Stone, 1985; Stone & Wertsch, 1984). The term "prolepsis" was introduced into modern psycholinguistics by Rommetveit (1974, 1979). Prolepsis refers to a communicative move in which the speaker presupposes some as yet unprovided information. Rommetveit argued that the use of such presuppositions creates a challenge for the listener, a challenge that forces the listener to construct a set of assumptions in order to make sense of the utterance. When the communication is successful, this set of assumptions recreates the speaker's presuppositions. Thus the listener is led to create for him- or herself the speaker's perspective on the topic at issue.

A simple example of prolepsis is contained in the following dialogue between a tourist and a guard in an art museum.

Tourist: Where is the Impressionist collection?
Guard: (*Pointing to a display case in the distance*) Down the hallway just
              beyond the kitchenware.
Tourist: I beg your pardon.
Guard: Just beyond the Oriental pottery.

In this interchange, the guard makes his opinion about Oriental pottery clear, but he does not do so explicitly. Instead, he presents his perspective by forcing his listener to infer it. The initial referring expression, "the kitchenware," is presumed by the tourist to be a response to his question, but its exact relevance is unclear – hence the request for clarification. The subsequent clarification by the guard then allows the tourist to create the equation between Oriental pottery and kitchenware that the guard has intended to convey. The important point here is that the guard has conveyed information to the tourist by forcing him to seek a meaning for his utterance.

Although many instances of prolepsis during adult–child interactions would not be so provocative as the museum example, the effect of such interactions on the child's understanding of the adult's perspective on the situation at hand may be just as powerful. Indeed, the notion of prolepsis can be readily applied to the interchanges that occur during the adult–child interactions characteristic of scaffolding. During a prototypical interaction (Palincsar, 1986; Palincsar & Brown, 1984; Rogoff & Gauvain, 1986; Wertsch, 1979; Wood & Middleton, 1975) the adult might begin with a general question such as, "What piece goes next?" Then, as necessary, the adult would follow that question with more directed verbal or nonverbal directives that, in effect, provide the meaning presupposed by the initial, general directive. In this way the child comes to understand what was presupposed by the initial directive and is led to construct the adult's under-standing of the task goal and of the appropriate means for achieving the goal.

An example of prolepsis in adult–child interaction may be of use. The example below is taken from a study of mother–child interaction (Rogoff & Gauvain, 1986) in which mothers were asked to assist their preschool chil-dren in placing pictures of everyday objects into groups in preparation for a memory test.

Mother:	(*Picks up the picture of a bucket and holds it in front of the child*) What's that?
Child:	It's a bucket and it helps you carry things and . . .
Mother:	Yeah, and *it helps you clean. (Looks at child*)
Child:	(*Nods and pauses*)
Mother:	(*While adjusting the broom in the box for cleaning materials*) OK, what else, do you see something else that helps you clean?
Child:	(*Watches his mother's hand on the bucket card, then points to the bucket and then to the broom*)
Mother.	(*Nods*) The broom. So it should be put in here. (*Holds the bucket in the cleaning box*)
Child:	(*Takes the bucket from his mother's hand and places it in the correct box*)

In this excerpt the mother is trying to help her child understand that a bucket goes with the partially assembled pile of other "cleaning materials." That is, the mother is trying to help the child see the value of using similari-ties in function as an organizing device. However, the approach is not one of explicit provision of a rule.

The mother's utterance "and it helps you clean" is proleptic in the same sense as the first example. That is, it assumes an understanding on the part of the child of the significance of functional information in this task. The child does not act on her hint for placing the picture, however, so the mother proceeds to help the child see the connection between the information about the object's function that she provided earlier and the correct placement of the broom. In this way, the child is led to place the picture correctly.

More importantly, for our purposes, it can be argued that the child has begun to appreciate the significance in the context of this task of information about an object's function. This goal has been accomplished by juxtaposing an underspecified (i.e., richly presupposing) utterance with its subsequent specification. The mother's initial utterance assumes a perspective on the task and an appropriate solution strategy that must be later spelled out for the child. The child, in turn, by making a connection between his mother's earlier proleptic remark and the task approach that it presupposed, is ex-posed to a new perspective on how to "play the game," which constitutes a heuristic for improving memory. Eventually, through repetitions of similar interchanges, there would be a transfer of responsibility for the memory strategy, a transfer motivated by the proleptic challenges. In the present case, the mother did not adopt this ploy intentionally (though she could have), but that fact does not diminish its potential utility.

The notion of prolepsis is similar in many respects to Grice's (1989)[3] concept of conversational implicature.[4] When introducing this concept, Grice attempted to point to a special class of implications conveyed during speaking. This class consisted of those implications that were conveyed *contextually* rather than logically. The key construct introduced by Grice in this context was termed the *cooperative principle*. Most simply, this principle holds that a speaker, when speaking on a given occasion, should make the contribution appropriate to the context, *and* that a listener should assume that it has indeed taken place. To specify what would count as "appropriate," Grice introduced a set of "conversational maxims," which hold that an utterance should be relevant, true, clear, and only as informative as is required. Grice's insight was to point out that, on the assumption that the maxims are generally obeyed, apparent violations of the maxims serve to convey additional meaning — meaning that is nowhere evident in the actual words uttered.

Grice gave a number of examples of implicatures[5] that illustrate the functioning of the various maxims. For example, note the following exchange (Grice, 1989, p. 32).

Speaker A: Smith doesn't seem to have a girlfriend these days.
Speaker B: He has been paying a lot of visits to New York lately.

In this example, Grice saw the maxim of Relevance at work. At first glance, this maxim appears to have been violated by B. It is actually not the case; and by assuming that B must be saying something that is relevant to the conversation, A is led to infer that B believes that Smith may indeed have a girlfriend in New York. Note that B's words themselves do not in any way imply this situation. It is his utterance *in context*, together with the maxim of Relevance, that invites the intended inference.

The following example illustrates that implicatures can also be created by intentional violations of the maxims (Grice, 1989, p. 37).

> Miss X produced a series of sounds that corresponded closely with the score of "Home Sweet Home."

In this case, the speaker has intentionally violated the maxim of Quantity. That is, he could have said simply:

> Miss X sang "Home Sweet Home."

It is by virtue of recognizing this intentional violation that we are led to infer something about the speaker's opinion of Miss X's performance.

Examples of prolepsis such as those presented earlier can be seen as special cases of conversational implicature. In the case of the museum guard, for example, his intended meaning goes forward only if the visitor assumes that his remark about kitchenware is relevant to the conversation. It differs from Grice's examples of implicature in one crucial respect: The shared context at that point in the conversation is not yet sufficient to allow the implicature to go through. Further specification is necessary, and the listener is motivated to seek it. Here is the element of anticipation characteristic of prolepsis. Thus prolepsis can be seen as a special type of conversational implicature in which the necessary context is specified *after* the utterance rather than before it. What is useful about the notion of prolepsis is its highlighting of the creative or transformative effect of such discourse turns via the communicative tension introduced by the speaker. . . .

In any specific communicative exchange involving constructive comprehension processes such as those sketched by Rommetveit and Grice, the result for the listener is a new perspective on the immediate context, or, a new "situation definition." This situation definition is, of course, not necessarily more sophisticated or more functional. It is merely more consistent with that presupposed by the speaker. However, when this process takes place between an adult, or "expert," and a novice, the result may have both of these characteristics.

In his discussion of prolepsis, Rommetveit (1974, 1979) added one additional element important to the general analysis of conversational inference. He argued not only that the process of prolepsis involves the construction of new understandings of a speaker's intended meaning but also that in situations characterized by what he termed "mutual trust" the process may increase the likelihood that the listener will adopt the speaker's perspective as his own. . . . Rommetveit's argument suggests that the process of creating presuppositions pulls the listener into a new perspective on the situation at hand, one that the listener may adopt as his own. Rommetveit referred to this process as the construction of a greater "intersubjectivity." He argued that the chances of advancing intersubjectivity are far less in situations in which prolepsis is not so centrally involved. Such situations might include instruction that relies on explanation or step-by-step demonstration. . . .

The potential value of exploring the semiotic dimensions of the interactions involved in scaffolding has been stressed by several authors. For example, the importance of a process similar to prolepsis has also been stressed by Rogoff (1986, pp. 32–33):

> In order to communicate successfully, the adult and child must find a common ground of knowledge and skills. Otherwise the two people would be unable to share a common reference point, and understanding would not occur. This effort toward understanding . . . draws the child into a model of the problem that is more mature yet understandable through links with what the child already knows.

Palincsar (1986) also stressed the importance of dialogue during scaffolding, drawing on examples from her own interactional studies of the fostering of reading comprehension via "reciprocal teaching." She argued that dialogue is the means by which support is provided and adjusted, and that it serves the function of "facilitating the collaboration necessary between the novice and the expert for the novice to acquire the cognitive strategy or strategies" (p. 95). . . .

Clearly, the semiotics of scaffolding are complex, and much work remains to be done to flesh out the picture of the communicative mechanisms embodied in successful scaffolding. Conversational implicature in general and prolepsis in particular are only two of many such mechanisms at work during adult–child interactions. . . .

Although the discussion to this point has focused largely on the linguistic dynamics involved in effective scaffolding, the semiotic devices involved are clearly not just verbal. Nonverbal communicative devices (including gestures, eye gazes, and pauses) have long been implicated by others as crucial components of the scaffolding process (Rogoff, 1990; Wertsch, McNamee, McLane, & Budwig, 1980; Wood et al., 1976). The undeniable role of such factors poses a challenge: How can we move beyond the assumption that the "dialogue" constituting scaffolding is verbal to develop an integrative framework capable of incorporating a broader notion of semiotic interactions in scaffolding situations?

A useful first step for such an enterprise is implicit in comments provided by Grice (1989). Although most discussions of his framework (and indeed, the bulk of his own discussion) are focused on implicatures created via speech situations, Grice did not limit his description of the "cooperative principle" and its effects to the verbal domain. He noted, for example, that "talking [is] a special case, or variety of purposive, indeed rational behavior," and that there are "analogues [to the maxims] in the sphere of transactions that are not talk exchanges" (Grice, 1989, p. 28). Thus the construct of implicature can (and should) be broadened to encompass nonverbal interactions as well.

. . . Working out an account of the dynamics involved in nonverbal proleptic challenges may provide a means of understanding the powerful instances of children's learning via observations noted by several cross-cultural researchers interested in scaffolding (John-Steiner, 1984; Rogoff, 1990; Tharp & Gallimore, 1988).

Another issue for the future development of our understanding of the semiotics of scaffolding relates to the role of individual and developmental differences in effective scaffolding. The notions of implicature and prolepsis assume a complex interpretive interchange between individuals. What learner characteristics mediate the effectiveness of such interchanges? What significance should be attributed, for example, to linguistic facility? Contrary to much current opinion, Vygotsky placed considerable emphasis on the role of the child's developmental status and cognitive integrity in the dynamics of the ZPD. . . .

One class of developmental factors that must be considered when a picture of the semiotic dynamics is being developed within the ZPD is the child's growing mastery of the comprehension and use of various linguistic devices. For example, there is some evidence from developmental psycholinguistics of age-related sensitivity to the meanings implicit in verbs encoding the speaker's stance with respect to the message being conveyed (e.g., *may* and *could*). Clearly, the child's mastery of such forms is intimately related to the success of conversational inferences.

Although the discussion so far serves to highlight the need to refine and elaborate our understanding of the mechanisms of effective scaffolding, it should serve also to indicate the potential utility of a semiotic perspective on such interactions. Much of the "work" of scaffolding is accomplished via the close communicative exchanges characteristic of these interactions. The following discussion explores the interpersonal aspects of these exchanges involved in scaffolding.

Interpersonal dimensions of scaffolding

If, as argued above, successful scaffolding involves the construction of shared situation definitions and if such construction involves a process of inference and trust, to use Rommetveit's (1979) terms, we must recognize that these interactions are not occurring between faceless functionaries. For the complex process of inferencing required in implicature and prolepsis to go forward, the individuals involved must share some minimal set of presuppositions about the situation at hand, and the two participants must respect each other's perspectives. The actors are engaged in an interpretive exchange, and the nature of the inferences involved in constructing a shared situation definition is a function of the past, present, and anticipated future interactions between the participants. This sequence, in turn, determines the range of perceived "fair" inferences and the context to be incorporated as ground for the inferences.

When developing a systematic perspective on the social dimension of the semiotics of scaffolding, at least two aspects of social interactions must be distinguished. The first relates to the situationally defined qualities of an interaction, and the second relates to a more enduring dimension of repeated interactions.

In his discussion of social relations, Hinde (1979) defined a relationship as "an intermittent interaction between two people" characterized by (1) interchanges over an extended period of time; (2) some degree of "mutuality" ("the behavior of each takes some account of the behavior of the other"); (3) a continuity between successive interactions; and (4) affective/cognitive as well as behavioral components. In this definition, Hinde has clearly chosen to emphasize the cumulative and enduring qualities of the social interactions constituting a relationship. . . .

These two aspects of a relationship – the current and the enduring – are closely related, both developmentally and situationally. . . . Using this perspective, the social relationships within a scaffolding situation can be seen as involving both a subjective relation defined by the current activity (the "here-and-now") and symbolic qualities of social interchange crystallized out of past interactions. This complex interpersonal context acts as a filter through which an individual's learning opportunities via scaffolding must be viewed.

The interpersonal dimension of scaffolding is receiving increasing attention from scholars. Forman (1989; Forman & Cazden, 1985; Forman & McPhail, 1993) for example, has argued that there is a close correspondence between the initial and evolving nature of the interpersonal relationship between the participants in a peer dyad and the degree of cognitive progress made by a dyad across a series of joint problem-solving sessions. Rogoff (1990), in her analysis of past findings regarding social interactional influences on children's learning, has identified the factors of the relative "status" (authority) and "expertise" of the participants as important determinants of the differential effectiveness of scaffolding across various studies of adult–child and child–child interactions.

The dimensions of authority and expertise highlighted by Rogoff are important components of the critical interpersonal factors that mediate the success of scaffolding. However, additional interpersonal factors must also be considered. One likely candidate in this regard is that of the affective dynamics of the relationship, that is, in Rommetveit's terms, the degree of mutual trust. A similar argument, based on a different set of premises, was presented by Verdonik and associates (Verdonik, Flapan, Schmit, & Weinstock, 1988) with respect to "power plays" between parents and children as a factor in the child's demonstration of competencies. Disagreements regarding who is defining and directing the activity would clearly influence the direction and success of scaffolding.

Another factor that should prove useful in determining the interpersonal dynamics of the ZPD is the symbolic status of the to-be-learned activity in the learner's world. Goodnow (1990), for example, stressed the need to consider the relation of a skill to its explicit or implicit value in a given culture on the one hand and to the individual's social identity within the culture on the other. The important point here is that there are symbolic values attached to ways of seeing and doing that, in turn, influence the participants' interactions in scaffolding situations. From the perspective presented here, this influence is mediated in part via its effect on the participants' provision and uptake of appropriate semiotic challenges. If adults place little value on a particular child's learning of some skill, their interchange in the context of that activity is unlikely to provide the finely tuned directives necessary to encourage the child's inferences. Similarly, if children (or adult learners) place little value on the activity at issue, they are not motivated to engage in inferential interactions.

Although this discussion has, of necessity, only skimmed the surface of the relevant issues, it does serve to highlight the key role of interpersonal dynamics in scaffolding. Surely, one virtue of a semiotic perspective is its clear implication of the importance of these dynamics when mediating the impact of potential scaffolding experiences. Our challenge for the future is the development of a theoretical framework that captures the essential features of this process.

Expanded metaphor

It is obvious that we have come a long way from the initial picture of scaffolding. The early discussions of scaffolding were focused primarily on describing a process of assisting the child in identifying, sequencing, and practicing subgoals for eventual guided assembly. We have moved away from this view of asymmetrical structuring of the passive child through a process of breaking down the task. We see now that scaffolding is a much more subtle phenomenon, one that involves a complex set of social and semiotic dynamics.

Currently, what we have is a picture of a fluid interpersonal process in which the participants' communicative exchanges serve to build a continually evolving mutual perspective on how to conceive the situation at hand. In the above discussion, two aspects of this process in particular have been emphasized. The first is the class of semiotic devices, such as implicature and prolepsis, that serve to encourage an interlocutor to construct and share the speaker's perspective. The second is the mediating influence of interpersonal relations and the social symbol value attached to situations and behaviors in this process of meaning construction. Both of these aspects are crucial components of a comprehensive understanding of the scaffolding process. It is my assumption that attempts to address these and other issues related to the semiotic dimension of scaffolding will prove fruitful conceptually and empirically. I hope that such an approach will help us to appreciate the implications of issues that Vygotsky only sketched for us.

Notes

1 The authors did note that the mechanism must rest on the child's ability to *recognize* the correct problem solution when it is achieved, even if he could not have produced it himself (Wood *et al.*, 1976).
2 Another shift evident in discussions of scaffolding is a move from an emphasis on asymmetrical relations in which the adult is directing the child to an emphasis on mutuality. This trend is evident in terms used to refer to the scaffolding process: guided participation (Rogoff, 1990), instructional conversation (Tharp &

Gallimore, 1988), and guided cooperative learning (Brown & Palincsar, 1989). This issue is discussed later in the chapter.

3 Grice's lectures on conversational implicature were originally delivered in 1967, but they were not published in complete form until 1989.

4 There is still debate among linguists about the exact "boundaries" of Grice's notion of conversational implicature. Thus, for example, whereas Grice distinguished conversational implicature from the more common pragmatic concept of presupposition (Levinson, 1983), Green (1989) has argued that implicature can actually account for presupposition (as well as other notions, such as reference and discourse cohesion).

5 The term "implicature" is used here as a shorthand for "conversational implicature." Actually, Grice distinguished conversational implicature (or, more exactly, "particularized" conversational implicature) from other, more conventional forms of implicature that share the general attribute of being less dependent on the utterance context and more tied to the actual words uttered.

References

Brown, A. L., & Palincsar, A. S. (1989). Guided cooperative learning and individual knowledge acquisition. In L. B. Resnick (ed.). *Knowing, learning and instruction*. (pp. 393–451). Hillsdale, NJ: Lawrence Erlbaum Associates.

Forman, E. A. (1989). The role of peer interaction in the construction of mathematical knowledge. *International Journal of Educational Research*, 13, 55–69.

Forman, E. A., & Cazden, C. (1985). Exploring Vygotskian perspectives in education: the cognitive value of peer interaction. In J. V. Wertsch (ed.). *Culture, communication, and cognition: Vygotskian perspectives* (pp. 323–47). Cambridge: Cambridge University Press.

Forman, E. A., & McPhail, J. (1993). Vygotskian perspectives on children's collaborative problem-solving activities. In E. A. Forman, N. Minick, & C. Addison Stone (eds.). *Contexts for learning: sociocultural dynamics in children's development* (pp. 213–29). Oxford: Oxford University Press.

Goodnow, J. J. (1990). The socialization of cognition. In J. W. Stigler, R. A. Schweder, & G. Herdt (eds.). *Cultural psychology: essays on comparative human development* (pp. 259–86). New York: Cambridge University Press.

Green, G. (1989). *Pragmatics and natural language understanding*. Hillsdale, NJ: Lawrence Erlbaum Associates.

Grice, H. P. (1989). *Studies in the ways of words*. Cambridge, MA: Harvard University Press.

Hinde, R. A. (1979). *Towards understanding relationships*. London: Academic Press.

John-Steiner, V. (1984). Learning styles among Pueblo children. *Quarterly Newsletter of the Laboratory of Comparative Human Cognition, 6*, 57–62.

Levinson, S. C. (1983). *Pragmatics*. Cambridge: Cambridge University Press.

Palincsar, A. S. (1986). The role of dialogue in providing scaffolded instruction. *Educational Psychologist, 21*, 73–98.

Palincsar, A. S., & Brown, A. L. (1984). Reciprocal teaching of comprehension-fostering and comprehension-monitoring activities. *Cognition and Instruction, 1*, 117–75.

Rogoff, B. (1986). Adult assistance of children's learning. In T E. Raphael (ed.). *The contexts of school-based literacy* (pp. 32–3). New York: Random House.

Rogoff, B. (1990). *Apprenticeship in thinking: cognitive development in social context.* New York: Oxford University Press.

Rogoff, B., & Gauvain, M. (1986). Analysis of functional patterns in mother–child instructional interaction. In J. Valsiner (ed.). *The role of the individual subject in scientific psychology* (pp. 261–90). New York: Plenum Press.

Rommetveit, R. (1974). *On message structure: a framework for the study of language and communication.* New York: Wiley.

Rommetveit, R. (1979). On codes and dynamic residuals in human communication. In R. Rommetveit & R. M. Blakar (eds.). *Studies of language, thought, and verbal communication* (pp. 163–75). Orlando, FL: Academic Press.

Stone, C. A. (1985). Vygotsky's developmental model and the concept of proleptic instruction: some implications for theory and practice in the field of learning disabilities. *Research Communications in Psychology, Psychiatry, and Behavior, 10*, 129–52.

Stone, C. A., & Wertsch, J. V. (1984). A social interactional analysis of learning disabilities remediation. *Journal of Learning Disabilities, 17*, 194–9.

Tharp, R. G., & Gallimore, R. (1988). *Rousing minds to life: teaching, learning, and schooling in social context.* New York: Cambridge University Press.

Verdonik, F., Flapan, V., Schmit, C., & Weinstock, K. (1988). The role of power relationships in children's cognition: its significance for research on cognitive development. *Quarterly Newsletter of the Laboratory of Comparative Human Cognition, 10*, 80–4.

Vygotsky, L. S. (1978). *Mind in society.* Cambridge, MA: Harvard University Press.

Vygotsky, L. S. (1987). *Thinking and speech.* In R. W. Rieber & A. S. Carton (eds.). *The collected works of L. S. Vygotsky. Vol. 1. Problems of general psychology* (N. Minick, translator). New York: Plenum (originally published in 1934).

Wertsch, J. V. (1979). From social interaction to higher psychological processes: a clarification and application of Vygotsky's theory. *Human Development, 22*, 1–22.

Wertsch, J. V., & Stone, C. A. (1985). The concept of internalization in Vygotsky's account of the genesis of higher mental functions. In J. V. Wertsch (ed.). *Culture, communication, and cognition: Vygotskian perspectives* (pp. 162–79). New York: Cambridge University Press.

Wertsch, J. V., McNamee, G. D., McLane, J. G., & Budwig, N. A. (1980). The adult–child dyad as a problem-solving system. *Child Development, 51*, 1215–21.

Wood, D., & Middleton, D. (1975). A study of assisted problem solving. *British Journal of Psychology, 66*, 181–91.

Wood, D., Bruner, J. S., & Ross, G. (1976). The role of tutoring in problem solving. *Journal of Child Psychology and Psychiatry, 17*, 89–100.

Experimental studies of collaborative learning and peer interaction

Part III

Experimental studies of
collaborative learning and
communication

Chapter 9

Cognitive approaches to group work*

Paul Light and Karen Littleton

In this chapter we shall give an account of research on cognitive development, conducted over the last fifteen years or so, which has addressed whether, when and how peer interaction facilitates children's learning and problem-solving and cognitive development. Other possible benefits of collaboration, such as its impact on children's social development or communication skills, will not be considered here, although we fully recognize their importance. Likewise we recognize that in classroom situations the continuing role of the teacher in structuring and managing group work may be of prime importance, but the studies to be discussed here focus only on the constructive processes of inter-action within small groups of children working autonomously. Classroom management of these groups raises issues which go beyond the present chapter (see Mercer and Fisher, 1992).

As with much of developmental psychology, our story starts with Piaget and his successors in the Genevan school. The first substantive section of the chapter will deal with the Piagetian legacy, and the idea of 'socio-cognitive conflict' as an explanation for the facilitation of cognitive development through peer interaction. As we shall see, the concept of 'constructive conflict' has played a key role in research in this field. The following section will cover the subsequent enrichment of this idea to encompass the role of social norms and expectations, under the label 'social marking'. We shall then broaden our range a little, moving away from Piagetian tasks to consider evidence relating to peer facilitation across a wide range of ages and types of cognitive task. Here we shall draw increasingly on the psychological perspective associated with the Russian psychologist Vygotsky, which emphasizes processes of mutual construction of knowledge and understanding.

As its title suggests, we shall concentrate in this chapter upon 'cognitive approaches', namely approaches which address the question of how group work impacts upon the intellectual skills and processes involved in children's

---

* This is an edited version of a chapter that appeared in *Groups in schools*, London: Cassell, 1994.

learning. Nevertheless, in our conclusion we shall draw on some recent findings to suggest that the analyses of cognitive processes in peer interaction cannot be pursued very far in isolation from the social, motivational and emotional dimensions of such interaction.

The research which we will be presenting in this chapter has not been directed primarily at influencing classroom practice. Nonetheless, there may be some implicit messages for how such practice might best be managed. We hope that familiarity with this research may inform (though it cannot prescribe) the way that teachers utilize group work in support of children's education.

Egocentrism and socio-cognitive conflict

Piaget began his research on the development of human understanding in the 1920s, and continued his work in the field for almost sixty years. Not surprisingly, then, 'Piaget's theory' is not a single, coherent position, and there are significant shifts of emphasis at different periods. The work for which Piaget is best known in the English-speaking world dates mostly from the 1940s to the 1960s. In this period he was intent on an exercise he called 'genetic epistemology', namely the production of an account of human reasoning in terms of its genesis or course of development. The detailed stage-by-stage account which resulted gave little attention to the question of what particular types of experience were necessary to induce progress. Where particular experiences were referred to, these tended to be encounters between the child and the physical world – for example, counting objects and then counting them again in a different order and then discovering that the number remained the same. Very little attention was paid to the social dimensions of experience, so that the Piagetian child could be seen almost as a solo child-scientist, single-handedly (re)discovering physics and mathematics by grappling with the puzzles and paradoxes of the natural world.

This is something of a parody of Piaget's position, of course, but it serves to contrast this later Piagetian work with his earliest researches conducted in the 1920s and 1930s. In these early studies, based for the most part on observations of his own children, Piaget developed the key concept of egocentrism. In his work both on *The Language and Thought of the Child* (1926) and on *The Moral Development of the Child* (1932), Piaget saw the principal barrier to the pre-school child's progress as being an inability to 'decentre': to take account of other people's points of view. The egocentric child, he suggested, does not understand the relativity of points of view, and takes his or her own view for reality. This egocentrism limits moral thinking and communication in fairly obvious ways, but also limits cognitive development in other more subtle ways. Since children cannot appreciate that the first thing that strikes them about a problem might not be the only way the problem can be thought about, they cannot reflect on alternatives or understand how different factors might interact with one another. Importantly, Piaget saw this egocentrism of children's thinking as being overcome through social experience of a particular kind.

The child's relations with adults (whether parents or others) were seen by Piaget as inherently asymmetrical, and the difference in power and status was such that children could not balance their own views against those of adults. But in more symmetrical relationships between the child and his or her peers, differences of viewpoint could provide both a divergence of views (different 'centrations' which would conflict with one another) and the social pressure to reach a resolution of this difference of view. By integrating the partial centrations in a higher-level perspective embracing both, the children could resolve their differences. Thus peer interaction was seen to hold a very special potential for helping egocentric ('pre-operational') children to overcome their egocentrism and make progress towards higher-level ('operational') thinking.

This idea lay dormant for many years, little explored in subsequent work either by Piaget or by his co-workers. But in the 1970s, at a time when social psychology was establishing itself in Geneva, these social dimensions of Piaget's theory began to be explored systematically. In these studies some of the 'hallmark' tests of operational thinking devised by Piaget in his later work were used to explore the argument that he had himself advanced many years earlier regarding the facilitatory role of peer interaction.

The principal architect of these experiments in peer interaction with Piagetian tasks was Willem Doise, together with his research associates Gabrial Mugny and Anne-Nelly Perret-Clermont. They worked extensively with a task which very obviously involved 'points of view', since it involved spatial rearrangements. The child's ability to co-ordinate different points of view was for Piaget a key index of the overcoming of egocentrism (Piaget and Inhelder, 1956). The 'three mountains' task (in which children had to reconstruct different views of an array of three papier-mâché mountains) became one of the best known 'indicators' of the achievement of decentred operational thinking.

In the version of the task used by Doise and colleagues (see Figure 9.1), a child was presented with an arrangement of model buildings on a cardboard base, making up a little village. The buildings were oriented in relation to a fixed mark on the base, such as a village pond. Another table stood to the side of the child, with another base, but this had no buildings on it, only the fixed mark. This might be in the same position vis-à-vis the child (Figure 9.1a) or, for example, rotated 180 degrees (Figure 9.1b). The child's task was to reconstruct the village using a second set of pieces on the second base in such a way that the buildings all stood in the same relation to the pond as they did in the original village. The task is fairly easy if the fixed mark is in the 'same' position on the second base as on the first, but much more difficult if it has been rotated relative to the child. Children's difficulties with this type of task

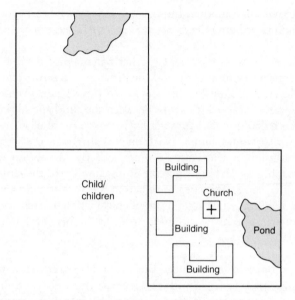

(a) Pond in same position for children viewing two tables

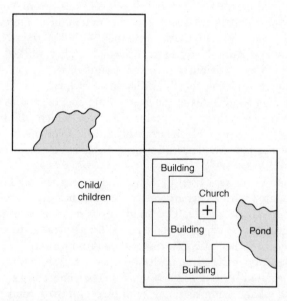

(b) Pond rotated 180 degrees

Figure 9.1a and b Village representations (adapted from Doise and Mugny, 1984)

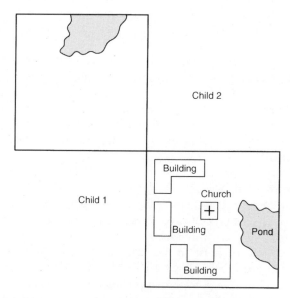

(c) Pond in same position, children in different positions

Figure 9.1c Village representations (adapted from Doise and Mugny, 1984)

can be used as an index of their egocentrism, since correct solution depends on the children decentring from their own point of view, allowing the fixed mark to provide the point of reference for placements.

Doise and colleagues (e.g. Doise and Mugny, 1984) used a three-step experimental design to investigate the effects of peer interaction on children's responses to this task. The first (pre-test) step involved all children being tested individually to establish their level of development in relation to the task. On the second step some children (the control group) were assigned to working alone again, while others (the experimental group) worked in pairs. Finally, the third step of the procedure (post-test.) involved all the children working alone again. This design allowed the researchers to ask two experimental questions. First, will the children who work together on step 2 produce better performances than those who work alone? Second, will those who worked together on step 2 show better individual performance at post-test than those who worked alone at step 2?

These two questions are both of interest, of course. In terms of the first question, there may be many situations in which the performance of the group as a group is the important thing for a teacher to foster. But the concerns of researchers in this area, and of teachers in many cases, have focused mainly on the second question, namely whether the experience of working in a pair will be of value in terms of subsequent individual performance. Here, perhaps, we see the influence of our profoundly individualistic culture!

Doise and colleagues experimented with a number of arrangements in these studies. They pre-tested children and retained only those who could solve simple versions of the task, where although the child had to turn through 90 degrees to look from one table to the other, the fixed mark was in the same position vis-à-vis the child on each of the tables. Their performances on the more complex items involving further rotations of the fixed mark were classified in three levels, from failure to take any account of such rotations (Level 1), through partial adjustment to such rotations (Level 2) to fully correct performance (Level 3).

Doise and Mugny (1984) report two studies which will serve to exemplify their work with this type of task. In the first, they pre- and post-tested 100 children aged 5–7 years individually, and in between allowed some of them (randomly chosen) to work on the task alone while others worked in pairs. The pairs included Level 1–Level 1 pairs, Level 1–Level 2 pairs and Level 1–Level 3 pairs. The partners were always from the same school class and were of the same gender. The pre- and post-tests took place about ten days before and after the experimental phase. Results showed that Level 1 subjects made rather little progress when paired with other Level 1 subjects, but also rather little when paired with Level 3 subjects. They made considerable gains when paired with a Level 2 partner. It seemed that the Level 3 subjects were rather sure of themselves and imposed their solution without much discussion, whereas the Level 1–Level 2 pairs were characterized by much more conflict and negotiation.

A second experimental design entailed creating conflicting points of view not by taking children at different levels but by placing children of the same cognitive level in different positions with respect to the array. With the tables corner to corner (see Figure 9.1c), it is possible to arrange the children's positions so that a child in one of the 'bays' has a 'simple' transposition to deal with while the child in the opposite bay has a complex rotation. If Level 1 subjects are paired together, each of them will try to impose a simple translation of positions, and these will conflict with one another, one being a correct solution and the other an incorrect solution.

Doise and Mugny (1984) report a study in which they compared pre- to post-test progress of Level 1 children, some of whom worked in pairs trying to tackle the problem together from different positions, while others worked alone but were able to move from one position to the other as they worked. The paired children made significantly more progress, lending further support to the idea that it is socio-cognitive conflict (the holding of different points of view by different partners in a social interchange) that holds the key to progress.

The other task which Doise and colleagues (but most especially Perret-Clermont, 1980) used for these experiments was the conservation task. In its best-known form this involves establishing the equality of amounts of liquid in two identical beakers and then pouring the contents of one of them into a differently shaped beaker, so that the liquid level is noticeably higher or lower. Then the child is asked whether the amounts of liquid in the two containers are still the same. Pre-operational children judge them not to be, basing their response on liquid level or some other salient cue (e.g. 'this jar's fatter'). In a similar way, Piaget's research indicated that young children do not appreciate that the length of a stick remains the same despite displacements of position, or that the weight (mass) of, say, a ball of clay remains the same despite changes in shape.

Perret-Clermont used the same three-step design as was used for the 'village' studies. For children assigned to the interactive condition at the second stage, she explored various arrangements. One which proved effective was to have three children work together. Two were selected as having shown a grasp of conservation at pre-test, the third was a non-conserver. The third child was then given a jug of juice and the task of sharing the juice equally between the three of them in variously shaped beakers, so that they would all agree that they had the same. Non-conserving children exposed to this experience not only succeeded with their partners in achieving 'fair shares', but typically went on to perform well on the individual post-test.

This arrangement involves a conflict between pre-operational and operational responses to the task, but progress was also demonstrated in situations where two different pre-operational centrations were brought into conflict. Thus with two rulers initially aligned with one another, children will agree that they are the same length. If one is then displaced relative to the other, children in different seating positions may both suppose the lengths to be different, but disagree as to which is now longest. Doise and Mugny (1984) report that such contradictions of equally wrong answers (whether offered by a child or an adult) can be effective in producing progress towards higher-level 'conserving' responses which resolve the lower-level conflicts.

These studies thus lent considerable weight to the idea that peer facilitation could have rather dramatic effects on children's cognitive development, and to the idea that such benefits could be explained in terms of socio-cognitive conflict. They also helped to stimulate a much wider interest in research on the facilitatory effects of peer interaction, including much of the research discussed in the remainder of this chapter. However, as is so often the case, the initially rather simple story these studies seem to tell has become a good deal more complicated as further research has accumulated.

Peer interaction and social marking

In part the need for some reappraisal of the interpretation of peer facilitation effects in terms of socio-cognitive conflict was suggested by the very effectiveness of peer interaction. For example, with conservation, it appeared that a session of only ten or twenty minutes of peer interaction around a conservation problem was often enough to shift a child from non-conserving to conserving responses. This shift is, in Piagetian terms, one of the major hurdles on the path to operational thinking, so it seems remarkable that it can be achieved so readily, with children even showing generalization to types of conservation not addressed in the group session (Perret-Clermont, 1980). Moreover, social class differences in children's responses were rather marked at pre-test, with middle-class children showing a significantly greater frequency of conserving responses, but this difference disappeared by post-test. Can we really suppose that the effects of years of differential socialization can be eclipsed by ten or twenty minutes of peer interaction?

An alternative explanation is that in some way or another the experience of working together with other children on the task changes the way the children understand the questions. The work of Margaret Donaldson (1978) and others suggests strongly that children often fail Piagetian tests not because they cannot work out the answer but because they misunderstand the question that they are being asked. With the conservation task, for example, the way in which the experimenter deliberately draws the child's attention to an irrelevant cue (e.g. by pointedly pouring the juice into different-shaped containers for no apparent reason) may lead the child to interpret the task in terms of appearances (which looks more now?) rather than in terms of actual amounts. In the peer interaction situation, where the children are sharing juice amongst themselves, this misleading cue is not available, and the need to establish fairness of distribution keeps the children's attention firmly focused upon the actual amounts. So it may be, as Light and Perret-Clermont (1989) have argued, that the standard individual pre-test actually gives a misleadingly poor impression of the abilities of the children, while the peer interaction condition allows them to be clearer about what is expected of them and thus to show themselves to better advantage.

One way of paraphrasing this argument is to say that it is the social norms or conventions associated with 'fair shares' that help the children to sort out what the task is about. In fact one of the main ways in which the work of Doise and his colleagues has developed since 1980 has involved recognition of the pervasive role of such norms and conventions. Doise uses the phrase 'social marking' to refer to the way that the ease or difficulty of a cognitive task can be affected by the extent to which it can be mapped on to social norms or rules with which the child is familiar.

In the case of the spatial rearrangement (village) task, social marking has been explored by, for example, replacing the houses, pond, etc. with a model classroom with pupils' desks facing the teacher's desk (the fixed mark). With these materials, if the children rearrange the materials incorrectly, the children will no longer be facing the teacher. Thus the usual cognitive strategy of the Level 1 or Level 2 child will lead to a conflict with certain social conventions which these Swiss children all shared. How this would work with British primary school children, accustomed to very different classroom organizations, is an open question!

Doise (1990) describes studies in which, for example, children are pre- and post-tested on the village tasks, while in between some of them have experience (alone or in pairs) with either the village materials or the classroom materials. Because the children were at the same level and shared the same physical relationship to the materials, not much progress was expected for those who worked with the village materials, and indeed not much was found. But the children who worked with the classroom materials did better, especially those who worked as pairs, and they carried over this advantage to the standard individual post-test a week or so later.

Another direction of work explored by Mugny et al. (1984) involved having an adult oppose a child's judgements in the interaction phase of the study. With the village materials, children usually gave way to adults, even when the adult was wrong. With the classroom materials, on the other hand, children tended to hold on to their own ideas more strongly, and argued for them even when the adult disagreed. In this condition, the children made significantly greater pre- to post-test progress than with the village materials.

In this more recent Genevan account, therefore, the effects of immediate face-to-face interaction between children working together on a task cannot be considered in isolation from the framework of social benefits and expectations that the participants bring to the situation. Peer interactions, in other words, are themselves seen to be conditioned by their social context.

Meanwhile, as we shall show in the next section, the initial studies of Doise et al. had begun to spawn a much wider interest in experimental research on peer interaction. This new research took from the Genevan work a general experimental approach (the three-step design, with individual pre- and post-tests) and a concern with the possible role of conflict. On the other hand, the non-Genevan research has typically shown much less interest in the Piagetian repertoire of tasks, and a much less exclusive concern with children at the boundary between pre-operational and operational thinking.

Peer interaction and problem solving

One of the tasks long beloved of cognitive psychologists interested in problem solving is the 'Tower of Hanoi'. This is usually presented in the form of a board with three vertical pegs in it; over one peg is slipped a number of different-sized tiles, with the largest at the bottom and the smallest at the top so that they form a pagoda-shaped stack (see Figure 9.2). The task is to

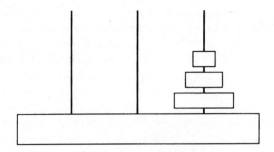

Figure 9.2 Original set-up of 'Tower of Hanoi'

dismantle the 'pagoda' and re-form it on one of the other pegs, but with the constraints that only one tile can be moved at a time and that a larger tile may never be placed on a smaller one. With three tiles, the problem is soluble in a minimum of seven moves.

Our own first exploration of peer interaction effects on problem solving began with this task (Glachan and Light, 1982: Light and Glachan, 1985). We pre-tested individual children, aged about 8, and then assigned them at random to either a control condition where they worked alone or an experimental condition where they worked in pairs, sitting opposite one another with the board between them. We then post-tested them all individually with a slightly different version of the task. In the first study, we obtained no evidence that the children who worked together gained any advantage from doing so. However, when we looked at what they were doing this offered no surprise. They were simply taking turns, having one move or a whole trial each, but taking little interest when it was 'not their go'. So we attached little handles to each side of the tiles and tried again with a rule which stipulated that they must co-operate on all moves and that no move could be made unless the two children moved the tile together. Under these conditions we did get evidence that children who worked together did better, and carried over some of this advantage to individual post-test.

We followed this up with a study in which the same task was presented on a computer. The children had to key in numbers to signal which tile they wanted to move where. Again, it was only when we modified the software so that both children had to key in each move that we saw any benefit for the children who worked together (Light *et al.*, 1988). What counts, seemingly, is for the children to be engaged with one another as well as with the task. Blaye (1988) came to the same conclusion on the basis of a series of studies involving 5- and 6-year-olds in a matrix-filling task presented to them on computer. Whilst the experience of working in a pair often led to greater individual progress than working alone, this was particularly noticeable when one of the children was required to indicate their choice with a lightpen while the other had to affirm their consent by using the keyboard. Once again it is co-ordinating the roles of the children that seems to be important.

In our own work we have experimented with a number of other computer-presented 'puzzles', one being a computer version of the pegboard code-breaking game 'Mastermind'. The computer generated a digital code sequence which the children had to 'break' by trying out different sequences and getting feedback (Light and Glachan, 1985). In this study the children who worked together again enjoyed some advantage over those who worked alone. In an attempt to understand the basis of this facilitation we tape-recorded the interaction between the children. We looked in particular for 'arguments', i.e. sequences where the children were offering differing sugges-tions as to what move to make next, and where at least one of them was offering some kind of justification. As it happened, such arguments were fairly common in about half of the pairs and rather scarce in the other half. The improvement of children's scores from pre-test to post-test was signifi-cantly greater in those pairs who engaged in frequent argument than it was for the remainder.

This study then offered some support for the view that 'socio-cognitive conflict', or at least disagreement, may be a necessary condition for progress in peer interaction situations. More evidence comes from a more recent series of studies by Christine Howe and colleagues at Strathclyde. These were con-ducted with secondary school-aged pupils using computer-based tasks related to the physics curriculum. The design of these studies has followed the famil-iar pattern of individual pre-tests and post-tests, and in between a session in which children work together in pairs or small groups.

Howe et al. (1991), in a study concerning trajectories of objects dropped from planes, formed pairs on the basis of pre-test responses such that students (12- and 14- year-olds) in a pair were either similar or different in terms of their initial predictions and conceptions. The pairs which showed the greatest pre- to post-test gains were those where the students differed both in terms of their predicted trajectories and the conceptions on which these predic-tions were based. In a subsequent study (Howe et al., 1992) the researchers differentiated between the actual judgements subjects made and the strategies they used in approaching the problem. In this case the problem concerned comparison of the speed of two trains under various conditions. One train (on the computer screen) ran at a constant speed, while the other accelerated or decelerated, with variations of direction, starting position and so on. Subjects were undergraduates. Pre-tests were used to establish the judgements made and strategies used by each subject, and then the pairs were made up so that the partners were either similar or different in judgements or strategies. The most productive group combination in terms of conceptual change was where partners differed in both strategy and judgement. How-ever, in this instance, the next most productive arrangement was where the partners were similar in both judgements and strategies, this being apparently more effective than where partners differ on only one of these dimensions. Although Howe and colleagues offer some speculations about how this comes about, it seems on the face of it a rather puzzling outcome.

While the work of Howe and colleagues lends support to the idea that socio-cognitive conflict may be the key ingredient in peer facilitation of learning, other researchers have raised more doubts about this and have criticized the concept of conflict as vague and ill-defined (Blaye, 1988). Some researchers have found that interaction between children at the same level is actually sometimes the most effective situation. Thus, for example, Light *et al.* (1994) found with a detour problem-solving task couched as a computer adventure game that working with a partner of the same pre-test score level was more effective than working with a lower-level or a higher-level partner. So, there appear to be at least some circumstances under which learners need to be evenly matched to maximize the productivity of the interaction. It may be that the fact that the task was wholly novel for both partners was important here: they were not coming to the situation with well-formed views of how the problem should be tackled, as they were in the case of Howe *et al.*'s study. In these circumstances, collaborative gains may have more to do with joint construction of understanding than with decentring through conflict in Doise's sense. In the next section we shall consider other research which bears on this issue.

Co-construction and the role of talk

Before turning to the main theme of this section, we ought to give brief consideration to an issue which may well have struck the reader by this stage, namely why computers seem to figure such a lot in this literature. In some ways this seems paradoxical, since computers were introduced into educational thinking back in the 1960s and 1970s largely in terms of a vision of individualized education. But the reality in schools, especially primary schools, is that most use of computers is by pairs or small groups often working collaboratively at the keyboard, largely independently of the teacher. Indeed, it seems that this may prove to be their greatest strength. Teachers have long seen advantages in group work, but the logistics of the classroom often militate against these advantages being realized. Research by Galton *et al.* (1980) and Bennett (1987) has revealed that, whilst children in classrooms may commonly be seen sitting together in groups, closer observation reveals that their mode of working is rarely collaborative – the children are typically found working 'in parallel' rather than in co-operation. There are indications, both in the classroom observation literature and in the experimental literature (see review by Light and Blaye, 1990), that computers may offer at least part of the answer, by providing sufficient structure and responsiveness to maintain the effective functioning of the group with the minimum of teacher intervention. This consideration, together with the practical advantages for the researcher of running experiments on the computer, has led to a heavy concentration in the peer interaction literature on facilitation of computer-based learning and problem solving.

We began this chapter with Piaget whose theory of cognitive development had such massive influence upon contemporary thinking. But there is, today, a countervailing influence represented by the Russian psychologist L. S. Vygotsky. . . . Vygotsky's work directs attention most obviously to asymmetrical interactions, between more and less expert individuals. His theory offers an account of tutoring, and draws attention to the fact that most of what children have to learn the adults around them already know. But the concepts of negotiation of meaning and co-construction of shared understanding can be applied to peer interaction as well as to adult–child interaction. They lead us to consider collaborative rather than conflictual processes, and in particular to focus on the constructive role of discussion.

Much of the research on peer interaction conducted within this tradition has been classroom-based, and has involved larger groups than the twos and threes typically used in the more experimental neo-Piagetian tradition. Greater 'ecological validity' gained by working in more naturalistic conditions is won at the cost of some control over the conditions of working, and such studies rarely include individual pre- and post-testing or individual control conditions.

Some studies have eschewed measuring 'cognitive outcomes' altogether and have focused instead on developing criteria for discussing the variety and 'educational quality' of talk arising during children's collaborative work. Dawes et al. (1992), for example, investigated the nature of primary school children's talk when they are working together at the computer and identified three qualitatively different types of talk in their data: disputational, cumulative and exploratory talk. Disputational talk is effectively unproductive disagreement. Such talk is characterized by an initiation (e.g. proposition, hypothesis, instruction) followed by a challenge (be this a direct rejection or a counter-proposition/hypothesis). Such challenges typically lack clear resolution or else result in resolution which is not supported by agreement. Cumulative talk simply adds uncritically to what has gone before. Initiations are typically accepted either without discussion or with only superficial amendments. In contrast, however, exploratory talk demonstrates the active joint engagement of the children with one another's ideas. Whilst initiations may be challenged and counter-challenged, appropriate justifications are articulated and alternative hypotheses offered. Where alternative accounts are offered they are developments of the initiation. Progress thus emerges from the joint acceptance of suggestions. Whilst Dawes et al. acknowledge that all three types of talk are appropriate in certain circumstances, they maintain that exploratory talk offers a potential for learning over and above that offered by the other categories. According to this analysis, then, collaborative activities should be designed to foster children's use of exploratory talk.

Other researchers have also put considerable resources into analysing the verbal exchanges and patterns of interactions in medium-sized groups (six or so). Thus, for example, Celia Hoyles and colleagues (Hoyles and Sutherland, 1989: Hoyles *et al.*, 1990) have made very detailed observational studies of groups of children working on an extended LOGO project in the context of their mathematics work. LOGO is a computer programming language, being used in this case to support 'Turtle graphics' – with children controlling the movements of a screen 'turtle' to produce geometric figures of various kinds. According to these researchers the critical role for discussion comes when there is some kind of mismatch between what a student is attempting to achieve and what their partner will allow or comprehends. The pivotal role for discussion between learners is said to occur when such 'conflict' arises, for it is here that the different perceptions of the problem and its solution have to be negotiated, articulated and made compatible within the demands and constraints of the task. Note that here the term 'conflict' is used in a wider sense than that intended by Doise and colleagues, being rather closely related to that of negotiation.

Negotiation and verbally explicit pre-planning are central to the analysis of interaction in problem solving offered by Barbieri and Light (1992). In this study we were able to show that pairs who negotiated most explicitly and made most extensive use of verbal pre-planning while working collaboratively on a detour task tended to be the most successful at individual post-test. However, such correlations do not provide unambiguous evidence that the quality of discussion which children engage in directly affects the quality of learning outcomes. It remains possible, for example, that it was the fact that particular children had 'cracked the task' that shaped the discussion, rather than vice versa. Sorting out cause and effect in this area is not easy. In our own work we are trying to replicate these findings in a study with pre- as well as post-test data, to see how far the verbal interaction measures predict gains as opposed to absolute levels of task performance. There have been some attempts to partial out prior abilities in this way. Webb *et al.* (1986), for instance, investigated the way in which 'explanations' were associated with learning outcomes amongst pupils learning programming. They found that the frequency of both giving and receiving explanations was associated with learning achievements.

In fact, getting children to talk their way through a problem without a partner present can itself be helpful to problem solving (Fletcher, 1985), while on the other hand some advantage can accrue to groups of students who work together on a problem even when they are not allowed to talk at all (e.g. Jackson *et al.*, 1992). So while language is part of the story, and probably a large part, it is certainly not all of it. A good deal more work will need to be done before we fully appreciate the ways language functions in facilitating understanding.

Limitations of a purely cognitive approach

As Hoyles *et al.* (1992) have noted, the majority of studies investigating effective group work have neglected interpersonal variables within the pairs or groups of children, such as the children's individual characteristics and self-perceptions, and their perceptions of one another, and of the task itself. Others have also remarked on the neglect of issues such as the relative status of pupils (Laborde, 1988) and other social psychological considerations which might affect performance (e.g. Saloman and Globerson, 1989), as well as the role of training for interaction.

Moreover, as indicated previously, some studies (e.g. Jackson *et al.*, 1992) have come up with findings which challenge any supposition that interaction and discussion alone underpin the beneficial effects of group work. Indeed, our own work investigating children's computer-based problem solving has revealed that working in the presence of other children who are similarly engaged can be facilitative even if the children are working on different machines without any overt interaction (Light *et al.*, 1994).

A striking paper by Robinson-Stavely and Cooper (1990), involving computer-based learning in adults with little computer experience, high-lights the effects of mere presence of a peer and draws attention to the power of expectancy of success in influencing both performance and the response to others in the learning situation. In their first study Robinson-Stavely and Cooper asked male and female students to complete a difficult computer task and a series of questionnaires in either the presence or the absence of another person. Those women who worked in the presence of someone else typically performed less well, reporting higher anxiety and expressing more negative attitudes towards computers than those women who were required to work alone. With the men, however, the presence of another person had the opposite effect. In a second study, Robinson-Stavely and Cooper manipulated expectations for success. Some students were given 'feedback' that they were likely to do well and others that they were unlikely to succeed. There was evidence of facilitation for 'positive expectancy' subjects and impairment for 'negative expectancy' subjects, as compared with those subjects who were required to work alone.

What emerges from Robinson-Stavely and Cooper's study is the significance of social comparison rather than simply social facilitation in the learning situation. Social comparison (and more generally the role of social representations in learning) is central to some recent French research (Monteil, 1991, 1992). This has focused on social comparison variables affecting learning in secondary school pupils. In a series of studies generating clear and replicable results, Monteil and colleagues have manipulated actual academic ability levels, inducing expectancies of success in pupils relative to their peers on particular tasks, and varying the public vs. private nature of the subsequent learning situation. Students for whom there is a mismatch (whether positive or negative) between their general academic standing and their induced perception of their own ability relative to their peers show good learning outcomes in private or 'anonymous' learning situations, whereas those who receive 'feedback' matching their expectations learn more effectively in situations where their performance is visible to their peers (Monteil, 1992). Whether the same results would be obtained in a British or North American context, where academic success and failure are typically less strongly 'marked' in schools, remains to be seen.

Monteil and colleagues interpret their results in terms of social comparisons within the peer-based learning situation, and interpret the effects of such comparisons as mediated by emotional responses to the situation, influencing the focusing of attention on task-relevant information. Their studies attest to the powerful influence of social representations (of self and of other) on school children's learning and highlight the need to pay closer attention to the ways in which children working in the various conditions we create construe the task and their own situation and ability in relation to it.

There are limitations, then, on how far we can expect to get with purely cognitive accounts of the benefits of group work. We have seen in this chapter that studies based on the cognitive-developmental theories of Piaget and Vygotsky have taken us a considerable distance in understanding how and when peer interaction facilitates children's understanding. To get much further, we shall need to integrate a fuller understanding of children's social perceptions and emotional responses with our cognitive accounts of 'how group work works'.

Even when we have this fuller picture we should not expect to establish group work as any kind of educational panacea. To the question of whether group work leads to better cognitive outcomes, the answer will always be 'it depends'. The studies we have reviewed in this chapter at least begin to illuminate some of the conditions for productive outcomes. For example, they illustrate the importance of ensuring joint engagement with the task. They also indicate that there will be no overall recipe for pairing or grouping children. For tasks which require children to arrive at correct judgements, interactions may only be productive where group members differ in their initial viewpoints. However, for novel tasks requiring constructive elaboration of solutions not heavily dependent on prior knowledge, balanced pairings are likely to prove more effective. As we foresaw at the outset, we are a long way from being able to prescribe the ways in which group work should be used to maximize cognitive gains. But the emerging research literature will, we hope, provide a valuable resource for teachers reflecting on the role of group work within their own classroom practice.

References

Barbieri, M. S. and Light, P. (1992) Interaction, gender and performance on a computer-based problem solving task. *Learning and Instruction*, 2, 199–214.

Bennett, N. (1987) Co-operative learning: children do it in groups – or do they? *Educational and Child Psychology*. 4, 7–18.

Blaye, A. (1988) Confrontation sociocognitive et résolution de problème. Unpublished doctoral thesis, University of Provence, Aix-en-Provence.

Dawes, L., Fisher, E. and Mercer, N. (1992) The quality of talk at the computer. *Language and Learning*, October, 22–5.

Doise. W. (1990) The development of individual competencies through social interaction. In H. Foot, M. Morgan and R. Shute (eds). *Children Helping Children*. Chichester: Wiley.

Doise, W. and Mugny, G. (1984) *The Social Development of the Intellect*. Oxford: Pergamon Press.

Donaldson, M. (1978) *Children's Minds*. London: Fontana.

Fletcher, B. (1985) Group and individual learning of junior school children on a microcomputer-based task. *Educational Review*. 37, 251–61.

Galton, M., Simon, B. and Croll, P. (1980) *Inside the Primary School*. London: Routledge.

Glachan, M. and Light, P. (1982) Peer interaction and learning. In G. Butterworth and P. Light (eds). *Social Cognition*. Brighton: Harvester Press.

Howe, C., Tolmie, A. and Anderson, A. (1991) Information technology and group-work in physics. *Journal of Computer Assisted Learning*. 7, 133–43.

Howe, C., Tolmie, A., Anderson. A. and MacKenzie, M. (1992) Conceptual knowledge in physics: the role of group interaction in computer-supported teaching. *Learning and Instruction*. 2, 161–83.

Hoyles, C. and Sutherland, R. (1989) *Logo Mathematics in the Classroom*. London: Routledge.

Hoyles, C., Healy, L. and Pozzi, S. (1992) Interdependence and autonomy: aspects of groupwork with computers. *Learning and Instruction*. 2, 239–57.

Hoyles, C., Sutherland, R. and Healy, L. (1990) Children talking in computer environments. In K. Durkin and B. Shire (eds). *Language and Mathematical Education*. Milton Keynes: Open University Press.

Jackson, A., Fletcher, B. and Messer, D. (1992) When talking doesn't help: an investigation of microcomputer-based group problem solving. *Learning and Instruction*. 2, 185–97.

Laborde, C. (1988) Divers aspects de la dimension sociale dans les recherches en didactique des mathématiques. In C. Laborde (ed.). *Actes du premier colloque franco-allemand de didactique des mathématiques et de l'informatique*. Grenoble: La Pensée Sauvage.

Light, P. and Blaye, A. (1990) Computer-based learning: the social dimensions. In H. Foot, M. Morgan and R. Shute (eds). *Children Helping Children*. Chichester: Wiley.

Light, P. and Glachan, M. (1985) Facilitation of problem solving through peer interaction. *Educational Psychology*. 5, 217–25.

Light, P. and Perret-Clermont, A.-N. (1989) Social context effects in learning and testing. In A. Gellatly, D. Rogers and J. Sloboda (eds). *Cognition and Social Worlds*. Oxford: Clarendon Press.

Light, P., Foot, T., Colbourn, C. and McClelland, I. (1988) Collaborative interactions at the microcomputer keyboard. *Educational Psychology*. 7, 13–21.

Light, P., Littleton, K., Messer, D. and Joiner, R. (1994) Social and communicative processes in computer-based problem solving. *European Journal of Psychology of Education*. 9, 93–109.

Mercer, N. and Fisher, E. (1992) How do teachers help children to learn? An analysis of teachers' interventions in computer-based activities. *Learning and Instruction*. 2, 339–55.

Monteil, J.-M. (1991) Social regulation and individual cognitive function: the effects of individuation on cognitive performance. *European Journal of Social Psychology*. 21, 225–37.

Monteil. J.-M. (1992) Towards a social psychology of cognitive functioning. In M. von Granach, W. Doise and C. Mugny (eds). *Social Representation and the Social Bases of Knowledge*. Berne: Hubert.

Mugny, G., DePaolis, P. and Carugati, F. (1984) Social regulation in cognitive development. In W. Doise and A. Palmonari (eds), *Social Interaction in Individual Development*. Cambridge: Cambridge University Press.

Perret-Clermont, A.-N. (1980) *Social Interaction and Cognitive Development in Children*. London: Academic Press.

Piaget, J. (1926) *The Language and Thought of the Child*. London: Routledge.

Piaget, J. (1932) *The Moral Development of the Child*. London: Routledge.

Piaget, J. and Inhelder, B. (1956) *The Child's Conception of Space*. London: Routledge.

Robinson-Stavely, K. and Cooper, J. (1990) Mere presence, gender and reactions to computers. *Journal of Experimental Social Psychology*. 26, 168–83.

Saloman, G. and Globerson, T. (1989) When teams do not function the way they ought to. *International Journal of Educational Research*. 13, 88–99.

Webb, N., Ender, P. and Lewis, S. (1986) Problem-solving strategies and group processes in small groups learning computer programming. *American Educational Research Journal*. 23, 247–61.

Chapter 10

Exploring Vygotskian perspectives in education

The cognitive value of peer interaction*

Ellice A. Forman and Courtney B. Cazden

Two important and related themes in Vygotsky's writings are the social foundations of cognition and the importance of instruction in development:

> An important point to note about Vygotsky's ideas on the social origins of cognition is that it is at this point that he uses the notion of internalization. He is not simply claiming that social interaction leads to the development of the child's abilities in problem-solving, memory, etc.; rather, he is saying that the very means (especially speech) used in social interaction are taken over by the individual child and internalized. Thus, Vygotsky is making a very strong statement here about internalization and the social foundations of cognition.
>
> (Wertsch, 1981, p. 146)

> If all the development of a child's mental life takes place in the process of social intercourse, this implies that this intercourse and its most systematized form, the teaching process, forms the development of the child, creates new mental formations, and develops higher processes of mental life. Teaching, which sometimes seems to wait upon development, is in actual fact its decisive motive force. . . . The assimilation of general human experience in the teaching process is the most important specifically human form of mental development in ontogenesis. This deeply significant proposition defines an essentially new approach to the most important theoretical problem of psychology, the challenge of actively developing the mind. It is in this that the main significance of this aspect of Vygotsky's enquiries lies.
>
> (Leont'ev and Luria, 1968, p. 365)

In all of Vygotsky's writings with which we are familiar, the social

---

* This is an edited version of a chapter that appeared in *Culture, communication and cognition: Vygotskian perspectives*, Cambridge: Cambridge University Press, 1985.

relationship referred to as "teaching" is the one-to-one relationship between one adult and one child. When we try to explore Vygotskian perspectives for education, we immediately confront questions about the role of the student peer group. Even if formal education takes place in a group context only for economic reasons, because no society can afford a teacher for each individual child, the presence of peers should not be ignored or relegated only to discussions of issues in classroom management and control.

We see two separate but related issues concerning the group presence. First, there are the problems posed for the teacher in carrying out direct teaching to a group of students; second, there are the questions raised for the teacher's more indirect planning for the social organization of all work-related talk in the classroom setting, specifically the contribution that peers can make to each other. . . .

Understanding this contribution has both practical and theoretical significance. Practically, despite the fact that school classrooms are unusually crowded social environments, group work is rarely encouraged (Galton, Simon, and Croll, 1980), perhaps in part because there has been no clear rationale for its value. (See Sharan [1980] for one review of arguments and evidence.) Theoretically, most developmental research studies in the United States have traditionally focused on the value of peer interactions in the socialization of behavior and personality and have said less about their possible value for cognition and intellectual learning. . . .

Peer collaboration

. . . Given the focus on individual achievement in most Western industrial societies, curricula that promote collaboration are rarely found in schools or studied by educators or psychologists. The major exception to this generalization is a body of research conducted by a group of Genevan psychologists (Doise, Mugny, and Perret-Clermont, 1975, 1976; Mugny and Doise, 1978; Perret-Clermont, 1980). They have conducted a series of experiments to examine the effect of peer collaboration on logical reasoning skills associated with the Piagetian stage of concrete operations: perspective taking, conversation, and so on.

Most of the Genevan research employs a training study design in which subjects are randomly assigned to treatment or control groups in which they are exposed to different social contexts. For example, the subjects in the treatment group may be asked to solve a conservation task in a small peer group composed of conservers and nonconservers, while subjects in the control group are asked to solve the same problem alone. All subjects are individually pretested and posttested on some standard measure of concrete-operational reasoning, and the effect of exposure to peer collaboration is assessed by comparing the pretest-to-posttest gains in concrete-operational reasoning found in each group. The Genevans have employed this same training study design across a number of studies in which the particular reasoning task chosen, the social groups assembled, and the criteria used to evaluate cognitive growth are systematically varied. After reviewing this entire body of research, Perret-Clermont (1980) concludes that peer interaction enhances the development of logical reasoning through a process of active cognitive reorganization induced by cognitive conflict. She claims also that cognitive conflict is most likely to occur in situations where children with moderately discrepant perspectives (e.g., conservers and transitional subjects) are asked to reach a consensus.

Two Russian researchers, Lomov (1978) and Kol'tsova (1978), and two Japanese investigators, Inagaki and Hatano (Inagaki, 1981; Inagaki and Hatano, 1968, 1977) have reached similar conclusions – that peer interaction helps individuals acknowledge and integrate a variety of perspectives on a problem, and that this process of coordination, in turn, produces superior intellectual results. For Kol'tsova, the results are precise, rich, and logically rigorous definitions of a social science concept. For Inagaki and Hatano, the results are generalizable and stable conservation concepts. For Perret-Clermont, the results are increased ability to use concrete operational logic.

In none of these studies were subjects' interactions during collaborative problem solving systematically observed. The studies provide only anecdotal evidence to support the hypothesis that peer interaction is capable of enhancing intellectual performance because it forces individuals to recognize and coordinate conflicting perspectives on a problem. To test this hypothesis, one would need to examine the process of social coordination that occurs during problem solving in order to isolate the social conditions that are the most responsible for cognitive growth. For example, one could observe the interactions that occur while the group is working in order to differentiate those groups in which members work closely together and frequently attempt to coordinate their differing perspectives from those in which members work largely on their own. Then one could examine how these different group interactional patterns affect the problem-solving strategies used. Just this approach is advocated by Perret-Clermont:

> We have also shown that, for the task to have educational value, it is not sufficient for it merely to engage children in joint activity; there must also be confrontation between different points of view. Are all the activities described as "cooperation" by research workers such as to induce real inter-individual coordinations which are the source of cognitive conflict? This question can only be answered by the systematic observation which remains to be done.
>
> (1980, p. 196)

In further studies of the psychology of intelligence, we should envisage not solely the effect of inter-individual coordination on *judgment* behavior, or on *performance* as an index of development . . . but also the impact of different types of social interaction, and in particular of partner's strategies, on the *strategy* which the subject adopts in order to carry out the task.

(1980, p. 192)

We will describe a recent study (Forman, 1981) in which videotapes of collaborative problem-solving sessions were analyzed for the social interactional patterns used and the problem-solving strategies employed. In addition, individual measures of logical reasoning were collected on this sample of collaborative problem solvers that were compared with similar measures collected on a previous sample of solitary problem solvers.

The research design used by Forman is a modification of the training study design utilized by Perret-Clermont and her colleagues. Instead of providing only one opportunity for children to solve a problem in a collaborative fashion, Forman exposed her subjects to a total of 11 problem-solving sessions. There are several reasons for using a longitudinal design to assess children's problem-solving skills. One can observe the process of cognitive growth directly, rather than having to infer it from pretest–posttest performance; and children can develop stable working relationships. In addition, a longitudinal design was chosen for this study so that the data collected on collaborative problem solving could be compared with similar longitudinal data collected by Kuhn and Ho (1980) on solitary problem solving.

Forman's study thus provides two kinds of information about collaboration: how the reasoning strategies of collaborative problem solvers differ from those of solitary problem solvers and how some collaborative partnerships differ from others in both social interactional patterns and cognitive strategy usage. In the following discussion, we will focus on these two kinds of data: comparisons of collaborators with solitary problems solvers and comparisons among different collaborative partnerships. We will then discuss the findings of Forman's study in light of Perret-Clermont's hypothesis and what seems to us the essential and complementary theory of Vygotsky.

Forman's study

Like Perret-Clermont, Forman asked children to cooperate in the solution of a logical reasoning task. Unlike Perret-Clermont, Forman selected a chemical reaction task that has been used to assess the ability to isolate variables in a multivariate context (Kuhn and Phelps, 1982). In addition, her subjects were older (approximately 9 years of age) than those selected by Perret-Clermont (4–7 years).

In both the study conducted by Forman (1981) and that conducted by Kuhn and Ho (1980) the subjects were fourth- to fifth-grade, middle class children – 15 singletons (Kuhn and Ho) and 4 pairs (Forman) – who showed no ability to isolate variables in a multivariate task known as the "simple plant problem." In addition to the pretest used for subject selection, all subjects were given an additional pretest: a combinations problem in which subjects were asked to arrange five kinds of snacks in all possible combinations. The singletons and pairs participated in 11 problem-solving sessions, approximately once a week over a three-month period. The two pretest measures were readministered as posttests within a week after the final problem-solving session. All pretests and posttests were administered individually.

The chemical reaction problem consisted of a series of seven chemical problems that were ordered in terms of logical complexity. Problem 1, the simplest, requires that subjects identify the one chemical from a set of five odorless, colorless chemicals that is necessary and sufficient for producing a specified color change when mixed with a reagent. In problems 2 and 3, two or three of the five chemicals are capable of producing the color change, either separately or together. In problem 4, two chemicals are capable of producing the change, but only when *both* of them are present; and so forth.

Problem 1, with a different operative chemical each time, was presented for the first four sessions. This procedure insured that the children were repeatedly exposed to the simplest problem in the series before more difficult problems were introduced. After the fourth session, a new problem in the series was presented whenever the previous problem had been solved once. Thus, progress through the problem series is one measure of the effectiveness of the subjects' problem-solving strategies.

Each of the 11 problem-solving sessions in both studies followed the same format. First, two demonstration experiments were performed by the experimenter. Then, the children were asked a standard set of questions about the demonstration, for example: "What do you think makes a difference in whether it turns purple or not?" Next, the children were invited to set up the experiments they wanted to try in order to determine what chemical(s) were responsible for the change. No mixing of chemicals was permitted during this setting-up phase of the task. After the experiments were set up and some additional questions about them were posed, the children were permitted to mix together the combinations they had selected. In Forman's study, the dyads were encouraged to work together on setting up and mixing the chemical experiments. Finally, after the results from the experiments had been observed, the experimenter repeated the original set of questions in order to assess whether the correct chemical(s) had been identified.

Forman analyzed only the part of the sessions devoted to planning and setting up the experiments. Four sessions for each of three subject pairs (George and Bruce: session 3, 5, 8, 11; Lisa and Linda: sessions 3, 5, 9, 11; Matt and Mitch: sessions 3, 5, 8, 10) – 12 tapes in all – were coded. (The fourth pair had been included only as insurance against illness, etc.) The two coding systems used in the analysis consisted of one set of social interactional categories and one set of experimentation categories. In this chapter, we will discuss only one type of social behavior code (procedural interactions) and three types of experimentation strategies (random, variable isolation, and combinatorial).

Procedural interactions occurred during most of the problem-solving sessions coded (a range of 71 per cent to 100 per cent of the available time). They were defined as all activities carried out by one or both children that focus on getting the task accomplished.[1] Examples of procedural interactions were distributing and arranging task materials, choosing chemical experiments, and recording experiments. Three levels of procedural interactions were identified: parallel, associative, and cooperative (adapted from Parten's [1932] study of social interaction). These three levels represent three qualitatively different approaches to the sharing of ideas and the division of labor. During parallel procedural interactions, children share materials and exchange comments about the task. However, they make few if any attempts to monitor the work of the other or to inform the other of their own thoughts and actions. Associative procedural interactions occur when children try to exchange information about some of the combinations each one has selected. However, at the associative level, no attempt is made to coordinate the roles of the two partners. Cooperative interactions require that both children constantly monitor each other's work and play coordinated roles in performing task procedures.

The experimentation strategy codes were adapted from Kuhn and Phelps (1982). Three basic types of experimentation strategies were observed: a random or trial-and-error strategy; an isolation-of-variables strategy; and a combinatorial strategy. The random experiments strategy represents a relatively ineffective, unsystematic approach to experimentation. The variable isolation strategy is effective for solving the first three problems only. The more advanced problems, 4 through 7, require both experimental isolation and combinatorial strategies. Thus, this experimentation coding system was devised to identify when or if this strategy shift (from only variable isolation to both variable isolation and combinatorial) occurred.

Experimental strategy codes were assigned to a dyad based solely on the type of chemical experiments set up. Neither the type of social organization used to select these experiments nor the kinds of conversations that occurred during the setting-up process affected the assignment of an experimentation code. Thus, the coding of experimentation strategies constituted an assessment of each dyad's behavior that was independent of that obtained by coding their social interactions.

For the comparisons of the problem-solving achievements of collaborators versus singletons, two kinds of data are available: the number of chemical problems solved during the 11 sessions and pretest-to-posttest change scores. The first comparison produced striking differences between collaboration and solitary problem solving. While Kuhn and Ho found that only 4 of the 15 singletons solved problems 1 through 3 in the 11 sessions, all 4 of Forman's dyads solved problems 1 through 4 in the same amount of time. In addition, one dyad (George and Bruce) solved problems 1 through 6 during this three-month period, an achievement approached by none of Kuhn and Ho's subjects.

The pretest–posttest comparison between singletons and dyads produced more mixed results. These results are displayed in Tables 10.1 and 10.2 (ignoring for now the initials in parentheses). On the simple plant problem (Table 10.1), the singletons showed greater progress than the pairs between the pretest and posttest. In contrast, subjects who had worked in pairs seemed to show greater progress on the combinations problem (Table 10.2) than did the subjects who had worked alone.[2] Thus, while the pairs seemed able to master the series of chemical problems at a much faster rate than did the singletons, they did not show consistently greater pretest–posttest gains.

One clear difference between these two comparisons (progress through the problems versus posttest performance) is that both partners were able to contribute to the solution of each chemical problem presented, but on the pretest–posttest measures the partners were on their own. The relatively sophisticated problem-solving strategies that collaborators were able to dis-

Table 10.1 Pretest and posttest category frequencies on the simple plant problem

Group	Predominantly concrete	Transitional	Predominantly formal	Total N
Pretest				
Singletons	15	0	0	15
Pairs	8	0	0	8
Posttest				
Singletons	4	5	6	15
Pairs	6 MI, L2, M2, G, KI, K2	I (B)	I (LI)	8

Table 10.2 Pretest and posttest category frequencies on the combinations problem

Group	Predominantly concrete	Transitional	Predominantly formal	Total N
Pretest				
Singletons	15	0	0	15
Pairs	8	0	0	8
Posttest				
Singletons	12	3	0	15
Pairs	5 K2, LI, MI, KI, G	3 L2, M2, B	0	8

play when they could assist each other were not as apparent when each partner was asked to work alone on similar problems.

Another reason why collaborators did not always outperform the singletons may lie in differences among the partnerships. Because of the very small number of dyads examined, large differences between dyads may obscure all but massive differences between dyads and singletons. Therefore, we turn to the second set of comparisons: those among dyads. First, we will discuss the types of social interactions that occurred over time in the three collaborative partnerships examined. Second, we will look at the experimentation strategies used by those same dyads. Third, we will reexamine their pretest–posttest data.

The most obvious difference among the social behaviors of the three dyads concerned the development of procedural interaction patterns. All procedural interactions were classified as either parallel, associative, or cooperative. Table 10.3 shows that all three dyads engaged in predominantly parallel and associative interactions during the first session coded (session 3 for all three dyads). Only Lisa and Linda showed any degree of cooperative behavior during this session. However, by sessions 5, 8, and 11 George and Bruce were entirely cooperative. Lisa and Linda retained some associative interaction patterns in session 5, but by sessions 9 and 11 they too were engaging in cooperative interactions. In contrast, Matt and Mitch never cooperated throughout the three-month period. The interaction pattern that Matt and

Table 10.3 Percentage of procedural time spent in parallel, associative, and cooperative activities

Subject pair	Type of procedural activity (%)		
	Parallel	Associate	Cooperative
George and Bruce			
Session 3	61	39	0
Session 5	0	0	100
Session 8	0	0	100
Session 11	0	0	100
Lisa and Linda			
Session 3	42	26	32
Session 5	0	44	55
Session 9	0	0	100
Session 11	0	0	100
Matt and Mitch			
Session 3	90	10	0
Session 5	85	15	0
Session 8	100	0	0
Session 10	100	0	0

Mitch seemed to prefer was either predominantly or entirely parallel in nature.

Table 10.4 summarizes the differences in experimentation strategies used in each pair's last two sessions. All three pairs used similar kinds of experimentation strategies during the earlier sessions. George and Bruce, the dyad who solved the greatest number of problems, used both an isolation of variables and a combinatorial strategy in the two later sessions. Lisa and Linda used only the variable isolation strategy in session 9 but both strategies by session 11. In contrast, Matt and Mitch produced either random experiments or experiments capable of isolating single variables throughout the study, despite the fact that neither of these strategies was sufficient for solving the advanced problems that were presented to them during sessions 8 and 10.

Returning to the pretest–posttest measures, we find that George and Bruce, who worked so well together, did not maintain this high degree of performance when they were tested individually. The initials on Tables 10.1 and 10.2 show the posttest status of the six children whose tapes were ana-lyzed: George(G), Bruce(B), Lisa(L1), Linda(L2), Matt(M1), Mitch(M2), plus the remaining unanalyzed fourth pair (Kl and K2). On the simple plant problem (Table 10.1), the children receiving the highest scores were Bruce and Lisa; on the combinations problem (Table 10.2), Bruce, Linda, and Mitch exhibited the most advanced/reasoning skills. Thus the clear differences among dyads that were apparent on the videotapes of collaborative problem-solving sessions were not reflected in the posttest results.

In summary, when pairs were compared with singletons, the pairs solved the chemical combination problems at a much faster rate. However, the pairs did not do better than the singletons on all of the posttest measures. Single-tons appeared to outperform the pairs on the simple plant problem, a test of a subject's ability to isolate variables, whereas the pairs seemed to do better on the combinations problem.

Table 10.4 Experimentation strategies used in chemical problems 4–7

Subject pair	Random combinations	Isolation-of-variables strategy	Systematic combinatorial strategy
George and Bruce			
Session 8		X	X
Session 11		X	X
Lisa and Linda			
Session 9		X	
Session 11		X	X
Matt and Mitch			
Session 8	X	X	
Session 10		X	

When comparisons were made between the pairs, it was found that George and Bruce solved more chemical combination problems than did the other pairs. In addition, George and Bruce were the first pair to switch to an entirely cooperative interaction pattern and to use a combinatorial experimentation strategy. On some of these variables, that is, the degree of cooperation shown and the use of a combinatorial strategy, Lisa and Linda appeared to hold an intermediate position between the two pairs of boys. However, these fairly consistent differences in interactional style and problem-solving strategy use were not reflected in the posttest performance of these children. In general, George and Bruce did not exhibit consistently higher levels of reasoning on their individual posttests than did the other subjects.

Discussion

What can these results tell us about the hypothesis proposed by Perret-Clermont that peer interaction can induce cognitive conflict that, in turn, results in cognitive restructuring and growth? Forman did find an association between high levels of social coordination (cooperative procedural inter-actions) and the use of certain experimentation strategies (combinatorial strategies). However, she did not devise a measure of cognitive conflict for her study, and her findings thus cannot establish that social coordination results in cognitive conflict, which then affects problem-solving skills.

One reason why cognitive conflict was not assessed was that overt indices of conflict, that is, arguments, were relatively rare during the portion of the problem-solving session examined – the setting-up phase of the task during which experimentation strategies were most apparent. In this portion of the session, hypotheses concerning the experiments could be proposed but not tested. During most of the setting-up time, children were busy working, separately or together, on laying out and sharing task materials and on planning and choosing experiments. Among the children who interacted at a cooperative level, a great deal of mutual support, encouragement, correction, and guidance was exchanged. For example, one child would select chemical combinations while the other checked for duplicates. Instead of conflicting points of view, one saw two people attempting to construct and implement a joint experimentation plan to be tested later on in the task.

Conflicting points of view were apparent later in the problem-solving session, when most or all of the results of the experiments were visible. At that time, one could observe children forming distinct and sometimes opposing conclusions about the problem solution. Just such a conflict occurred in problem-solving session 3 between George and Bruce. Here is a summary of their interaction taken from a videotape record.

In this session, chemical C alone was the solution to the chemical problem. The two boys set up and mixed the following set of experiments: B, C, BE, CD, CE, DE, BDE, CDF, DEF. In addition, they could examine the results of the two demonstration experiments: BCE, DEF. All experiments containing chemical C turned purple, the rest remained clear.

After all the experiments were mixed, the experimenter asked both children, "What makes a difference in whether it turns purple?" Bruce initially concluded that the answer was C and E. George expressed his surprise that a single element, for example C, produced the desired color change. In response to the standard prompt from the experimenter, "Can you be sure it's C and E?" Bruce reexamined some experiments and found one that contained E (and not C) that did not change color. Bruce, however, did not conclude at this point that C was the only operative chemical. George then asked Bruce whether all the experiments containing C produced the desired color change. Bruce scanned each experiment containing C and announced that each did change color.

Based on the experimental evidence and some information remembered from previous sessions, George concluded that C was the solution to the problem. Bruce, however, contradicted George by asserting it was F. At this point, they both reexamined the experiments. Afterward, George still concluded it was C and Bruce concluded it was C and F.

The experimenter asked whether they could be sure of their answers. George replied that he was sure of C but not of F. Once again, the evidence was examined. This time, Bruce identified the experiment CDF as indicating that F was an operative chemical. George countered this argument by comparing it with experiment DEF that did not produce the desired reaction. Bruce responded that D and E were more powerful liquids than F and therefore prevented F from working. George then tried another approach by asking Bruce how he could tell it was F and not C that made the mixture CDF turn purple. Bruce replied by asking George how he could tell it wasn't both C and F that made CDF turn purple. George's concluding remark was an assertion that he just knew it was C alone.

This interchange shows the kinds of activities that conflicting solutions to the problem seemed to induce. The children returned repeatedly to the experimental evidence for supporting data. Because their conclusions differed, they were forced to acknowledge information that refuted their own inferences as well as data that supported them. These data then had to be integrated into a convincing argument in support of their own point of view. Counterarguments to their partner's position also had to be constructed. Bruce, in particular, was forced to revise his conclusions based on the evidence George brought to his attention. Despite his efforts, George was unable to convince Bruce to accept his conclusion. Unfortunately, they had not provided themselves with enough of the appropriate experimental evidence in session 3 to enable them to reach a consensus about the solution.

Collaboration on the chemical reaction task thus seems to involve two different types of social interactive processes. The first process, which occurs during the setting-up or planning stage of the task, involves either separate (parallel) working patterns or closely coordinated cooperative patterns. Cooperation during the setting-up stage consists of mutual guidance, encouragement, and support. Often during this phase of the task, complementary problem-solving roles are assumed.

Later on in the task, when experimental evidence is being examined, the second kind of interactive process occurs. At this time, each child seems to be reaching independent conclusions about the solution of the task that are based on all or only some of the available experimental evidence. After each child comes to a conclusion, he or she may find that his or her partner does not agree. In this circumstance, overt conflicting perspectives on the experimental evidence are expressed in the form of an argument. Arguments capable of producing a consensus seemed to be those that made use of appropriate supporting evidence.

It appears that Perret-Clermont's notion that cognitive conflict is the mediator between peer interaction and cognitive reorganization can be tested best in contexts where overt manifestations of conflict are likely. These contexts seem to occur when children have access to a wealth of empirical evidence, when this evidence is capable of suggesting at least two distinct solutions to the problem, and when a consensual solution is solicited.

Perret-Clermont's hypothesis about the importance of cognitive conflict comes from Piaget's theory concerning the role of social factors in development. Most of the past research on the topic of peer collaboration has been based upon Piaget's ideas. Piaget placed more importance on peer interaction than upon adult–child interaction, so it is not surprising that the bulk of research on collaboration has shared a Piagetian perspective.

In order to understand the limitations as well as the strengths of this perspective on collaboration, one needs to appreciate the role that peer interaction plays in Piaget's theory. Piaget (1970) identified four factors that he believed are necessary for a theory of cognitive development: maturation, experience with the physical environment, social experiences, and equilibration or self-regulation. In addition, Piaget claimed that equilibration is the most fundamental of the four factors. Peer interaction, and social experiences in general, derive their importance from the influence they can exert on equilibration through the introduction of cognitive conflict. Perret-Clermont shares this view of development when she writes:

> Of course, cognitive conflict of this kind does not create the *forms* of operations, but it brings about the disequilibriums which make cognitive elaboration necessary, and in this way cognitive conflict confers a

special role on the social factor as one among other factors leading to mental growth. Social–cognitive conflict may be figuratively likened to the catalyst in a chemical reaction: it is not present at all in the final product, but it is nevertheless indispensable if the reaction is to take place.

(Perret-Clermont, 1980, p. 178)

When Piaget looks at peer interaction, therefore, he looks for evidence of disequilibrium, that is, cognitive conflict. He is not interested in describing or explaining social interactional processes as a whole. Piaget's theory is most helpful in explaining those situations where cognitive conflict is clearly and overtly expressed in external social behaviors, for example arguments. However, in situations where overt conflict is not apparent and where mutual guidance and support are evident, his theory provides few clues concerning the role of social factors in development. Fortunately, Vygotsky's writings on adult–child interaction offer insights into the intellectual value of these kinds of peer interactions.

To illustrate how Vygotsky's ideas shed light on some of the processes involved in peer collaboration, we will discuss another set of observations of George and Bruce. One of the most puzzling findings from Forman's study was the discrepancy between how a dyad functions as a unit and how the partners function separately. George and Bruce were clearly the most successful collaborators, yet they did not show the same consistently high level of functioning when they were posttested separately. This discrepancy between dyadic and individual performance levels was also apparent when subjects who collaborated were compared with those who worked alone. On the posttest measures, which were individually administered, collaborative problem solvers did not do better than solitary problem solvers. Nevertheless, collaborative partners were able to solve many more chemical problems than could solitary problem solvers during the same period of time.

. Vygotsky acknowledged that a discrepancy might exist between solitary and social problem solving when he developed his notion of the zone of proximal development. He defined this zone as "*the distance between the actual developmental level as determined by independent problem solving and the level of potential development as determined through problem solving under adult guidance or in collaboration with more capable peers*" (1978, p. 86). Thus, Vygotsky hypothesized that children would be able to solve problems with assistance from an adult or more capable peer before they could solve them alone. This seemingly obvious observation was then used to reach several original conclusions. One conclusion was that the zone of proximal development could be used to identify those skills most amenable to instruction. Another was that learning consists of the internalization of social interactional processes. According to Vygotsky, development proceeds when interpsychological regulation is transformed into intrapsychological regulation.

Returning to Forman's data, it appears that a similar process of interpsychological to intrapsychological regulation may also occur in collaborative contexts where neither partner can be seen as objectively "more capable," but where the partners may assume separate but complementary social roles. One child may perform an observing, guiding, and correcting role while the other performs the task procedures. This observing partner seems to provide some of the same kinds of assistance that has been called scaffolding by Wood, Bruner, and Ross (1976). Such support from an observing partner seems to enable the two collaborators to solve problems together before they are capable of solving the same problems alone.

In addition, one can see in Forman's data instances where problem-solving strategies first appear as social interactional procedures and are later internalized. Remember that a combinatorial problem was administered to each child individually at three different times (as a pretest, as an immediate posttest and as a delayed posttest). In addition, these same children were presented with a similar combinatorial problem in each problem-solving session when they were asked to decide jointly which chemical mixtures to set up. Therefore, a comparison can be made between the combinations generated by each child when he or she worked alone or in pairs.

Both George and Bruce used an empirical strategy to generate combinations during their pretest – for example, selecting a combination at random and then basing the next combination on the first by adding, subtracting, or substituting one of its elements. The third combination would then be produced by copying, with another minor revision, the second combination. Pairwise checking of each new combination with each previous combination was the empirical procedure used for guarding against duplications.

In their early collaborative problem-solving sessions, George and Bruce worked in parallel and each used an empirical strategy similar to the one used on the pretest to generate combinations. After about a month of working together, they devised a social procedure for generating combinations empirically by assuming complementary problem-solving roles: one selected chemicals and the other checked their uniqueness.

After two months, they had begun to organize their combinations into groups based on their number of elements. In addition, they had devised a deductive system for generating two-element combinations. This deductive procedure enabled the child who had previously done the checking to prompt, correct, and reinforce the selections of his partner. Higher-order combinations were produced empirically using the familiar social procedure.

At the last session, the boys continued to assume complementary roles but now used the blackboard as a recording device. They produced combinations in a highly organized fashion – singles, two-element combinations, three-element combinations, and so on – and were able to generate almost all of the 31 possible combinations. They used a deductive procedure for generating the two-element combinations but still relied on their empirical procedure for the higher-order combinations.

At the first posttest one week after the last collaborative session, the degree to which each boy had internalized a deductive combinatorial system was assessed by asking them to generate combinations independently. Bruce was able to generate all 10 two-element combinations deductively on his own, but George was not. George used an empirical system to generate combinations. On the second posttest four months later, however, both boys had internalized a deductive procedure for producing two-element combinations.

It appears that these two boys were able to apply a preexisting intrapsychological rule, an empirical combinatorial procedure, to a collaborative context by dividing the procedure into complementary problem-solving roles. With repeated exposure to the problem, these boys were able to progress to a deductive procedure for generating simple, two-element combinations. At first, deductive reasoning was clearly a social activity for George and Bruce. Each time one partner selected a series of combinations, the other guided, prompted, and corrected his selections. Later, one partner was able to demonstrate that he had internalized this deductive procedure by using it to generate all possible two-element combinations on his own. Four months later, both partners were able to generate all possible pairs of five objects deductively by themselves. Thus, for these two boys, deductive combinatorial reasoning first appeared in a collaborative context. Only one of the two boys was initially able to show that he had internalized this procedure when he generated combinations alone. Months later, however, both boys had internalized this deductive process.

In summary, a Piagetian perspective on the role of social factors in development can be useful in understanding situations where overt indices of cognitive conflict are present. However, if one wants to understand the cognitive consequences of other social interactional contexts, Vygotsky's ideas may be more helpful. In tasks where experimental evidence was being generated and where managerial skills were required, by assuming complementary problem-solving roles, peers could perform tasks together before they could perform them alone. The peer observer seemed to provide some of the same kinds of "scaffolding" assistance that others have attributed to the adult in teaching contexts.

Thus, the Vygotskian perspective enables us to see that collaborative tasks requiring data generation, planning, and management can provide another set of valuable experiences for children. In these tasks, a common set of assumptions, procedures, and information needs to be constructed. These tasks require children to integrate their conflicting task conceptions into a mutual plan. One way to achieve a shared task perspective is to assume complementary problem-solving roles. Then each child learns to use speech to guide the actions of her or his partner and, in turn, to be guided by the partner's speech. Exposure to this form of social regulation can enable children to master difficult problems together before they are capable of solving them alone. More importantly, experience with social forms of regulation can provide children with just the tools they need to master problems on their own. It enables them to observe and reflect on the problem-solving process as a whole and to select those procedures that are the most effective. When they can apply this social understanding to themselves, they can then solve, independently, those tasks that they had previously been able to solve only with assistance.

Thus, collaborative problem solving seems to offer some of the same experiences for children that peer tutoring provides: the need to give verbal instructions to peers, the impetus for self-reflection encouraged by a visible audience, and the need to respond to peer questions and challenges.

Conclusion

In conclusion, in these analyses we are not talking about a children's culture separate from adults'. What Leont'ev and Luria discuss as the "most important specifically human form of mental development" – namely, "the assimilation of general human experience in the teaching process" – must ultimately be grounded in adult–child interactions. But peer (and cross-age) relationships can function as intermediate transforming contexts between social and external adult–child interactions and the individual child's inner speech.

Although such peer interactions take place in home and community as well as at school, they may be especially important in school because of limitations and rigidities characteristic of adult–child interactions in that institutional setting. Cazden (1983) argues for the value to child development of a category of parent–child interactions of which the peek-a-boo game and picture book reading are familiar examples. In interactions such as these, there is a predictable structure in which the mother initially enacts the entire script herself and then the child takes an increasingly active role, eventually speaking all the parts initially spoken by the mother. The contrast between such learning environments and the classroom is striking. In school lessons, teachers give directions and children nonverbally carry them out; teachers ask questions and children answer them, frequently with only a word or a phrase. Most importantly, these roles are not reversible, at least not within the context of teacher–child interactions. Children never give directions to teachers, and questions addressed to teachers are rare except for asking permission. The only context in which children can reverse interactional roles with the same intellectual content, giving directions as well as following them, and asking questions as well as answering them, is with their peers.

Notes

1 Other social interactional codes were used to identify conversations that served to plan, reflect upon, or organize these procedural activities (metaprocedural inter-actions), task-focused jokes (playful interactions), task-focused observations (shared observations), and off-task behavior.

2 A second set of posttests was administered to both samples four months after the first posttest. The pairs constantly outperformed the singletons on both second posttest measures. However, the interpretation of these findings is problematic due to the fact that this four-month period occurred during the school year for the pairs but during the summer for the singletons.

References

Cazden, C. B. 1983. Peekaboo as an instructional model: Discourse development at school and at home. In B. Bain (Ed.), *The sociogenesis of language and human conduct: A multi-disciplinary book of readings*. New York: Plenum, pp. 33–58.

Doise, W., Mugny, G., and Perret-Clermont, A. N. 1975. Social interaction and the development of cognitive operations. *European Journal of Social Psychology, 5*(3), 367–383.

Doise, W., Mugny, G., and Perret-Clermont, A. N. 1976. Social interaction and cognitive development: Further evidence. *European Journal of Social Psychology, 6*, 245–247.

Forman, E. A. 1981. The role of collaboration in problem-solving in children. Doctoral dissertation, Harvard University.

Galton, M., Simon, B., and Croll, P. 1980. *Inside the primary classroom*. Boston: Routledge & Kegan Paul.

Inagaki, K. 1981. Facilitation of knowledge integration through classroom discus-sion. *Quarterly Newsletter of the Laboratory of Comparative Human Cognition, 3*(3), 26–28.

Inagaki, K., and Hatano, G. 1968. Motivational influences on epistemic observation. *Japanese Journal of Educational Psychology, 6*, 191–202.

Inagaki, K., and Hatano, G. 1977. Amplification of cognitive motivation and its effects on epistemic observation. *American Educational Research Journal, 14*, 485–491.

Inhelder, B., and Piaget, J. 1958. *The growth of logical thinking from childhood to adolescence*. New York: Basic Books.

Kol'tsova, V. A. 1978. Experimental study of cognitive activity in communication (with specific reference to concept formation). *Soviet Psychology, 17*, 23–38.

Kuhn, D., and Ho, V. 1980. Self-directed activity and cognitive development. *Journal of Applied Developmental Psychology, 1*(2), 119–133.

Kuhn, D., and Phelps, E. 1982. The development of problem-solving strategies. In H. Reese (Ed.), *Advances in child development* (Vol. 17). New York: Academic Press.

Leont'ev, A. N. 1981. The problem of activity in psychology. In J. V. Wertsch (Ed.), *The concept of activity in Soviet psychology*. Armonk, New York: Sharpe, pp. 37–71.

Leont'ev, A, N., and Luria, A. R. 1968. The psychological ideas of L. S. Vygotsky. In B. B. Wolman (Ed.), *Historical roots of contemporary psychology*. New York: Harper & Row.

Lomov, B. F. 1978. Psychological processes and communication. *Soviet Psychology, 17*, 3–22.

Mugny, G., and Doise, W. 1978. Socio-cognitive conflict and structure of individual and collective performances. *European Journal of Social Psychology, 8*, 181–192.

Parten, M. 1932. Social participation among preschool children. *Journal of Abnormal and Social Psychology, 27*, 243–269.

Perret-Clermont, A. N. 1980. *Social interaction and cognitive development in children*. New York: Academic Press.

Piaget, J. 1970. Piaget's theory. In P. H. Mussen (Ed.), *Carmichael's manual of child psychology* (3rd ed., Vol.1). New York: Wiley, pp. 703–732.

Sharan, S. 1980. Cooperative learning in small groups: Recent methods and effects on achievement, attitudes, and ethnic relations. *Review of Educational Research, 50* 241–271.

Simon, B. (Ed.), 1957. *Psychology in the Soviet Union*. Stanford, Calif.: Stanford University Press.

Simon, B., and Simon, J. (Eds.). 1963. *Educational psychology in the USSR*. Stanford, Calif.: Stanford University Press.

Slavina, L. S. 1957. Specific features of the intellectual work of unsuccessful pupils. In B. Simon (Ed.), *Psychology in the Soviet Union*. Stanford, Calif.: Stanford University Press, pp. 205–212.

Vygotsky, L. S. 1978. *Mind in society*. Edited by M. Cole, V. John-Steiner, S. Scribner, and E. Souberman. Cambridge, Mass.: Harvard University Press.

Vygotsky, L. S. 1981. The genesis of higher mental functions. In J. V. Wertsch (Ed.), *The concept of activity in Soviet psychology*. Armonk, New York: Sharpe.

Wertsch, J. V. (Ed.). 1981. *The concept of activity in Soviet psychology*. Armonk, New York: Sharpe.

Wood, D., Bruner, J. S., and Ross, G. 1976. The role of tutoring in problem-solving. *Journal of Child Psychology and Psychiatry, 17*, 89–100.

Chapter 11

Peer interactive minds

Developmental, theoretical, and methodological issues*

Margarita Azmitia

> Collaboration operates through a process in which the successful intellectual achievements of one person arouse the intellectual passions and enthusiasms of others, and through the fact that what was at first expressed only by one individual becomes a common intellectual possession instead of fading away into isolation.
>
> From an interview by John-Steiner (1985, p. 187)

The potential synergy of peer interactive minds has been the subject of scholarly debate for many centuries. Whether concerning adolescents in Socrates' ancient Greek Academy, contemporary children collaborating on a school project, two grandmothers solving a moral dilemma, or a team of scientists creating and testing a theory, the age-old question remains: How do peers create intellectual synergy and cognitive development? By cognitive development I mean both adding to and revising our knowledge and strategies. Considerable research (for reviews, see Gilovich, 1991; Kuhn, 1991) has shown that revising our knowledge or abandoning old views is especially difficult, regardless of whether we are talking about scientific theories or social stereotypes. Knowledge revision is difficult because we tend to ignore or devalue information that is inconsistent with our beliefs. Peers can help us revise our knowledge by focusing our attention on information that we would not otherwise consider and forcing us to question or explain our views.

The first goal of this chapter is to review work that addresses processes and outcomes of peer interactive minds in childhood and adolescence. Because the work on childhood and adolescence has proceeded relatively independently from research on adulthood and old age, the second goal is to suggest potential linkages between these two bodies of work. The final goal is to highlight some of the methodological and theoretical challenges that currently confront

* This is an edited version of a chapter that appeared in *Interactive Minds: Life-span perspectives on the social foundation of cognition*, Cambridge: Cambridge University Press, 1997.

research on peer interactive minds. To foreshadow my conclusion, I will propose that, although the past two decades have brought considerable advances, many challenges remain, both in theory construction and in the application of our findings to classrooms, work places, and other environments of daily living.

Before proceeding with the first goal, it may be useful to review the many ways that peers can influence knowledge acquisition and revision. First, their influence may be at the motivational or affective level, increasing each other's willingness to attempt difficult tasks and reducing frustration when the work becomes too challenging. Second, peers may observe and imitate the behaviors and strategies of others. Third, a more expert peer might tutor a novice. Not only does the novice increase his or her knowledge, but through teaching the expert also refines his or her understanding and learns to communicate it effectively. Fourth, peers can engage in lively discussions and negotiations that may result in mutually shared and potentially higher levels of understanding (Azmitia & Perlmutter, 1989; Winegar, 1988). In this chapter, I devote special attention to this fourth notion of peer interactive minds.

Because most researchers have focused on a single age group or a limited age period (e.g. childhood, adolescence, adulthood), we currently lack models of peer interactive minds across the life span. When I began writing this chapter, I had the overambitious goal of proposing a life-span model of peer interacting minds. Many months later, I had the more modest aim of simply setting forth some candidate processes and issues that may frame this life-span model. In particular, I will propose that understanding how age-related changes in communicative, metacognitive, and negotiation skills work together to influence the processes and outcomes of collaborations between peers may provide the foundation for this life-span model. Because my research has focused on childhood and adolescence, I will devote more attention to these periods.

One of the many lessons that we have learned while researching peer interactive processes and outcomes is that context matters. Context effects may include cultural differences (Ellis & Gauvain 1992: Tharp & Gallimore, 1988), societal or institutional norms and prescriptions for social interaction (Perret-Clermont, Perret, & Bell, 1991), the nature of the relationship between collaborators (Nelson & Aboud, 1985; Goodwin, 1993), and the characteristics of the task or the setting (Cooper, Ayers-Lopez, & Marquis, 1982; Ellis & Rogoff, 1986).

The chapter is organized as follows. First, I review research on peer interacting minds in childhood and adolescence. I pay special attention to how age-related changes in negotiation skills affect the dynamics and products of peer collaboration. I also consider how the difficulty of the task and the nature of the relationship between the collaborators (i.e. friends vs. acquaintances) moderate these processes and outcomes. Second, I make some suggestions about what researchers studying peer interactive minds at different points of the life span can learn from each other's work. Finally, I offer some thoughts on theoretical and methodological issues that currently confront the field.

Peer interactive minds in childhood and adolescence

In an earlier piece of work, Marion Perlmutter and I (Azmitia & Perlmutter, 1989) sketched a developmental framework for studying social influences on cognition. Because this chapter elaborates on that framework, I will first summarize its main points. We suggested that children's task performance depends on their skill level relative to the difficulty of the task, and that the impact of social input on their performance and, more broadly, their cognitive growth also depends on these variables. For example, when children's skill level is very low, they may be able to follow simple directions and imitate behaviors, but may not be able to see how these behaviors facilitate problem solving. Difficult tasks might also absorb so much of their attention and thinking that sustained and meaningful social interaction is precluded. As will be discussed, it is possible that young children often find themselves in this situation, thus accounting for the fragility of peer interacting minds and their cognitive outcomes during the preschool years (see Brownell & Carriger, 1991). As their communicative, collaborative, metacognitive, and negotiation skills increase during middle childhood and adolescence and become more routinized or automatic, individuals may be less hampered by task difficulty and derive greater benefits from peer collaborative problem solving.

Our model also addressed the mechanisms through which social interaction leads to the creation and revision of knowledge. Like others before us, we proposed that imitation, conflict and its negotiation, tutoring or apprenticeship, and co-construction (i.e., the elaboration and integration of the perspectives of the different collaborators into a mutually shared view) can mediate the cognitive outcomes of peer collaboration. However, we took issue with the practice of pitting the effects of one mechanism against those of another in order to decide which is the best mechanism of facilitation, because this practice can obscure the possibility that each mechanism might facilitate a specific kind of cognitive change. For example, imitation might be sufficient for adding knowledge or strategies, but conflict, negotiation, and co-construction may be necessary for revising knowledge or abandoning old strategies in favor of better tools. An additional reason for our reservations about this competitive strategy was that it draws attention away from the possibility that different mechanisms may be salient at different points of the life span. We speculated, for example, that during the preschool years, imitation may be the most powerful mechanism for promoting knowledge acquisition because children's limited interactive skills constrain their ability to sustain collaborative dialogues, coordinate views, or resolve conflicts (see Hartup, 1983; Selman, 1980). As children hone their collaborative and nego-tiation skills, other mechanisms of facilitation may become salient, although imitation will still be an important mechanism of knowledge construction (but perhaps not of knowledge revision).

In framing our developmental model, we devoted special attention to dis-cussing how age-related changes in children's and adolescents metacognitive skills influenced processes, mechanisms, and outcomes of peer interacting minds. We were especially interested in these metacognitive skills because they are key elements of knowledge construction and revision, as they allow individuals to allocate cognitive resources effectively to both the task and the collaboration, to plan, implement, and monitor a problem-solving strategy, and to evaluate the proposed solution for the problem.

Although Garton (1992) agreed with our view that age-related changes in metacognitive skills have implications for the processes and outcomes of peer interactive minds, she quite rightly faulted us for not devoting sufficient attention to the influence of age-related changes in children's and adolescents' communicative skill. She suggested that it is important to consider these changes not only because discourse is one of the pathways through which metacognitive skills are constructed, but also because age-related changes in communicative skills affect the process of negotiation and co-construction of knowledge.

In this chapter, I address Garton's criticism by discussing age-related changes in two aspects of communication – conflict and its negotiation – that influence collaboration and knowledge construction and revision. I pay special attention to conflict negotiation processes because they figure prominently in Piaget's (1965) and Vygotsky's (1978) theories, which have dominated child developmental work on peer interactive minds. . . .

Age-related differences in collaborative skills

Collaborative skills include all the tools that allow us to engage in social interaction and create a shared understanding of our task and our roles and goals. It is not enough to start a dialogue. This dialogue must be moved along and repaired when confusions, misunderstandings, or conflicts ensue. Simi-larly, we must monitor each other's actions, anticipating movements, offering assistance, or "backing off," when our partner appears to have matters under control or assistance would not be welcome. Finally, we must also keep in mind the goals of the collaboration so that we can accomplish them or change them if they no longer seem tenable or a better alternative emerges.

Before reviewing the specific age-related changes in collaborative skills, it is important to point out that even though our ability to collaborate increases with age, collaboration is challenging across the life span. All of us would probably agree with the proposal that it takes considerable time and effort to build and maintain a truly collaborative interaction, and even more time and effort to build a truly collaborative *relationship* (see Hinde, 1979). One of the biggest challenges is that, like any other relationship, this collaboration must evolve and grow, as otherwise it would become stagnant and unfulfilling (Fogel, 1993). Because most of our work on peer interactive minds in childhood and adolescence has focused on interactions (as opposed to relationships), except for a brief section on collaborations between friends, I too will be focusing on peer interactions over one or a small number of sessions.

Before 2 years of age, children are able to coordinate their actions and goals with another peer at only a rudimentary level, and even then they do so infrequently. Often, successful interaction depends on the presence of a supportive context, such as an adult who facilitates communication and coordinations between the infants (Rogoff, 1990) or a task that requires cooperation, provides many clues to its solution, or is more open-ended, such as symbolic play (Hartup, 1983; Verba, 1993).

Around 2 years of age, however, there is a dramatic shift in children's ability to sustain interactions. In particular, they begin to engage in reciprocated play and to collaborate to solve simple problems, particularly those that do not depend heavily on discussion or require children to take on more than one role (Brownell & Carriger, 1991; Tomasello, Kruger, & Ratner, 1993). Brownell and Carriger suggest that this shift in children's ability to establish a shared understanding may be mediated, at least in part, by the growth of symbolic and representational skills. Children's increasing mobility, exposure to other children, and communicative skill also contribute to these changes in peer interaction and collaborative problem solving.

Although preschoolers are more skilled than infants or toddlers at managing interaction and creating a shared understanding, their skills are fragile and are often tied to specific familiar contexts. For example, numerous scholars have detailed the synergy of peer interactive minds during play. During play, young children create scenarios, negotiate and coordinate complex roles, justify their views, flexibly shift the discourse and interaction toward new goals, and, on occasion, compromise (Corsaro, 1985; Garvey 1987). However, young children's ability to coordinate their behaviors during collaborative problem-solving tasks is more limited. Although they can share resources and take turns, preschoolers are often unable to explain their views, repair breakdowns in interaction and understanding, and refrain from attempting to dominate the problem-solving process, a tendency that is also reflected by their frequent reliance on unilateral conflict resolution strategies such as blocking and insistence (Azmitia, 1988; Miller, 1987; Selman, 1980).

Garvey (1987) suggests that these difficulties may be due, at least in part, to the fact that problem solving requires that peers focus their actions and attention toward a specific, single goal, that is, the solution of the problem. Because play allows flexible alteration of goals, children may avoid breakdowns by redefining their aims whenever they encounter an obstacle. The fragility of peer interactive minds during the preschool years may also be due to difficulties in resisting distraction, coordinating joint attention, or shifting attention to other strategies or dimensions of the problem (Cooper & Cooper, 1984; Ellis & Siegler, in press).

It is important to point out, however, that although during the preschool years collaborative problem solving can be fragile, the degree to which limitations in communicative and interactive skills will affect peer interactive minds depends on the nature of the problem and its difficulty. For example, collaborations involving pairs of experts proceed more smoothly and are more resistant to disruption than those involving pairs of novices (Azmitia, 1989). Children are also better able to sustain collaboration when the task is familiar or when it provides feedback that supports a particular view more than another (Rogoff, 1990).

During middle childhood, peers become increasingly able to initiate, maintain, and repair collaboration and achieve a shared understanding of their problem-solving roles and goals. Also, cognitive gains following the collaboration are evident over a wider range of tasks. A variety of explanations have been offered to account for these improvements in the processes and outcomes of peer collaborative minds. These explanations include general proposals concerning development, such as declines in egocentrism (Piaget, 1965), or suggestions targeting more specific processes or abilities, such as an increased understanding of fairness and reciprocity (Youniss, 1980), improvements in the regulation of their own and others' affect to reduce frustration and increase task enjoyment (Hartup, 1996), and advancements in perspective taking such that collaborators recognize the need to justify their positions and reach mutually agreeable resolutions of conflicts (Hartup, 1996; Miller, 1987; Selman, 1980).

However, once again the task context influences the processes and outcomes of peer interactive minds. If the task is too difficult, it may absorb all the individuals' processing resources, thus increasing the fragility of collaboration (Azmitia & Perlmutter, 1989; Ellis & Rogoff 1986). An additional reason for the difficulty children may have in maintaining collaboration and a shared understanding in very difficult tasks is that their frustration and anxiety may lead to hostility and to defensiveness or rigidity in perspectives. Given this unpleasant state of affairs, children may prefer to withdraw from the interaction and work by themselves. However, because of the developmental changes discussed in the preceding paragraphs, these task difficulties will decrease as children progress through the middle childhood years.

Forman (1992) and Selman (1980) have suggested that it is not until early to middle adolescence that the impact of task difficulty (and task context) on peer interacting minds becomes attenuated due to dramatic growth in communicative, collaborative, and metacognitive skills. Put more simply, on average, adolescents are able to achieve a shared understanding of the collaboration and the task across a wider variety of situations. Bos (1934) and

Forman and McPhail (1993) have provided detailed analyses of two key processes that can facilitate knowledge acquisition and revision. First, partners can elaborate on each other's perspectives and work to integrate their positions and build a joint understanding of the problem (i.e., co-construct the solution). Second, partners can challenge each other's reasoning, justify their challenges, and attempt to resolve their differences (i.e., conflict and negotiation). Subsequent research has shown that in late childhood and early adolescence, conflict is more likely to lead to knowledge acquisition, revision, and generalization than to co-construction (Kruger, 1993).

It is important to point out, however, that neither co-construction nor conflict and its negotiation necessarily lead to better solutions or higher levels of understanding. Indeed, like collaborating adults, at times adolescents co-construct a new *misunderstanding* of the problem (Forman & McPhail, 1993; Levin & Druyan, 1993). Regardless of its accuracy, however, this new understanding reflects the synergy of interacting minds, as it is often impossible to isolate the contributions of each adolescent. Bos notes:

> The same things happen in cases where, in lively exchange of thoughts, adults discuss a problem. Through the interpretation of the other, which is rejected by us, we arrive at ideas, which in turn are taken over, eventually are further elaborated, and thereby lead to a result. Whom shall we give credit for the solution? It was fortunate that our young candidates did not bother about the authorship and after intensive collaboration simply declared that they had worked out the problems *together*.
>
> (1934, p. 364)

Despite these age-normative changes in adolescents' skills, it is the case that many adolescents are unable to create and transform knowledge during collaboration, and that even when they do, not all adolescents display these discoveries at a later time (e.g., subsequent interactions, their next project, an exam, or an individual posttest). Some of this variability reflects individual differences in cognitive skills and knowledge about a domain. These variations may also reflect differences in the ability and willingness of collaborators to negotiate and renegotiate collaborative roles and construct a shared understanding of the task or problem. I will return to this issue later, when I distinguish between the potential and the reality of children's and adolescents' interacting minds. For now, I want to focus on the age-related changes in negotiation processes that mediate knowledge construction and revision. I first discuss role negotiations and renegotiations and then knowledge construction and revision.

Age-related differences in the negotiation and renegotiation of roles

Role negotiations and renegotiations maintain and repair social interaction. As mentioned, these processes are also linked to the cognitive outcomes of peer interactive minds. For example, individuals who make joint decisions and coordinate their problem-solving activities make greater cognitive gains than those who do not (Rogoff, 1990; Tharp & Gallimore, 1988). Also, the acquisition of competence by novices during collaborations with more expert partners is mediated by the renegotiation of problem-solving roles such that the novices gradually increase their participation in the task until they become capable of solving the problem independently (Vygotsky, 1978).

Role negotiation and renegotiation can be especially problematic for preschoolers because they frequently experience difficulty sharing, compromising, and balancing the demands of the task with the demands of managing the collaboration. Negotiating problem-solving roles may also be challenging for children, adolescents, or adults with limited collaborative experience or who prefer to work on their own. Although there certainly is wide within-culture variability, it is generally the case that U.S. schools and universities emphasize individual work. However, even though individuals in U.S. society may have limited opportunities to collaborate in academic contexts, from an early age they collaborate in games, relationships, and social interactions. The collaborative and negotiation skills acquired in these contexts may be transported to academic settings, such as when children transport the turn-taking strategies from games into the classroom. However, transporting these strategies into the classroom is not enough; they must be adapted to the characteristics of academic problem solving. For example, unlike games, relationships, and social interactions, in which roles are often familiar and routinized, this is usually not the case for academic tasks. Also, while even young children are able to establish problem-solving roles, what is tricky, and consequently shows significant improvements with age, is (1) renegotiating roles during the course of collaboration and (2) establishing a style of interaction wherein individual contributions or strict accounting of turns are deemphasized in favor of a joint goal.

I base these two suggestions on the results of a series of studies in which my student colleagues and I (Azmitia, 1989; Azmitia & Linnet, 1995; Azmitia, Lopez, Conner, & Kolesnik, 1991; Azmitia & Montgomery, 1993) have been studying ontogenetic and microgenetic changes in children's and young adolescents' ability to negotiate and renegotiate mutually agreeable problem-solving roles with acquaintances. Across all the age groups (4 to 11 years of age) and tasks (copying models, writing, isolating causal variables), most collaborators initially adopted a "let's take turns" strategy. However, the ability to adhere to this strategy increased with age. Age-related differences in the ability to sustain this strategy were especially evident in collaborations that involved partners with different skill levels, such as experts and novices.

The nature of the task may have contributed to the fragility of this egalitarian collaboration strategy. In particular, preschoolers had more difficulty sustaining turn taking in tasks that provided clear feedback about each participant's competence level, such as reproducing designs or copying Lego models. Within minutes, preschool-age experts attempted to persuade their more novice partners to allow them to take control of the task. Although initially the novices accepted their secondary roles (thus achieving a shared understanding of roles and goals), as their competence increased they attempted to renegotiate their roles to increase their participation. Their expert partners typically resisted their renegotiation attempts, the novices persisted, and often the collaboration disintegrated into a battle of wills and disruptive behaviors such that either the task was not completed, one child withdrew from the interaction, or both, as illustrated in the following example from a task in which children were building a copy of a Lego house:

Novice:	You gotta let me help. You said you would.
Expert:	I will, after I finish this [the door].
Novice:	(*Sighs, sits back, crosses arms around chest, and frowns. Twenty-two seconds later, takes some blocks and begins building a section of the model [correctly]. After the section is completed, he hands it to the expert.*) I built this for our house.
Expert:	(*Looks over.*) I'm the builder, you find Legos [for me] when I tell you, OK? Give me a yellow two-dot.
Novice:	I wanna be a builder too. She [experimenter] said work together. My window is good (*points to model and back to section he built*).
Expert:	Well, it's not going on my house (*moves copy of model out of the reach of the novice*).
Novice:	(*Starts shaking the table, making it impossible for expert to continue building.*)
Expert:	Stop it! If you don't quit it we won't get finished. I'm almost done with the door.
Novice:	(*Stops shaking the table, observes the expert until he finishes the door.*) My turn! My turn!
Expert:	It's not time for your window yet.
Novice:	But it's the only thing [left]. . . and the roofs but the window goes first (*points to model*). How about I do the window and you [do] the roofs? Here (*offers roof pieces*).
Expert:	You'll mess it up [the window]. I gotta do it.
Novice:	No, I know how. See (*points to his completed window*)? It's the same (*points to model*).
Expert:	(*Looks*) Well, you don't know how to put it on.
Novice:	Yeah I do!
Expert:	If you want me to use your window you gotta let me put it on.

Novice: (*Sighs, puts head down on arms, and disengages from the interaction. Eighteen seconds later, starts pelting the expert with Legos, and when the expert lifts his hands to protect himself from the Legos, he quickly reaches over and smashes the copy of the Lego house to pieces.*)

One might assume that the attempts at role renegotiation made by novices were ineffective because their negotiation strategies were unilateral (e.g., insisting, grabbing, avoiding, blocking). As evident in the preceding example, however, this hypothesis is untenable because novices often used nonegocentric strategies such as justifying their position, bartering, or proposing a compromise (see Selman, 1980). It is possible that these nonegocentric strategies failed to persuade the experts because any renegotiation would have entailed their giving up resources or power. Moreover, because the experts had the skill to complete the task independently, they had little to gain from agreeing to renegotiate the problem-solving roles. Possibly, if the experts had had a stronger motivation for relinquishing control, such as realizing that time was running out and the task was far from complete, or their partners alluded to the obligations of friendship, they would have been more responsive to the role renegotiation attempts made by the novices.

A small pilot study that explored role renegotiation in pairs of experts and novices who were close friends revealed that friendship was a more powerful motive for persuading the expert to renegotiate the problem-solving roles than time constraints, perhaps because preschoolers have a limited understanding of time. However, although novices who alluded to the obligations of friendship were more likely to persuade their partners than novices who alluded to efficiency or time pressures, their success was short-lived. Soon, the experts reasserted their dominance. In many cases, what ensued was a pattern in which the novice reminded his or her friend about their agreement, the expert honored the agreement for a short time, and then regained control of the task, at which point he or she was chastised by the novice, and so on and so forth until the task was completed or time expired. It is possible that this inability to sustain more egalitarian roles even when collaborating with friends may reflect preschoolers' understanding of the goals of a collaborative problem-solving task. In particular, experts might have viewed the goal of solving the problem as more important than the goal of solving it together, even when their partner was a close friend. This suggestion receives some support from an additional pilot study in which we emphasized in our instructions that collaboration was more important than task completion. In this situation, experts still took control of the task and resisted the requests for role renegotiation of their novice partners. It appears then, that if one wants to promote more egalitarian problem-solving roles during the preschool years, one should avoid pairing children whose skills differ substantially or use tasks in which the discrepancy in the skills of the partners is not so obvious.

During middle childhood and early adolescence, peer collaborators became more capable of adhering to the turn-taking strategy and negotiating and renegotiating their problem-solving roles even when feedback from the task made it obvious that their expertise differed dramatically. However, it was still the case that expertise affected role negotiations, since, at least initially, experts took a leadership role in the task. This leadership role may have been essential to keep the problem-solving process on track. Pozzi, Healy, and Hoyles (1993) found that groups in which someone initially took the lead in coordinating the planning and decision making were able to collaborate and learn more effectively than those in which no one took the lead or was allowed to do so. Groups in which there was no leader were less effective because either many avenues were pursued and abandoned, or collaborators were unable to agree on which plan to follow. Especially pertinent to my point that successful collaborations require flexibility in roles over time, Pozzi and others found that the most successful groups were those in which the leader relinquished control once the plan was in place and group members had negotiated acceptable roles. We have observed a similar result in our studies. In particular, collaborations between experts and novices during middle childhood and early adolescence are more successful than those between expert and novice preschoolers because the experts, and especially girls, are more open to increasing the role of the novice once he or she exhibits increased understanding and skill.

In the case of these older peers, nonegocentric strategies such as justifications and a willingness to compromise were more successful for role negotiation than egocentric strategies, such as insistence, threatening, grabbing, or blocking. On the surface, this statement might seem to contradict my earlier point that nonegocentric, collaborative negotiation strategies do not necessarily increase the success of negotiations. However, I think that the age-related increase in the effectiveness of these strategies was due, at least in part, to an increase in expert children's and adolescents' willingness to listen to and consider the justifications, bargains, and compromises offered by their novice partners. Thus, and it should not come as a very surprising conclusion, the success of role renegotiation strategies is not independent of the receptivity of partners to renegotiate the problem-solving roles even though such renegotiation may result in their giving up some of their resources or power.

Older children's and young adolescents' openness to role renegotiation may have stemmed from age-related increases in the understanding of social conventions, reciprocity, and fairness (see Youniss, 1980). For example, they often yielded when their partner alluded to the rules of the task (e.g. "She [the researcher] said we were supposed to work together"), a type of justification that was seldom effective when used by preschoolers.[1] Age-related increases in successful role renegotiation may also have been due to age-related improvements in the ability to monitor the negotiation process and switch strategies or drop the issue if success appeared unlikely. Dropping the bid for renegotiation before the partner becomes too frustrated and aroused may repair the interaction and increase the probability that the renegotiation bid will work if introduced at a later time. We saw ample evidence of this increased flexibility in role negotiation and renegotiation by the late elementary school years (10 or 11 years of age). Teasley and Roschelle (1993) have noted a similar pattern when collaborators are exchanging ideas and opinions about a task, which suggests that this flexibility and adaptiveness of negotiation extends beyond role renegotiation to the renegotiation of knowledge.

Finally, in addition to their greater mutuality and flexibility in role negotiation, older collaborators also appeared to have a more relaxed approach to turn taking. Preschoolers had aimed for strict equality: They kept track of each other's contributions by counting block placements and impeding placements when someone was trying to extend his or her turn. They also kept a running commentary about the division of labor and often reminded each other about what they had agreed upon. Eight- and 11-year-olds, in contrast, negotiated the division of labor at the start of the session and subsequently paid less attention to each other's specific contributions; the division of labor became an issue only when one of the partners seriously violated a previous agreement or attempted to renegotiate it. Finally, older children and young adolescents were also more likely than younger children to talk about the goals of the task. For example, they discussed whether the experimenter's relatively vague exhortation to "work together" meant cooperate, divide the labor, or simply try to do the task as efficiently as possible, even if this meant that the more competent partner would do all the work and the less competent partner would act as gopher and cheerleader. Their discussion of the goals might suggest that these older children and young adolescents were more aware of the need to establish a shared understanding of the goals of the task. These shared goals not only sustained and repaired collaboration, but also increased the probability that these collaborations would lead to the joint creation and revision of knowledge.

Age-related differences in the negotiation and renegotiation of knowledge

Peer collaborative processes can provide insights not only into how collaborators negotiate their roles and the goals of the task, but also into the processes of knowledge construction and revision (see Miller, 1987; Rubtsov, 1981). Negotiations will succeed and affect individuals' knowledge only if the negotiators enter into the process in "good faith," that is, with the goal of finding a joint solution to the problem. Although these cooperative argumentation processes are evident by toddlerhood, they show considerable development across childhood and adolescence. One major developmental shift, which occurs during elementary school years, involves the ability to operate on the reasoning of others and create a joint understanding of a problem.

Numerous researchers have demonstrated that peers who engage in transactive dialogues, that is, dialogues in which they operate on each other's reasoning, are more likely to increase their conceptual understanding. These dialogues can take the form of coordinating ideas into a general theory or rule that is then applied and tested (e.g., Tolmie *et al.*, 1993) or resolving disagreements and evaluating the merits of contrasting approaches to the problem (e.g. Azmitia & Montgomery, 1993; Berkowitz & Gibbs, 1985; Kruger, 1992).

Drawing on Piaget (1965), Berkowitz and Gibbs (1983, 1985) suggested that when peers operate on each other's reasoning, they become aware of contradictions and inadequacies in their thinking. This awareness promotes internal disequilibrium, the resolution of which results in cognitive growth. Although transactive dialogues have largely been investigated from a neo-Piagetian perspective, they can also be investigated within Vygotsky's framework, which has the advantage of focusing attention on how transactive dialogues create knowledge (Forman & McPhail, 1993).[2]

Because Piaget (1965) believed that the capacity to engage in transactive discussion and reasoning is attained only during the formal operational period, early studies of the relation between transactive dialogues and cognitive development (e.g., Berkowitz & Gibbs, 1983) were focused on adolescents and young adults. Recently, however, Kruger (1992) and Berkowitz and Gibbs (1985) have explored transactive dialogues in younger children. Although their results suggest that peer interacting minds create transactive dialogues long before the formal operational stage, it is the case that younger (elementary school-aged) children produce not only fewer but different kinds of transacts than adolescents and adults. Children's transactive dialogues consist largely of representational transacts, which tend to be paraphrases of their partner's reasoning. Adolescents' and young adults' transactive dialogues, in contrast, contain a high proportion of operational transacts, which transform and challenge their partner's thinking. Because operational transacts are associated with greater conceptual change than representational transacts, Berkowitz and Gibbs (1985) and Berkowitz and others (1987) suggest that, at least in tasks that tap reasoning skills, collaborations between adolescents or young adults may have a greater developmental potential than those between younger children.

Berkowitz and others' (1987) framework represents one of the few attempts to map developmental changes in peer interacting minds across the life span. They propose that, despite large individual differences during adolescence and adulthood, operational transactive dialogues increase in density and become vehicles for the synthesis of well-documented conceptual frameworks or scientific theories. (The final stages in their theory probably represent the potential of peer interactive minds; it is especially unlikely that many individuals will reach their final stage, *ideal discourse*.)

At this ideal stage, dialogue is focused on developing the best position, without concern for personal views, power, or status. Because few individuals are able to keep these concerns in check, the capacity to create and maintain ideal discourse may be a defining feature of wisdom. However, while an individual might have the capacity to create ideal discourse, he or she would need a wise partner actually to instantiate it. That is, as argued earlier, an individual's strategies, no matter how sophisticated, will not succeed in the absence of a receptive partner. Hence, to create and maintain ideal discourse both partners need to keep their personal views, power, or status in check so as to develop the best possible theory or position.

Berkowitz and others' (1987) model provides a useful framework for capturing age-related changes in transactive dialogues. It now remains to be demonstrated empirically that these transactive processes lead to specific cognitive outcomes. Studies that link transactive dialogues to cognitive *outcomes* are rare, in part because of the current emphasis on the importance of focusing on developmental *processes*. . . .

To develop practical applications of our findings, we must consider both outcomes and processes of peer interacting minds. Effective peer collaborative programs are surprisingly difficult to implement or reproduce in schools and universities, and thus, unless we can explain in detail how to create processes and outcomes, many teachers will not be receptive to our proposals. In the following section, I will highlight some of the differences between the potentials and the realities of peer interacting minds, to explore the issue of practical application further.

From potential to reality

As our understanding of peer interactive minds grows, it is reasonable to ask ourselves whether our findings generalize beyond the relatively controlled problem-solving contexts or tasks we have tended to study. This question is especially relevant given the considerable interest of educators in using our findings to engineer peer collaborative and tutoring programs in schools and universities. . . . We seldom admit that, while we know what kinds of peer interactive minds promote cognitive development, many of us are not yet sure of how to replicate these interactive minds in the "wilds" of the classroom without completely restructuring the schools.[3] I now turn to some factors that lead to this variability and may pose obstacles for creating and maintaining the synergy of peer interactive minds.

One problem with our models is that we have conceptualized the negotiation of roles and knowledge too romantically. For example, following Piaget (1965), our models often assume that, at least by middle childhood or adolescence, peers will adhere to principles of reciprocity and equality. The reality is that, across the life span, peer negotiations during collaborative problem solving (or in other arenas, for that matter) are often Machiavellian – that is, motivated by power and self-interest more than by the desire to find the best solution. The negotiation process is also affected by the social status of the collaborators. Even in the laboratory, it is often the case that an expert will maintain the status quo by deferring to a novice partner with higher social status. During informal conversations with these experts, some told us that they saw the collaboration as an opportunity to interact and potentially develop a relationship with a more popular peer who would not otherwise be open to an extended interaction. Other experts explained that they had deferred to the more popular novices because they were afraid of the consequences of challenging them. For example, one boy told us he worried that if he did not let his partner "run" things during our laboratory task, his partner would tell others not to play with him when they returned to the classroom. Taken together, these disclosures by experts suggest that we need to consider that processes and outcomes of peer interactive minds are embedded within the larger context of peer relationships.

The processes and outcomes of peer interactive minds also depend on the meaning that collaborators attribute to the task. While our laboratory research suggested that by middle childhood most children were capable of collaborating effectively with a peer, when we studied these same children's and adolescents' collaborations and role negotiations in the classroom (Azmitia & Linnet, 1995) we observed numerous power struggles and breakdowns that interfered with problem solving and task completion. Interestingly, some of the children and adolescents who had viewed working together and exploring a variety of perspectives as more important than task accuracy in the laboratory were more concerned with task accuracy in the classroom. When we queried them informally about these situational differences, they pointed out that while their performance in our laboratory tasks would not show up in their report cards, their performance in the classroom would. Thus, we must also consider how individuals' personal stakes in the outcome of the problem-solving process influence their willingness or ability to display their collaborative and negotiation competencies.

A final problem is that our models of the links between negotiation and cognitive development are too simple. For example, perhaps spurred on by finding positive correlations between transactive negotiations and cognitive growth, we have often assumed a causal connection between them. However, this is an empirical question that must be addressed by future work. The positive correlations between some aspects of dialogues and cognitive growth may have also led us to assume that "more is better," but our current models do not have a way of accounting for the common finding that progress, or insight, occurs during one dramatic moment during which the timing and process is indistinguishable from other transactive negotiations. We also have a poor understanding of why ideas and issues that were unresolved during inter-action influence the subsequent posttest performance of individuals. Consider the following negotiation between two 11-year-olds who were trying to decide which pizza ingredients, if any, had led to the death of a subset of diners:

C1:   So it has to be onions and green olives.

C2:   Yeah, onions but it can't be green olives. See, this dead one doesn't have it (*points to dead one*).

C1:   That doesn't matter, it [green olives] just has to be in the dead but not in the alive. See, no green olives, no green olives, no green olives (*points to alive*).

C2:   But it has to be in all of them [the dead]. Otherwise they wouldn't all die. What killed this one then? (*points to dead diner that didn't eat green olives*).

C1:   The onions, see, they [dead] all have onions.

C2:   Well, I'm writing just onions.

C1:   And green olives. Onions *and* (*emphasizes*) green olives.

C2:   Let's just go on to the next one.

C1:   OK. (*Whispers*) But it was onions and green olives.

Although Child 2 was unconvinced during the negotiation, his performance in a subsequent individual posttest indicated that he understood that an ingredient did not have to be in all the pizzas consumed by the dead diners to be a causal factor. Piaget's followers would not be puzzled by this finding, because they would propose that this conflict provoked an internal disequilibrium that Child 2 subsequently resolved on his own. However, this explanation suffers from circularity, as at present we lack the tools to measure internal disequilibrium. Perhaps a different way of looking at this delayed effect on knowledge revision is to ask what motivated Child 2 to reconsider his position. As will be seen in the next section, one possibility is that because these adolescents were close friends, the respect of Child 2 for Child 1 may have led him to puzzle over his friend's position after the problem-solving interaction had ended. This added opportunity for reflection increased the potential that Child 2 would recognize the validity of his partner's argument, thus abandoning his less adequate belief. This explanation, of course, will also suffer from circularity until we are able to devise a way to test it empirically. It does appear, however, that, at least in some situations, by early adolescence the interacting minds of friends can be more powerful contexts for change than those of acquaintances.

The interacting minds of friends

To date, we know very little about the dynamics and cognitive products of different peer relationships, and, in particular, acquaintanceship and friendship. This gap in our knowledge is unfortunate, because, as Moss suggests, "It is evident that different relationship contexts fundamentally will affect collaborative cognitive endeavors with respect to participants' motivations for engaging in joint activity and how responsibility is shared during interaction" (Moss, 1992, p. 118).

There are several features of friendship that may promote the negotiation and renegotiation of roles and knowledge. First, conversations between friends are characterized by greater mutuality than collaborations between acquaintances (see Gottman, 1983; Hartup, 1996), which may indicate that friends are more attuned to each other's needs and goals and are thus better able to establish a shared understanding. Second, because friends trust each other, they may be more willing than acquaintances to expose their views and challenge each other (Nelson & Aboud, 1985; Shantz & Hobart, 1989). Third, because friends have great respect for each other, they might attend closely to each other's points, thus increasing the possibility of influence (Hartup, 1996). Finally, because friends are concerned with equality and fairness, they may put greater effort into negotiating and renegotiating roles and meaning.

Up until recently, most research on the developmental affordances of friendship focused on socioemotional development. There are several reasons for this state of affairs. First, Piaget (1965) and Vygotsky (1978), the most influential theorists on research on peer learning, did not elaborate on the cognitive affordances of different peer relationships. Researchers following in their footsteps have thus focused on assessing the impact of factors that play a role in Piaget's and Vygostky's models, such as expertise, power, and onto-genetic constraints. Second, up until recently researchers were in search of universal processes and outcomes of peer interacting minds. Third, the dynamics of children's friendships are not well understood, and given the tremendous variability that is already inherent in peer interactive minds, researchers may have been reticent to introduce yet another wild card into the equation. Finally, as Damon (1990) observed, teachers often assume that children or adolescents will not work effectively with friends. Because research on peer interacting minds has often been driven by educational considerations, our laboratory tasks have modeled the classroom – that is, explored collaborations between acquaintances.

Increasingly, however, researchers interested in cognitive development have explored the processes and outcomes of the interactive minds of friends. Their findings are mixed. Some (e.g., Azmitia & Montgomery, 1993; Hartup, 1996; Nelson & Aboud, 1985) have found that collaborations between friends lead to greater equality in roles, more transactive discourse, and larger increases in knowledge than collaborations between acquaintances, but others (e.g., Berndt et al., 1988; Newcomb et al., 1979) have failed to find differences in the processes and outcomes of the collaborations of friends and acquaintances. After reviewing these studies, Ryan Montgomery and I speculated that the nature of the task and its difficulty may mediate differences in the processes and outcomes of the collaborations of friends and acquaintances. In particular, it appeared that studies that yielded support for the cognitive advantage of working with a friend had employed challenging tasks or tasks that drew heavily on metacognitive skills such as planning, monitoring, and evaluating evidence.

To test these speculations, we carried out a study of young adolescents' (11-year-olds) collaborations on problems of isolating causal variables (e.g., which pizza ingredients, if any, caused the death of some of the members of a group of diners, and an adaptation of Kuhn & Brannock's, 1977, plant problem, which asks individuals to look at an array of healthy and sick plants and isolate the variable(s) that are responsible for keeping the plants healthy). We chose the isolation of variables problem because the mature understanding of causality figures prominently in theories of cognitive development. Also, age-related differences in the ability to isolate causal variables have received considerable attention by Kuhn and her colleagues. Because they have provided detailed descriptions of the microgenetic processes through which individuals acquire an understanding of causality, we could use their descriptions to identify the peer discourse events that would provide a window into the negotiation of knowledge and its potential internalization into the individual minds of collaborating peers.

As predicted, we found that adolescents who collaborated with a friend exhibited greater pretest to posttest change than adolescents who collaborated with an acquaintance. When we analyzed the videotaped collaborations, we found that friends were more likely than acquaintances to justify their proposals, work collaboratively, engage in transactive discussions of task concepts and solutions, and evaluate their outcomes. Although all these discourse and interaction features were positively correlated with problem-solving accuracy during both the collaboration and posttest sessions, only the correlation between transactive conflicts and problem-solving accuracy was statistically significant.

These findings were mediated by task difficulty. In particular, the differences between friends and acquaintances regarding transactive dialogues and task performance were significant only in the most difficult isolation of variables problems. Further analyses of the interactions revealed that, in the more difficult problems, the collaborations of acquaintances tended to disintegrate. For example, adolescents often became absorbed in the task and began to work individually and produce self-directed (private) speech. There was also an increase in power struggles and conceptual conflicts characterized by unilateral negotiation strategies, such as insistence, physical blocks, or verbal aggression. Most pairs of friends, in contrast, were able to sustain and repair the collaboration in these difficult circumstances. They maintained their partner's involvement by asking questions, offering encouragement, and making statements to the effect that "We're in this together" or, as one girl told her partner, "They [the experimenters] are trying to trick us, but we'll show 'em." During conceptual conflicts, they justified their positions, were receptive to criticism and to their partner's proposals, and refrained from personal attacks.

Although one could argue that these differences in the collaborations of friends and acquaintances reflect differences in their social and cognitive competencies, the adolescents were randomly assigned to the friends or acquaintances conditions, and subsequent analyses revealed no differences in the pretest scores of the two groups. I suggest that it is more likely that the differences in collaboration processes and outcomes reflect variations in adolescents' motivations to achieve a shared understanding of their roles, goals, and the task, as well as the ease with which they could achieve such understanding. For example, adolescents' respect for their friends and eagerness to work with them may have led them to work harder at repairing the collaboration and resolving conflicts of roles or ideas. It is also possible that because of their longer interaction history, the interaction routines of friends were more automatized, and thus they were able to maintain the collaboration even when the problem made high demands on their cognitive resources. . . .

I do not want to leave the reader with the impression that in order to maximize the synergy and cognitive outcomes of children's and adolescents' interactive minds, we should try to ensure that they collaborate with their friends. Collaborating with an acquaintance might allow individuals to stretch their skills in the service of accommodating to the interactive and cognitive skills of an unfamiliar partner (see Rogoff, 1990). Moreover, because in both childhood and adulthood there is a decline in the incidence of negotiations among close friends and romantic partners (Clark, 1984; Krappmann, personal communication, October 1993), this factor will have to be taken into account in our models about the relation between negotiation and cognitive development. It is possible that this decline in negotiations is domain-specific (e.g., confined to duties and responsibilities). It seems likely that negotiations about knowledge, ideas, and values remain an active component of friendships. If such were not the case, the relationship would not evolve, and over time, individuals would feel bored and stifled and search for new, more exciting relationships (see Fogel, 1993).

Peer interactive minds across the life span

As mentioned earlier, work on children and adolescents has proceeded relatively independently from work on adults and the elderly. Given this state of affairs, one might ask what researchers studying peer collaborative cognition at different points of the life span could learn from each other's work. I suggest that those of us who have focused on childhood and adolescence would do well to take note that we have to study both interacting minds and solitary reflection. Staudinger (1996), for example, found that adults who were allowed a few minutes of solitary reflection following their discussion with a peer gave more sophisticated solutions to uncertain life situations than adults who worked alone or participated in peer discussions but were not allowed these moments of solitude before the posttest. Perhaps we have lost sight of the importance of solitary conscious or unconscious activity for cognitive growth as a result of the contemporary emphasis on the social construction of knowledge. Individual posttests are not enough. We have to explore the genesis and ontogenesis of knowledge longitudinally, trying, as Staudinger (1996) suggests, to capture the delicate balance between interactive and solitary activities.

It might be useful to study informal discussions of issues or problems in which children and adolescents are not constrained by the demands of generating a tangible product, because this "cognitive play" seems essential for the genesis and ontogenesis of knowledge. We also need to increase our understanding of the situatedness (see Suchman, 1993) of peer interactive minds, paying greater attention to the fact that our task and the participants' interaction processes are embedded in a larger cultural setting that influences task solutions and collaboration dynamics.

In addition, we should move beyond relying exclusively on analyses of verbal processes to studying other ways in which peer interactive minds communicate and learn from each other. Hutchins and Paley (1993), for example, have shown how incorporating actions and nonverbal messages into the analyses can help us not only to illuminate dimensions of knowledge construction and revision that talk does not capture, but also to contextualize the meaning of the talk. Finally, because tolerance for ambiguity and flexibility in considering alternatives may be one of the hallmarks of adulthood, and perhaps the major difference between children's and adults' interactive minds, we must begin to study other types of tasks, especially problems with ill-formed or, at the very least, multiple solutions. Even in adulthood, however, flexibility, and tolerance of ambiguity is not guaranteed. Indeed, truly sophisticated problem solving that takes into account ambiguities and what is within the realm of possibility may be a defining feature of wisdom (Baltes, 1993).

Scientists studying peer interactive minds in adulthood and old age might emulate the work on childhood and adolescence insofar as they pay more attention to age-related changes in the processes and outcomes of peer interactive minds. There are both improvements and declines in communicative, metacognitive, and negotiation skills over adulthood (see Baltes, 1993), but at this point we do not know how these normative and non-normative developmental changes influence the processes and products of peer interactive minds. An interesting question is whether one compensatory strategy for remaining productive and creative is to enlist the collaboration of others, and thus, in some cases, older adults may benefit more from collaboration than younger adults. If so, the benefits of collaboration would be greater in older than younger adulthood. . . .

Peer interactive minds: theoretical and methodological issues

Despite our progress in understanding the processes and outcomes of peer interactive minds, we currently face several obstacles that make it difficult to create a life-span developmental theory of peer collaborative cognition. First, as mentioned earlier, one challenge is that the work on children and adolescents for the most part has proceeded independently from the work on younger and older adults. Often, different questions, methodologies, and problems characterize research on early and later parts of the life span. Thus, it will not be easy to link the findings together. Second, regardless of which part of the life span we focus on, the formulation of powerful concepts and mechanisms for the co-construction of cognition has not been accompanied by empirical documentation of how the social discourse becomes the internal discourse that leads to knowledge construction and revision. It is not that such documentation has not been attempted. Rather, we are still hampered by our inability to look inside minds to explain the puzzle that even in cases where partners appear to have the same amount of knowledge before the collaboration, the same discourse events promote cognitive growth in some individuals but not in others.

I will suggest that part of the problem is that we need to rethink our pretest–collaboration–posttest designs in such a way that they are adapted to the slow, nonlinear pace of cognitive development. As mentioned, we should also consider whether our fascination with peer interacting minds may have led us to underestimate the contribution of solitary work and reflection to cognitive development, or at least to fail to recognize that cognitive development requires both social interaction and solitary reflection.[4] Finally, concerning an issue that I will not discuss further because I cannot offer a solution, we need to develop more sensitive measures of our research participants' knowledge and competencies. For example, our current penchant for assessing mastery or knowledge from the products of pretest, interactive, and posttest sessions may over- or underestimate the competence of our participants. We often also make the incorrect assumption that if individuals are exposed to a more sophisticated, well-justified view, they will recognize its import and revise their own thinking, or alternatively, if their partner's view is less sophisticated, they will challenge it and through the process of explaining their objections, increase their confidence in their own beliefs. The fact is that we still know very little about the impetus for knowledge construction and revision during and following social interaction. . . .

Our lack of progress is not due to a lack of powerful mechanisms or metaphors – for example, co-construction, internalization, appropriation, and transactive discussion – but rather at least partly to our failure to specify these mechanisms at both the theoretical and empirical level. Lawrence and Valsiner's comment concerning the limitations of our current treatment of internalization can also be applied to our other mechanisms:

> This general concept of internalization is not sufficient for elaborated theoretical use, nor is it helpful in deriving empirical research methodologies. To go beyond generalities, it is necessary to specify what

"materials" are imported from society into the intra-personal world of any individual and *in what ways* it operates.

(1993, p. 151)

In his commentary on Lawrence and Valsiner's paper, Wertsch (1993) makes a radical proposal: If we really want to understand the cognitive outcomes of social interaction, we need to stop using metaphors such as internalization, which imply a dualism between the social and the individual. He suggests that we substitute the concept of mastery for internalization and focus our efforts on mapping how the performance of individuals changes over the course of a social interaction and beyond (e.g. during future individual or collaborative encounters with the problem or task). . . . If we do decide to go the "task performance equals mastery" route, then we need to gain a better understanding of how contextual and developmental factors influence the processes and outcomes of peer interactive minds and use our findings to develop a well-specified theoretical model. In addition, as mentioned, we should reconsider our current ways of assessing mastery or knowledge.

I have been one of the proponents of the advantages of the pretest–collaboration–posttest design for assessing the cognitive outcomes of peer interactive minds. As mentioned earlier, upon reflection I have come to recognize that there are several problems with this design. First, it is often the case that improvements in children's and adolescents' performance during the collaboration fail to materialize in the posttest. Rogoff, Radziszewska, and Masiello (in press) have proposed that the finding that gains observed during the collaboration session do not generalize to the individual posttest is not surprising because the collaboration and the posttest represent different social contexts. They add that it is unreasonable to assume that posttest performance is the best characterization of the "true inner state" of our participants, and suggest that following the collaboration, we should assess their participation in a variety of social and individual contexts to get a better estimate of conceptual change. . . .

An additional problem with the posttest design is that it is based on the assumption that we have a grasp of the pace of development and thus know when we should measure it – that is, when to administer the posttest and how much change to expect. In a series of studies, Christine Howe and her colleagues (Howe, Tolmie, & Rodgers, 1992; Tolmie *et al.*, 1993) have explored children's, adolescents', and young adults' co-construction of understanding in the domain of physics. Their work is unique in that they administer more than one posttest following the collaboration session. What initially intrigued me about their findings was that they demonstrated that the cognitive benefits of the collaboration did not materialize immediately. In the first posttest, peers who had engaged in transactive discussions showed a similar level of mastery to those who had not engaged in these types of dialogues. In the posttest that was administered two months later, however, peers who had engaged in transactive dialogues showed significantly more sophisticated understanding of physics than those who had not. Howe and her colleagues proposed that this delayed effect may index the time that it takes individuals to re-equilibrate their cognitive structures or to reflect on the understanding that they co-constructed during the collaboration and put it into practice.

In the context of an electronic discussion sponsored by the Laboratory of Comparative Human Cognition (San Diego, California), Steve Draper, one of Tolmie and Howe's colleagues, pointed out in jest that their data suggest that the process of fermentation may provide the new metaphor for cognitive development. That is, the products of peer interactive minds may need to ferment for a while before they are incorporated into existing cognitive structures and begin to guide performance. . . . To track the fermentation process empirically, we need to carry out longitudinal research. The value of carrying out such research is illustrated by the contributions that Deanna Kuhn and her colleagues (e.g., Kuhn, 1991; Kuhn, *et al.*, 1988; Kuhn & Phelps, 1979) have made to mapping microgenetic changes in the scientific reasoning of individuals. An important contribution of their research is to show that change is not linear; that is, it is subject to false starts, regressions, and resistance to change. In many cases, individuals also fail to realize the significance of their findings, thus ignoring potential insights or solutions (Kuhn & Phelps, 1979).

Carrying out longitudinal studies of peer interactive minds, both in terms of including multiple collaborative sessions and a series of posttests spaced over several months, is not the only (or perhaps even the best) solution for linking the processes and cognitive products of peer collaboration, but it is at least an alternative that is worth pursuing. Without stronger and better specified theoretical and measurement models, however, even this alternative may fail to help us make significant progress in our understanding of peer interactive minds. One of our biggest challenges, and the one that I would like to explore in my future work, is understanding enough about tasks, collaboration processes and outcomes, and their developmental patterns to create the situations in which peer interactive minds produce, revise, and appropriate knowledge both in the laboratory and in the "wilds" of the classroom, the work place, or any environment of daily living.

Notes

1 This strategy, however, was often effective when paired with a threat to tell the experimenter that the child was not following his or her instructions to work together.

2 Piaget's and Vygotsky's frameworks are not as far apart as they are often portrayed in the literature. Process analyses are quite common in contemporary research that follows from Piaget's theory, and researchers in the Vygotskian tradition are

increasingly considering the role of ontogenetic constraints in negotiation. Moreover, there is a growing trend to integrate both approaches to generate a tighter framework for conceptualizing the cognitive products of peer collaboration.

3 Of course, one solution to this problem *is* to restructure the schools (e.g. Tharp & Gallimore, 1988). However, mounting evidence suggests that the change brought about by restructuring is remarkably difficult to sustain, and that over time the institutions often revert to their initial state. Moreover, most of us do not have the experience or resources needed to restructure the schools.

4 Of course, there is no such thing as a solitary mind: the individual always hears the "voices" of others who have influenced his or her thinking and problem-solving competencies (see Wertsch, 1991). By solitary reflection I simply mean thought that occurs when one is by oneself.

References

Azmitia, M. (1988). Peer interaction and problem solving: When are two heads better than one? *Child Development, 59*, 87–96.

Azmitia, M. (1989, April). Constraints on learning through collaboration: The influence of age, expertise, and interaction dynamics. Paper presented at the biennial meetings of the Society for Research in Child Development, Kansas City, KS.

Azmitia, M., & Linnet, J. (1995). Elementary school children's conflicts with friends and acquaintances. Unpublished manuscript.

Azmitia, M., Lopez, E. M., Conner, S., & Kolesnik, K. (1991, July). Children's negotiation of collaboration and learning. Paper presented at the biennial meetings of the International Society for the Study of Behavioral Development, Minneapolis, MN.

Azmitia, M., & Montgomery, R. (1993). Friendship, transactive dialogues, and the development of scientific reasoning. *Social Development, 2*, 202–221.

Azmitia, M., & Perlmutter, M. (1989). Social influences on children's cognition: State of the art and future directions. In H. W. Reese (Ed.), *Advances in child development and behavior* (Vol. 22, pp. 89–144). New York: Academic Press.

Baltes, P. B. (1993). The aging mind: Potential and limits. *Gerontologist, 33*, 580–594.

Berkowitz, M. W., & Gibbs, J. C. (1983). Measuring the developmental features of moral discussion, *Merrill-Palmer Quarterly, 29*, 399–410.

Berkowitz, M. W., & Gibbs, J. C. (1985). The process of moral conflict resolution and moral development. In M. W. Berkowitz (Ed.), *New directions for child development: Peer conflict and psychological growth* (pp. 71–84). San Francisco: Jossey-Bass.

Berkowitz, M. W., Oser, F., & Althof, W. (1987). The development of sociomoral discourse. In W. M. Kurtines and J. L. Gewirtz (Eds.), *Moral development through social interaction* (pp. 322–352). New York: Wiley.

Berndt, T. J., Perry, T. B., & Miller, K. E. (1988). Friends' and classmates' interactions on academic tasks. *Journal of Educational Psychology, 80*, 506–513.

Bos, M. C. (1934). Experimental study of productive collaboration. *Acta Psychologica, 3*, 315–426.

Brownell, C. A., & Carriger, M. S. (1991). Changes in cooperation and self–other differentiation during the second year. *Child Development, 61*, 1164–1174.

Clark, M. S. (1984). Record keeping in two types of relationships. *Journal of Personality and Social Psychology, 47*, 549–557.

Cooper, C. R., Ayers-Lopez, S., & Marquis, S. (1982). Children's discourse during peer learning in experimental and naturalistic situations. *Discourse Processes, 5*, 177–191.

Cooper, C. R., & Cooper, R. G. (1984). Peer learning discourse: What develops? In S. Kuczaj (Ed.), *Children's discourse* (pp. 77–97). New York: Springer.

Corsaro, W. M. (1985). *Friendship and peer culture in the early years.* Norwood, NJ: Ablex.

Damon, W. (1990). Social relations and children's thinking skills. In D. Kuhn (Ed.), *Perspectives on teaching and learning thinking skills: Contributions to Human Development* (pp. 95–107). Basel: Krager.

Ellis, S., & Gauvain, M. (1992). Social and cultural influences on children's collaborative interactions. In L. T. Winegar & J. Valsiner (Eds.), *Children's development within social context: Vol 2. Research and methodology* (pp.155–180). Hillsdale, NJ: Erlbaum.

Ellis, S., & Rogoff, B. (1986). Problem solving in children's management of instruction. In E. C. Mueller & C. R. Cooper (Eds.), *Process and outcome in peer relationships* (pp. 301–325). New York: Academic Press.

Ellis, S., & Siegler, R. S. (in press). The development of problem solving. In *Handbook of perception and cognition.*

Fogel, A. (1993). *Developing through relationships: Origins of communication, self and culture.* Chicago: University of Chicago Press.

Forman, E. A. (1992). Discourse, intersubjectivity, and the development of peer collaboration: A Vygotskian approach. In L. T. Winegar & J. Valsiner (Eds.), *Children's development within social context: Vol. 2. Research and methodology* (pp. 143–160). Hillsdale, NJ: Erlbaum.

Forman, E. A., & McPhail, J. (1993). Vygotskian perspective in children's collaborative problem solving activity. In E. A. Forman, N. Minick, & C. A. Stone (Eds.), *Contexts for learning: Sociocultural dynamics in children's development* (pp. 213–229). Oxford: Oxford University Press.

Garton, A. F. (1992). *Social interaction and the development of language and cognition.* Hillsdale, NJ: Erlbaum.

Garvey, C. (1987, April). Creation and avoidance of conflict. Paper presented at the biennial meetings of the Society for Research in Child Development, Baltimore, MD.

Gilovich, T. (1991). *How we know what isn't so: The fallibility of human reason in everyday life.* New York: Free Press.

Goodwin, C. (1993, November). Seeing as a situated phenomenon. Paper presented at the NATO sponsored workshop Discourse, Tools, and Reasoning: Situated Cognition and Technologically Supported Environments, Lucca, Italy.

Gottman, J. (1983). How children become friends. *Monographs of the Society for Research in Child Development, 48* (3, Serial 201).

Hartup, W. W. (1983). Peer relations. In E. M. Hetherington (Ed.) & P. H. Mussen (Series Ed.). *Handbook of child psychology: Vol. 4. Socialization, personality, and social development* (pp. 103–196). New York: Wiley.

Hartup, W. W. (1996). Cooperation, close relationships, and cognitive development. In W. M. Bukowski, A. F. Newcomb, & W. W. Hartup (Eds.), *The company they keep: Friendships and their developmental significance.* New York: Cambridge University Press.

Hinde, R. A. (1979). *Towards understanding relationships.* New York: Academic Press.

Howe, C., Tolmie, A., & Rodgers, C. (1992). The acquisition of conceptual knowledge in science by primary school children: Group interaction and the understanding of motion down an incline. *British Journal of Developmental Psychology, 10,* 113–130.

Hutchins, E., & Paley, L. (1993, November). Constructing meaning from space, gesture, and talk. Paper presented at the NATO sponsored workshop Discourse, Tools, and Reasoning: Situated Cognition and Technologically Supported Environments, Lucca, Italy.

John-Steiner, V. (1985). *Notebooks of the mind.* New York: Harper.

Kruger, A. C. (1992). The effect of peer and adult–child transactive discussions on moral reasoning. *Merrill-Palmer Quarterly, 38,* 191–211.

Kruger, A. C. (1993). Peer collaboration: Conflict, cooperation, or both? *Social Development, 2,* 165–183.

Kuhn, D. (1991). *The skills of argument.* Cambridge: Cambridge University Press.

Kuhn, D., Amsel, E., & O'Loughlin, M. (1988). *The development of scientific thinking skills.* New York: Academic Press.

Kuhn, D., & Brannock, J. (1977). Development of the isolation of variables scheme in experimental and natural experiments' contexts. *Developmental Psychology, 13,* 9–13.

Kuhn, D., & Phelps, E. (1979) A methodology for observing development of a formal reasoning strategy. In D. Kuhn (Ed.), *New directions for child development: Intellectual development beyond childhood* (pp. 45–58). San Francisco: Jossey-Bass.

Lawrence, J. A., & Valsiner, J. (1993). Conceptual roots of internalization: From transmission to transformation. *Human Development, 36,* 150–167.

Levin, L., & Druyan., S. (1993). When sociocognitive transaction among peers fails: The case of misconceptions in science. *Child Development, 63,* 1571–1591.

Miller, M. (1987). Argumentation and cognition. In M. Hickmann (Ed.), *Social and functional approaches to language and thought* (pp. 225–249). San Diego, CA: Academic Press.

Moss, E. (1992). The socioaffective context of joint cognitive activity. In L. T. Winegar & J. Valsiner (Eds.), *Children's development within social context: Vol 2. Research and methodology* (pp. 117–154). Hillsdale, NJ: Erlbaum.

Nelson, J., & Aboud, F. (1985). The resolution of social conflict between friends. *Child Development, 56,* 1009–1017.

Newcomb, A. F., Brady, J. E., & Hartup, W. W. (1979). Friendship and incentive condition as determinants of children's task-oriented social behavior. *Child Development, 50,* 878–881.

Perret-Clermont, A. N., Perret, J. F., & Bell, N. (1991). The social construction of meaning and cognitive activity in elementary school children. In L. B. Resnick, J. M. Levine, & S. D. Teasley (Eds.), *Perspectives on socially shared cognition* (pp. 41–62). Washington, DC: American Psychological Association.

Piaget, J. (1965). *The moral judgement of the child.* New York: Basic Books.

Pozzi, S., Healy, L., & Hoyles, C. (1993). Learning and interaction in groups with computers: When do ability and gender matter? *Social Development, 2,* 222–241.

Rogoff, B. (1990). *Apprenticeship in thinking: Cognitive development in social context*. New York: Oxford University Press.

Rogoff, B., Radziszewska, B., & Masiello, T. (in press). Analysis of developmental process in sociocultural activity. In L. Martin, K. Nelson, & E. Tobach (Eds.), *Cultural psychology and activity theory*. Cambridge: Cambridge University Press.

Rubtsov, V. V. (1981). The role of cooperation in the development of intelligence. *Soviet Psychology, 19*, 41–62.

Selman, R. L. (1980). *The growth of interpersonal understanding*. New York: Academic Press.

Shantz, C. U., & Hobart, C. J. (1989). Social conflict and development: Peers and siblings. In T. J. Berndt & G. W. Ladd (Eds.), *Peer relationships in child development* (pp. 71–94). New York: Wiley.

Staudinger, U. M. (1996). Wisdom and social-interactive foundation of the mind. In P. B. Baltes & U. M. Staudinger (Eds.), *Interactive minds: Life-span perspectives on the social foundation of cognition* (pp. 276–318), Cambridge: Cambridge University Press.

Suchman, L. (1993, November). Centers of coordination: A case and some themes. Paper presented at the NATO sponsored workshop Discourse, Tools, and Reasoning: Situated Cognition and Technologically Supported Environments, Lucca, Italy.

Teasley, S. D., & Roschelle, J. (1993). Constructing a joint problem space: The computer as a tool for sharing knowledge. In S. P. Lajoie & S. D. Derry (Eds.), *Computers as cognitive tools* (pp. 229–258), Hillsdale, NJ: Erlbaum.

Tharp, R., & Gallimore, R. (1988). *Rousing minds to life*. Cambridge: Cambridge University Press.

Tolmie, A., Howe, C., Mackenzie, M., & Greer, K. (1993). Task design as an influence on dialogue and learning: Primary School work with object flotation. *Social Development, 2*, 183–201.

Tomasello, M., Kruger, A. C., & Ratner, H. H. (1993). Cultural learning. *Behavioral and Brain Sciences, 16*, 495–552.

Verba, M. (1993). Construction and sharing of meanings in pretend play. In M. Stanback & H. Sinclair (Eds.), *Pretend play among 3-year-olds* (pp. 1–29). Hillsdale, NJ: Erlbaum.

Vygotsky, L. S. (1978). *Mind in society*. Cambridge, MA: Harvard University Press.

Wertsch, J. V. (1991). *Voices of the mind*. Cambridge: Cambridge University Press.

Wertsch, J. V. (1993). Commentary, *Human Development, 36*, 168–171.

Winegar, L. T. (1988). Children's emerging understanding of social events: Co-construction and social process. In J. Valsiner (Ed.), *Child development within culturally structured environments: Vol. 2. Social co-construction and environmental guidance in development* (pp. 3–27). Norwood, NJ: Ablex.

Youniss, J. (1980). *Parents and peers in social development*. Chicago: University of Chicago Press.

Part IV

Collaborative learning and peer interaction in the classroom

Chapter 12

Sociocultural processes of creative planning in children's playcrafting*

Jacquelyn Baker-Sennett, Eugene Matusov, and Barbara Rogoff

Leslie:	(*complaining about making too many changes in the play*) If we make up the whole thing over again it will be too hard.
Carol:	No it won't.
Robin:	No it won't.
Leslie:	We can't do it all right now.
Robin:	Yes we can. We almost already have. When we think of the parts, we think of the play!
Kim:	Yeah!
Carol:	Yeah!
Kim:	We just think of who the people are and . . .
Robin:	. . . and what they're going to do . . . And then we can organize it.

(*Snow White*, Session 3)

This chapter explores the sociocultural processes of creative planning through an examination of the process of children's collaborative creation of a play. We argue that creative planning processes are grounded in practical considerations of sociocultural activity, in a wedding of imagination and pragmatics. Original, workable ideas evolve from a process that is the synthesis of spontaneous improvisation and organized, directed activity, as individuals participate with others in sociocultural activities. We examine how a collaborative interactional system develops in the process of planning, and how this social organization is essential to the planning process, as a group of young children plan a play. We follow the germs of the children's ideas as they are offered, critiqued and elaborated by each other, and consider the role of classroom structure, teacher support, and fairy-tale scripts as cultural aspects of the event.

Our purpose is to develop the argument that creative planning involves flexible use of circumstances in the pursuit of goals. We work from a

* This is an edited version of a chapter that appeared in *Context and Cognition: Ways of learning and knowing*, Hemel Hempstead: Harvester-Wheatsheaf, 1992.

contextual perspective in which individual cognitive and social activity is seen as constituting and constituted by sociocultural processes. That is, the development of original and workable ideas can better be understood when we consider the social, cultural and institutional contexts in which creative planning takes place. We make the case that creative planning involves an active, dynamic social process that itself involves both advance planning and on-line improvisation. In order to follow the creative planning process we must trace the development of the social and cultural conditions in which creative planning occurs.

Creating as a social cognitive activity

Traditionally, researchers have considered both planning and creating as *individual* endeavours. This assumption can be attributed, in part, to the methodologies that have been employed. Researchers have typically examined children's ability to arrive at problem solutions under contrived circumstances, working on a task alone, under the direction of an adult experimenter in controlled conditions. But firm experimental control and focus on solitary thinking is ill-suited to an investigation of children's flexible and spontaneous problem solving. In everyday activities taking place outside the laboratory context, creative planning is often a flexible, collaborative venture (Csikszentmihalyi, 1988; John-Steiner, 1985; Rogoff, 1990; Vygotsky, 1978).

Planning typically occurs in elaborate sociocultural systems that may be invisible under isolated laboratory conditions. Although recent research suggests that collaborative processes may facilitate planning and creating (Bouchard, 1971; Weisberg, 1986; Azmitia, 1988; Radziszewska and Rogoff, 1988, 1991), there is limited information on how children plan under their own direction, outside the laboratory context. Likewise, there is little work that focuses on how personal, interpersonal and cultural processes together contribute to the development of creative plans. The present study focuses on how the interpersonal and cultural processes of an activity constitute and are constituted by planning processes when children engage in a collaborative long-term project with a fluid product.

Our use of the word 'social' relates to the sociocultural contexts in which cognitive processes such as creative planning are embedded and to the process of the emergence of relations between children that are essential to group creative planning. When planning a play, children need to develop the play itself and to develop a means of co-ordinating with each other to design the play. Their planning of the play is inherently embedded in their planning of how they, as a group, are going to plan the play; their interpersonal processes are organized towards the goal (among other goals) of producing an entertaining play. This is consistent with Gearhart's findings (1979) that 3-year-olds planning pretend shopping trips learned to adjust their planning process to take each other's plans into account, rather than simply expecting other children to serve as pliable tools for the execution of their own plans.

A sociocultural approach focuses us on the *process* (rather than the products) of creative planning and brings to attention the importance of flexibility in creative planning. Planning is inherently a creative process that involves foresight as well as improvisation in the face of changing circumstances. It also involves anticipating, and being able to take advantage of, unpredictable events. Although research on skilled planning emphasizes the development of planning in advance (Brown and DeLoache, 1978; Wellman, Fabricius and Sophian, 1985), successful planning involves flexibly and opportunistically altering plans in process (Gardner and Rogoff, 1990; Pea and Hawkins, 1987). Since we cannot anticipate all aspects of our planning endeavours, it is often both advantageous and efficient to plan opportunistically, developing and adjusting plans during the course of action (Hayes-Roth, 1985; Rogoff, Gauvain and Gardner, 1987). The necessity of flexibility in planning is made much more apparent when research examines the sociocultural context of planning, in which co-ordination with others, cultural tools, institutional constraints and opportunities, and unforeseen events are the objects of study rather than being seen as 'noise' to be controlled, as has been the case in most research on planning to date.

An investigation of children's playcrafting

Our discussion is based on videotaped observations of children's collaboration in developing a play. The group involves six 7- to 9-year-old girls who planned and performed their own take-off on a fairy-tale in their 2nd/3rd grade classroom during ten planning sessions extending over one month.

This study departs from most previous studies in following the creative planning process from start to finish, in studying group collaborative processes rather than individual or dyadic problem solving, and in examining problem solving in an open-ended project rather than as a problem that involves a pre-existing script or algorithm for solution. Our goal was to examine the playcrafting process in as natural a situation as possible, to tape the playcrafting process as it unfolded in a setting that was not of our design.

Playcrafting sessions, rather than individual subjects, are our unit of analysis. We followed the group's ideas as they developed across time, with individual contributions woven together. We are not attempting to separate out individual contributions to examine the characteristics of individuals as independent units, although we do, of course, attend to how each child's contributions are woven together in the whole effort. Our focus on the development of the event is consistent with a contextual event approach (Rogoff, 1982; Rogoff and Gauvain, 1986).

Our analysis concentrates on one play, *Snow White*, that was produced as part of the writing curriculum in a 2nd/3rd grade classroom in an 'open' nontraditional school where creative activities such as playcrafting are common and children are routinely expected to collaborate on classroom projects and to organize their own activities. Interpersonal problem solving and management of one's own learning activities are an explicit part of the curriculum. The classroom teacher serves as a resource and guide in a 'community of learners'. Thus, the cultural context of the children in this classroom is one that includes sustained attention and creativity in child-managed collaborative projects, with comfortable use of adult assistance and guidance but not dependence on adult management.

Children were assigned by their teacher to plan and perform their own versions of a fairy-tale. (The class chose four tales to make into plays; *Snow White* was one of two in which the group attempted to create a new version of the play rather than just to enact a traditional version.) Over the course of one month each group planned and practised its play with intermittent assistance from the classroom teacher and a student teacher, and then performed its play for classmates and adult visitors.

The teacher's role in structuring the task

Preparing the planning and writing task

Before initiating the project the teacher conducted library research on fairy-tales, set up a fairy-tale reading centre in a corner of the classroom, showed students a video presentation of *Rumpelstiltskin*, and 'piggy-backed' this group project with an individual fairy-tale writing assignment. The teacher explained: 'I see this as a learning experience that you will learn all sorts of skills from. You will be doing some reading and some writing. You will do planning and organizing. These are all skills that we are trying to learn.'

The teacher, in conjunction with the students, structured the task by listing common elements of fairy-tales (e.g. begins 'Once upon a time', has a happy ending). This list was later copied from the blackboard to a poster-board and remained visible to the students throughout the month. The teacher also provided the groups with an important organizational tool for their planning of the plays: a coloured sheet of paper on which each group was to list the participants, the play's title, the characters, the setting and main events (including problem and solution).

Structuring the collaborative process

The teacher viewed this project not only as a cognitive task (it was clearly part of the reading and writing curriculum for teacher, students and parents alike), but also as a challenging social task. She attempted to maximize student success on the interpersonal problem-solving processes as well as the planning of the plays themselves.

Groups were formed with attention to the academic and interpersonal strengths of the individual children. After the teacher helped the students generate a list of fairy-tales and select four to produce, she asked the students to select their first and second choices. During recess the teacher (assisted by a parent volunteer) grouped students according to their preferences and according to her perception of individual cognitive and social strengths and weaknesses:

Parent:	I think that would balance the group.
Teacher:	Uh huh. We haven't put anybody in here with real strong writing skills.
Parent:	Sarah's pretty good, isn't she?
Teacher:	Mmmm, she's OK, but she won't take a leadership role. Um, who . . . I'm kind of wondering is if we got Jason in there, he could be a leader.

When the students returned from recess the teacher told them which group they were in, and emphasized that their task would be socially as well as cognitively challenging. She offered suggestions for successfully working as a group and for managing inevitable social struggles:

Teacher:	You'll vote as a group and you'll say, 'OK, do we want to do it the old way or the modern way?' and everybody will have to discuss it and say the pros and the cons. When having a little group there are certain things that make it positive and certain things that make it hard. One guy has an idea and says, 'MODERN! MODERN! I want it modern.' Does that help the group?
Kids	(*in unison*): No!
Teacher:	Or if some kids just sit there and don't say anything, does that help the group?
Kids	(*in unison*): No!
Teacher:	OK, so you have to figure out a way to make the group work. What if I said, 'I have seen groups that have too many chiefs and no Indians?' What do I mean? Leslie . . .
Leslie:	That means that too many people are taking over the group.
Teacher:	Everybody wants to be the boss and nobody listens. So that might be a problem that you might have to solve with your group. Because you always need some workers and some listeners. Part of this will be figuring out how to make your group work. . . . There will be some adults in the room to help but a lot of the time it will just be up to you to say 'wait a minute, we need to compromise' or 'we need to vote on it', rather than just one guy taking over.

Thus, by establishing groups that she believed would be cognitively and socially balanced and by providing students with a number of organizational strategies for planning and managing social relations, the teacher prepared the groups to embark on their project.

Once the groups began their projects, the teacher occasionally served as a mediator of disputes, stepping in to ask the children how they could decide issues and encouraging their reflection on the *process* of solving interpersonal problems. At a key point in the first session of *Snow White*, she suggested that departing from the traditional tale (an idea she had earlier suggested in encouraging creative adaptations of the tales) might help the girls to escape from their difficulties, which had to do with differences in recall of the traditional tale. The idea of creating an adaptation brought the girls together and formed the basis of the rest of their sessions.

From across the room the teacher observed the group to make sure that all was going well, and during some later sessions she observed and made practical suggestions. She was occasionally asked for information (on spelling and on whether minor changes were allowed in the assignment). Her role was to monitor and support the girls' efforts; the decisions on how to plan and develop the play belonged to the group. During a number of later sessions the student teacher attempted to organize the group, but his efforts were generally rejected, as the group was already organized in a way that he did not seem to detect, and his style was one of intervention rather than of observation and support. (The classroom teacher informed us that the student teacher's over-zealous attempts to manage are a typical strategy used by student teachers, who feel responsible for doing something, but are not yet skilled in observing and subtly assisting a group to solve its own problems.)

Method for examining the course of events

To examine how the girls' organization and ideas evolved over the course of the project, we first described their discourse and actions throughout each of the sessions (ten records of twenty to eighty single-spaced pages each). Each of the authors checked and corrected the transcripts against video and audio-taped records of the sessions, usually clarifying some points but seldom disagreeing on the overall interpretation of the events. Then with the use of the transcripts and videotapes, we abstracted a summary of the creative planning activities (a forty-five-page document). This summary version of the ten sessions was further abstracted to produce a chart of the events as they occurred over the ten sessions. Figure 12.1 presents the chart of the creative planning activities of the group during ten planning sessions, concentrating on transitions in the group's focus of planning. The classification system of Figure 12.1 emerged from our successive abstractions of the planning process over the ten sessions, as well as from concepts of planning derived from the literature and previous research on planning. It represents the transitions of the group from abstract levels of planning, to determining the events of the play,

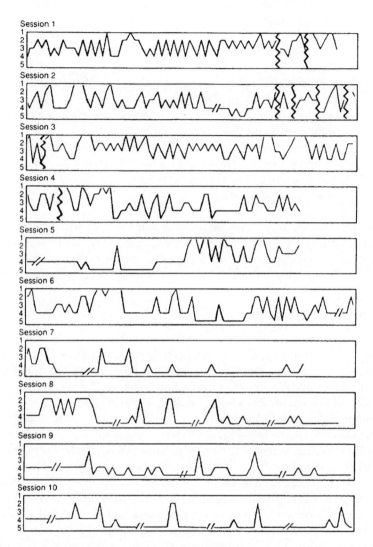

Figure 12.1 Levels of planning across sessions 1 to 10

Key

Level 1 How to plan planning the play/establish rules for handling disputes

Level 2 How to plan the play/co-ordinate pieces/resolve different ideas/keep on track

Level 3 Deciding main themes and events/coherence and motivation of the events

Level 4 Deciding props, costumes, dialogue and action/who plays what

Level 5 Acting what has already been decided/with local improvisation and adjustment.

Each point indicates a topic change, either within a level or across levels

⟩ indicates a breakdown in group planning; a dead end with high feelings

–//– indicates that the level continued longer than shown

to detailed decisions regarding specifics of the production and practice of the actions that have been decided:

Level 1   How to plan planning the play and establish rules for handling disputes;

Level 2   How to plan the play, co-ordinate pieces, resolve competing ideas, and keep on track in planning;

Level 3   Deciding on the main themes and events and ensuring coherence of the events and their motivation;

Level 4   Deciding on specifics such as props, costumes, dialogue and action, as well as who will play what character;

Level 5   Acting on what has already been decided, with only local improvisation and adjustment.

The events abstracted by these five levels account for almost 100 per cent of the ten sessions in which the children prepared their play, with the exception of one brief segment noted below. In the following sections, we describe the group's use of these levels of planning as the children develop the play.

The course of planning

During the ten planning sessions, activities proceeded for the most part from the general to the specific (Levels 1 and 2 to Level 5, in Figure 12.1). On the first day the group spent most of their time developing a general story framework (Levels 2 and 3), trying to arrive at consensus based on individual memories of the traditional version of *Snow White*. However, each girl had seen either one or two different versions of the tale (one produced by Disney and the other by Fairy Tale Theater). Thus, they could not arrive at a consensus by referring to *the* traditional version of the fairy-tale. Since the two versions are quite different, the task was complicated and the girls could not decide which production to adopt. With assistance from the teacher in attempting to resolve disputes regarding the 'real' story, at the end of the first session the girls decided to modify the traditional story model and collaboratively to develop 'twists' on the traditional story (Levels 1, 2 and 3).

During the second and third sessions, there was still a great deal of planning how to plan (Levels 1 and 2), with greater emphasis on deciding the main theme and events of the play (Level 3). In the second planning session the girls moved from the creation of a general story model to the development of a script of lines and actions Levels 3 and 4). In the third session there was still great attention on how the play should be planned, deciding how to divide and distribute roles, and attempting to make these decisions (Levels 1 and 2).

A shift in activities took place about the fourth session, as can be seen in Figure 12.1. During the first three sessions the groups planned in advance, 'out of action', sitting round a table and discussing many ideas that would later be incorporated into their play. During the fourth session, the girls began to practise what they had planned. While practising, they improvised, planned 'in character', and practised planned events. The shift was entirely managed by the children, as were almost all the moves between levels of planning in the first sessions (the major exception being the teachers' intervention in suggesting a modification of the tale at the end of the first session).

Essential to the first four sessions was building a *social foundation* to allow the girls both to complete the cognitive aspects of their task and to work effectively as a group. Once this foundation was built, the group was able to communicate and plan 'in action' during the course of the remaining sessions, which they treated as practice sessions. From the fourth session, the girls spent a great deal of time practising – a phase that they marked by labelling it as such, as well as by changing the physical setting from working around a table to rehearsing in the hallway outside the classroom. From sessions four through ten the group spent incrementally more time rehearsing, planning in character and improvising, and less time planning out of action (see Figure 12.1).

Advance planning and planning during action

The girls engaged in flexible, opportunistic planning (Hayes-Roth and Hayes-Roth, 1979; Rogoff, Gauvain and Gardner, 1987), beginning with more weight being given to advance planning (especially Levels 1, 2 and 3) during the first four playcrafting sessions and then focusing to a greater extent on planning during action (especially Levels 3, 4 and 5). During the course of action old plans were modified, new plans developed and improvisations emerged. Planning during action is not an appendage or consequence of advance planning, but rather an integral aspect of opportunistic planning.

Advance planning involved the organization of future activity through building action sequences, co-ordinating participants, and considering material resources either before the activity started or during a pause. During the first four playcrafting sessions when the *Snow White* team planned the story theme and main events, and checked the coherence of the events and their motivation, they worked out of character and usually without action. This advance planning was necessary for the group to establish a consensus regarding the theme and events of the play as well as to develop a group working relationship that was necessary for the planning process. Although the girls often plunged into planning at a detailed level during the first four days, one or another of them soon brought the group back to the more abstract levels of planning the theme, events and motivation of the play as a whole, without which the concrete levels of planning could not be co-ordinated.

The girls each took leadership roles in managing the return of the group to advance planning at different times. On the first day, one girl repeatedly moved the group back to planning main events when the group spent too long planning props or other specifics; however, when she mentioned that she forgot to list the dwarves under 'characters', another girl took the responsibility for maintaining the more abstract planning level, as she suggested staying at a general level: 'Just say dwarves; don't give the names.' On the second day, a third girl showed a consistent pattern as peacemaker and organizer, by turning the conversation away from disputed topics to fun or simple topics, and then reorganizing at a higher level of planning soon after. Each of the other girls also provided leadership to the group in moving the work along at a general planning level, with comments on not bothering with costumes or props *yet* and on not taking too long improvising a particular scene (e.g. 'We can figure that out later'; 'This is good enough for now'; 'Pretend the scene's over, and then . . .').

Much of what occurred during the ten playcrafting sessions involved planning during action. Some of this improvisational planning was necessary, when the group needed to cope with their plans being derailed by the absence of group members, who later could not agree or failed to understand what the group was trying to do. They also needed to plan the time so as to avoid running out of time at the end of a session before a process came to a conclusion. While these 'inconveniences are carefully controlled in most laboratory planning sessions, during everyday endeavours they are the occurrences that make the creative planning process a challenge and provide opportunities for breaking into new patterns. The skill, for many, is being able to turn unplanned events into opportunities. Take, for example, Kurt Vonnegut's description of his reliance on improvisation during the writing process:

> [Writing is] like make a movie: All sorts of accidental things will happen after you've set up the cameras. So you get lucky. Something will happen at the edge of the set and perhaps you start to go with that; you get some footage of that. You come into it accidentally. You set the story in motion, and as you're watching this thing begin all these opportunities will show up.
>
> (Vonnegut in Winokur, 1990, p. 252)

Creativity in planning

The 'trick' for both experienced writers and novice playcrafters is to be able flexibly to anticipate change and adapt to unexpected occurrences throughout the course of the planning process. Plans often do not go as anticipated, and it is virtually impossible to anticipate all the obstacles and opportunities that will arise during the course of events. Thus planning during action, involving flexibility and alertness to new opportunities and problems, provides fertile ground for creative solutions. Perkins (1981) discusses how Picasso's creation of *Guernica* involved 'accident and intention, the balance of luck and foresight in creative process' (p. 21). Perkins quotes Arnheim's description of the work:

> An interplay of interferences, modifications, restrictions, and compensations leads gradually to the unity and complexity of the total composition. Therefore the work of art cannot unfold straightforwardly from its seed, like an organism, but must grow in what looks like erratic leaps, forward and backward, from the whole to the part and vice versa.
>
> (p. 19)

Most of the planning during action that we observed was not in response to intruding events, but was instead the means by which the girls managed the complexities of creating a complex play and of co-ordinating their often discrepant ideas. On many occasions, the girls elaborated on the idea mentioned by another person, with the collaborative product reflecting a creative advance that is more than the sum of the individual contributions.

For example, the development of the idea of having the evil stepmother give Snow White a poisoned banana instead of a poisoned apple can be followed across a number of events and ideas from different individuals across the ten sessions. At the end of the first session, when the teacher suggested making an adaptation of the play to resolve their dispute, one girl's immediate response was to suggest using a poisoned lemon to change the original version. The girls together brainstormed other poisoned foods that could be used, among which was the poisoned banana; this was what got written on their planning sheet. In the second session, the girls discussed the adaptation written at home by one of the girls, which involved the prince punching the princess in the stomach and her throwing up all over him. Another girl suggested using chewed-up banana to create the effect, and the girls all wrote down 'banana' on their papers. Then they practised the play in the later sessions, the evil queen gave the princess a poisoned banana and the princess pretended to vomit when the prince kissed (not punched) her. However, the pretend vomiting deterred all the girls from playing the prince, a role they otherwise wanted. In the final performance, the poisoned banana remained but the vomiting had disappeared. Thus the development of several events involving the banana reflected the girls' adjustment to practical constraints, their creative use of each other's ideas to advance the group product, and the process of adjustment of the plan over time.

Another example involved the use of a fortuitous circumstance in creating a scene. During the first session, the girls considered how they could have a talking mirror, and a number of possibilities were discussed, one of which was to have a hole in a mirror with an actor speaking in the hole. All six girls participated in this discussion, which ended without resolution as one girl brought them back to the need to focus on main events. Nothing more was done with the mirror issue until the ninth session, when the evil queen went to look in a pretend mirror but was inconvenienced by the student teacher who was right where she wanted the mirror to be. She told him to move. But his being there seemed to have prompted the idea of having a person play the mirror, and she asked a classmate to come over to be the mirror and told her the mirror's line. This feature was replayed in the tenth session, and appeared in the final performance as well. In this example, the creative planning built on an intrusion to develop a creative germ that had been mentioned long before. Related processes have been observed in children's pretend play in early childhood (Göncü and Kessel, 1988).

Planning during action: in character or improvisation

We observed two types of planning during action: planning 'in character' and improvisation. Planning in character took place during activity, within the context of rehearsals or planning of script lines. It typically involved filling in gaps in dialogue or action or communicating the need for a character to appear on stage without breaking the momentum of the rehearsal. In the following example from the seventh session, the group had not yet discussed an ending for the play. Since it was inefficient to stop the rehearsal in order explicitly to plan an ending, Robin (as the wicked stepmother) took the initiative and summarized the finale, in character and without interrupting the course of action: 'Then the prince gets his wizard to turn all my mirrors black every time I look in them. So that I die if I look in them. OK?' Once this plan had been devised, during subsequent rehearsals the group was able to remember the course of events and add dialogue and action through improvisational techniques.

When improvising, the girls planned and carried out actions and events simultaneously, performing 'according to the inventive whim of the moment' (McCrohan, 1987; Dean, 1989). Improvisation differs from planning in character in terms of communicative focus. In the previous example, Robin explicitly communicated the plan to the group. However, in the following improvisational example the action and the plan were synonymous. In earlier sessions the group had decided on using a poisoned banana and that the dwarves would carry the princess over to a glass coffin. During the seventh session, the group improvised the dialogue:

Carol: It's a banana! She's not breathing.
Stacy: It looks a bit peculiar.
Carol: She's not breathing! Come on let's carry her.
Stacy: Try CPR!
Carol: Let's carry her off.

Improvisation allows for spontaneous modifications and elaborations without the need to reflect verbally on the plan and often without the need to establish verbally mediated consensus. If an improvised line or move seemed jarring, this led to discussion either in character or out of character.

Since the group had established consensus early on about the play's overall structure and had developed shared modes of communication, during the later playcrafting sessions they could short-cut many of the formal negotiations and plan during the course of action.

Choosing advance planning and planning during action

The group evidenced struggles in managing a flexible adjustment of planning to blend the advantages of both advance planning and planning during action. On a number of occasions, the group evidenced tension between proceeding through advance planning or through planning during action. They had numerous discussions about writing the script all out versus putting the play together through acting, as in this example from the fifth session:

> Leslie asks: 'Do you want to write scripts or do you want to take the play part by part?'
>
> Heather suggests writing part of the script, then doing that part, then writing more script.
>
> Leslie urges writing a script to avoid forgetting their lines, and suggests getting out of costume to write scripts. Eventually the girls write scripts.
>
> Robin suggests: 'Why don't we all work together on one big script and then we can get it copied? So we can all work together on one script.' (a solution to the problem of co-ordination)
>
> The girls write, agreeing to focus on the first part of the play and just listing the names in abbreviated fashion.
>
> Leslie remains concerned with co-ordination: 'What if one person wants to say something and the other. . . ?'
>
> Robin reassures: 'It will probably be all right.'
>
> They write some more, and again Leslie worries about advance planning: 'I just figured out our problem. We don't know how the story *goes*.'
>
> Robin reassures that planning in action will work: 'We are just kinda making the story up as we go – as we act.'
>
> Leslie is content: 'Oh. OK.'

At times, the student teacher intervened to encourage more advance planning, urging the group to resolve each conflict before going on. However, the girls largely ignored him. His suggestions would have been likely to lead to stalemates, with the group stuck on disputes, rather than to creative solutions. . . .

Social organization of creative planning

In our use of the playcrafting event as the unit of analysis, we consider the roles of individuals involved as they constitute and are constituted by the coherence of the overall event. It is relevant to ask how the individuals co-ordinated their efforts and their relative responsibilities for the management of planning, and the extent to which their thinking was shared.

Although the six girls differed in writing skill and leadership strength, and they varied in friendship histories, they consistently worked together throughout the sessions. Even when they attempted to work independently, each writing her own lines or developing her own character, they consulted each other constantly on fitting their contributions together, assisting each other in spelling and reminding each other of decisions that had already been made or of the basic story model in which they were working.

Working together was not easy – early sessions were full of conflict and mismatches of assumptions and ideas. At times subgroups worked together simultaneously or several girls worked actively while others observed. There were four girls who played a more dominant role in decision making, but the other two were always attentive and all six contributed ideas and manage-ment at one point or another. (Of the two girls who were less dominant, one was the only 2nd grader in the group and the other was quieter than the other four 3rd graders. After the teacher had put this group together, she noticed that it was composed of a number of strong personalities and expressed concern about the potential for explosion in the group.)

In any case, the girls were all engaged, with shifting leadership from day to day. There were *very* few moments spent off-task, by any of the six girls. On a few occasions the group fooled about around play development, but this seemed often to serve a function of reducing tension or getting past an impasse in planning. The only occasion when the group really spent time off-task was a three to four minute period when the student teacher interrupted the group in an attempt to organize it in his own fashion.

Initial anchors for planning

To begin the process of planning, the girls faced the problem of anchoring their imaginations so that they could work from common ground. Without such anchors, there would be little hope of co-ordinating their individual efforts. Some of the anchors drew upon the constraints and resources of the cultural institution in which the children worked – school. Before the first session, the teacher provided anchors for the planning process in her man-agement of the classroom to choose four plays as a basis for the projects and to determine with the children who was to work on which play, after lessons on the structure of fairy-tales. Her requirement to produce a written script also channelled the process.

Another means of anchoring the process, and of encouraging planning at higher levels, was the teacher's provision of the planning sheet requesting the children to determine the characters, the setting and the main events. The use of this sheet was managed in the first session by Stacy, who repeatedly directed the group back to determining characters or main events when they strayed into too much detail on planning props or dialogue, as in the following example:

> When the girls got involved in discussing how to make a talking mirror, Stacy tried to get them back to general planning. She interrupted, tapped the girl who was leading the mirror discussion with her pencil, and said 'Main Events'.
> But the discussion remained on the mirror topic.
> Stacy tried again, exasperated: 'We are going to do the Main Events.'
> When the others continued discussing the mirror, Stacy asked: 'What are the Main Events?'
> Finally the girls turned to reconstructing their memories of the main events of the tale. But after some progress, the girls began to worry about how they would produce the setting.
> Stacy tried to move away from this level of planning, insisting: 'We aren't doing this right now. We are on the Main Events right now.' And the girls returned to listing the main events.

At the end of the first session, the main events for *Snow White* were written as:

> the queen wats snow white
> kiled. Snow wite eats a pousand
> banana snow white gets strageld
> snow white gets bered and the
> price comes and they get meryd.

The girls also used the traditional story line of the play as an anchor for their planning during the first day, relying on cultural knowledge outside the structure provided by the teacher. However, since the girls did not share a common story line (due to having seen two different video versions of the tale), their common ground here was not solid. Intersubjectivity was repeatedly disrupted, until the girls understood the basis of the misunderstanding. Eventually they checked understandings with each other.

> In Session 2, when Heather and Robin disagreed on how the dwarves should carry their shovels, Heather checked, 'Have you seen the Walt Disney one?' before going on with a proposal; 'OK, well you know how they swing back? {*she demonstrated*] They go like that.'

Many of the girls' disputes could be traced to *apparent* consensus but with different underlying assumptions that later surfaced as problems. The problem of differing assumptions was resolved when the teacher suggested that they make up a modern version of the play, and the girls eagerly accepted this solution to their interpersonal trouble.

Hence the decision to create rather than reproduce a play resulted from interpersonal difficulties in establishing a common ground. The idea of modifying the traditional tale had been suggested before the beginning of the sessions by the teacher, and during the session by several girls. But it was not until it appeared as a solution for the difficulties in co-ordinating ideas across people that it was adopted:

> The teacher suggested: Why don't you guys think up a totally new version? A modern-day version?'
>
> The group made favourable comments, and Robin supported the idea: 'I think that it would be neat to come up with a modern-day version. Like Snow White eats a poison lemon or something.'
>
> After further discussion, Robin gave more support to the idea of a new version as a way of achieving consensus: 'We could have a whole new thing and then everybody would be figuring it out all together and then nobody would have seen it [i.e. quarrel about the "real" story].'
>
> The group began immediately to brainstorm.

For the second session, the anchor for planning was elaborated by Robin's production, at home, of a modified story line in which many events were made to be opposite to the original tale. She reported to the group that she was following their group decision: 'I just totally changed it. Remember how we were going to make a new one? So I just did that.' When she read the story to the group they were largely enthusiastic.

Although this version did not persist intact, Robin's play served as a new anchor point, both for those who accepted it and for those who argued against it. The argument derived from a girl who had been absent at the previous session and was not pleased with changes occurring in her absence: 'Well, she shouldn't have done it until all of us like it. . . . It's supposed to be *Snow White*, not *Black Night*.' With the teacher's support, the group pulled together to reach a new agreement, and this resulted in a change of the name of the play, from the revised name offered by Robin:

> The teacher probed: 'What could you do to solve the problem?'
>
> Leslie suggested: 'We could change it? . . . Could we just change the name instead of *Black Night*? Would that help?'
>
> The girls discussed alternative names. After much more discussion, and attempts by the group to have each girl write individual ideas to be

mixed together, Leslie offered an efficient compromise: 'If we have a little of Robin's *Black Night*, if you want to, we could have *Snow White Black Night.*' In discussion, the idea of *Blue Sky* came up, and Leslie suggested: 'How about *Blue Night*? Cuz, some of your [Robin's] idea and some of their idea?'

At this suggestion, all agreed and planning moved along collaboratively. The group's solution was to combine parts of each idea, to form a new one. This is a recipe for creative planning, and it is essential to note that interpersonal processes were central to the process of mixing ideas and guiding the resulting creative elaboration.

Means of co-ordinating efforts

Over the course of the playcrafting sessions the group was able to develop effective ways to manage both the play-planning task and the social relationships.

Division of tasks

One collaborative method the group attempted involved the division of various tasks. Here, a task is divided into subtasks and individuals are assigned to perform one or more of the subtasks. Once the subtasks have been performed, individual products are integrated to form a whole. Sometimes, tasks were divided, with parallel contributions from all, by distributing character roles and having each participant create her own actions, dialogue and motivations, as in the following proposal in the second session: 'Everybody get a piece of scratch paper . . . *write down their parts*, and what they want to say. Then we'll discuss them . . . and see if everybody likes it.' On some occasions, subgroups divided tasks and worked simultaneously within subgroups. For example, the three dwarves worked on their dialogue and actions, speaking across the table through the conversation of the king and queen who were developing their piece of the script.

At other times, the division involved specialization, with distribution of individual jobs (e.g. playwright, director, set designer), and later integration of the products according to a master plan. This social organizational model is common in professional theatre (see Schechner, 1985, for an anthropological discussion of theatre). One advantage of this model is that it takes into consideration variation in individual skills. For example, a child who has difficulty writing can create props. However, the group must decide who will divide the task and who will integrate individual products once they have been created. Without a clear distinction in resources or status, it is difficult to determine who should take what role. In fact, during the planning of *Snow White* a great deal of the conflict revolved around one or another of the four dominant girls protesting about one or another of them adopting too much of a dominant leadership role.

A cultural tool – writing – was often used by the girls to take control of the planning process. As in ancient times, the scribe and the literate had power over those who did not write or read. In the first session, Stacy took the job of writing down decisions on the teacher's planning sheet. She also kept the group on task by reminding them of the need to make decisions at the level of the planning sheet (e.g., main events). However, this gave her a dominant role about which other girls later protested. Leslie scolded: 'You are supposed to be writing down what we *all* want!' and later Heather asked Stacy if she could write the next part, since Stacy had written everything so far (but Stacy did not yield the pencil and paper).

In other sessions, other girls also used writing as a means of influence – Robin writing the play at home, Carol gaining authority in decision making as the only girl who could find her script from the session before, and Leslie later being nominated to be the writer of the script (with admonitions to write the group consensus) on the basis of her more complete manner of writing. When there were difficulties in establishing group consensus, the written word was often used as an anchor point and as a way of exerting leadership. Perhaps because the group members were basically similar in resources and skills and involved four girls who vied for the leadership role, asymmetry in roles was often rejected, in favour of discussion, negotiation and compromise.

Shared decision making

This collaborative method was used throughout the creation of *Snow White* with ideas developed through a process of brainstorming and evaluated and adapted for use. Each child has a say in the decision-making process even though individual children do not make equivalent contributions to proposals or to carrying them out. During one dispute, the girls complained that Leslie was being bossy in protesting about the inclusion of a part that was not her character's; she replied, 'it's my play, too', disputing the idea that decisions could be made unilaterally by people playing specific parts.

The process was often chaotic, filled with interruptions, topic and task changes. Likewise, the play under construction was sometimes disjointed, since the individual parts often did not comprise a coherent whole. This was complicated by the likelihood that individuals were working from differing models of the goal or differing background information.

To progress, the group must be able to work together on a shared task, with shared attention, shared communication, and the ability to adjust individual activities to facilitate the group. At times the girls proposed ways of co-ordinating their individual or subgroup ideas:

Teacher:	Can you think of how you would like it [the play]?
Stacy:	I'd like to change the form. Like make [the ideas] exactly opposite . . .
Robin:	Why don't we mix them up? . . . Like we can get everybody to make the ideas so everybody will have their own idea and then we can mix them up together. . . . We can figure out a way to mix them all up on somebody's piece of paper.

The social–cognitive collaborative methods of division of tasks and shared decision making that the group used to create their play served both as a planning *process* that propelled the group to its goal and as a *tool* that facilitated the creation of the play, with indivisible social and cognitive processes. During the initial four playcrafting sessions sociocognitive vehicles for the co-ordination and generation of ideas were built by the group, and as they were built, the group was able to use them to create its play. On the fourth day the group was able to achieve a coherence between cognitive activities and social organization. After the fourth day it spent most of its time planning specific dialogue and action, and rehearsing.

The *Snow White* group's methods and product contrasted with many of the other groups' playcrafting sessions, which did not employ a method of shared decision making. For example, in one of the other fairy-tale groups an adult needed to remain with the group for all ten sessions in order to dictate the method of collaboration and to structure the task The adult became responsible for generating ideas, negotiating conflict, and attempting to motivate the group's efforts. Another group elected not to collaborate on a joint project, but rather to work on individual products that were later performed separately. In these instances the groups did not develop a means of collaborative management of ideas, and their interactions and plays were of a much different nature from those of *Snow White*, in which the group developed successful interaction patterns and used them to develop a play together, working almost independently of adult direction. We argue that collaborative methods of social organization were essential to the group's handling of a variety of cognitive tasks.

Summary

In this chapter we have argued that creative planning can best be understood as a sociocultural process involving both advance and improvisational planning. Whereas many traditional perspectives view creativity and planning as cognitive products, mental possessions or individual traits, our purpose has been to explicate sociocultural processes in children's collaborative creative planning. We emphasize both the process and the sociocultural nature of planning by arguing that in order to plan collaboratively children need to develop ways of managing both social relations and the cognitive problems inherent in the project. Social interaction patterns constitute the cognitive course of the creative process and, in mutual fashion, cognitive processes constitute social organizational patterns.

We stress the dynamic, sociocultural nature of the processes of creative planning. Sociocultural contexts provide fertile ground for the development of new ideas and structure creative planning as ideas emerge and evolve in new ways. Regardless of whether we investigate artistic, scientific or everyday creative planning, all take place within sociocultural communities. The individual contribution to creative planning is only a part of a broader dynamic sociocultural process, in which the whole is greater than the sum of the parts.

References

Azmitia, M. (1988), 'Peer interaction and problem solving: when are two heads better than one?', *Child Development*, 59, pp. 87–96.

Bouchard, T.J. (1971), 'Whatever happened to brainstorming?', *Journal of Creative Behavior*, 5, pp. 182–9.

Brown, A. and DeLoache, J. (1978), 'Skills, plans, and self-regulation', in R. Siegler (ed.), *Children's Thinking: What develops?* (Hillsdale, NJ: Erlbaum), pp. 3–35.

Csikszentmihalyi, M. (1988), 'Society, culture, and person: a systems view of creativity', in R.J. Sternberg (ed.), *The Nature of Creativity* (Cambridge: Cambridge University Press), pp. 325–39.

Dean, R.T. (1989), *Creative Improvisation: Jazz, contemporary music and beyond* (Philadelphia: Open University Press).

Gardner, W. and Rogoff, B. (1990), 'Children's deliberateness of planning according to task circumstances', *Developmental Psychology*, 26, pp. 480–7.

Gearhart, M. (1979), 'Social planning: role play in a novel situation', paper presented at the meetings of the Society for Research in Child Development, San Francisco.

Göncü, A. and Kessel, F. (1988), 'Preschoolers' collaborative construction in planning and maintaining imaginative play', *International Journal of Behavioral Development*, 11, pp. 327–44.

Hayes-Roth, B. (1985), 'A blackboard architecture for control', *Artificial Intelligence*, 26, pp. 251–322.

Hayes-Roth, B. and Hayes-Roth, F. (1979), 'A cognitive model of planning', *Cognitive Science*, 3, pp. 275–310.

John-Steiner, V. (1985), *Notebooks of the Mind: Explorations of thinking* (New York: Harper & Row).

McCrohan, D. (1987), *The Second City: A backstage history of comedy's hottest troupe* (New York: Putnam).

Pea, R. and Hawkins, J. (1987), 'Planning in a chore scheduling task', in S. Friedman, E. Scholnick and R. Cocking (eds), *Blueprints for Thinking: The role of planning in psychological development* (New York: Cambridge University Press), pp. 273–302.

Perkins, D.N. (1981), *The Mind's Best Work* (Cambridge, MA: Harvard University Press).

Radziszewska, B. and Rogoff, B. (1988), 'Influence of adult and peer collaborators on children's planning skills', *Developmental Psychology*, 24, pp. 840–8.

Radziszewska, B. and Rogoff, B. (1991), 'Children's guided participation in planning errands with skilled adult or peer partners', *Developmental Psychology*, 27, pp. 381–9.

Rogoff, B. (1982), 'Integrating context and cognitive development', in M.E. Lamb and A.L. Brown (eds), *Advances in Developmental Psychology*, vol. 2 (Hillsdale, NJ: Erlbaum).

Rogoff, B. (1990), *Apprenticeship in Thinking: Cognitive development in social context*, (New York: Oxford University Press).

Rogoff, B. and Gauvain, M. (1986), 'A method for the analysis of patterns, illustrated with data on mother–child instructional interaction', in J. Valsiner (ed.), *The Individual Subject and Scientific Psychology* (New York: Plenum), pp. 261–90.

Rogoff, B., Gauvain, M. and Gardner, W. (1987), 'The development of children's skills in adjusting plans to circumstances', in S. Friedman, E. Scholnick and R. Cocking (eds), *Blueprints for Thinking: The role of planning in psychological development* (New York: Cambridge University Press), pp. 303–20.

Schechner, R. (1985), *Between Theater and Anthropology* (Philadelphia, PA: University Pennsylvania Press).

Vygotsky, L.S. (1978), *Mind in Society* (Cambridge, MA: Harvard University Press).

Weisberg, R.W. (1986), *Creativity: Genius and other myths* (New York: Freeman).

Wellman, H., Fabricius, W. and Sophian, C. (1985), 'The early development of planning', in H. Wellman (ed.), *Children's Searching: The development of search skill and spatial representation* (Hillsdale, NJ: Erlbaum), pp. 123–49.

Winokur, Jon (1990), *Writers on Writing* (Philadelphia: Running Press).

Chapter 13

Constructing scientific knowledge in the classroom*

Rosalind Driver, Hilary Asoko, John Leach, Eduardo Mortimer and Philip Scott

The core commitment of a constructivist position, that knowledge is not transmitted directly from one knower to another, but is actively built up by the learner, is shared by a wide range of different research traditions relating to science education. One tradition focuses on personal construction of meanings and the many informal theories that individuals develop about natural phenomena (Carey, 1985; Carmichael *et al.*, 1990; Pfundt & Duit, 1985) as resulting from learners' personal interactions with physical events in their daily lives (Piaget, 1970). Learning in classroom settings, from this perspective, is seen to require well-designed practical activities that challenge learners' prior conceptions, encouraging learners to reorganize their personal theories. A different tradition portrays the knowledge-construction process as coming about through learners being encultured into scientific discourses (e.g., Edwards & Mercer, 1987; Lemke, 1990). Yet others see it as involving apprenticeship into scientific practices (Rogoff & Lave, 1984). Our own work has focused on the study of ways in which school students' informal knowledge is drawn upon and interacts with the scientific ways of knowing introduced in the classroom (e.g., Johnston & Driver, 1990; Scott, 1993; Scott, Asoko, Driver, & Emberton, 1994). Clearly there is a range of accounts of the processes by which knowledge construction takes place. Some clarification of these distinct perspectives and how they may interrelate appears to be needed.

A further issue that requires clarification among science educators is the relationship being proposed between constructivist views of learning and implications for pedagogy. Indeed, Millar (1989) has argued that particular views of learning do not necessarily entail specific pedagogical practices. Furthermore, the attempts that have been made to articulate "constructivist" approaches to pedagogy in science (Driver & Oldham, 1986; Fensham, Gunstone, & White, 1994; Osborne & Freyberg, 1985) have been criticized on the grounds that such pedagogical practices are founded on an empiricist view of the nature of science itself (Matthews, 1992; Osborne, 1993), an argument that is examined later in the chapter.

* This is an edited version of an article that appeared in *Educational Researcher*, October 1994.

In this chapter we shall present our view of the interplay among the various factors of personal experience, language, and socialization in the process of learning science in classrooms, and discuss the problematic relationships between scientific knowledge, the learning of science, and pedagogy.

The nature of scientific knowledge

Any account of teaching and learning science needs to consider the nature of the knowledge to be taught. Although recent writings in the field of science studies emphasize that scientific practices cannot be characterized in a simplistic unitary way, that is, there is no single "nature of science" (Millar, Driver, Leach, & Scott, 1993), there are some core commitments associated with scientific practices and knowledge claims that have implications for science education. We argue that it is important in science education to appreciate that scientific knowledge is both symbolic in nature and also socially negotiated. The objects of science are not the phenomena of nature but constructs that are advanced by the scientific community to interpret nature. Hanson (1958) gives an eloquent illustration of the difference between the concepts of science and the phenomena of the world in his account of Galileo's intellectual struggles to explain free-fall motion. For several years Galileo collected measurements of falling objects representing acceleration in terms of an object's change in velocity over a given distance, a formulation that led to complex and inelegant relationships. Once he began to think about acceleration in terms of change of velocity in a given time interval, then the constant acceleration of falling objects became apparent. The notion of acceleration did not emerge in a nonproblematic way from observations but was imposed upon them. Scientific knowledge in many domains, whether explanations of the behavior of electrical circuits, energy flow through ecosystems, or rates of chemical reactions, consists of formally specified entities and the relationships posited as existing between them. The point is that, even in relatively simple domains of science, the concepts used to describe and model the domain are not revealed in an obvious way by reading the "book of nature." Rather, they are constructs that have been invented and imposed on phenomena in attempts to interpret and explain them, often as results of considerable intellectual struggles.

Once such knowledge has been constructed and agreed on within the scientific community, it becomes part of the "taken-for-granted" way of seeing things within that community. As a result, the symbolic world of science is now populated with entities such as atoms, electrons, ions, fields and fluxes, genes and chromosomes; it is organized by ideas such as evolution and encompasses procedures of measurement and experiment. These ontological entities, organizing concepts, and associated epistemology and practices of science are unlikely to be discovered by individuals through their own observations of the natural world. Scientific knowledge as public knowledge is constructed and communicated through the culture and social institutions of science. . . .

The view of scientific knowledge as socially constructed and validated has important implications for science education. It means that learning science involves being initiated into scientific ways of knowing. Scientific entities and ideas, which are constructed, validated, and communicated through the cultural institutions of science, are unlikely to be discovered by individuals through their own empirical enquiry; learning science thus involves being initiated into the ideas and practices of the scientific community and making these ideas and practices meaningful at an individual level. The role of the science educator is to mediate scientific knowledge for learners, to help them to make personal sense of the ways in which knowledge claims are generated and validated, rather than to organize individual sense-making about the natural world. This perspective on pedagogy, therefore, differs fundamentally from an empiricist perspective.

Learning science as an individual activity

Although Piaget did not refer to himself as a "constructivist" until later in his life (Piaget, 1970), the view that knowledge is constructed by the cognizing subject is central to his position. As his statement "l'intelligence organise le monde en s'organisant elle-même" (intelligence organizes the world by organizing itself; 1937, p.311) reflects, Piaget's central concern was with the process by which humans construct their knowledge of the world. In broad terms, Piaget postulated the existence of cognitive schemes that are formed and develop through the coordination and internalization of a person's actions on objects in the world. These schemes evolve as a result of a process of adaptation to more complex experiences (through the process Piaget called *equilibration*). New schemes thus come into being by modifying old ones. In this way intellectual development is seen as progressive adaptation of individual's cognitive schemes to the physical environment. Piaget acknowledged that social interaction could play a part in promoting cognitive development through, for example, making different viewpoints available to children through discussion. For development to occur, however, equilibration at the individual level is seen as essential.

Although later in life Piaget addressed the relationship between individual knowledge schemes and the history of science (Piaget & Garcia, 1989), and indeed his underlying quest was essentially epistemological, the focus of much of his research program was on how individuals make sense of the physical world through the development of content-independent logical structures and operations. By contrast, the research program into children's scientific reasoning that has emerged over the last 20 years has focused on domain-specific knowledge schemes in the context of children's learning of science. Children's conceptions of physical phenomena have been documented in a wide range of science domains (Carmichael *et al.*, 1990; Driver, Guesne, & Tiberghien 1985; Pfundt & Duit, 1985; West & Pines, 1985). Although this field of research focuses on domain-specific knowledge rather than general reasoning schemes, it shares a number of commonalities with a Piagetian perspective and can lead to similar perspectives on pedagogy. Both view meaning as being made by individuals, and assert that meaning depends on the individual's current knowledge schemes. Learning comes about when those schemes change through the resolution of disequilibration. Such resolution requires internal mental activity and results in a previous knowledge scheme being modified. Learning is thus seen as involving a process of conceptual change. Teaching approaches in science based on this perspective focus on providing children with physical experiences that induce cognitive conflict and hence encourage learners to develop new knowledge schemes that are better adapted to experience. Practical activities supported by group discussions form the core of such pedagogical practices (see, for example, Nussbaum & Novick, 1982; Rowell & Dawson, 1984). From this personal perspective, classrooms are places where individuals are actively engaged with others in attempting to understand and interpret phenomena for themselves, and where social interaction in groups is seen to provide the stimulus of differing perspectives on which individuals can reflect. The teacher's role is to provide the physical experiences and to encourage reflection. Children's meanings are listened to and respectfully questioned. In the following passage Duckworth describes clearly the kinds of interventions that are helpful:

> What do you mean? How did you do that? Why do you say that? How does that fit in with what she just said? Could you give me an example? How did you figure that? In every case these questions are primarily a way for the interlocutor to try to understand what the other is understanding. Yet in every case, also, they engage the other's thoughts and take them a step further.
>
> (1987, pp. 96–97)

The teacher's activities and interventions are thus portrayed as promoting thought and reflection on the part of the learner with requests for argument and evidence in support of assertions. There is, in our view, a significant omission from this perspective on knowledge construction. Developments in learners' cognitive structures are seen as coming about through the interaction of these structures with features of an external *physical* reality, with meaning-making being stimulated by peer interaction. What is not considered in a substantial way is the learners' interactions with *symbolic* realities, the cultural tools of science.

Furthermore, in viewing learning as involving the replacement of old knowledge schemes with new, the perspective ignores the possibility of individuals having plural conceptual schemes, each appropriate to specific social settings. (Scientists, after all, understand perfectly well what is meant when they are told "Shut the door and keep the cold out" or "Please feed the plants.") Rather than successive equilibrations, it is argued that learning may be better characterized by parallel constructions relating to specific contexts (Solomon, 1983). Bachelard's (1940/1968) notion of "conceptual profile" can be drawn on usefully here. Instead of constructing a unique and powerful idea, individuals are portrayed as having different ways of thinking, that is, a conceptual profile, within specific domains. For example, in everyday life a continuous view of matter is usually adequate in dealing with the properties and behavior of solid substances. Different perspectives can, however, be drawn upon: a quantum view of matter is epistemologically and ontologically different from an atomistic view, and both of these are different from a continuous model. These three perspectives might form an individual's conceptual profile for solids, and each will be appropriate in different contexts. Thus, a chemist dealing with a synthesis reaction might find it more useful to consider atoms as material particles rather than as a set of mathematical singularities in fields of force (Mortimer, 1993).

Learning science as the social construction of knowledge

Whereas the individual construction of knowledge perspective places primacy on physical experiences and their role in learning science, a social constructivist perspective recognizes that learning involves being introduced to a symbolic world. This is well expressed in Bruner's introduction to Vygotsky's work:

> The Vygotskian project [is] to find the manner in which aspirant members of a culture learn from their tutors, the vicars of their culture, how to understand the world. That world is a *symbolic world* in the sense that it consists of conceptually organized, rule bound belief systems about *what exists*, about how to get to goals, about what is to be valued. There is no way, none, in which a human being could possibly master that world without the aid and assistance of others for, in fact, that world *is* others.
>
> (Bruner, 1985, p. 32)

From this perspective knowledge and understandings, including scientific understandings, are constructed when individuals engage socially in talk and activity about shared problems or tasks. Making meaning is thus a dialogic process involving persons-in-conversation, and learning is seen as the process by which individuals are introduced to a culture by more skilled members. As this happens they "appropriate" the cultural tools through their involvement in the activities of this culture. A more experienced member of a culture can support a less experienced member by structuring tasks, making it possible for the less experienced person to perform them and to internalize the process, that is, to convert them into tools for conscious control.

There is an important point at issue here for science education. If knowledge construction is seen solely as an individual process, then this is similar to what has traditionally been identified as discovery learning. If, however, learners are to be given access to the knowledge systems of science, the process of knowledge construction must go beyond personal empirical enquiry. Learners need to be given access not only to physical experiences but also to the concepts and models of conventional science. The challenge lies in helping learners to appropriate these models for themselves, to appreciate their domains of applicability and, within such domains, to be able to use them. If teaching is to lead students toward conventional science ideas, then the teacher's intervention is essential, both to provide appropriate experiential evidence and to make the cultural tools and conventions of the science community available to students. The challenge is one of how to achieve such a process of enculturation successfully in the round of normal classroom life. Furthermore, there are special challenges when the science view that the teacher is presenting is in conflict with learners' prior knowledge schemes.

Informal science ideas and commonsense knowledge

Young people have a range of knowledge schemes that are drawn on to interpret the phenomena they encounter in their daily lives. These are strongly supported by personal experience and socialization into a "commonsense" view. Research that has been conducted worldwide has shown that children's informal science ideas are not completely idiosyncratic; within particular science domains there are commonly occurring informal ways of modeling and interpreting phenomena that are found among children from different countries, languages, and education systems. One of the areas that has been most thoroughly studied is informal reasoning about mechanics. Here there is a commonly held conception that a constant force is necessary to maintain an object in constant motion (Clement, 1982; Gunstone & Watts, 1985; Viennot, 1979). This notion differs from that of Newtonian physics, which associates force with *change* in motion, that is, acceleration. It is not, however, difficult to understand how experiences such as pushing heavy objects across a floor or pedaling a bicycle can be seen to fit with a "constant motion implies a constant force" notion. In another domain, that of reasoning about material substance, children see no problems in considering matter as appearing and disappearing. When a log fire burns down to a pile of ash, children state that matter is "burnt away" (Andersson, 1991). Older children may acknowledge that there are gaseous products from the fire. These, however, are not seen as substantive, but as having different etherial properties (Meheut, Saltiel, & Tiberghien, 1985). "Gases, after all, cannot have mass or weight; otherwise, why don't they just fall down?" Indeed, for many young people the idea that air or gas can have weight is most implausible. Many even postulate that they have negative weight in that they tend to make things go upwards (Brook, Driver, & Hind, 1989; Stavy, 1988). A similar form of reasoning is used about the role of gases in biological processes such as photosynthesis, respiration, and decay (Leach, Driver, Scott, & Wood-Robinson, in press).

These are just some examples of the types of informal ideas that are pervasive in the reasoning of young people and adults. In the domains such as the ones referred to here, we argue that there are commonalities in informal ways of reasoning partly because members of a culture have shared ways of referring to and talking about particular phenomena. In addition, the ways in which individuals experience natural phenomena are also constrained by the way the world is.

As far as people's everyday experiences are concerned, the informal ideas are often perfectly adequate to interpret and guide action. Fires *do* burn down to result in a small pile of ash – a widely used way of getting rid of unwanted rubbish. If you want to keep a piano moving across the floor you *do* need to keep up a constant push. It is not surprising that ideas that are used and found useful are then represented in everyday language. Phrases such as being "as light as air" or something being "completely burned up" both reflect and give further support to underlying informal ideas. We argue, therefore, that informal ideas are not simply personal views of the world, but reflect a shared view represented by a shared language. This shared view constitutes a socially constructed "commonsense" way of describing and explaining the world.

During the years of childhood, children's ideas evolve as a result of experience and socialization into "commonsense" views. For very young children (aged 4–6), air only exists as a wind or a draft – young children do not conceptualize air as a material substance. The notion of air as *stuff* normally becomes part of children's models of the world by age 7 or 8. This stuff is then conceptualized as occupying space but as being weightless or even having negative weight or *upness* (Brook *et al.*, 1989). This example illustrates a much more general point: that the entities, such as air-as-stuff, that are taken as real by children, may be quite different at different ages. In other words, children's everyday ontological frameworks evolve with experience and language use within a culture. This change corresponds with what others describe as radical restructuring of children's domain specific conceptions (see Carey, 1985; Vosniadou & Brewer, 1992).

"Commonsense" ways of explaining phenomena, as pictured here, represent knowledge of the world portrayed within everyday culture. They differ from the knowledge of the scientific community in a number of ways. Most obviously, common sense and science differ in the ontological entities they contain: the entities that are taken as real within everyday discourse differ from those of the scientific community. Second, commonsense reasoning, although it can be complex, also tends to be tacit or without explicit rules.

Scientific reasoning, by contrast, is characterized by the explicit formulation of theories that can then be communicated and inspected in the light of evidence. In science, this process involves many scientists in communication with one another. Although tacit knowledge undoubtedly has a place in science, the need for explicitness in theory formulation is central to the scientific endeavor. Third, everyday reasoning is characterized by pragmatism. Ideas are judged in terms of being useful for specific purposes or in specific situations, and, as such, they guide people's actions. The scientific endeavor, on the other hand, has an additional purpose of constructing a general and coherent picture of the world. The scientific commitment, therefore, is not satisfied by situationally specific models, but strives for models with the greatest generality and scope.

Learning science as involving individual and social processes

We now consider what we see as the implications of the distinctions between common sense and scientific reasoning for the learning of science. We have argued that learning science is not a matter of simply extending young people's knowledge of phenomena – a practice perhaps more appropriately called nature study – nor of developing and organizing young people's commonsense reasoning. It requires more than challenging learners' prior ideas through discrepant events. Learning science involves young people entering into a different way of thinking about and explaining the natural world; becoming socialized to a greater or lesser extent into the practices of the scientific community with its particular purposes, ways of seeing, and ways of supporting its knowledge claims. Before this can happen, however, individuals must engage in a process of personal construction and meaning making. Characterized in this way, learning science involves both personal and social processes. On the social plane the process involves being introduced to the concepts, symbols, and conventions of the scientific community. Entering into this community of discourse is not something that students discover for themselves any more than they would discover by themselves how to speak Esperanto.

Becoming socialized into the discourse practices of the scientific community does not entail, however, abandoning commonsense reasoning. Human beings take part in multiple parallel communities of discourse, each with its specific practices and purposes. There is considerable interest in the science education community at present in the process of conceptual change. Learning science is being characterized in some quarters as promoting conceptual change from students' informal ideas to those of the scientific community (Hewson, 1981; Posner, Strike, Hewson, & Gertzog, 1982; West & Pines, 1985). We see a problem in this characterization in that we would not expect students necessarily to abandon their commonsense ideas as a result of science instruction. As argued earlier, students still have such ideas available to them for communication within appropriate social contexts (Solomon, 1983).

Some researchers portray students' learning in science as reflecting similar patterns of change as have occurred in science itself, through progressive restructuring of students' underlying theories (Carey, 1985; Chinn & Brewer, 1993; McCloskey, 1983; Vosniadou & Brewer, 1987). Although we recognize that learning science does involve some restructuring of ideas, we argue that viewing learning as theory change puts too great an emphasis on the theory-like nature of students' informal ideas. We argue that their tacit and situated nature distinguishes them from scientific theories. Furthermore, learning science in school means more than changing from one set of theories to another; it means being consciously articulate about what constitutes theories in the first place.

A social perspective on learning in classrooms recognizes that an important way in which novices are introduced to a community of knowledge is through discourse in the context of relevant tasks. Science classrooms are now being recognized as forming communities that are characterized by distinct discursive practices (Lemke, 1990). By being engaged in those practices, students are socialized into a particular community of knowledge, a process described as a cultural apprenticeship (Rogoff & Lave, 1984; Seely Brown, Collins, & Duguid, 1989). The discursive practices in science classrooms differ substantially from the practices of scientific argument and enquiry that take place within various communities of professional scientists; this is hardly surprising when one considers the differences between schools and the various institutional settings of science in terms of purposes and power relationships. This disjunction has been recognized, and some science education researchers are experimenting with ways of organizing classrooms so as to reflect particular forms of collaborative enquiry that can support students in gradually mastering some of the norms and practices that are deemed to be characteristic of scientific communities (Eichinger, Anderson, Palincsar, & David, 1991; Roseberry, Warren, & Conant, 1992).

Learning in the science classroom

In this section we identify some of the discursive practices that support the co-construction of scientific knowledge by teachers and students and that also reflect features of scientific argumentation. We present brief episodes of teaching and learning in science classrooms and draw upon both personal and social perspectives on learning to interpret what is happening in each case. The examples are taken from studies that we have conducted in collaboration with teachers, in science classrooms in the United Kingdom, in which explicit attention has been given to the differences between students' informal thinking about a particular topic and the science view (Scott, Asoko, & Driver, 1992).

The episodes are not intended to present exemplary instances of teaching and learning. Rather, they have been selected to illustrate the ways in which students develop personal meanings in the social context of the classroom, how scientific meanings are appropriated and how ontological and epistemological differences between informal and science views can create obstacles to personal understanding.

Light rays: negotiating "new conceptual tools" – new ontological entities

A class of 8–9-year-old pupils was involved in an introductory series of lessons on light (see Asoko, 1993). Children at this age tend to consider light as a source or an effect (Guesne, 1985) but are less likely to conceptualize light as existing in space and traveling out from a source. The teacher, Michael, was interested in helping the class to develop the idea that light travels through space and that it travels in straight lines. Once he had established agreement that light travels in straight lines, he planned to introduce the conventional representation of light "rays."

Initially, Michael invited the class to consider the light in their classroom, which the children all agreed was sunlight. He then explored this notion with them further by asking where the sunlight comes from.

Pupil 1:   From the Sun.

Michael: You mean that the light that's coming through that window has come from the Sun? (*several simultaneous replies*)

Pupil 2:   It's from the heat – because it is so hot it makes a bright light.

Michael: So how does it get here? If the light is at the Sun, how come it is here as well? Martyn?

Pupil 3:   'Cause the Sun's shining on us.

Michael: But it is 93 million miles away – so how come the light from the Sun is here on the table?

Pupil 4:   Is it because of the ozone layer? (*There then followed a short exchange in which several pupils contributed ideas about the hole in the ozone layer allowing more sunlight through, after which Michael reposed the question.*)

Michael: But how does the sunlight get here?

Pupil 5:   It travels here.

Michael: Coulton says, and his exact words are, that "it travels here." In other words, light moves from the Sun to here . . .

Pupil 5:   Yes.

Michael: 93 million miles. Is that right?

Pupils: Yes (*chorus of many voices*).

In this interchange, Michael indicated that the Sun "shining" could be further elaborated and, with contributions from the class, focused on the idea of light as something that travels out from the source through space. His interaction with the class as this idea was explored gives an indication that the idea is generally accepted as plausible, an important feature in the co-construction of classroom knowledge.

The idea that light travels was further developed through a practical activity carried out in groups. Each group of 3–4 children had a set of equipment comprising a 12-volt bulb placed centrally under an octagonal cardboard box about 35 cm in diameter, placed on a large sheet of paper. A slit about 12 cm high and 0.5 cm wide was cut in each of the eight faces. The children were asked to think about what they would see when the bulb was switched on and to draw what they expected to see on the paper. Almost all the children drew lines at 90° to the faces extending from the slit to indicate the path of the light. The lines varied in length from 2–3 cm to about 30 cm. When all the children had made at least one prediction, all the lamps were switched on simultaneously in the darkened room. The spectacular effect caused some excitement and not a little surprise when children realized that instead of travelling only a short distance, the beams of light continued across the paper and could be seen, in a vertical plane, when they met a surface such as the wall or a child's body.

Michael called the class together to discuss their observations. He drew a plan view of the octagonal box on a flip chart. Drawing a line to represent the path of the light, he commented that everyone had made predictions about the position of the line that agreed with what they saw, but commented that many people in the class thought the light would stop.

Michael:	Is that right?
Pupil 1:	No, it carries on.
Michael:	It carries on. How long would it carry on?
Pupil 2:	Right to the end. Just keeps carrying on.
Pupil 3:	Just keeps carrying on, is that . . .
Pupil 4:	It can't stop. You can't stop light without turning it off.

In this sequence, the notion that light "keeps carrying on" is again interpreted in part of a shared discourse. Michael then invited children to come up and draw more lines on his drawing to show where the light would go. After the children had done this Michael began using the words *ray of light* to describe the path of light.

In this extended set of sequences, Michael was introducing the children through discourse to the scientific *way of seeing*, making it plausible to them in the context of a memorable experience. Once he had satisfied himself that the children had a mental representation for "the path the light travels along," he introduced the convention or symbolic representation of the light ray, a cultural tool that would be used in subsequent lessons. Throughout the sequence, a coherent story evolved, a story that Michael, through feedback, checked was shared by the class. This process of developing shared meaning between teacher and students is at the heart of making what Edwards and Mercer (1987) call *common knowledge* in the classroom. This common knowledge or shared discourse then referred to a new ontological framework about light, a framework in which light travels, and travels in straight lines (represented symbolically by "light rays") over long distances.

Air pressure: scaffolding "a new way of explaining" – conflict between common sense and scientific views

The process by which new ways of explaining are developed by students can involve dialogic interactions between the teacher and individuals, or small groups of students. In these interactions, the adult (or a more competent peer) provides what Bruner (1986) called "scaffolding" for the students' learning as they construct new meanings for themselves.

In an instructional sequence on air pressure with 11–12-year-old students (Scott, 1993), the teacher had developed, through demonstrations and discourse with the class, a new way of explaining a range of simple phenomena (such as why a plastic bottle collapses inward when air is withdrawn from it). This new way of explaining was based on differences in air pressure inside and outside the bottle, and the class was then asked to work in groups to use the pressure difference idea to explain further phenomena, such as how suction cups hold on to surfaces and how a liquid can be drawn into a teat pipette.

In the following passages, we see examples of an adult "expert" attempting to "scaffold" students' reasoning in terms of a pressure difference model. We also see the ways in which students' existing informal theories, such as "vacuums suck," influence their personal sense making.

Christa and Adele completed an activity with the suction cups and were surprised at the amount of force needed to pull them off a smooth surface. They considered their explanation for this:

Christa: It's a flat surface and there's no air in the cup there, so there's less air in than there is on the outside, so it'll stick down.
Adult: So what *does* this pushing . . . this sticking it down?
Christa: Air.
Adele: Suction.
Adult: What's suction?
Adele: It's something that pulls . . . it's something that pulls it down . . .
Adult: A minute or two ago, you said it was something to do with pushing the air out here.
Adele: Yeah.
Adult: And then you also said it was something to do with suction. Are these the *same* explanations, or are they different?

Adele: They're nearly . . . (*Adele is not sure and comes to a halt.*)

The adult then referred the two girls to the earlier demonstration of the collapsing plastic bottle that they explained in terms of the difference in air pressure inside and out. The girls then returned to consider the case of the suction cups.

Adult: Now, where's the inside and the outside of this?
Adele: Well . . . that's the inside (*indicates the underside of the suction cup*).
Adult: Yes . . . right.
Adele: Yeah, and that's the outside.
Adult: Uh huh – can you use the explanation like the one used for the bottle to explain what happens here? (*The adult refers once again back to the collapsing plastic bottle.*)
Adele: Has it got anything to do with gravity?
Adult: What makes you say that?
Adele: Pulling it down.

After further exchanges, Adele and the adult agreed that you can have gravity acting even when there is no air, so they are really different things. They continued considering the suction cups:

Adele: It's sticking to the bottom of there – it [air] all comes out of the sides.
Adult: All right, and what about the air on the outside?
Christa: And the air on the outside's pushing it *down*.
Adele: So it's hard to pull up.

In this extract, the adult structured the course of the reasoning, first reminding the girls of the explanation the class constructed for the collapsing plastic bottle and then supporting the girls in making the link to the case of the suction cup by guiding them to consider the air inside, and the air outside.

Shortly afterwards, Adele raised a further question.

Adele: How is it when you put it down and then you pull a little corner up it slips up?
Adult: Oh, that's a very good question. Do you want to think about that for a minute?
Adele: It's, it's . . .
Christa: No, I'll show you what it is. It's the air, it can get back in, can't it?
Adele: Yeah, it's getting back in it, so the air's pushing it upwards, isn't it?
Both: Yeah!

Here, the adult withdrew support or scaffolding from the girls, except for being an interested audience, and the girls confidently used the pressure difference explanation by themselves. However, a final question from Christa suggests that problems may still exist:

Adult: Now . . . (long pause) . . . do you have any questions about this?
Christa: Why . . . why does air push it down . . . when air's come out of the side? Why does air push it down?

Christa's question suggests that although she had been successful (with the support of the adult) in constructing the pressure difference explanation in this case, it may still lack plausibility for her ("Why does air push it down?"). In fact, it is highly unlikely that any previous experience or talk about static air would support the idea that it creates such large pressures. The new way of explaining challenges the students' ideas about what air can and cannot do; it challenges their personal ontologies of air.

The examples presented here draw attention to the fundamental (but frequently overlooked) point that different domains of science involve different *kinds* of learning. In the first example, the young students appeared to experience little difficulty in understanding and believing that light travels and keeps on traveling unless blocked. They adopted the scientific discourse and used the ideas productively. The situation in the second example appears to be rather different. The teacher had carefully engaged students in activities and discourse to support them in constructing the science view, and yet we see students experiencing real difficulties in making those science models meaningful and appropriating them for themselves. We suggest that these differences in student response can, in part, be accounted for by considering the ontological and epistemological demands of learning in the separate science domains in question. What is common to both cases, however, is the process whereby a teacher, familiar with the scientific way-of-seeing, makes the cultural tools of science available to learners and supports their (re)construction of the ideas through discourse about shared physical events.

Summary and final comments

The view that scientific knowledge is socially constructed, validated, and communicated is central to this chapter. We have presented a perspective on science learning as a process of enculturation rather than discovery, arguing that empirical study of the natural world will not reveal scientific knowledge because scientific knowledge is discursive in nature. We have shown that learners of science have everyday representations of the phenomena that science explains. These representations are constructed, communicated, and validated within everyday culture. They evolve as individuals live within a culture. We have shown that there are epistemological and ontological differences between everyday and scientific reasoning. Although learning science involves social interactions, in the sense that the cultural tools of science have to be introduced to learners, we have argued that individuals have to make personal sense of newly introduced ways of viewing the world. If everyday representations of particular natural phenomena are very different from scientific representations, learning may prove difficult. We have argued that the relationship between views of learning and pedagogy is problematic, and that no simple rules for pedagogical practice emerge from a constructivist view of learning. There are, however, important features of the mediation process that can be identified. If students are to adopt scientific ways of knowing, then intervention and negotiation with an authority, usually the teacher, is essential. Here, the critical feature is the nature of the dialogic process. The role of the authority figure has two important components. The first is to introduce new ideas or cultural tools where necessary and to provide the support and guidance for students to make sense of these for themselves. The other is to listen and diagnose the ways in which the instructional activities are being interpreted to inform further action. Teaching from this perspective is thus also a learning process for the teacher. Learning science in the classroom involves children entering a new community of discourse, a new culture; the teacher is the often hard-pressed tour guide mediating between children's everyday world and the world of science.

What is presented here differs fundamentally from the positivist program in education with its emphasis on technical rationality and a nonproblematic portrayal of the knowledge to be acquired. By participating in the discursive activities of science lessons, learners are socialized into the ways of knowing and practices of school science. This presents a major challenge for educators: the challenge lies in fostering a critical perspective on scientific culture among students. To develop such a perspective, students will need to be aware of the varied purposes of scientific knowledge, its limitations, and the bases on which its claims are made. A crucial challenge for classroom life is therefore to make these epistemological features an explicit focus of discourse and hence to socialize learners into a critical perspective on science as a way of knowing.

References

Andersson, B. (1991). Pupils' conceptions of matter and its transformations (age 12–16). *Studies in Science Education, 18*, 53–85.

Asoko, H. (1993). First steps in the construction of a theoretical model of light: A case study from a primary school classroom. In *Proceedings of the Third International Seminar on Misconceptions in Science and Mathematics Education*. Ithaca, NY: Misconceptions Trust.

Bachelard, G. (1940/1968). *The philosophy of no.* (G. C. Waterston, Trans.). New York: Orion Press. (Original work published 1940.)

Brook, A., Driver, R., & Hind, D. (1989). *Progression in science: The development of pupils' understanding of physical characteristics of air across the age range 5–16 years.* Centre for Studies in Science and Mathematics Education, University of Leeds, United Kingdom.

Bruner, J. (1985). Vygotsky: A historical and conceptual perspective. In J. Wertsh (Ed.), *Culture, communication and cognition: Vygotskian perspectives* (pp. 21–34). Cambridge: Cambridge University Press.

Bruner, J. (1986). *Actual minds, possible worlds.* Cambridge, MA: Harvard University Press.

Carey, S. (1985). *Conceptual change in childhood.* Cambridge, MA: MIT Press.

Carmichael, P., Driver, R., Holding, B., Phillips, I., Twigger, D., & Watts, M. (1990). *Research on students' conceptions in science: A bibliography.* Centre for Studies in Science and Mathematics Education, University of Leeds, United Kingdom.

Chinn, C., & Brewer, W. (1993). The role of anomalous data in knowledge acquisition: A theoretical framework and implications for science instruction. *Review of Educational Research, 63*(1), 1–50.

Clement, J. (1982). Student preconceptions in introductory mechanics. *American Journal of Physics, 50*(1), 66–71.

Driver, R., Guesne, E., & Tiberghien, A. (1985). *Children's ideas in science.* Milton Keynes, Bucks.: Open University Press.

Driver, R., & Oldham, V. (1986). A constructivist approach to curriculum development in science. *Studies in Science Education, 13*, 105–122.

Duckworth, E. (1987). *"The having of wonderful ideas" and other essays on teaching and learning.* New York: Teachers' College Press.

Edwards, D., & Mercer, N. (1987). *Common knowledge.* London: Methuen.

Eichinger, D., Anderson, C. W., Palincsar, A. S., & David, Y. (1991, April). An illustration of the roles of content knowledge scientific argument, and social norms in collaborative problem solving. Paper presented at the Annual Meeting of the American Educational Research Association, Chicago, IL.

Fensham, P., Gunstone, R., & White, R. (Eds.). (1994). *The content of science.* London: Falmer Press.

Guesne, E. (1985). Light. In R. Driver, E. Guesne, & A. Tiberghien, *Children's ideas in science* (pp. 10–32). Milton Keynes, Bucks.: Open University Press.

Gunstone, R., & Watts, M. (1985). Children's understanding of force and motion. In R. Driver, E. Guesne, & A. Tiberghien (Eds.), *Children's ideas in science* (pp. 85–104). Milton Keynes, Bucks.: Open University Press.

Hanson, N. R. (1958). *Patterns of discovery.* Cambridge: Cambridge University Press.

Hewson, P. (1981). A conceptual change approach to learning science. *European Journal of Science Education, 3*(4), 383–396.

Johnston, K., & Driver, R. (1990). *A constructivist approach to the teaching of the particulate theory of matter: A report on a scheme in action.* Centre for Studies in Science and Mathematics Education, University of Leeds, United Kingdom.

Leach, J., Driver, R., Scott. P., & Wood-Robinson, C. (in press). Children's ideas about ecology 2: Ideas about the cycling of matter found in children aged 5–16. *International Journal of Science Education.*

Lemke, J. (1990). *Talking science.* Norwood, NJ: Ablex.

McCloskey, M. (1983). Intuitive physics. *Scientific American, 248,* 122–130.

Matthews, M. (1992). Constructivism and empiricism: An incomplete divorce. *Research in Science Education, 22*, 299–307.

Meheut, M., Saltiel, E., & Tiberghien, A. (1985). Pupils' 11–12 years old) conceptions of combustion. *European Journal of Science Education, 7*(1), 83–93.

Millar, R. (1989). Constructive criticisms. *International Journal of Science Education, 11*(5), 587–596.

Millar, R., Driver, R., Leach, L., & Scott, P. (1993) *Students' understanding of the nature of science: Philosophical and sociological foundations to the study.* Working Paper 2 from the project "The development of understanding of the nature of science." Centre for Studies in Science and Mathematics Education, The University of Leeds, United Kingdom.

Mortimer, E. F. (1993). Studying conceptual evolution in the classroom as conceptual profile change. *Proceedings of the Third International Seminar on Misconceptions in Science and Mathematics Education.* Ithaca, NY: Misconceptions Trust.

Nussbaum, J., & Novick, S. (1982). Alternative frameworks, conceptual conflict and accommodation. *Instructional Science, 11,* 183–208.

Osborne, J. (1993). Beyond constructivism. *Proceedings of the Third International Seminar on Misconceptions in Science and Mathematics Education.* Ithaca, NY: Misconceptions Trust.

Osborne, R., & Freyberg, P. (1985). *Learning in science: The implications of children's science.* Auckland: Heinemann.

Pfundt, H., & Duit, R. (1985). *Bibliography: Students' alternative frameworks and science education.* Kiel, Staffs.: IPN.

Piaget, J. (1937). *La construction de réel chez l'enfant.* Neuchâtel Delachaux & Niestlé.

Piaget, J. (1970). *Genetic epistemology.* (E. Duckworth, Trans.). New York: Columbia University Press.

Piaget, J., & Garcia, R. (1989). *Psychogenesis and the history of science.* New York: Columbia University Press.

Posner, C. J., Strike, K. A., Hewson, P. W., & Gertzog, W. A. (1982). Accommodation of a scientific conception: Toward a theory of conceptual change. *Science Education, 66*(2), 211–227.

Rogoff, B., & Lave, J. (1984). *Everyday cognition: Its development in social context.* Cambridge, MA: Harvard University Press.

Roseberry, A., Warren, B., & Conant, F. (1992). *Approaches to scientific discourse: Findings from language minority classrooms* (Working Paper No. 1–92). Cambridge, MA: TERC.

Rowell, J. A., & Dawson, C. J. (1984). Equilibration, conflict and instruction: A new class-oriented perspective. *European Journal of Science Education, 7*, 331–334.

Scott, P. (1993). Overtures and obstacles: Teaching and learning about air pressure in a high school classroom. *Proceedings of the Third International Seminar on Misconceptions in Science and Mathematics Education.* Ithaca, NY: Misconceptions Trust.

Scott, P., Asoko, H., & Driver, R. (1992). Teaching for conceptual change: A review of strategies. In R. Duit, F. Goldberg, & H. Neidderer (Eds.), *Research in physics learning: Theoretical issues and empirical studies* (pp. 310–329). Keil, Germany: Schmidt & Klannig.

Scott, P., Asoko, H., Driver, R., & Emberton, J. (1994). Working from children's ideas: An analysis of constructivist teaching in the context of a chemistry topic. In P. Fensham, R. Gunstone, & R. White (Eds.), *The content of science.* London: Falmer.

Seely Brown, J., Collins, A., & Duguid, P. (1989). Situated cognition and the culture of learning. *Educational Researcher, 18*(1), 32–42.

Solomon, J. (1983). Learning about energy: How pupils think in two domains. *European Journal of Science Education, 5*(1), 49–59.

Stavy, R. (1988). Children's conception of gas. *International Journal of Science Education, 10*(5), 552–560.

Viennot, L. (1979). Spontaneous reasoning in elementary dynamics. *European Journal of Science Education, 1*(2), 205–222.

Vosniadou, S., & Brewer, W. F. (1987). Theories of knowledge restructuring in development. *Review of Educational Research, 57*, 51–67.

Vosniadou, S., & Brewer, W. F. (1992). Mental models of the earth: A study of conceptual change in childhood. *Cognitive Psychology, 24*, 535–585.

West, L., & Pines, A. (Eds.). (1985). *Cognitive structure and conceptual change.* Orlando, FL: Academic Press.

Chapter 14

Sharing cognition through collective comprehension activity*

Giyoo Hatano and Kayoko Inagaki

In this chapter we will examine two important questions in constructive group interaction: how a collective attempt to acquire knowledge takes place, and how much knowledge comes to be *shared* (acquired in common) through this attempt. We will be concerned particularly with the generation, revision, and elaboration of explanations for a set of facts, a rule, or a procedure. In other words, our focus is collective comprehension activity and the sharing of its product by group members.

As will be shown, a large number of members of a group can be involved in enduring, coherent discourse about a target issue. Moreover, the group may generate "respectable" cognitive products, for example, a plausible explanation, that any individual member is unlikely to produce. The first question we will explore is how this phenomenon is possible.

The second question we will examine is: How much of the knowledge offered during the discourse is acquired by members differing in prior knowledge and in the extent of participation? When they do not know who knows best? How can group members pick out valid pieces of information and reject others? If the collective attempt succeeds in producing a plausible explanation about the target, is it acquired by all or almost all the members?

This chapter consists of three parts. First, we will examine in what type of groups constructive interaction is likely to occur. After discussing a few conditions necessary for a group to engage frequently in constructive interaction, we will offer a prototype of such interaction: a class taught by Hypothesis–Experiment–Instruction. Second, we will present some experimental data related to the above two questions. We will rely primarily on our own research findings but will refer to studies by our Japanese colleagues as well. Finally, we would like to propose our own answers to these questions in speculative ways.

Before we turn to these three major parts, however, it is important to define

---

* This is an edited version of a chapter that appeared in *Perspectives on socially shared cognition*, Washington, DC: American Psychological Association, 1991.

terminology. Throughout this chapter "comprehension" is defined as the solution of the problem of "the 'how' and 'why' of the connections observed and applied in action" (Piaget, 1978). In other words, to *comprehend* means to achieve insight *(nattoku* in Japanese) or to find satisfactory explanations for the occurrence of a series of events, the validity of a rule, or the success of a procedure. *Comprehension activity* is a term for the process of achieving insight and thus, as described by Collins, Brown, and Larkin (1980) and Hatano and Inagaki (1987), includes generating inferences, checking their plausibility (by seeking further information from outside or by retrieving another piece of stored information), and coordinating pieces of old and new information, all to build an enriched and coherent representation of what is going on behind a given set of information, a representation that will serve as the basis for insight.

Sometimes comprehension activity is an individual enterprise initiated when a person becomes aware that his or her comprehension is inadequate, although within his or her reach, and is terminated when this person feels he or she has found satisfactory explanations (Hatano & Inagaki, 1987). On other occasions, comprehension takes a collective form. At least some members of a given group become interested in the how and why and ask a question or invite others' comments on their own relevant ideas. The committed members go on by presenting additional information they have gathered, drawing attention to pieces of shared information that seem to support their ideas, and so forth, until all group members are satisfied with some proposed explanations or are convinced that no plausible explanation is forthcoming (or are just bored with the activity). The exact nature of this activity will be discussed in greater detail later.

Where shall we look for constructive group interaction?

It is now generally accepted that social interaction plays an important role in the acquisition of knowledge. However, constructive interaction, that is, the collective invention of knowledge that none of a group's members has acquired or is likely to produce independently, occurs frequently only in some types of groups. We think the following four parameters are important to characterize such groups.

Horizontal in terms of the flow of information

Of the two distinguishable types of interactions, many more researchers have studied *vertical* interaction (represented by adult–child interaction), partly because of the influence of Vygotsky (1978). Current conceptualizations of apprenticeship (Collins, Brown, & Newman, 1989) also concern interaction that is vertical in nature. These researchers assume that one member (i.e., the developed person) continues to be more capable than the other (i.e., the developing individual) at every moment of interaction. Moreover, they have paid much more attention to the reproduction than to the invention of knowledge, if not simply the transmission of knowledge from the more mature to the less mature.

We believe that the construction of knowledge through social interaction can be observed much more often in the other type of interaction, that is the *horizontal* (as in peer interaction). Speaking generally, the less mature member in vertical interaction is not highly motivated to construct knowledge, because he or she believes that the other member possesses or can construct that knowledge more easily (Inagaki, 1981). Even when asked for an explanation, he or she will concentrate on looking for the more capable member's desired answer, instead of figuring it out, as is often observed between a teacher and student. The more mature member may offer some explanation but is unlikely to elaborate or revise it, because the idea is not challenged in interaction.

In contrast, in horizontal interaction, members' motivation to disclose their ideas tends to be natural and strong, because no authoritative right answers are expected to come immediately. Therefore, the members often express fearlessly a variety of ideas, which are likely to be examined, sorted out, and elaborated in interaction. What is critical here is the horizontality in terms of (perceived) expertise as to the target issue among those who participate in the exchange of ideas.

Characterizing a relationship as *horizontal* does not exclude the possibility that some members are more capable than others at some given moment. It only means that roles among members are changeable in interaction. Thus the vertical–horizontal distinction should be taken as a continuum rather than a dichotomy.

Three or more members

We maintain that, although "two heads are better than one," dyads are far from optimal for the construction of knowledge, and that it is preferable to study interactions in groups consisting of at least three and preferably a few more persons. In other words, we believe that the presence of a third party is an essential component of group process through which knowledge is constructed. Even when only two persons are actively involved in discussion or debate, they seldom ignore other people. Instead, they often talk to the third party or audience, because it may have the potentially deciding vote.

The presence of an audience can enhance the collective construction of knowledge for social and cognitive reasons. Socially, it makes discussion or debate livelier and more enduring, because discussion or debate becomes an intellectual game for gaining supporters to form the majority. Cognitively, it divides the roles of proposing and evaluating ideas among the members.

Third parties give, either explicitly or implicitly, clues for evaluating arguments offered by the proponent and opponent: the proponent and opponent can evaluate how persuasive their ideas are by observing reactions of the audience. This is certainly easier than monitoring their own arguments by reflection only.

Does the presence of an audience always facilitate the construction of knowledge? Certainly not. It may lead those speakers who care about the audience's reactions too much to avoid any risky or adventurous attempt and may undermine their motivation for knowing. It may also induce superficial or even sensational arguments if speakers "play to a gallery." We believe, however, that the presence of an audience tends to be advantageous for the construction of knowledge to the extent that the audience is rational.

Involvement of empirical confirmation

We assert that, because comprehension activity includes seeking further external information, constructive group interaction usually includes seeking information from outside the group. As Piagetians have revealed (e.g., Doise & Mugny, 1984), although social interaction *per se* may enable its participants to acquire knowledge, it probably does so only when the correct idea is so salient that it comes out promptly to solve cognitive conflict produced by the interaction. People are not always ready to incorporate information offered by others. Unless the information is persuasive in terms of logic or given by someone known to be an authority, people, especially those forming the majority, will not assimilate the information until external feedback proves its plausibility. Miyake's study (1986) has shown that empirical confirmation by inspection played a significant role in facilitating joint comprehension of how a sewing machine makes stitches, even for her academically sophisticated subjects.

Furthermore, we believe that constructive group interaction is often induced when group members talk about a set of clearly articulated alternatives that are falsifiable by empirical means. In other words, the construction of knowledge occurs often when group activity is "situated" in a specific context. Otherwise, sharing the meaning of what is discussed requires much effort and cost. People may agree (or disagree) prematurely with very different interpretations about the target. For example, our unpublished study revealed that, when asked to comprehend jointly why a given series of steps was needed to make *bonito sashimi*, dyads of female college students rarely spent more than 10 minutes developing an answer. They thought they had comprehended and that their comprehension was shared. Only when asked whether the same procedure should be followed under slightly different conditions was the discrepancy in their interpretations uncovered.

Room for individual knowledge acquisition

A group as a whole usually has a richer database than any of its members for problem solving. It is likely that no individual member has acquired or has ready access to all needed pieces of information, but every piece is owned by at least one member in the group. For example, when a dyad of two experts – one in the language in which a target passage is written and the other in its content – is required to translate a written passage, their joint product is much better in quality than either of the individual products (Sugimoto, 1988). Thus, if pieces of information distributed among a group's members are aptly collected, group problem solving should be more effective than individual enterprise.

However, problem solving by a group may not result in all individual members' acquisition of its product. Individual group members may not be able to solve on their own a problem that they have solved collectively. Pieces of information distributed among members can be used to solve a given problem without being coordinated into a new piece of knowledge in each member's head. This is because the knowledge has not been invented or represented in an explicitly stated and usable form for individuals.

Individual knowledge acquisition is possible in everyday life in loosely organized groups that are supposed to fulfill several different functions, even when knowledge acquisition itself is not the primary goal. Because human beings have an intrinsic motivation to understand (Hatano & Inagaki, 1987), they are likely to seek the meaning of what they and others do in the group and, thus, to get relevant pieces of knowledge without any explicit request to do so. However, this motivation can be undermined by the expectation of extrinsic rewards, external evaluation, or even the authorized "right" answer (Hatano & Inagaki, 1987). Moreover, because engaging in comprehension activity is seldom the shortest or quickest way to solve a specific problem, it is discouraged when efficiency in getting the solution is emphasized.

Therefore, we assume that, if the group activity is to pursue goal(s) other than knowledge acquisition, if the procedure to achieve the goal(s) has been well established, and if the group's members are required to perform the procedure with utmost efficiency, the members are not likely to engage in persistent comprehension activity. As a result, they are not likely to advance their individual knowledge even when they are repeatedly involved in the group. Readers will find this assumption plausible if they imagine themselves working in a factory under the Taylor system or in a military unit in which what each person should do is specified in detail. Collective problem solving occurs in these groups, but not the collective construction of knowledge.

Sharing cognition in a group: an example

One concrete example of a group in which constructive interaction takes place is a class taught by a Japanese science education method called

Hypothesis–Experiment–Instruction (Itakura, 1967), originally devised by K. Itakura and used in science classes in elementary and junior high schools. The following procedure is usually adopted with this method:

1 Pupils are presented with a question having three or four answer alternatives. The question specifies how to confirm which alternative is right.
2 Pupils are asked to choose one answer by themselves.
3 Pupils' responses, counted by a show of hands, are tabulated on the blackboard.
4 Pupils are encouraged to explain and discuss their choices with one another.
5 Pupils are asked to choose an alternative once again. They may change their choices.
6 Pupils are allowed to test their predictions by observing an experiment or reading a given passage.

A teacher, after presenting the problem, acts as a chairperson or moderator who tries to stay neutral during students' discussion. Thus, although he or she has control over what kinds of activities students engage in, none of the discussion participants is regarded as more capable or expert than any other. Throughout the interaction, information flows horizontally. In step 4 above, students are often engaged in lively discussions in a large group of 40 to 45 people. Several students may express their opinions often, but a majority of them tend to participate vicariously in the discussion, nodding or shaking their heads or making brief remarks. There is empirical confirmation in step 6 that can demonstrate clearly which answer alternative is correct. Moreover, discussion in step 4 is about which alternative will prove to be correct in step 6: in other words, discussion is situated in the context of empirical confirmation.

The group is not expected to perform this task efficiently. Rather, its members are expected to acquire knowledge, because this method is for learning science and, above all, for learning basic concepts and principles in science. However, unlike the dyads in Miyake (1986), students are not explicitly asked to achieve comprehension as a final task outcome. They are encouraged only to discuss which alternative is correct. Enduring comprehension activity is initiated primarily by their being presented a problem, the answer alternatives of which represent plausible yet erroneous ideas (i.e., common misconceptions held by pupils) as well as the correct answer, and is amplified through discussion.

Consider the following example from the first lesson on buoyancy, taught by Mr. Shoji to fifth graders (Inagaki, 1981). Mr. Shoji started the lesson with a question: "Suppose that you have a clay ball on one end of a spring. You hold the other end of the spring and put half of the clay ball into water. Will the spring (a) become shorter, (b) become longer, or (c) retain its length?" Response frequencies before discussion are shown in Table 14.1.

Table 14.1 Tabulation of pupils' response frequencies before and after discussion

Response	Before discussion	After discussion
(a) Spring becomes shorter	12	21
(b) Spring becomes longer	8	5
(c) Spring retains its length	14	8

Note
From "Facilitation of Knowledge Integration through Classroom Discussion" by K. Inagaki, 1981, *The Quarterly Newsletter of the Laboratory of Comparative Human Cognition, 3.* No. 2, p. 27. Copyright 1981 by LCHC. Reprinted by permission.

As you can see, each alternative was chosen by several students, indicating that all three alternatives were plausible to the students. The following are examples of reasons for choosing alternative *a*, *b*, or *c* that were given by students before entering the discussion:

(a) "The water has the power to make things float. Therefore, I think the water will make the clay ball float to some extent." "I feel myself lighter in water. I have this experience when I take a bath."
(b) "The spring will be longer because the clay ball will sink." "Because the water will be absorbed into the tiny particles which the clay ball consists of."
(c) "The nature of the clay will not change when we put it into the water." "The water has the power to make completely immersed things float, but not if they are only half immersed."

The teacher then elicited group discussion by encouraging students to give counter-arguments against other opinions. Students actively engaged in discussion, refuting other opinions or defending their own. For example, one of the supporters of *a* opposed a supporter of *c* by saying, "Your opinion is strange to me. You said, 'The weight of the clay ball will not change because it is only half immersed in water.' But you know, when a person's head is above the water, his weight is lighter in water." Another supporter of *a* said, "I don't agree with the idea that the clay ball is as heavy in water as in air. I think the water has the power to make things float." One of the supporters of *c* objected: "Even if the water has the power to make things float, the clay ball will not float, I suppose." Another student supporting *a* insisted, "If the clay is a very small lump, I think the water can make it float."

After the discussion, the teacher retabulated the pupils' responses by asking whether there were any pupils who had changed their choices. As shown in Table 14.1, opinions of supporters of option *a* made nine students change their predictions, but about 40 percent of the students still had incorrect predictions. Finally, the pupils observed an experiment to test their predictions. The result supported the pupils who had chosen alternative *a*.

Which arguments made by the supporters of *a* might have won over some of their classmates before the demonstration? Could the remaining supporters of *b* or *c* incorporate these arguments after the demonstration? To our regret, no detailed information is available about the individual cognitive processes or social dynamics involved in discussions by the above class. (Generally speaking, there have been only a few analytic studies on Hypothesis–Experiment–Instruction. We will present one of them in the next section.)

Let us discuss briefly the representativeness of our example, that is, a class taught by Hypothesis–Experiment–Instruction, for constructive interaction in general. Can we observe more or less similar interactions among "just plain folks" (Lave, 1988)? We think it is likely that ordinary people, as well as students, engage in a collective attempt to determine which of the alternative ideas confronting them is best, although they pick out their own problem and propose their own alternatives instead of being presented with a ready-made problem and answer alternatives. In our daily conversation, for example, we may talk about such things as which bar serves the best *sushi* and what is the fastest route for going to Dokkyo University from Chiba University. Although we are not primarily interested in the problem of *why*, we may try to formulate some justifications for our choice. We also believe it is universal across cultures that groups of people discuss their own choices and elaborate their explanations for their choices through discussion, although how well the Hypothesis–Experiment–Instruction method works may be culture-bound.

Some experimental findings

Motivational and cognitive effects of discussion

Our earlier studies on constructive interaction aimed at examining the effectiveness of the Hypothesis–Experiment–Instruction method for Japanese schoolchildren. All of these studies were typical group comparisons between experimental and control subjects, and we did not analyze in detail either collective comprehension activity or patterns of sharing. However, the findings can serve as a basis for constraining the range of answers to the questions we posed at the beginning of this chapter.

Let us consider one study (Inagaki & Hatano, 1968) in which fourth graders received a science lesson concerning the conservation of weight when sugar is dissolved in water. Subjects were randomly divided into experimental and control groups (44 and 43 students, respectively) on the basis of their performance on the target task at pretest. Two-thirds of the members in each group were nonconservers. In the experimental condition, the six steps outlined previously were followed in groups of about 20 students each, whereas in the control condition, steps 3, 4, and 5 were omitted. Thus, the difference between the conditions was in the extent of the exchange of ideas among the pupils, or, more specifically, of the information about who (or how many students) supported each of the alternatives and how they justified their choices, not in the amount of authoritative information given.

Using audiotapes and relying on informal observations, we obtained group protocols, that is, transcribed sequences of members' utterances (with salient nonverbal behaviors recorded). Unlike individual thinking-aloud protocols, group protocols are too coarse to allow us to analyze all major mental events occurring in any individual's brain, even when he or she speaks very often and the group is very small. Utterances in a group are almost always preceded by editing and, thus, cannot be taken as concurrent indexes of mental events. The larger the group, the more editing is done and the longer is the delay. However, these protocols suggest at least two elements to be included in the answer to our first question regarding how a collective attempt to acquire knowledge takes place.

First, students' enduring comprehension activity was pushed forward by their social, or more specifically "partisan," motivation, as well as by cognitive or "epistemic" motivation. In other words, their collective attempt is not a "pure" comprehension activity but aims at winning an academic competition as well as at comprehension. As soon as the whole group was divided (psychologically, not spatially or socially) into a few parties according to their choice of answer alternatives, the students seemed to be motivated to work for the party they belonged to, that is, to collect more supporters and eventually win the argument by persuading all others. Most of the utterances were arguments against other parties that ranged from pointing out errors in reasoning to noting overlooked facts that they thought were critical. Speakers often gave signs of solidarity to supporters who had chosen the same alternative, and the supporters returned signs of agreement. When their prediction proved to be correct, students were quite excited and again exchanged signs of companionship. When it turned out to be wrong, they were greatly disappointed but tried to console each other.

This is not to say that the classroom discussion was driven solely by the competitive desire to be academic winners. Epistemic motivation, the desire to know and understand, remained strong and underlay all the partisanship. In addition to the general situational emphasis on individual learning, the freedom to change one's prediction and, thus, one's affiliation to a party, and also the agreed reliance on experiment as the means for confirming or disconfirming predictions seemed to enhance this motivation. Thus, the students were all seeking to share better comprehension, as well as competing between parties.

The second element that the protocols suggest is that this partisanship made pupils' comprehension activity more effective, because it served to divide the task into several manageable parts. It is hard for any individual to collect arguments both for and against each alternative and to assess them impartially. In collective comprehension activity, participants do not have to do this. Supporters of one alternative have only to try to defend it (offer arguments "for") by elaborating justifications, because supporters of other alternatives naturally try to criticize them (propose arguments "against"). In fact, in response to other parties' criticisms, most committed supporters could think of more plausible and sophisticated explanations than they had had at the beginning, while maintaining a more or less consistent standpoint. Moreover, assessing the strength of each argument, which would have been very hard to do on a purely cognitive basis, was helped by social cues. The effectiveness of one's own or a comrade's argument could be judged by whether it made opponents silent or attracted more supporters. Here reactions of the third party would also be considered. Unlike the arrangement of partners in Miyake's experiment (1986), the division of labor in this experiment was possible in part on a competitive basis.

Division of labor was also possible within a party. Because those students belonging to the same party shared many relevant opinions, they could easily add to or elaborate what had been said by their comrades. The students could make their explanation increasingly clear, more persuasive, and more detailed in the course of discussion, although each of the individual contributors added only a little.

Let us derive suggestions from this study for our second question regarding how much knowledge is shared through collective comprehension activity. In contrast to the few shifts in the choice of alternatives before the experimental confirmation, when given a posttest immediately after the observation of the experiment, all but a few of the previously mentioned children in the experimental condition acquired conservation responses to the target sugar-and-water task, as did most of the control condition children. Moreover, the experimental condition children could give adequate explanations about why the weight of dissolved sugar was conserved more often than could the control condition children. For example, 26 percent of the experimental subjects gave atomistic or quasiatomistic explanations, whereas none of the control subjects gave such reasons. In addition, experimental subjects showed greater progress in applying the principle of weight conservation to a variety of situations.

However, what experimental subjects could learn depended on what had been discussed, especially what explanations had been offered by the proponents of the correct alternative. For example, most of the atomistic reasons given at the posttest were found in one class in which one of the students had justified his prediction of the conservation of weight by relying on atomism (i.e., a lump of sugar consisted of a large number of very small particles, and these particles still existed in water). It is reasonably clear that explanations offered in group discussion could be assimilated when students were given external feedback informing them which alternative was correct. In other words, through collective comprehension activity, they had been able to share a set of possibly correct explanations despite apparent opposition. Thus, effects of group discussion must vary from class to class, because the content of the discussion necessarily varies.

Analyses of group protocols

Our recent studies have been concerned with individual *learning history*, that is, how each student in a group elaborates or revises his or her idea by incorporating and reacting to information presented in discussion. Therefore, the results of these studies are more informative concerning the two questions posed at the beginning of this chapter. One of these studies (Inagaki & Hatano, 1989) dealt with characteristics of monkeys in relation to their lives in a tree.

First, three experimental groups of about 20 fifth graders each read a short passage about relationships between animals' characteristics and their ways of living, using lions and moles as examples. Next, they were given a problem in multiple choice form about the monkey's characteristics. An example problem was: "Do the thumbs of monkeys' forefeet oppose the other 'fingers' (like in human hands) or extend in parallel to other 'fingers' (like in human feet)? How about the thumbs of their hind feet?" Answer alternatives included: (a) the thumbs are never opposing; (b) the thumbs are opposing only in the forefeet; and (c) the thumbs are opposing in both fore and hind feet. (Alternative (c) is correct.) Then, pupils' response frequencies were tabulated on the blackboard, and group discussion followed. After about 15 minutes of discussion, the pupils chose an answer alternative once again. (These three steps correspond to steps 3–5 in our earlier studies.) Finally, students were given a short passage stating the correct answer, instead of observing an experiment. This passage described only the relevant facts about monkeys and contained no explanations about why these characteristics had evolved. The control condition was also provided to assess how likely it was that those pupils would construct knowledge without social interaction. Three control groups of about 20 pupils read the same passage immediately after they chose, for the first and only time, an answer alternative to the multiple choice problem.

We again made group protocols, and this time they were supplemented by retrospective data obtained by a questionnaire given after the group interaction. In addition to the points made in the preceding section, the following pieces of evidence were obtained for the presence of the partisan motivation. First, in the questionnaire, 47 of the 65 experimental students (72 percent) nominated no one belonging to other camps as having stated reasonable but not agreeable opinions. Second, only 11 children out of the 65 (17 percent) changed their predictions at the second choice (before the feedback). Third, levels of confidence were significantly elevated after the discussion, and there was also significantly elevated interest in reading the passage. This combination clearly contradicts Berlyne's theory (e.g., 1963), which attributes curiosity to uncertainty, and suggests that both confidence and interest reflect children's commitment to their party more than their cognitive incongruity.

Learning histories of vocal and silent participants

After reading the passage about the characteristics of monkeys, both experimental and control subjects were asked in a questionnaire format to explain why monkeys had a thumb opposing other fingers. When the degree of elaborateness of the explanations was rated on a 4-point scale, the experimental subjects gave significantly more elaborate explanations than did the control subjects (mean rated score for the experimental group was 1.88 with an SD of 1.04, and was 1.44 with an SD of 1.06 for the control group, $t(126) = 2.36$, $p < .05$), by connecting the given facts in the passage to some of the ideas expressed in discussion.

However, this picture as a whole does not tell much about the variety of learning histories. Even within the experimental condition, there occurred different series of learning events for different groups and different students, and the overall difference of the experimental subjects from the control subjects reflects only in a global fashion the aggregate of these histories.

Discussions developed differently in the three experimental groups, depending on the distribution of the children's initial responses, which were tabulated on the blackboard. In Group A, supporters of option b formed the majority (three students supported option a, 13 students option b, and five students option c) and spoke most actively. Their opinion, that thumb-opposing forefeet would be convenient for grasping a branch or an object, but thumb-opposing hind feet would be inconvenient for walking, dominated the discussion. In Group B, supporters of options b and c were in the mainstream with competing pluralities (four students chose option a, 10 students option b, and eight students option c). Discussion in this group was on the monkey's hind feet, and the two sides stood evenly divided at the end of the session. In Group C, supporters of a and b were most numerous (10 students chose option a, 10 option b, and two option c). Their arguments were exclusively between two opinions, that is, "A monkey has thumb-opposing forefeet because they are convenient for grasping an object," and "A monkey should not have such feet because they are not good for walking."

Each of the subjects in the three experimental groups was placed into one of four cells of a 2 × 2 design, according to whether the subject belonged to the majority (of combined pluralities) or minority at the beginning of the discussion and whether the subject spoke at least once or not at all during the discussion. These groups were compared in terms of rated elaborateness of their explanations (see Table 14.2). A two-way ANOVA indicated that the explanations given by vocal participants were slightly more elaborate than those of silent ones, and the minority participants' explanations were as elaborate as those of the majority participants.

This suggests that the vocal participants tended to be somewhat more involved in the discussion and thus better able to integrate various pieces of information than the silent participants. However, some vocal participants

Table 14.2 Degree of elaborateness of explanations given by each type of participant after discussion

Type of participant	N	M	SD
Majority-vocal	18	2.22	0.85
Majority-silent	33	1.58	1.05
Minority-vocal	7	2.29	0.88
Minority-silent	7	2.00	1.10

belonging to the majority failed to give elaborate explanations on the posttest. Even when they started with good ideas, they did not seem to have learned much, probably because they belonged to the mainstream during the discussion, and the difference between their prediction and many others' ideas seemed small.

Although silent participants tended not to learn as much from discussion, some of them actively tried to find agent(s) who spoke for them in discussion, and if they could, they tended to give elaborate explanations afterward. M.Y., described in the next paragraph, is representative of such children. Even when silent participants (such as T.I., described after M.Y.) could not find such an agent because they belonged to a minority, some of them seem to have responded with their opponents arguments in mind and elaborated their explanations by incorporating challenging ideas into their initial choice.

M.Y. (a boy) from Group B belonged to the majority; he chose *b* before the discussion. In the questionnaire he referred to two vocal supporters of *b* as those whose opinions had been the same as his. At the same time he named a girl who had supported *c* as a proponent of a reasonable explanation. He did not change his prediction, and his curiosity and confidence after the discussion increased. His explanation on the posttest was rated elaborate: "A monkey cannot climb a tree nor grasp an object unless its fore and hind feet are thumb-opposing." This suggests that he incorporated information from the supporter of *c* when he read the material and found out that his idea was correct for the forefeet but not for the hind feet

T.I. (a girl) from Group A did not try to find an agent in discussion; she did not name anybody whose opinion had been plausible. She chose alternative *c* both before and after the discussion, and wrote in the questionnaire that she had not changed her answer because she had been confident in herself. Her explanation on the posttest was, "Because [monkeys] have not walked on the ground often, [their feet] have become suitable for holding on to branches." Because no control group pupils gave such explanations, we can infer that she was responding to the argument by supporters of *b*, who made up the majority, that "thumb-opposing hind feet are inconvenient for walking."

Data-constrained speculations

How collective comprehension activity takes place

In the following paragraphs, we will discuss how collective comprehension activity takes place with some success even among students who are academically unsophisticated, basing our discussion on the data presented above. Our answer to the first question we posed in this chapter is as follows: Collective comprehension activity often takes place when cognitive motivation and social motivation work in a concerted fashion. The activity is performed successfully when it is divided, on the basis of social motivation, between proponents, opponents, and a third party, as well as within each party.

Collective comprehension activity is different from individual comprehension activity in its social nature in a dual sense: (a) it is energized by social (partisan) motivation; and (b) there are social constraints on which part of the hypothesis space is explored and what types of evidence are considered. Our studies clearly demonstrated that social motivation made collective comprehension activity lively, enduring, and cheerful. The studies also showed that the partisan motivation gave a basis for effective division of labor in the pursuit of comprehension. It enabled students to take partial charge of the hard task of collecting and evaluating arguments both for and against each alternative between parties and within each party.

Partisan motivation, however, is by no means the sole motivation for collective comprehension activity. Comprehension activity, whether it is collective or individual, is induced by epistemic curiosity or motivation for comprehension. In this sense, the activity is radically different from ordinary party politics, which is almost exclusively driven by partisan motivation. The epistemic motivation is amplified, not superseded, by the partisan motivation, because in the constructive group activities one's affiliation with a party is cognitively based and is changeable depending on cognitive change, and the group discussion proceeds under the shared metacognitive belief in empirical confirmation as the means to decide which answer is correct.

The collective comprehension activity examined so far has at least two components in common with the collective scientific discovery by children in day care that we studied earlier (Inagaki & Hatano, 1983). First, in both cases, information seeking was initiated not only by epistemic curiosity but also by social motivation: the desire to help one's party win in the collective comprehension activity and the desire to induce a socially useful event in the collective discovery. Second, in both cases, knowledge could be acquired through group interaction, although group members did not yet have enough cognitive capability to do so by themselves, mainly because the task of knowledge acquisition was divided into easier steps. Although the two cases differed in many aspects – for example, the children in day care could not formulate a hypothesis verbally – they can shed light on the how and why of the occurrence of a collective attempt to acquire knowledge and its success.

How much knowledge is shared

As for the knowledge acquired through group discussion, our experimental data suggest three points. First, students often produce knowledge that can seldom be acquired without such interaction. Second, what a majority of them acquires varies from group to group, even when the interaction is induced by one and the same procedure. Third, knowledge differs considerably, even among those students who have been in the same group. Therefore, we must conclude that two processes are involved in the construction of knowledge through interaction: (a) individual invention of knowledge, motivated by group interaction; and (b) assimilation of information proposed by others in the preceding interaction, with some individual editing.

Group discussion often induces individual comprehension activity following it; that is, it motivates people to collect more pieces of information about the issue of the discussion and to understand the issue more deeply. Our cognitive Berlynean theory (Hatano & Inagaki, 1987) assumes that, when people recognize that their comprehension is not yet adequate, they are likely to engage in activity for seeking adequate comprehension, as long as they believe the target is worth understanding and its adequate comprehension is within reach. Group discussion on an issue is likely to make students recognize that their comprehension is not adequate. In the course of discussion, students may be surprised to find out that there exists a number of ideas that are plausible although different from their own. In addition, they may be perplexed by being unable to decide which of the alternative ideas is most tenable. More important, when asked for clarification of their views or when they are directly disputed, students may become aware of the lack of coordination among the bits of knowledge they possess. Through these processes, students often begin to feel a healthy dissatisfaction with the adequacy of their comprehension.

At the same time, group discussion offers much information valuable for deepening comprehension if one assimilates it appropriately. Because group members have been exposed to plausible explanations in the process of discussion, they can revise or elaborate their knowledge easily by incorporating some of them when the feedback reveals the falsity of their predictions.

Our data strongly suggest that silent members may be actively participating. They can learn much by observing the ongoing discussion or debate carefully. This is often characterized as a vicarious process, but it is more than that. In a sense, these students are all trying to find an agent, someone who really speaks for them. A good agent or vocal participant can articulate what a silent member has been trying without success to say and, through clarity of expression, can confirm the validity of the assertion for everyone involved.

Such a participant not only persuades opponents but also convinces supporters that they are on the right track.

We would like to emphasize that, although not competent enough to understand the target issue without group activity, people usually try to interpret and incorporate what has been achieved collectively. However, we would also like to emphasize that comprehension is essentially a private achievement, because exactly what and how much explanation is satisfactory may vary from individual to individual. Moreover, there can usually be at least several plausible interpretations and explanations for a given set of facts, rules, or procedures. In fact, Miyake (1986) found that, even after an hour-long joint comprehension activity that resulted in a subjective feeling of complete sharing, members of dyads, when individually queried, gave very different explanations.

Thus our answer to the second question we posed can be summarized as follows: People who have been involved in collective comprehension activity need not have uniform representations; they may well have different ways of comprehension. However, many of those ways of comprehension can be achieved only after constructive interaction – more accurately, interaction in a particular group in which the participants have expressed certain opinions. Only in this sense can we claim that they share comprehension through their collective attempt.

References

Berlyne. D. E. (1963). Motivational problems raised by exploratory and epistemic behavior. In S. Koch (Ed.), *Psychology: A study of a science* (Vol. 5, pp. 284–364). New York: McGraw-Hill.

Collins, A., Brown, J. S., & Larkin, K. M. (1980). Inference in text understanding. In R. J. Spiro, B. C. Bruce, & W. F. Brewer (Eds.), *Theoretical issues in reading comprehension* (pp. 387–407). Hillsdale, NJ: Erlbaum.

Collins, A., Brown, J. S., & Newman, S. E. (1989). Cognitive apprenticeship: Teaching the crafts of reading, writing, and mathematics. In L. B. Resnick (Ed.), *Knowing, learning, and instruction: Essays in honor of Robert Glaser* (pp. 453–494). Hillsdale, NJ: Erlbaum.

Doise, W., & Mugny, G. (1984). *The social development of the intellect.* Oxford: Pergamon Press.

Hatano, G., & Inagaki, K. (1987). A theory of motivation for comprehension and its application to mathematics instruction. In T. A. Romberg & D. M. Stewart (Eds.), *The monitoring of school mathematics: Background papers, Vol.2: Implications from psychology; outcomes of instruction.* (Program Report 87–2), (pp. 27–46). Madison: Wisconsin Center for Education Research.

Inagaki, K. (1981). Facilitation of knowledge integration through classroom discussion. *The Quarterly Newsletter of the Laboratory of Comparative Human Cognition, 3,* 26–28.

Inagaki, K., & Hatano, G. (1968). Motivational influences on epistemic observation.

Japanese Journal of Educational Psychology, 16, 191–202. (In Japanese with English summary)

Inagaki, K., & Hatano, G. (1983). Collective scientific discovery by young children. *Quarterly Newsletter of the Laboratory of Comparative Human Cognition, 5,* 13–18.

Inagaki, K., & Hatano, G. (1989). Learning histories of vocal and silent participants in group discussion. Paper presented at the annual meeting of the Japanese Psychological Association, Tsukuba, Japan. (In Japanese)

Itakura, K. (1967). Instruction and learning of concept "force" in static based on Kasetsu–Jikken–Jigyo (Hypothesis–Experiment–Instruction): A new method of science teaching. *Bulletin of National Institute for Educational Research, 52,* 1–121. (In Japanese)

Lave, J. (1988). *Cognition in practice.* Cambridge: Cambridge University Press.

Miyake, N. (1986). Constructive interaction and the iterative process of understanding. *Cognitive Science, 10,* 151–177.

Piaget, J. (1978). *Success and understanding.* London: Routledge & Kegan Paul.

Sugimoto, T. (1988). Substantive and linguistic knowledge in translation. Paper presented at the annual meeting of the Japanese Cognitive Science Society, Osaka. (In Japanese)

Vygotsky, L. S. (1978). *Mind in society.* Cambridge, MA: Harvard University Press.

Chapter 15

Learning and teaching mathematics in the information era*

Kathryn Crawford

A Vygotskian view of education in the information era

Vygotsky's (1962, 1978, 1986) view of human learning, and the developmental experience of being and acting in a cultural context, challenges many of the epistemological beliefs and assumptions underlying educational practice. In particular, it challenges traditional views of mathematics as value free, objective and divorced from everyday personal concerns.

In his view the subjective and personal views of individuals, their location in a context, and their knowledge derived from past experience all shape their conceptions of needs and their interpretations of the purposes or goals of an activity. The needs and purposes of people, their actions and the meanings that they attach to an activity, their relationships with other people in the socio-cultural arena in which they think, feel and act, and the presence of culturally significant artefacts, all become important as determinants of multiple consciousnesses and evolving cognitive structures. They also determine individual interpretations of the 'reality' of the experience and their choices about later action.

Paradoxically, a Vygotskian view, while acknowledging the essential subjectivity of all conscious experience, also shifts attention away from the traditional psychological focus on descriptions of individual characteristics or states and measures of performance towards a greater focus on maturing patterns of change and the processes by which people are changed. The focus is on the connections between people and the cultural context in which they act and interact in shared experiences and communication aimed at inter-subjectivity – a shared consciousness of culturally significant phenomena mediated by the use of language and other symbolic tools.

Vygotsky's insistence on non-absolute forms of consciousness seems less rad-

* This is an edited version of an article that appeared in *Educational Studies in Mathematics*, vol. 31, 1996.

ical in an era of computerised 'virtual reality' for auditory, visual and, most recently, tactile sensory domains. Mathematics, through information technology, is now used increasingly to create the sensation of reality or to re-represent and model information beyond sensory experience (e.g. in mathematical models in the physical and social sciences). Vygotsky's claims about the social ontogeny of knowledge and cognitive structures also seem less radical in an era where human activity in urban settings is increasingly circumscribed by cultural artefacts and the creative symbolism of a consumer society.

Schools are constituted as a part of the wider cultural activity – they form the culture and are formed by it. An interactive, systemic view of learning in context acknowledges the multiple perspectives and actions of the participants and the extent to which such settings are constituted within and influenced by the wider culture and the wider patterns of activity of the time. That is, educational institutions are both a part of wider cultures influencing the development of their populations and also have an identity of their own which is defined by the wider culture. Figure 15.1 below summarises the elements and influences and their connectedness for a teacher (T) and a group of pupils (P1. . . n) in a mathematics class, in a school, in a culture, during the information era. The experiences, perceptions, needs and goals of each participant are influenced by many interacting factors. These include each person's unique history of experience and awareness, the more generally recognised characteristics of the era, the culture, the ethos of the school environment, the role definitions of *teachers* and *students*, the ways in which activity in a mathematics class is defined, and the interactions between people in the immediate social context.

Mathematical knowledge also has a socio-cultural ontogeny. For math-

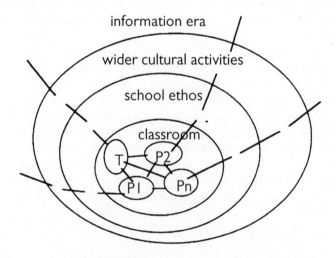

Figure 15.1 Human development in school: a socio-cultural context

ematics educators, Vygotsky's cultural historical method of research – in which attention is paid to the history of individual and group activity and the socio-cultural context in which it occurs – provides a possible source of insight about the tensions and inconsistencies emerging in mathematics education. New forms of mathematical knowledge, constituted through new forms of human activity using new tools, and changes in the ways mathematics is used in technologically based societies, present challenges to educators. They have a learning history from another era. In many cases, they work in institutions with very stable forms of organisation that have become somewhat isolated from the wider community. In the past, mathematics may have been an erudite activity of the academic elite – now, particularly in its mechanised form, it is becoming a fundamental aspect of organisation, creativity and opportunity at all levels of society.

Most people have learned mathematics in a form that is decontextualised from the human activities that engendered it. Brousseau (1992: p. 22) uses the term 'didactical transposition' to describe the shift in meaning that occurs when knowledge is learned in contexts separate from where it is generated and used in the wider community. He suggests that knowledge is recontextualised in educational institutions but '. . . the restoration of intelligible situations (recontextualisation) has as a price the shift in meaning (didactical transposition)'. That shift in meaning is experienced by teachers of mathematics in both their own mathematical education and in the ongoing context of their profession.

A Vvgotskian view suggests a new set of questions for research in mathematics education which reflect the fact that mathematical knowledge increasingly shapes and is shaped by human activity and communication in new technologically sophisticated contexts. In such a view, mathematics learning becomes an integral and essential part of human development and consciousness in an era at once fraught with ecological peril and new opportunities for creativity and understanding on a global scale. Some of these questions are:

- What is the nature of mathematical activity in the information era?
- What is the history of mathematical activity for individuals and groups in a culture – including teachers.
- What is the effect of mathematical activity of various kinds on cognitive development?
- How is mathematics used in a culture? – by whom?
- How do people experience mathematics? – at school? – at home? – at work?
- What are the goals or purposes of mathematical activity in educational settings? – in the wider community?
- What needs and purposes are met by such activity? – For whom? How?

- What is the range of mathematical activity for different people working together in a particular setting?
- What is the distribution of activity among people doing mathematics in any setting?
- What difference does the use of tools such as computers and calculators make to the quality of human activity and learning?
- How are different learning experiences related to different forms of mathematical knowledge and later dispositions to think and act mathematically?
- What is the effect of computerisation and increased use of mathematics on the nature of knowledge and human activity in many fields?

A systemic view of human learning in a cultural context which now includes the powerful cultural artefacts associated with information technology suggests a view of mathematics education as a lifelong experience inextricably connected to other forms of cultural activity including significant patterns of social interaction. The beginnings of these processes can be seen in early childhood.

The social ontogeny of mathematical development in early childhood

Computers provide a new context for children's activity with different opportunities for and constraints on the development of cognitive structures. Educational tools such as paper, pencils, paints and computers, according to Vygotsky, are cultural artefacts. They have a socio-cultural ontogeny and their significance for individual or group patterns of development depends on how they are culturally defined, the social context in which they are encountered, and the ways in which they are used. Booth (1984) has described how spontaneous pattern making of young children with paint and paper follows the edge of the paper (usually rectangular). The cognitive structures that are formed through individual and group activity with computers are also influenced by the features of a computational environment and the socio-cultural context in which the activity occurs. In an information era, computational environments influence children at an early age.

A study of pre-school children's use of Logo (Crawford, 1988) provides an illustration of the social ontogeny of knowledge and the tensions and opportunities for learning that are created by a new context for mathematical exploration. The study forms a part of a larger study of the social context of mathematics learning for young children. The children (N = 25) attended an informal pre-school setting twice a week in which they were encouraged to choose from a range of activities, which included exploration of a modified form of Logo, for a period of twelve weeks. At the beginning of the program the children's ages ranged from 54 to 60 months. Gender differences in skills and expectations were already evident in the group – boys spent more time with block building, puzzles and gross motor activity, girls spent more time playing with dolls, negotiating, chatting and creating detailed drawings. For this group and their teacher this was an initial introduction to a computer. Some children's parents used computers at home or at work.

The time spent on the computer was described as 'drawing on TV' in an effort to associate the activity with other cultural experiences of free expression and exploration. This definition, or *sign* in Vygotsky's terms, caused initial tensions and contradictions because the teacher and other adults had quite different expectations of computing activities. Initial plans to have the activity closely supervised by an adult were abandoned because the adult felt a need to instruct the children according to their more formal expectations of programming and to 'help' children 'do it correctly'. Girls in particular responded to this social context with help seeking and dependent learning behaviour – boys lost interest and moved off to another activity.

The program was modified. After the introduction of basic commands the children were told to seek help as they needed it and encouraged to explore the new medium freely with less close supervision by an adult. Activities were observed and records were kept for each child of the time spent, knowledge of commands, planning, discussion and whether the child initiated or followed ideas. With the exception of one child, all the children *chose* to spend time on the activity at least once a week.

In the initial weeks the children generally followed a pattern of activities which included:

- random and impulsive experimentation with commands (Logo scribble);
- purposeful investigation of the two aspects of the medium that were most different from paper and pencil. The children played 'hide the turtle' and attempted to predict where the turtle was after using commands. They also explored the wraparound effect by continuously using the F (fd 10) command;
- a gradually increasing focus on control of direction. Horizontal and vertical lines were the first indication of this stage. The terms quickly became part of the children's vocabulary as they discussed what was happening on the screen.

The public nature of the screen meant that new ideas and things to do were open to scrutiny by other children and 'spread' through the group very rapidly. No matter who was 'playing' with the computer, other children came to see what was happening and later tried out new ideas for themselves. The new context was defined socially in terms of related experiences with other cultural artefacts and the reactions of members of the group, including adults. Notions of left and right, horizontal, vertical distance and direction were useful in the Logo environment. They were also greeted very positively by adults in the context and by the children's parents. The phenomena were socially meaningful and the language signs to describe them and the ability to recognise and name them quickly became important in the wider social context as well as in the computer context. The children had gained early access to ideas and cognitive structures that are not usually established at pre-school. The new knowledge not only empowered them in the Logo medium but also in their social relationships. Adults responded positively to their new knowledge and ideas.

After four weeks, the children's conceptions of the social and technological possibilities of the Logo environment were extended. They were given a session in which they played at using the same commands to 'control' a turtle-robot on the floor. They were initially startled and delighted to find that the same commands could be used with the robot. They spontaneously built the turtle-robot a house and some shops to visit and moved it about in a much more planned way in their imaginary suburb. They soon tired of the robot's slow movement and returned to the computer screen. However, the robot-turtle activity had involved co-operative building and playing where planning was an important element. Back on the computer screen there was a substantial change in the form of their activities.

- There was more collaboration and discussion.
- Closed curves of various kinds began to appear and there was much discussion of ways to make shapes of various kinds.
- Planned filling of the available space occurred. For boys this involved use of geometric patterns – for girls, detailed representation of people and events.

The experience with the turtle-robot had recontextualised the computer activity in association with other cultural knowledge and activities.

By the end of the study there were no substantial differences between boys and girls, in either enthusiasm for or competence in the Logo medium. However, the gender differences in social experience and expectations, that were generally evident at the beginning of the program, were reflected in the expressed goals and needs of children and thus in their interpretation of the meaning and potential uses of the new cultural artefact after a few weeks. Boys were most interested in translation and rotation of shapes and the repetition of procedures – they were fascinated with the pattern making that was possible. The girls were more interested in representing people and events. They were frustrated that the L and R commands (Lt 30, Rt 30) were cumbersome and were interested in more precise ways to form angles. Both groups were able to articulate the mathematical ideas underlying these needs in ways normally expected of much older children.

For the children, the meaning and purposes of the computer activities were defined through the lens of their existing cultural consciousness. The 'drawing on TV' activity was initially associated with expressive and creative activities. The use of the robot-turtle extended the children's view of the possibilities through association with planning, rule making and exploratory activities in play. The personal dispositions and the knowledge of culturally approved meanings constituted through these activities were a far cry from the forms of mathematical knowledge constituted through the more intellectually limited and less personally meaningful imitation and memorisation of techniques in early mathematical activities at school. The results of the project suggest that, for young children, exploration of and playing with a mathematic artefact in an informal educational setting had a positive effect on their development of and inclination to talk about and use mathematical knowledge.

Human development in educational settings: history, activity and change

Vygotsky wrote about Activity in general terms to describe the personal and voluntary engagement of people in context – the ways in which they subjectively perceive their needs and the possibilities of a situation and *choose* actions to reach personally meaningful goals. In translations of Vygotsky's writings, the Russian word translated as 'activity' denotes levels of personal involvement, meaningfulness and intent that is not conveyed in English. His compatriots developed the notion of Activity (e.g. Leont'ev, 1981: Davydov *et al.*, 1983; Davydov and Radzikhovskii, 1985; Semenov, 1978) and made a clear distinction between conscious *actions* and relatively unconscious and automated *operations*. An *action* involves conscious behaviour that is stimulated by a need subordinated to a goal. An operation is an action that is transformed as a means of obtaining a result under given conditions. Operations are habits and automated procedures that are carried out without conscious intellectual effort. Both actions and operations form part of any Activity by groups or individuals. Luria (1973) developed a theory of brain function in a social context and was influenced by Vygotsky's ideas. My own early research (Crawford, 1986a, 1986b) investigated the relationships between cognitive abilities (based on psychometric tests drawing on the work of Luria), social experience and mathematical problem solving. The results supported the notion of an activity relationship between socio-historical factors, cognitive processes, subjective perceptions of roles, needs and goals, and mathematical problem solving.

The study raised serious questions about the limits of student activity during traditional mathematics instruction within traditionally organised schools. In particular, it suggested that traditional forms of instruction were effective in establishing student abilities to implement standard mathematical techniques – or *operations*. However, students in the sample showed almost no spontaneous disposition to engage personally with mathematical tasks – Activity. They were inexperienced and unskilled in interpreting the meaning of mathematical information, defining a problem, selecting strategies, and evaluating the results of problem-solving efforts. That is, they were inexperienced in mathematical *actions*. When students were prompted to undertake such activities, many lacked the conceptual framework in mathematics to 'make sense of' non-standard problems.

More recently, a study of first-year university students (Crawford *et al.*, 1993) found that more than 80 per cent of the sample studied viewed mathematics as a set of rote learned rules and techniques and approached mathematics learning in a fragmented fashion with the intent to reproduce, using paper and pencil, axioms and standard techniques for examination. That is, the majority of the most successful students of mathematics, at the end of their school experience, viewed mathematics as a series of operations – techniques and rules to be implemented.

The conceptions of mathematics and student orientations to mathematical tasks that are revealed in the above studies were not those intended by curriculum experts and educational administrators. They are the results of the informal learning with a socio-cultural ontogeny in the particular characteristics of the mathematical Activity in schools. In most parts of the world, curriculum documents now state the importance of active learning, problem solving, modelling, investigation and communication in mathematics. However, in Australia at least, there is evidence that, in many schools, the way in which mathematics is taught has changed very little in the past 20 years (see Speedy, 1989). Papert (1994: p. 2) notes that: 'In the wake of the startling growth in science and technology in our recent past, some areas of human activity have undergone a megachange. . . . School is a notable example of an area that has not.'

Educational policy reflects the learning needs of students entering the information era. Educational practice still reflects nineteenth-century ideas of mathematics education in which culturally approved knowledge and operational skills are passed from an expert to a novice. Too often, in schools, 'active learning' is interpreted as more 'work' under greater pressure of time, 'on task' behaviour and conformity to extended teacher expectations. 'Problem solving' is an extra thing to teach – teachers select the 'problems' and evaluate the solutions. A transition to an emphasis on personally meaningful mathematical Activity for students would require a radical transformation of cultural definitions of 'teacher' and 'student', their roles and the relationships between them, the organisation and resourcing of educational institutions and stronger connections between educational settings and other cultural activity.

In cultural historical terms we have operationalised schooling in ways that were appropriate in a former era. The traditional notions of expertise and authority are still implicit in teacher education and the organisation of educational institutions at all levels. Shared cultural conceptions about mathematics and how it is learned stem from shared experiences of mathematical activity in school and university – in countries where schooling is compulsory, almost everyone learns mathematics at school.

There are generational and organisational tensions and inconsistencies between the new opportunities for human development and historical notions of learning and teaching in all fields. Nowhere are these tensions and inconsistencies more evident than in mathematics education. This is because the new technologies have both changed the nature of and opportunities for human mathematical activity in fundamental ways and also widened the use and influence of mathematical information at all levels of society.

Cultural historical tensions: schools and information technology

We know that schools are slow to change. The introduction of exploratory activities using Lego-Logo materials to a group of 12-year-olds in a traditional girls' school (Crawford, 1992b) provides a situation calculated to highlight the tensions between historically based stable forms of educational practice, gendered experiences of mathematics and technology (Walkerdine, 1988; Crawford, Groundwater-Smith and Milan, 1990), and the fundamental challenges and opportunities for new forms of activity and development that are presented by information technology.

The school environment, in Vygotsky's terms, formed a micro-culture which formed and was formed by all members of the educational community. All staff at the school were aware of the parents' conservative beliefs about child rearing, schooling and work. Discipline, conformity to community expectations and values, and order were highly valued. Uniforms were worn by all students. Observations of the classrooms consistently revealed a highly teacher-centred mode of classroom organisation where neatness, accurate reproduction of demonstrated procedures and orderly predictable behaviour were highly valued. The girls generally worked alone. 'Cheating' by getting help from a friend was discouraged and all peer interaction was closely scrutinised. Most communication – indeed, most relationships during lessons – was restricted to that between the teacher and each individual child. Paper-and-pencil tests and percentage marks for achievement were the only forms of assessment and reporting in mathematics. Teachers expressed a transmission model of learning mathematics. They talked of 'covering the content' and ensuring that the students had learned 'the basics' – mostly well-automated arithmetic computation procedures. For the students, 'schoolwork' was defined in terms of following instructions precisely and doing what was required. Figure 15.2 presents a simplified diagram of the major aspects of the social interaction in the characteristic setting of classrooms in the school.

Vygotsky's notion of the 'zone of proximal development' (ZPD) has generally been interpreted by Western psychologists as an individual characteristic constituted within a particular activity in context. However, from a more

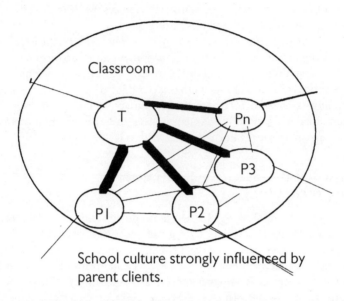

Figure 15.2 Patterns of interaction in traditional classrooms

systemic view, these common patterns of communication and interaction also defined the nature and dimensions of a shared ZPD for students in mathematics classes – the possibilities and probabilities of mathematical activity and development. In general, formal instruction was communicated by the teacher to the students. Most staff assumed that their needs, goals and intentions in a lesson were shared by the students. Little attention was paid to the personal experience of the students – to their individual needs and goals – to the subjective meaning of the experience for each learner. The students understood their role as 'finding out what she wants', memorising and practising with an intent to reproduce accurately the culturally approved information and procedures. Some students demonstrated their competence by answering questions in class 'discussions'. Most remained silent.

At the beginning of the project it was clear that, in such a context, exploratory 'playing with computers and lego blocks' was marginal to the 'real' purposes of the curriculum. A 'computer club' was formed so that students could choose to extend the range of their activity through using technological materials after school in a less formal setting. An aim of the project was to investigate learning through creative construction, exploration and collaborative problem solving. Figure 15.3 illustrates the different patterns of social interaction that were fostered as the students were encouraged to work collaboratively in groups to engage actively with the materials and take greater responsibility for problem solving and self-evaluation. Note the stronger

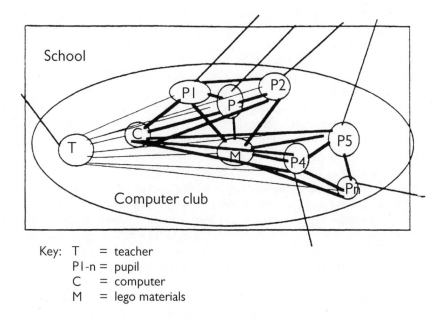

Key: T   = teacher
      P1-n = pupil
      C   = computer
      M   = lego materials

Figure 15.3 Social interaction for collaborative learning in groups

connections with the context outside the school, and the materials at hand, and the reduced focus on teacher–student interaction.

The girls in the computer project had no experience of independent or collaborative activity in school. Despite the fact that the computer activities were available after normal school lessons, the girls were initially almost paralysed with anxiety about the discontinuity between the usual teacher direction and suggestions that they might like to plan a project for themselves. The response of the girls to the new setting was in marked contrast to the response of the younger children with no experience of learning in school. They expressed concern about 'making mistakes'. Probe questions revealed that a 'mistake' was 'not doing what the teacher wants'. It also became clear that their mathematics curriculum in which they had 'done lots of work on three-dimensional shapes', and their informal experiences of cultural activity outside school had left them with neither the language nor the spatial knowledge needed to build models with the lego material. They initially had difficulty naming the new materials and discussing their projects. There was much muddled talk of 'thingies' and 'whatsits'. One student wrote in her diary after a session in which her group had attempted to build a simple four-wheeled vehicle: 'We made a snow machine thing with small and big wheels . . . we had trouble working and trying to move the darn thing . . . it was hard!'

They all had many examples of applications of information technology in their homes, but until the project started they had not paid any attention to them or to the logic of how they worked. They were also very inexperienced in model building. They suggested that model building and technology were things that concerned their fathers and brothers. Their school experience of 'doing' 3D shapes in geometry and gears in science had not equipped them for using such knowledge with actual blocks, gears and machines. Actually selecting bricks of appropriate length and width was a challenge for many. One group had real difficulty deciding where to attach a light sensor to a simple vehicle so that it could detect a black line on the floor. For a long time the sensor was pointing forwards.

In the informal setting of the computer club, the girls' confidence gradually grew. As they 'played' with the new artefacts, their ownership and personal involvement in their building projects grew, and their efforts were recognised and supported by project staff. Another journal entry by the same child later in the project indicates the changes in attitude, personal commitment and involvement in an Activity. It also suggests a more integrated and relational understanding of the elements of the problem. She wrote:

> I worked with Nadine and our project was a tower with a flashing light and three gears with a smaller gear that go faster and a bigger gear that goes slower. This tower had a helicopter like top and if it had no gears to make it go slower, it would spin off . . . which happened last week . . . Our new thing we did was to make gears . . . to make the helicopter (top) not fly off. It was fabulous that we made gears. I feel fabulous and proud that we made this creation.

The blocks were associated with self-directed play activities by the teaching staff. However, the programming activities were seen as part of the 'real curriculum'. Thus, as the project evolved, the social characteristics of the setting – the shared ZPD – for learning through building with the blocks involved problem definition, argument, strategic decision making, risk taking and experimentation and self-evaluation in a collaborative peer group. In contrast, when it came to developing programs for their models a more teacher-directed instructional setting evolved around programming activities. The girls were 'helped' with programming solutions. Consequently, in this domain, the range of their activity was reduced in terms of personal involvement and cognitive activities.

The differences in personal ownership and awareness associated with experiences of qualitatively different forms of Activity in the two aspects of the social context were clearly reflected in the diaries that were kept by each student – their subjective reality of the project. All the diaries contain initial typed instructions for Logo programming pasted in. These are followed by increasingly enthusiastic reports about what they have learned from building with their models – details of difficulties – joyful exclamations about the resolutions achieved. Few diary entries mention programming problems or their resolution. Follow-up interviews revealed that, whereas the model building was their own and enjoyable, the programming was 'real work' and not their own. They could not write about it because 'they could not understand the teacher's solutions'. The block activities had become part of their consciousness; the programming generally had not.

This project clearly illustrates the tensions between traditional forms of educational practice with traditional educational technologies and the new forms of cultural activity associated with the creative possibilities of new and complex technological systems.

First, the students' experience of their role as actors, during teacher-centred instruction in paper-and-pencil geometrical activities, resulted in knowledge about how to reproduce a series of culturally approved procedures and axioms and knowledge of the cultural symbols to denote shapes of various kinds. This narrow range of operational activity did not result in knowledge that was part of each student's own consciousness and a basis for creative problem solving. Second, creativity and exploration demand a setting in which the explorer/creator/learner is able to own the project, grapple with it, and take responsibility for the outcomes of the activity. In schools, such a context implies radical rearrangement of the power relationships between teachers, administrators and students and of traditional forms of social organisation.

Teachers' knowledge and information technology

It is little wonder that the majority of successful students enter university with a view of mathematics as a set of axioms and techniques that must be learned by rote and reproduced on demand – that is their school experience of mathematics. The conceptions of mathematics and how it is learned, of first-year students at university level, have been mentioned above. The social ontogeny of such conceptions and their relationship to the quality of mathematical experience in school is evident from the discussion in the above section. The transmission model of learning is more strongly represented at high school level, reinforced by the measurement needs of matriculation examiners, and persists strongly at university level. Academics are experts in their field. The usual university forms of course delivery reinforce the model of learning the culturally approved knowledge from experts.

However, the new technological tools make possible new forms of academic activity that are changing the nature of the knowledge and expertise of people working in universities. This change is most evident in mathematics and the physical sciences. New knowledge generation is now possible as mathematical models are tested and abstract concepts represented within computational environments. However, an equally radical change in the nature of knowledge generation has also occurred in the humanities and in most professional fields (Fugita, 1993). In archaeology, for example, computer-based models and data organisation and new dating techniques have revolutionised research processes. As yet, there is little indication of similar changes in the ways in which universities present courses at under-graduate level. Thus, in universities also, the nature and meaning of knowledge generated in one form of Activity, through research and creative theorising, is changed or transposed as academics 'transmit' information to undergraduate students, in a different social context, about other people's discoveries and techniques.

In education, a growing body of expertise is emerging as researchers grapple with the design and use of technologically based learning contexts. These changes are placing substantial pressure on staff at university level to update their expertise and rethink old conceptions of knowing, teaching and learning. To the extent that information technology has enhanced our powers of data organisation and analysis, the traditional place of mathematical activity in a university micro-culture has been changed. For example, some conceptual understanding of statistics, and in particular an understanding of non-linear, multi-level relationships is needed in most professional and academic fields. The pressure for change is not merely to teach more mathematics to more students in more fields, but to prepare students through experience of a new sort of mathematical *Activity* that has investigation and problem resolution as its goal and in which the *operations* are technologically supported. For those mathematics departments engaged in the development of new courses of this kind, there are tensions and challenges associated with the cultural history of mathematical activity of both academics and students.

The education of mathematics teachers at all levels now needs to involve learning to use information technology effectively as an educational aid. For teacher educators that will also mean learning to guide student-teachers in a social context that fosters a greater depth in intellectual, emotional and enact-ive involvement and responsibility. This is required because in the new forms of mathematical activity, in the wider culture, people use mathematics in a social context and their mathematical actions to meet their personal and political needs and goals are operationally supported by powerful information technologies. Mathematics educators now need to be able to create a range of new learning environments that foster Activity rather than merely oper-ational techniques in order to meet new societal needs for informed and critical use of mathematics in all fields. Some of these settings may involve information technologies but such culturally potent artefacts are not a prerequisite for changes in the intellectual depth and social and personal relevance of mathematics education, merely a reason for such changes.

Recent research (Crawford, 1992a) suggests that the experiences of creating and changing learning contexts, with or without the use of new technologies, is also a powerful learning activity. From a Vygotskian point of view, the

Activity of reproducing a set lesson, using a textbook as a source of information and using well-automated teaching strategies in the usual way involves little conscious intellectual activity for the teacher – the process involves *operations* within an assumed conceptual framework. On the other hand, experience in creating a new learning context in a classroom, experimenting with and refining strategies to foster new kinds of learning activity among students, representing mathematical information in new ways, changing the nature of mathematical activity, and being responsible for an evaluative account of the resulting learning and development requires intense personal involvement. Personal strengths and weaknesses and personal needs and goals are important. For most student-teachers at university such new requirements are a challenge. One such student wrote the following account in her journal at the beginning of the semester:

> During the first tutorial I noticed that many people began to feel threatened. . . . It was apparent that students did not feel comfortable with a view of mathematics education that took the power away from them. People view the role of teaching as a powerful one and beginning teachers feel most comfortable with this power. Perhaps it is because this mirrors our own experience at school.

Such purposeful Activity by student-teachers involves problem definition, interpretation, strategic thinking and evaluation in and of the kind of fluid and changeable social context in which teachers work. It results in a well-developed rationale for decision making about the design of learning experiences and a disposition to creative approaches to enhancing student involvement in meaningful mathematical activity through investigation and problem solving. A journal entry by the same student-teacher at the end of the semester illustrates the impact of the experience and her recognition of the more active involvement by schoolchildren that has been facilitated by changes in teaching practice. Note in the two entries the pattern of initial confusion and lack of involvement and later commitment to the processes and a more dynamic and dialectic understanding of teaching and learning as part of a single interactive process:

> This last session in school was a very positive experience for both students and teachers. . . . At this stage, they (*the students*) knew exactly what information they wanted to present on their posters. There was less in-group fighting when teachers were not present. . . . During this session little intervention was required. They worked very diligently and it was obvious that their co-operative group skills had vastly improved. . . . It was wonderful for us to be part of this change. [Italics added]

Opportunities to represent mathematical ideas in new ways, whether or not information technologies are part of the context, deepens mathematical understanding. All student-teachers reported the need to grapple with and extend their mathematical concepts. In addition, learning to create new contexts for mathematical learning in technological settings provides a motivating problem base for student-teachers to develop skills in ways that they see as relevant. Most importantly, during such an experience student-teachers have a new glimpse of themselves as one powerful element in a whole system of collective activity in which the history of each person, their existing knowledge and their intellectual, enactive and emotional involvement, and individual conceptions of the goals of the activity and of personal needs, are all part of the learning experience.

Conclusions

Vygotsky's systemic view of human development and consciousness mediated through action in a cultural context was formed in another era of social change. In the present era, another time of rapid change in the nature and purpose of human activity, his insights may be valuable as a lens through which to view modern dilemmas and challenges.

Now that we have built machines to carry out the forms of mathematical technique that have dominated the curriculum at all levels, it is time to reconsider the traditional narrow operational focus of students' mathematical activities. Now that information is stored on databases and standard techniques are carried out by machines, it is particularly inappropriate that the 'zone of proximal development' in mathematics classrooms still orients students towards imitation, memorisation and practising techniques with the intent to reproduce them in obedience to authority figures and without any reference to their personal needs and goals.

The full mathematical potential of information technology will only be fulfilled when the social ontogeny of 'school mathematics' is recognised and the socio-cultural context of mathematical development, in educational institutions, is changed in ways which recognise the new tools and the new ways in which mathematical knowledge is made and used through human activities.

References

Booth. D.: 1984, 'Aspects of logico-mathematical intuition in the development of young children's spontaneous pattern painting', in *The Proceedings of the Eighth Annual Conference for the Psychology of Mathematics Education, Sydney, Australia,* 224–232.

Brousseau, G.: 1992. 'Didactique: what it can do for the teacher', in: R. Douady and A. Mercier (Eds.). *Research in Didactique of Mathematics*, La Presse Sauvage, Paris, 7–39.

Crawford, K.P.: 1986a, 'Simultaneous and successive processing, executive control and social experience: individual differences in educational achievement and problem solving in mathematics', unpublished Ph.D. thesis, University of New England, Armidale, NSW, Australia.

Crawford K.P.: 1986b, 'Cognitive and social factors in problem solving behaviour', in *The Proceedings of the Tenth Conference of the International Group for the Psychology of Mathematics Education*, London, July, 415–421.

Crawford, K.P.: 1988, 'New contexts for learning mathematics', in *The Proceedings of the Eleventh Annual Conference of the International Group for the Psychology in Mathematics Education*, Vesprem, Hungary, August, 239–246.

Crawford, K.P.: 1992a, 'Applying theory in teacher education: Changing practice in mathematics education' , in W. Geeslin and K. Graham (Eds.), *The Proceedings of the Sixteenth Annual Conference of the International Group for the Psychology of Mathematics Education*, University of New Hampshire, Durham, NH, 161–167.

Crawford, K.P.: 1992b, 'Playing with Lego/Lego: School definitions of work and their influence on learning behaviour'. in L. Nevile (Ed.), *Proceedings of the Logo and Mathematics Education Conference*, LME5 Lake Tineroo, Queensland, Australia, April 1991, 45–55.

Crawford, K.P., Gordon. S., Nicholas, J. and Prosser, M.: 1993, 'Learning mathematics at university level', in W. Atweh (Ed.), *Contexts in Mathematics, The Proceedings of the Mathematics Education Research Group of Australasia*, Annual Conference, Brisbane, Australia, July 1993, 209–214.

Crawford, K., Groundwater-Smith, S. and Milan, M.: 1990, *Gender and the Evolution of Computer Literacy*, a revised research report to the NSW Ministry of Education, Canberra, Government Printing Office.

Davydov, V. and Radzikhovskii, L.A.: 1985. 'Vygotsky's theory and the activity-oriented approach in psychology'. in J. Wertsch (Ed.), *Culture Communication and Cognition: Vygotskian Perspectives*, Cambridge University Press. New York, 35–66.

Davydov, V.V., Zinchenko, V.P. and Talysina, N.F.: 1983, 'The problem of activity in the works of A.N. Leont'ev (1)'. *Soviet Psychology*, Summer 21(4), pp. 31–43.

Fugita, H.: 1993, 'Principles in organising university and pre-university mathematics curricula for scientists and engineers', a paper presented at the South East Asian Congress on Mathematics Education, Surabaya, Indonesia, 7–11 June,

Leont'ev, A.N.: 1981, 'The problem of activity in psychology', in J.V. Wertschz (Ed.), *The Concept of Activity in Soviet Psychology*, Sharpe, Armonk, NY, 37–71.

Luria, A.R.: 1973, *The Working Brain*, Penguin Books, Harmondsworth.

Papert, S.: 1994, *The Children's Machine Rethinking School in the Age of the Computer*, Harvester/Wheatsheaf, Brighton, Sussex.

Semenov, I.N.: 1978, 'An empirical psychological study of thought processes in creative problem solving from the perspective of the theory of activity', *Soviet Psychology*, 16(1), pp. 3–46.

Speedy, G.: 1989. 'Chair, the discipline review of teacher education in mathematics and science'. Government Printing Office. Canberra.

Vygotsky, L.S.: 1962, *Thought and Language*, MIT Press, Cambridge, MA.

Vygotsky, L.S.: 1978, *Mind in Society* (M. Cole, S. Scribner, V. John-Steiner and E. Souberman, Trans.), Harvard University Press, Cambridge, MA.

Vygotsky, L.S.: 1986, *Thought and Language* (Newly revised – translated and edited by A. Kozulin), MIT Press, Cambridge, MA.

Walkerdine, V.: 1988, *The Mastery of Reason*, Routledge, London.

Index